Luminous presence

Manchester University Press

Luminous presence

Derek Jarman's life-writing

Alexandra Parsons

MANCHESTER UNIVERSITY PRESS

Copyright © Alexandra Parsons 2021

The right of Alexandra Parsons to be identified as the author of this work has been asserted by them in accordance with the Copyright, Designs and Patents Act 1988.

Published by Manchester University Press
Oxford Road, Manchester M13 9PL
www.manchesteruniversitypress.co.uk

British Library Cataloguing-in-Publication Data
A catalogue record for this book is available from the British Library

ISBN   978 1 5261 4475 1 hardback
ISBN   978 1 5261 7157 3 paperback

First published by Manchester University Press in hardback 2021
This edition published 2023

The publisher has no responsibility for the persistence or accuracy of URLs for any external or third-party internet websites referred to in this book, and does not guarantee that any content on such websites is, or will remain, accurate or appropriate.

Typeset
by New Best-set Typesetters Ltd

For Elsie Long –
and in memory of Keith Collins and Catherine Silverstone

Contents

Illustrations	viii
Acknowledgements	xii
Introduction	1
1 'The porter into forgotten landscapes': *A finger in the fishes mouth*	30
2 *Dancing Ledge*: 'An autobiography at forty'	40
3 *Derek Jarman's Caravaggio*: 'Reading between the lines of history'	58
4 Becoming Pasolini: Derek Jarman in *Ostia*	79
5 *Kicking the Pricks*: 'Forward into an uncertain future …'	87
6 Self-projection in film: *The Last of England* and *The Garden*	104
7 *Modern Nature*: Haunting, flowers and personal mythologies	129
8 *Queer Edward II*: 'Are you a closet bigot?'	149
9 *At Your Own Risk*: A Saint's Testament	166
10 *Smiling in Slow Motion*: Testimony and elegy	183
11 'A kind of bliss': *Blue* and *Chroma*	196
12 *Derek Jarman's Garden*: A therapy and a pharmacopoeia	213
Conclusion: 'The past is the mirror'	223
Bibliography	228
Filmography	251
Index	253

Illustrations

Plates

1. Jarman in front of a rainbow, 1993. Photograph by Howard Sooley.
2. Jarman in a cameo role as a cardinal in *Caravaggio*. Photograph by Gerald Incandela.
3. Spread from Jarman's sketchbook 'The Last of England'. Copyright and courtesy of Keith Collins Will Trust (trustees: Diane Gelon, Karl Lydon and Amanda Wilkinson).
4. Jarman sleeps on an iron bed in the sea, watched over by figures with flaming torches. Still from Dungeness shoot of *The Garden*. Photograph by Liam Daniel. Copyright and courtesy of Basilisk Communications.
5. Jarman. Still from Dungeness shoot of *The Garden*. Photograph by Liam Daniel. Copyright and courtesy of Basilisk Communications.
6. Jarman lying in *Crambe maritima*. Still from Dungeness shoot of *The Garden*. Photograph by Liam Daniel. Copyright and courtesy of Basilisk Communications.
7. Pages from Jarman's journal 'The Garden', showing a planting plan, a prose journal entry and a pressed daffodil from his garden. Copyright and courtesy of Keith Collins Will Trust.
8. Set of contacts from Priory Road, summer 1965. Photographs by Raymond Dean.
9. and 10 Jarman at work on *Blood* in Richard Salmon's studio, 1992. Photographs by Howard Sooley.
11. Jarman in front of *Dead Sexy*, May 1993. Photograph by Howard Sooley.
12. Jarman, *One Day's Medication*, 1993. Copyright and courtesy of Keith Collins Will Trust.
13. Jarman in the garden at Prospect Cottage in the snow. Copyright and courtesy of Keith Collins Will Trust.

14	The Prospect Cottage garden in full bloom, June 2014. Photograph by Alexandra Parsons.	
15	The sunroom in Prospect Cottage, looking out onto part of the garden, June 2018. Photograph by Alexandra Parsons.	
16	Jarman's profile in front of a screening of *Blue*. Photograph by Liam Daniel, 1993.	
17 and 18	Jarman in Monet's garden at Giverny, 1993. Photographs by Howard Sooley.	

Figures

1	Jarman in *Dollar Bill Cape* and mitre. Photograph by Raymond Dean, 1970.	xiv
2	An early version of Jarman's 'Assisi' from 'untitled sketchbook', 1964. BFI National Archive, box 49, item 2. Copyright and courtesy of Keith Collins Will Trust.	31
3	*A finger in the fishes mouth*, poem no. 30. Copyright and courtesy of Keith Collins Will Trust.	35
4	Jarman in front of one of the GBH series of paintings, ICA exhibition, 1984. Photograph by Sharon Temple and Meisha Masche for *Performance Magazine*. Copyright and courtesy of Keith Collins Will Trust.	41
5	Spread from *Derek Jarman's Caravaggio*, pp. 24–5. Courtesy of Thames & Hudson.	62
6	Cover image of *Derek Jarman's Caravaggio*. Photograph by Gerald Incandela. Courtesy of Thames & Hudson.	65
7	Jarman includes another full-size photograph of David with the Head of Goliath in *Derek Jarman's Caravaggio*, p. 49. Photograph by and courtesy of Gerald Incandela.	67
8	Spread from *Derek Jarman's Caravaggio*, pp. 60–1. Courtesy of Thames & Hudson.	70
9	Pier Paolo Pasolini (Jarman) in *Ostia*. Screengrab.	81
10	Pasolini (Jarman) and Pino Pelosi (David Dipnall) in *Ostia*. Screengrab.	81
11 and 12	Jarman working at his journals in *The Last of England*. Screengrab. Copyright Anglo International Films.	98

13	Jarman and others in front of Spillers' Millenium Mills during the filming of *The Last of England*. Photograph by Mike Laye courtesy of Sandra Ross.	100
14	Jarman writes in his sketchbooks in *The Last of England*. Screengrab. Copyright of Anglo International Films.	107
15	Jarman wearing a sailor's hat in *The Last of England*. Screengrab. Copyright of Anglo International Films.	107
16	Jarman's mother and sister in the garden in front of their housing area at an RAF station. Home movie inserted into *The Last of England*. Screengrab. Copyright of Anglo International Films.	110
17	Jarman sleeps on his desk at Prospect Cottage as water drips down from the ceiling in *The Garden*. Screengrab. Copyright and courtesy of Basilisk Communications.	118
18	Jarman sleeps on his desk at Prospect Cottage in *The Garden*. Screengrab. Copyright and courtesy of Basilisk Communications.	118
19	Jarman sleeps on an iron bed in the sea at Dungeness, watched over by five figures. Still from Dungeness shoot of *The Garden*. Photograph by Liam Daniel. Copyright and courtesy of Basilisk Communications.	124
20	Jarman standing in the doorway of Prospect Cottage, 1990. Photograph by Howard Sooley.	130
21	Spread from Jarman's sketchbook 'Borrowed Time', 1987. Copyright and courtesy of Keith Collins Will Trust.	130
22	Prince Edward (Jody Graber) in *Queer Edward II*, p. 33. Photograph by and courtesy of Liam Daniel.	154
23	Prince Edward (Jody Graber) in *Edward II*. Screengrab. Copyright of Working Title Films.	157
24	Prince Edward (Jody Graber) dancing on the caged Queen Isabella (Tilda Swinton) and Mortimer (Nigel Terry) in *Edward II*. Screengrab. Copyright of Working Title Films.	157
25	Spread from one of Jarman's 'Edward II' journals, showing a collage of personal and work material.	

	The photograph on the verso is by Raymond Dean. Copyright and courtesy of Keith Collins Will Trust.	162
26	Jarman writing at Barts Hospital. Photograph by Howard Sooley, early 1993.	184
27	Simplified version of a page from Jarman's journal 'The Garden', printed on the inside front cover of *Derek Jarman's Garden*. Courtesy of Thames & Hudson.	216

Acknowledgements

I am indebted to the energy, humour and generosity of Keith Collins, who invited me to potter in Prospect Cottage and tirelessly corresponded with me. Thank you, Keith. I also count myself very lucky that Catherine Silverstone provided great support for both me and my work over the years. Thank you, Catherine. This book is dedicated to both of their memories.

With grateful thanks to Peter Swaab for his astute judgement and kindness, and to Robert Mills, Hugh Stevens and Melissa Zeiger for their ongoing support of my work on Derek Jarman. My thanks to the trustees of the Keith Collins Will Trust, Diane Gelon, Karl Lydon and Amanda Wilkinson. I also extend my thanks to Liam Daniel, Raymond Dean, Colin MacCabe, Gerald Incandela, Seán Kissane, James Mackay, Tony Peake, Sandra Ross, Andrew Shanahan, Donald Smith, Howard Sooley, Michael Warner, Ed Webb-Ingall, Edmund White and Michael Carroll. I also thank Matthew Frost, Paul Clarke and the reviewers for Manchester University Press.

This book has been supported by a postdoctoral fellowship from the Paul Mellon Centre for Studies in British Art, as well as by a period as an exchange scholar in the Department of English and Lesbian, Gay, Bisexual, and Transgender Studies at Yale University. I would also like to acknowledge financial support from University College London, Universität Tübingen and *The Literary Encyclopaedia* Travel Fund. My thanks to the librarians at BFI Archives and the Beinecke Rare Book and Manuscript Library for giving me generous access to resources.

I am also grateful to those who read early versions of this research: Juliette Atkinson, Matthew Beaumont, Sarah Brophy, Mark Ford, Julia Jordan, Eric Langley, Max Saunders and Mark Turner. Thanks also to everyone who kindly provided encouragement, support, opportunities and welcome feedback: Pascale Aebischer, Ardis Butterfield, Ben Campkin, Zara Dinnen, Rachael Gilmour, Ingrid Hotz-Davies, Mark Mathuray, Sam McBean, Aleksandr Prigozhin, Jordan Rowe, Andrew van der Vlies and Declan Wiffen.

Thank you, Annette-Carina van der Zaag and Daniel O'Gorman, for your consistent support, illuminating conversations and careful readings, above and beyond the call of duty. With special thanks to my parents, Judith and David Parsons. I am grateful for the support of my work, friendship and encouragement from Abigail Woodfin, David Anderson, James Bide-Thomas, Christopher de Bie, Martin Nyx Brain, Letitia Calin, Jess Cotton, Elsa Court, Luke Davies, Rachele Dini, Flora Dunster, Paulo Gonçalves, Amy Greenbank, Becky Hahn, Matt Ingleby, Karina Jacubowicz, Roberta Klimt, Brandon Menke, Holly Nyx, Nellie Nutt, kitt price, Alastair Reed, Heather Scott, Robert Stagg, Simon Trafford and Bethany Winning. Finally, many thanks to my colleagues at Wellcome Trust for providing space for my writing during its final stages.

A different version of sections of Chapter 8 has been published in a special issue of *Shakespeare Bulletin*, 'Derek Jarman and "the Renaissance"' (2014), and segments from Chapter 11 have been published in a special issue of *a/b: Auto/Biography Studies*, 'Embodiment' (2018).

Figure 1 Jarman in *Dollar Bill Cape* and mitre, 1970.

Introduction

Fragments of memory eddy past and are lost in the dark. In the yellowing light half-forgotten papers whirl old headlines up and over dingy suburban houses, past leaders and obituaries, the debris of inaction, into the void. Thought illuminated briefly by lightning.

(Derek Jarman, *Modern Nature*)[1]

> As she disappears
> I toast my ghost
> In acqua vite
> Luminous presence
> Here and gone.

(Derek Jarman, *Chroma*)[2]

The absence of the past

'WHEN I WAS YOUNG THE ABSENCE OF THE PAST WAS A TERROR that's why I wrote autobiography'.[3] So explains queer filmmaker, writer, artist and activist Derek Jarman in *At Your Own Risk*, his polemical history of homophobia in Britain. Writing from the standpoint of 1992, at which point he had published multiple parts of his serial, dispersed life-writing project, his statement is a distillation of the sharply politicised rationale for his continued focus on autobiographical writing. His use of the definite article here – 'the past' – implies that the past he refers to is the only possible past for him: the history of queer desire. In a compact way, he indicates the alienation of growing into a life with no visible forebears. 'Terror' is a strong word, but it communicates the severity of his childhood need. He recalls that 'In 1982, my friend Nicholas told me to write it "out"' (*At Your Own Risk*, p. 30), and he set about composing the first of his books of life-writing, *Dancing Ledge*, the first published manifestation of the life-writing that would continue apace until his death from AIDS-related illnesses in 1994.[4]

Jarman's understanding of the past, which inflects all his work, is reflected through his own body – always understood as linked to a history of other queer bodies. In repeated acts of experimental self-representation (see Figure 1), Jarman blended visionary queer politics and a commitment to rehabilitating queer pasts, which always made a claim for the vital importance of first-person accounts. He consistently created art from material drawn from his own life. The ways in which his queer identity and personal history intersect with his political activism frame almost all his projects, across visual art, film and written texts. Jarman's artistic output, from his first poems, Super 8s and journals to his late illness narratives, paintings and posthumously published diaries, all tell a story of a rich life full of friendship, generosity and creativity lived out in the bars, bedrooms, heaths and studios of London, and later the harsh landscape of the Kentish coast at Dungeness.

Jarman's statement at the start of this introduction indicates the reparative impulse within his life-writing. By producing narratives that explore his own queer past, he attempts to counter some of the harm he suffered growing up in a Britain where sex acts between men were illegal, prejudice was rife and information was hard to come by.[5] In his life-writing, Jarman sought to redress 'the terrible dearth of information, the fictionalisation of our experience' by demonstrating that 'the best of it is in our lives' (*Modern Nature*, p. 56). Writing retrospectively of his own experience of coming of age in the 1960s, he comments: 'It was very important to me to find the "I": *I* feel this, this happened to *me*, *I* did this. I wanted to read that. My obsession with biography is to find these "I"s. The subtext of my films ha[s] been the books, putting myself back into the picture' (*At Your Own Risk*, p. 30).

But Jarman's life-writing project also looks outwards. It provides a social act for those of us who are younger than him. Paul de Man has argued that 'autobiographical discourse is a discourse of self-restoration', yet Jarman's preoccupation with life-writing makes use of this 'self-restoration' for socially concerned ends.[6] Sarah Brophy reads the impulse as pedagogical, which is certainly a part of it, but Jarman's life-writing project goes further than this: it is a commitment to the transformational imagination – or queer futurity – that derives from embodied practice.[7] Repeatedly using his own life as material in his art is a practice that works towards a future in which queer lives are no longer a cause for public concern or debate. As the HIV/AIDS crisis gathered momentum, Jarman became more sharply engaged with the urgent need to provide visible forebears to younger generations and to create alternative scripts to understand queer experience. His autobiographical production is as much about pedagogy, responsibility and queer futurity as it is about self-reflection. His status as a highly visible queer man in the media, who had become famous through his idiosyncratic films, enabled him to take a stand and put material from his own life to use as a social act. From Jarman's HIV-positive diagnosis in December 1986 onward, his work developed militancy and urgency. It was imperative that he produce work quickly as he knew his time was now limited.[8]

'The problem of so much of the writing about this epidemic is the absence of the author', Jarman comments in *At Your Own Risk* (p. 5), frustrated with impersonal and damaging media accounts. He sought to counter some of this absence by bearing witness to the fraught historical moment in his life-writing, for example by sharing the debilitating effects of the AIDS-related illnesses he started to develop for the first time in his journal *Modern Nature*. When, in a late interview for *Face to Face*, Jeremy Isaacs asked Jarman how he would like to be remembered, he quipped that he would simply like to disappear: he'd like to take all his works and just evaporate.[9] His irreverent tone here shows an ambivalence in Jarman, as he makes a claim against his own centrality. Yet throughout his later work, he always places himself in view as witness and subject, and as an artist who excavates queer moments in history with utter seriousness and urgency to construct possible queer futures.

Like a number of New York artists and writers, including David Wojnarowicz, Peter Hujar and Edmund White, Jarman consistently created art with material drawn from his own life, using it as a generative activist force. He used what Joan Scott terms the 'authority of experience' by relating the material effects of AIDS-related illnesses on his own body during this time of crisis.[10] In doing so, Jarman demonstrates his belief in the power of a public process that makes use of life narratives to enact politically necessary work. In *Epistemology of the Closet*, Eve Kosofsky Sedgwick attributes the prevalence of overlapping public misrepresentations of HIV/AIDS and the resurgence of homophobia to 'a medicalized dream of the prevention of gay bodies' in the public's imaginary.[11] Simon Watney argues that it is only logical that media representations, courting their imagined publics, would play on 'the forward slippage from corruption theories of homosexuality to contagion theories of AIDS'.[12] It is here that Jarman sought to intervene. By generating powerful art to counter these discourses, he did activist work to battle social injustice where he found it, in particular against the harmful governmental and media responses to the AIDS crisis (from the mid-1980s onwards), the UK legislative initiative known as Section 28 (1988) and the resultant damaging silence in education regarding LGBTQ+ lives.[13]

As well as using his own past to counter the harmful dominant narratives circulating in mainstream discourse, Jarman was also committed to excavating the history of queer desire. His compulsive learning across the wealth of

Western thought is put to use alongside material from his own life in his work to counter a homophobic post-war Britain. The quotation with which I start this introduction declares Jarman's personal investment in a queer history project. He connects his own past to a wider queer past: by contributing his own 'autobiography', he hoped to counter some of the 'ABSENCE OF THE PAST' – by which he means the gay past – of his upbringing (*At Your Own Risk*, p. 30). Rehabilitating the queer past is a means for him to correct the absence he had felt as a child. The statement is an escalation of the elegiac well-known opening line of homosexual writer L. P. Hartley's *The Go-Between* (1953), written while Jarman was a child: 'The past is a foreign country: they do things differently there'.[14] By challenging official versions of history and uncovering its excised queer content, not in the form of the novel but the more spontaneous and immediate scrapbooked forms he favoured, he can stake his claim on it. In films such as *The Tempest*, *The Angelic Conversation* and *Edward II* he draws from the canonical Renaissance playwrights William Shakespeare and Christopher Marlowe, placing the queer content at the fore. In films such as *War Requiem* (based on the work of Benjamin Britten and Wilfred Owen), *Caravaggio* and *Wittgenstein*, he traces a new queer lineage.

The same reparative impulse is evident throughout his published life-writing, made evident in the beautifully illustrated books published alongside two of the films – *Derek Jarman's Caravaggio* and *Queer Edward II* – which at once extend the arguments made in the films and advance an understanding of the political importance of a reparative queer history project. He sometimes explores history in unexpected ways. For example, he unearths a queer history of colour in his final works: 'the forward exploration of Colour is Queer', Jarman announces in his introduction to the Wittgenstein script, 'Leonardo in his notebook, Newton's *Optics* and Ludwig's *Remarks on Colour*'.[15] Here, he draws a lineage between his work on colour and that of precursors who also worked on colour and desired men. He extends this lineage in *Chroma: A Book of Colour*, collaging evidence to support his assertion from Neoplatonist Marsilio Ficino, bisexual Johann Wolfgang von Goethe, bachelor Isaac Newton and homosexual Ludwig Wittgenstein. He also responded to Section 28 by constructing queer genealogies in his art.

Jarman's life-writing is remarkable for its experimental range as it develops its powerful, imaginative response to the HIV/AIDS crisis. Jarman constructs a varied autobiographical voice that calls on a range of intensities, often juxtaposing images and written text, and collaging quotations from many sources. His varied life-writing and self-making constitute a series of shifting gestures performed publicly that cite, expand and acknowledge existing modes of queer self-representation. Jarman extended the scope of AIDS literature, film and ways of bearing witness by repeatedly using particular images and symbols, creating transhistorical, allegorical forms of self-representation that take inspiration from diverse historical periods. He used interdisciplinary methods, collage and montage to create urgent life-writing work that owes much to experimental filmmakers including Andrei Tarkovsky, Sergei Parajanov and Kenneth Anger, as well as to experimental artists such as Robert Rauschenberg and Cy Twombly. Jarman is interested in the ways that he can reflect his memory, identity and embodiment in his life-writing. His life-writing works are far more than straightforwardly autobiographical. As Brophy suggests, they 'may be read as confrontational theoretical reflections on subjectivity, activism, art, and the overlapping representational contracts of testimony, obituary, and elegy'.[16] Their multiple modes and aims together create life-writing of wide appeal.

In the first epigraph to this introduction, I quote Jarman describing the transience of scattered, partial, almost intangible memories: 'Fragments of memory eddy past' and become 'lost in the dark'. He is concerned here with highlighting the impermanence of thought – the briefest moments in which it becomes 'illuminated [...] by lightning'. His written work is testimony to his attempt to retain some of these fragments; the politically inflected content of his life-writing is a counter to 'the debris of inaction', a hex against 'the void' (*Modern Nature*, p. 20). The second epigraph is taken from the final stanza of the final poem in *Chroma*, the final book that Jarman would see almost to completion. Jarman describes his ghost, whom he imagines as a willowy character who shifts gender, 'With a beard of spun glass', who 'dazzles', 'Rippling with laughter' (*Chroma*, p. 150), even as his body encounters these final months. He imagines his ghost as a 'Luminous presence', a bright yet fragile remnant of his vitality at the time of writing, a reminder of the nearness of his mortality. Reading back from the perspective of today, the 'ghost' that remains is the 'Luminous presence' found in his self-representations. Scattered across media, the 'fragments of memory' (*Modern Nature*, p. 20) that remain available to us offer us the 'ghost' of an alchemist both 'Here and gone' (*Chroma*, p. 150). Jarman's life-writing forms testimony that bears witness to a terrible time. In doing so, it offers ways to harness the impermanence of thought and of memory to fuel utopian dreaming.

Jarman's vision was embedded in temporal concerns. He uncovered traces of the past in order to critique the present, with the aim of contributing towards a brighter future. The vision we encounter across Jarman's life-writing is the embodiment of a wider queer affect. Writing two decades after the advent of queer theory, José Esteban Muñoz argues movingly that 'forward-dawning futurity' is the fundamental attribute of queerness: 'Queerness is not yet here. Queerness is an ideality. Put another way, we are not yet queer. We may never touch queerness, but we can feel it as the warm illumination of a horizon imbued with potentiality. We have never been queer, yet queerness exists for us as an ideality that can be distilled from the past and used to imagine a future.'[17] He reads an anticipatory trend in queer artists and writers who, while looking to the past, illuminated paths towards the future in politically critical ways. Their commitment to the future – conceived of as 'a horizon imbued with potentiality' – requires the outright 'rejection of a here and now and an insistence on potentiality or concrete possibility for another world'.[18] Jarman writes of his ghost's 'Luminous presence', which is a means not only to signal the haunting of his present by the knowledge of his future death, but also to signal the possibility of ephemeral parts of himself haunting and perhaps lighting the way towards the future. Muñoz's manifesto about queer futurity demonstrates the perseverance of the same persistent engagement with queer temporality we see in Jarman: queer art, using his life as material, as 'not simply a being but a doing for and toward the future'.[19]

'A doing for and toward the future'

In what follows, I will offer an overview and theorisation of Jarman's self-representations as a series of performative acts that form a larger project. They are forged through acts of collaboration, community-building and witnessing, and reflections on premature illness, death and mourning throughout the queer community in the wake of the HIV/AIDS crisis. This book argues that the life-writing process made visible through the way Jarman uses techniques of juxtaposition, or collage, is a queer practice of survival that also seeks to change the terms of his representation. Through his collaging process, he explores the performative power of life-writing, for example by engaging with the ways his varied self-making calls on that of others. But he nevertheless seeks to represent his lived experience, insisting on the referentiality of the text to his embodied life. Jarman's unique approach helped create cultural scripts that might offer new ways to communicate about queer lives – scripts that have been taken up by younger generations of writers, filmmakers and artists.

Jarman's powerful, imaginative response to the AIDS crisis in his life-writing was vitally important: his body of writing changed the cultural terms of HIV/AIDS representation. It is absolutely critical that he wrote in the first person about the effects of the crisis on his own life. He strongly believed that first-person accounts are far more politically effective. In his writing, he provides an imaginative means of performing the AIDS Coalition To Unleash Power (ACT UP) refrain: 'Stop looking at us. Start listening to us'.[20] Andrew Moor cites Jarman's decision not to document visually and display his body as 'an urgent, politicized response to other unsatisfactory representations of the AIDS crisis'.[21] Jarman's project in his late writing, as well as in his final film *Blue*, enacts the message from the ACT UP demonstrators. The written and audible expressions of the corporeal are here intentionally mediated to avoid an audience that gives precedence to the biological over the political, discursive aspects of his self-representations. The accumulated project of his life-writing was to intervene in the collective, ongoing cultural history of the HIV/AIDS crisis, with the aim of changing the social and political terrain for those who would follow.

I provide analyses of his strategic life-writing in his books, as well as his visual self-representation in film and his use of material from his life in his art. I read Jarman's self-representations across his literary and visual outputs as a queer utopian project recorded across journals, published books and films. It is intended to be read in terms of its process, whether engaging with particular historical characters or the contemporary political moment. Each text, film, work of art or public statement is an instance in a serial, dispersed and fragmentary project, which places emphasis not on the polish of the finished product, but on the process of its production.

Jarman composed serial life-writing because doing so enabled him to share a subjectivity undergoing profound shifts as the HIV/AIDS crisis worsened, he had his own HIV-positive status confirmed, became a public figurehead for AIDS-related issues, and began to suffer from AIDS-related illnesses. His responses are swift, as he did not know how long he would be able to work, and provisional, as his experiences and perspectives changed. Reflecting on the virus early in 1989 in *Modern Nature*, he comments, 'my whole being has changed' (p. 25), as he attempts to compare the rhythms and expectations of his life pre-diagnosis to those of his life in the present. As well as being serial, Jarman's life-writing is also dispersed. He describes his life-writing in *At Your Own Risk* as 'a series of introductions to matters and agendas unfinished. Like memory, it has gaps, amnesias, fragments of past, fractured present' (*At Your Own Risk*, p. 5). It is incomplete, fragmented and 'a series of introductions' rather than a relation of polished statements.

Analysing Jarman's work from the perspective of his life-writing is an act of reading on my part that is based on Jarman's own practice. His work is intensely embodied. Acting as Pier Paolo Pasolini in Julian Cole's student film about the poet-filmmaker's death, he repeats Pasolini's refrain: 'I'd like to [...] throw my body into the struggle'.[22] For Jarman, although this struggle only sometimes meant putting his body on display, the refrain contains exactly the sense one gets from an appreciation of Jarman's work: his art and life are intrinsic to one another. The struggle in his life not only informs but also directs the work. Reading this work through the lens of life-writing is not only suggested by Jarman himself but is also an evocative way to draw out how the diverse areas of his artistic and political practice work to support one another.

Luminous presence unpacks the complexity of Jarman's queer historical project. I consider how he writes back to mainstream discourse, reinstates the queer aspect of our pasts and starts to construct a brighter future during this dispiriting time. It affirms the unsettling value of his engagement with pedagogy and commitment to queer futurity in the wake of Section 28, one of the most repressive laws to have been passed in the Western world in the last fifty years. This research contributes to debates at the juncture of queer studies and life-writing studies concerning the role of memory, identity, embodiment and form as holding disruptive potential and political resonance.

The raw material of the research determines the manner of analysis. Given the multiple and intersecting sites of the autobiographical across Jarman's work in visual art, film and written text, no single-discipline approach is sufficient. I therefore interpret these diverse autobiographical practices in an interdisciplinary way. *Luminous presence* gives a close reading of Jarman's self-representations through a variety of theoretical standpoints, among them those of cultural studies, queer theory and life-writing studies. Rather than viewing life-writing as an introspective and ordinarily solitary articulation, I read it as generated by encounters that are social, collaborative and contestatory.

Although Jarman's films have received critical attention and he is viewed as one of the most influential British filmmakers of the late twentieth century, his work has nonetheless been under-researched. In particular, there is one rich area of his work that is yet to receive sustained analysis. Scholars to date have not yet attended to the wide-ranging body of his autobiographical work. His life-writing, however, has enduring relevance: it is a testament to optimism and belief in community in a time of crisis, it provides a demonstration of the power of politically engaged literature and art to speak out against inequalities, and it is a unique body of work that is committed to experimentation in its engagements with self-representation. Nevertheless, *Luminous presence* is the first full-length study to focus on his life-writing and self-representations. It explores this important part of Jarman's legacy, teasing out the complexity of his sustained experiments with self-representation in his work across literature, art and film.

Jarman's continued significance within our cultural life has recently been demonstrated by the activity to mark both the twentieth and twenty-fifth anniversaries of his death.[23] Four of his books of life-writing have recently been republished by Vintage Classics, with new introductions by Neil Bartlett, Olivia Laing, Ali Smith and Matthew Todd.[24] Their republication has drawn welcome attention to these beautiful texts and has allowed them to reach new audiences. A major retrospective in 2019–20 at the Irish Museum of Modern Art (IMMA) curated by Seán Kissane, 'Derek Jarman, PROTEST!', brought together Jarman's art with the different strands of his work, and was accompanied by a beautifully illustrated new publication reflecting on his life and legacy.[25]

Catherine Silverstone has reflected on how Jarman's death and memory are invoked in public discourse, and what's at stake in remembering him in public acts of commemoration. She points to pieces of work such as Isaac Julien's *Derek* (2008), in which Jarman's life and vision are remembered and celebrated. She raises the critical point that the loss of Jarman has come to 'signal [...] more than the loss of a particular life': his death, she points out, 'becomes a means through which to remember the HIV/AIDS crisis from the mid-1980s to early 1990s, queer civil rights activism, and changes in the conditions of experimental filmmaking'.[26] She rightly points to the overlapping personal memories of those who knew Jarman, and the public memories we have as a result of his work and its critical place in many of our lives. 'Legacy', Silverstone points out, 'is never complete but an on-going iterative process, without end, always already remaking the end.' This book focuses primarily on Jarman's shared personal history in his published books, but one should keep in mind the ambivalent ways in which personal, private and public memories overlap in any consideration of his life and legacy.

Jarman's published 'Queerlife' began with *Dancing Ledge* (1984) and includes the lavishly illustrated books published alongside the release of his films: *Derek Jarman's Caravaggio* (1986) and *Queer Edward II* (1991).[27] He published a series of hybrid autobiographical works that mix polemic with poetry: *Kicking the Pricks* (1987), *At Your Own Risk: A Saint's Testament* (1992), *Chroma: A Book of Colour* (1994) and *Blue* (1994).[28] His journals are collected in *Modern Nature: The Journals of Derek Jarman* (1991) and the posthumously published *Smiling in Slow Motion* (2000).[29] Diary entries also pepper the visual record of his garden, *Derek Jarman's Garden with Photographs by Howard Sooley* (1995), also published posthumously.[30] He also published an early chapbook of poetry, *A finger in the fishes mouth* (1972), which uses material from his life and travels. His late paintings include self-referential text and words relating to his illness. A number of books of Jarman's paintings have also been collated. Late paintings feature in the collectors' calendar *Today and Tomorrow* (1991), and in books to accompany exhibitions, *Queer* (1993) and *Evil Queen* (1994). He appears in several of his films, making a brief cameo appearance in *Caravaggio* (1986), and playing the role of dream poet in *The Last of England* (1987), which also features home-movie footage from his childhood. He returns to the role of dream poet in *The Garden* (1990).[31] Lastly, his voice is one of the four that speak in his final film, *Blue* (1993).

Why life-writing?

This book uses the term *life-writing* to encompass Jarman's capacious, varied autobiographical project. It is a collective term that describes the significant proportion of Jarman's diverse work that includes representations of himself, narratives from his life and stories from the lives of others. *Life-writing* can be used to signal what Smith and Watson refer to when they choose *life narrative* – as 'a general term for acts of self-presentation of all kinds and in diverse media'.[32] It can also refer to that 'which provide[s] materials out of which lives or parts of lives are composed'.[33] The term is often traced to Virginia Woolf, who used it in her autobiographical outline 'A Sketch of the Past' when stressing the importance of delineating the 'immense forces society brings to play upon each of us' in one's 'life-writing'.[34]

Premised on the expanded concept of the autobiographical signature or trace, the term *life-writing* encompasses every instance of cultural production that involves the representation of a body, relation of life stories or inscriptions that form a record of a life.[35] It is this generic inclusiveness that is important: the term *life-writing* encompasses any and every example of cultural production involving the representation or relation of life stories: autobiographical or texts, memoirs, letters, testimony, medical narratives or using parts of a life on canvas. The presentation of the body itself forms part of this category: cameos in films, self-portraiture, sharing the marks of ageing, trauma and illness, and the deployment of the various symbolic functions the body might enact at different times.

My intention in this book is to think across media, as Jarman does, presenting a reading that begins in his writing but takes into account the ways he shifts media to highlight different effects. The generic inclusiveness of the term *life-writing* allows for the inclusion of a rich collection of source material, but it is also a political decision to prioritise a reading that seeks to encompass the nuanced, embodied politics Jarman enacts through his multiple roles. Echoing Jarman's commitment to 'politics in the first person' (*At Your*

Own Risk, p. 121), *Luminous presence* thinks across generic boundaries in order to evaluate how and why Jarman deploys self-representations.

Queer life-writing

Michel de Certeau comments, 'Social life multiplies the gestures and modes of behavior *(im)printed* by narrative models; it ceaselessly reproduces and accumulates "copies" of stories'.[36] We are continual authenticators of our own lives, relentlessly constructing and reproducing narratives about them. Yet we also consume personal narratives on an everyday basis. Smith and Watson argue that 'we imbibe the heterogeneous "lives" authorized by and authenticated in the institutions through which we negotiate daily existence'.[37] As a consequence, the stories we tell about our own lives are likely to fall within the frameworks available to us for their construction: our own narratives cite and recite cultural norms.[38] Smith and Watson argue that 'In telling their stories, narrators take up models of identity that are culturally available'.[39]

However, as Judith Butler observes, 'If the "I" is not at one with moral norms, this means only that the subject must deliberate upon these norms, and that part of deliberation will entail a critical understanding of their social genesis and meaning'.[40] Those of us with marginal identities or characteristics that mark us as other from mainstream society in some way, such as our sexualities, illnesses or disabilities, race, religion, or histories of addiction or of surviving abuse, have reason to intervene in dominant cultural scripts where we can. Life-writing becomes a means of self-actualisation: by rewriting, for example, the script of a particular autobiographical form to match one's own past, one begins to validate experiences outside of the mainstream.

Jarman believed that life-writing held a particular political importance over other forms of writing. Its claims to representing reality were in his mind crucial in undoing harm and rewriting alternative forms of history. Recent discussions of life-writing often focus on the way autobiographical writing can give socially and politically marginalised subjects access to discourses of identity that will facilitate cultural and political recognition.[41] By publishing a memoir, such subjects gain access to authoritative speaking positions and, in some instances, use the form to test the limits of existing discourses.[42]

Yet publishing accounts of queer lives requires several conditions to be met. First, a legal climate that will not seek to intervene in the public accounts of the lives of its author. Second, a social climate that is unlikely to put its author at undue risk. Third, a publishing climate that shows interest in selling accounts like these because publishers believe there to be a market for them – often resulting in books written by those who were already well-known in literary, political or celebrity circles.[43] Consequently, there were very few queer autobiographical books published in Britain at around the time Jarman started publishing his life-writing, although of course there is a rich though partially occluded history of poetry, performance, novels and art.[44] When Edmund White published his first semi-autobiographical novel *A Boy's Own Story* in 1982, it was presented as fiction. Although Alan Hollinghurst sees 'the liberating potential of a closely autobiographical kind of novel, where the testamentary force of memoir is coupled with the artifice of fiction', there were pragmatic reasons for its genre as well.[45] White commented that it would have been impossible to get an autobiography published in the early 1980s as a little-known gay writer early in his career – writing autobiography or memoir was the preserve of the famous, or of politicians.[46] Jarman, on the other hand, had gained sufficient notoriety to give him a platform from which he could write non-fiction about his life. Although *Dancing Ledge* did not sell well in 1982 and quickly slipped out of view, Jarman continued to be offered publishing contracts as the decade progressed – and through these, the opportunity to try to change the terms of his representation as queer and as living with HIV/AIDS. By the late 1980s, he was sufficiently famous to have accrued a broad audience.

Jarman cared deeply that autobiographical and biographical books about queer experience should exist in large numbers. In a 1984 interview in the gay magazine *Square Peg*, Jarman comments that there were not nearly enough autobiographies 'where the gay aspect is put fairly to the fore'.[47] In Britain, John Addington Symonds' memoirs, written between 1889 and 1893, were finally published in 1984, the same year as *Dancing Ledge*. The philosopher Goldsworthy Lowes Dickinson wrote his autobiography in 1921, which was published posthumously in 1973. Quentin Crisp's witty memoir *The Naked Civil Servant* (1968) describes his life from childhood to middle age, covering his experiences as a rent boy, a nude model and a book designer. J. R. Ackerley's memoir, styled as a detective story about his own father's past, private life and sexuality but also detailing his own, *My Father and Myself*, emerged in 1968.

Following his early, coded autobiography *Lions and Shadows* (1938), Christopher Isherwood published an autobiography in 1976, *Christopher and his Kind*. His friend and lover Stephen Spender's *World Within World* (1951) emerged much earlier, but describes his homosexuality in terms Paul Robinson describes as 'coy frankness' that 'uniquely combines candor with obfuscation' and which ends at the point that Spender decides to marry Inez Pearn.[48] Jarman mentions Tom Driberg, the Labour MP and journalist, whose exploits were published posthumously in *Ruling Passions:*

The Autobiography of Tom Driberg (1977). It explores the development of his sexuality alongside other elements of his personality, especially his early involvement with left-wing politics and what he saw as a contradictory obsession with Catholicism. A progressive account from a confident, well-educated and well-connected man, it declares an absence of shame even in the face of censure from authority. Despite this, Driberg suppressed the book until after his own death. The filmmaker Terence Davies published the melancholy *Hallelujah Now* in 1984, which was marketed as a novel but explores its author's working-class background and geographical location (Liverpool, rather than London). Joe Orton's diaries from 1966 to 1967 would not be edited and published until 1986. By the time that Neil Bartlett's autobiographical reflection on gay lives in the 1890s and 1980s, *Who Was That Man? A Present for Mr Oscar Wilde*, was released in 1988, Jarman had published two sustained memoirs, *Dancing Ledge* and *Kicking the Pricks*.

As a result, Jarman felt he was remarkable for writing candidly about his own life at the time he started doing so, and the above portrait of the queer or homosexual lives published in Britain prior to the moment Jarman published *Dancing Ledge* in 1984 is reasonably brief. There simply had been very little else published that might be firmly classed as autobiography. However, having to locate biography in fiction does not necessarily lead to Jarman's conclusion that his generation 'had a lack of information', at least not by the early 1980s (*At Your Own Risk*, p. 72). Jarman's main barrier when he was growing up seems to be not that books did not exist, but his lack of access to them until he was introduced to writing by Jean Genet and Jean Cocteau at university.[49] His desire that life stories were contained within autobiographies rather than transformed into fiction or poetry meant that he was quick to discount the growing number of mainstream novels dealing with queer experience. This says more about his own priorities and interests than it does about gay and lesbian literary culture at the time. Indeed, Angus Wilson's prominent first novel *Hemlock and After* (1952) sought to advance a socially progressive agenda in which the homosexual protagonist was no happier or unhappier than anyone else. However, Jarman strongly believed that the relationship of life-writing to the real, however fraught and contested, gave it a specific importance in enabling political contestation.

AIDS writing

As the 1980s and 1990s drew on, the dearth of queer life-writing available in print that Jarman had lamented began to be reversed. As the HIV/AIDS crisis gathered momentum, HIV/AIDS narratives originating from the US, France and Britain about the lives of gay men proliferated and, in some cases, achieved respectable sales figures. However, G. Thomas Couser's extensive survey of predominantly US AIDS narratives, written from the perspective of 1997, soon after the release of protease uptake inhibitors to the market changed the prognosis for some, draws attention to the relative paucity of first-person accounts in comparison to those written by relatives or partners.[50] He focuses on examples including those by sisters (such as Susan Wiltshire's *Seasons of Grief and Grace: A Sister's Story of AIDS*, 1994), children (such as Susan Bergman's *Anonymity: The Secret Life of an American Family*, 1994), parents (such as Barbara Peabody's *The Screaming Room: A Mother's Journal of Her Son's Struggle with AIDS*, 1986) and wives (such as Elizabeth Cox's *Thanksgiving: An AIDS Journal*, 1990). Couser concludes that these narratives, often their authors' only forays into writing for publication, unfortunately 'tend unwittingly to [...] reinforce negative stereotyping'.[51] His analysis was corroborated by texts that followed, including Jamaica Kincaid's account of her sibling Devon Drew in *My Brother* (1997).

Of the first-person accounts, many are similarly problematic. For example, the celebrity actor Rock Hudson, who concealed his homosexuality until AIDS-related illnesses rendered that impossible, published *Rock Hudson: His Story* (1986), in an attempt to regain control of his public image. Though promoted as co-authored with Sara Davidson, it is in effect a biography based on a series of interviews between Hudson and Davidson, as Hudson was too unwell and not sufficiently experienced a writer to compose it himself. The book displays his conservative politics (he was an old friend of Ronald Reagan) and relentless preoccupation with himself – giving the impression he lived in a vacuum with no friends or lovers. Worse, *The Golden Boy* (1992), written by the model and Wall Street banker James Melson, occasionally reveals its author's loathing of other gay men and offers a conversion narrative upon its author's HIV-positive diagnosis, wherein the prodigal son returns to family and to Christianity. Jerry Arterburn's *How Will I Tell My Mother? A True Story of One Man's Battle With Homosexuality and AIDS* (1990) and Thomas B. Stribling's *Love Broke Through: A Husband, Father, and Minister Tells His Own Story* (1990) offer more focused conversion narratives in which their homosexuality is displayed as an aberration from which they recover following the crisis of their diagnosis, resulting in their being welcomed back into their conservative, religious families. On a different note, Edmund White, although he has written prolifically – including his autobiographical novels commencing with *A Boy's Own Story*, and a series of excellent essays on HIV/AIDS – only published *My*

Lives, purporting to finally offer readers his unfictionalised autobiography, in 2005.

Nevertheless, several important texts counter these problematic accounts. One of the most prominent examples is Paul Monette's 'labour of grief', *Borrowed Time: An AIDS Memoir* (1988), which details his partner Roger Horwitz's failing health, foregrounding the difficulty of narrating illness, and which achieved relatively high sales figures in the US.[52] Fenton Johnson's *Geography of the Heart: A Memoir* (1996) similarly describes his relationship with his partner, as does Mark Doty's *Heaven's Coast* (1996). The anthropologist Eric Michaels detailed the last year of his life in *Unbecoming*, a startling and forceful text that appraises what it means to resist ideas of victimhood and the figure of the patient. It was written in 1987 but published a decade later. From 1994 until his death in 1996, Oscar Moore wrote a column in the *Guardian* describing his AIDS-related illnesses and his experiences with London's hospitals, collected in *PWA: Looking AIDS in the Face*. In France, Emmanuel Dreuilhe's *Corps à Corps (Mortal Embrace)* (1988) is an unusual, highly literary autobiographical account that reads as a series of essays reflecting on AIDS. Hervé Guibert also published numerous AIDS-related texts, the most famous of which is *À l'ami qui ne m'a pas sauvé la vie* (1992).[53]

The individual most similar to Jarman in terms of his intense, interdisciplinary response to political crisis is New York artist, filmmaker, writer and performance artist David Wojnarowicz. He produced a series of powerful works that stand in productive contrast to Jarman's. His two most famous books, *Close to the Knives – a Memoir of Disintegration* (1992) and *Memories that Smell like Gasoline* (1992), are responses to the AIDS crisis in America and searing critiques of the US government's handling of it. They are also collections of what Richard Maguire terms 'versions of his life': *Close to the Knives* is a collection of essays that tells and retells his life-story from childhood in the 1950s to the AIDS-related illnesses that afflicted him in the late 1980s and early 1990s.[54] Eric Waggoner argues that the book's 'collection of journal fragments, interviews, sketches and creative essays is a singularly difficult book to engage with as autobiography, largely because of the resolutely visceral nature of its writing and the "pastiched" construction of its narrative'.[55] Some of these energies and the resulting interpretative difficulties for readers are similar to those found in Jarman's late life-writing: both use personal narrative published as life-writing as an activist tactic, within texts that are important due to their engagement with AIDS, and with queer autobiography more widely.

Commenting in the context of the virus on the new urgency of publishing queer life stories – about the whole range of experience, including childhood, coming out and adult lives, not just experiences with HIV/AIDS – Paul Monette writes in his later memoir *Becoming a Man: Half a Life Story* (1992) that 'every mention now is a kind of manifesto, as we piece together the tale of the tribe. Our stories have died with us long enough. We mean to leave behind some map, some key, of the gay and lesbian people who follow – that they may not drown in the lies.'[56] Although Cindy Patton argues that sustained narratives did not play a major role in the backlash against mainstream media – and Couser is also careful not to overstate the ability of these texts to do activist work – I argue, in contrast, that this understates the case in relation to the prominent, affective, activist texts by those who created unusual, self-reflexive responses to the AIDS crisis, such as Paul Monette, David Wojnarowicz and Derek Jarman.[57]

Brophy points to the 'shifting dynamics of mourning and memory, blend[ed] […] with a good deal of polemic' in the AIDS memoirs she analyses, reflecting that this is 'a tendency that often makes them seem like essays as much as life stories'.[58] AIDS testimony is not solely preoccupied with the effects of the virus on the individual, but exists in anticipation of its relational nature: books such as these are written as an address to a reader, listener or witness. Ross Chambers argues that 'they look forward as enunciations to a future in which they will be read', echoing Holocaust survivor and clinical psychologist Dori Laub's suggestion that it is in the act of being heard by an empathetic reader or listener that testimony enters reality.[59] Laub explains that the reader or listener is 'the enabler of the testimony – the one who triggers its initiation, as well as the guardian of its process and of its momentum'.[60]

The focus of all Jarman's late texts – the late diaries *Modern Nature* and *Smiling in Slow Motion*, the polemic *At Your Own Risk*, and the image-heavy Dungeness garden book *Derek Jarman's Garden* – is the HIV/AIDS crisis, the loss of his friends, and the effects of AIDS-related illnesses on his body, bearing witness to this terrible time. Repeatedly returning to the same subjects or memories, he juxtaposes elements from his reading of history and philosophy, memories of his own life and recollections of friends to collage a powerful and thought-provoking response to the HIV/AIDS crisis. By finding unusual ways to respond to the crisis, he sought to change the cultural terms of HIV/AIDS representation and intervene in the collective, ongoing cultural history of the HIV/AIDS crisis, with the aim of changing the social and political terrain for those who would follow.

Collage

Luminous presence provides a study of Jarman's intensive exploration of particular self-making practices, most notably *collage*, especially as he negotiates the structures of interpretation that inform our understanding of HIV/AIDS writing. It is also an exploration of his self-representations as an instantiation of the profound shift in the conception and experience of subjectivity that occurred between the moment of composition of much of Jarman's collection of poetry (many of the poems originate from 1964) and the striking shifts that took place from 1987 onwards, following his HIV-positive diagnosis. Jarman's work fits in with a wider trend that Amelia Jones highlights, in which 'artists in the 1990s construct fragmented, dispersed, and explicitly particularized subjects that encourage the spectator's committed engagement'.[61] Through persistent juxtaposition, Jarman insists on the interrelatedness of subjects and objects, our inevitable simultaneous existence as subject and object, and our interdependence with our environment, resulting in 'a multiplicitous and dispersed, but fully embodied, social and political subject'.[62] A note on terminology: I am using *collage* to mean the juxtaposition of found materials in art or in scrapbook form.

Luminous presence argues that Jarman's repeated use of *collage* technique in his life-writing is a queer activist art project. In Convolute N of *The Arcades Project*, Walter Benjamin touches upon his notion of *collage*, which he terms *literary montage*:

> Method of this project: literary montage. I needn't *say* anything. Merely show. I shall purloin no valuables, appropriate no ingenious formulations. But the rags, the refuse – these I will not inventory but allow, in the only way possible, to come into their own: by making use of them.[63]

It is via this method that Jarman seeks to construct new registers for living. Jarman's life-writing has three interlinked foci: his reparative work rehabilitating queer histories, his construction of AIDS testimony and his activist work in the cultural arena. The vitality and idiosyncrasy of his varied self-making project underpin these concerns. Foremost, Jarman was an artist – irreverent, experimental and, at times, hasty. Jarman's *collage* technique was an essential tool in creating his swiftly constructed blend of autobiography, history of queer experience and contestatory politics. We see the repository of much of his initial thinking and the source of many of his printed texts in his scrapbooks, which are built from the juxtaposition of disparate found objects, thoughts, projects, words and images. Versions of their contents were pared down then published at speed to provide a swift response to the impact of HIV/AIDS, Section 28 and a homophobic press.

Collage has a central role in the relationship between representation and the real. Donald Kuspit notes that collage 'implies an easy shift from the material of life to the material of art – the self-evidence of the relationship between the two'.[64] However, although an 'easy shift' between life and art is suggested, there is complexity behind this seeming directness. Writing about Marianne Moore's collage poems, Bartholomew Brinkman argues that 'The scrapbooker is not simply a passive conduit for information, but an active participant in reshaping and re-presenting content'.[65] Indeed, as Marjorie Perloff has argued, collage 'incorporates directly into the work an actual fragment of the referent, thus forcing the reader or viewer to consider the interplay between preexisting message or material and the new artistic composition that results from the graft'.[66] Far from being a direct (if fragmented or partial) translation from one form to another, the complex conversation between the newly juxtaposed material in the *collage* and its origins make it a critical site for the re-evaluation of existing scripts for identity, and their adjustment or reconstruction. Anna Poletti argues: 'the potential of collage puts assumptions about representation under pressure, making it a powerful technique for life writers who aim to produce life narrative while responding to the normative ideas about life that underpin the autobiographical speaking position'.[67] Jarman's self-representations use the formal technique of juxtaposition as a practice.

Thomas Brockelman argues that 'Collage intends to represent the intersection of multiple discourses'.[68] More than this, the *collage* is compiled to put pressure on discourses and, perhaps, to shift their terms. In 'Critically Queer', Judith Butler argues that it is in the act of citation and reiteration that discourse produces power: 'there is no power, construed as a subject, that acts, but only a reiterated acting that *is* power in its persistence and instability'.[69] As I discussed in the section on AIDS writing above, discussions of life-writing often focus on the unique ability of autobiographical writing to give socially and politically marginalised subjects access to discourses of identity that can facilitate cultural and political recognition. However, the limitation of writing memoirs or other autobiographical forms is that it co-opts a pre-existing form through which to write one's life, rather than creating another that may be more capacious and well-suited to the kinds of stories and subjectivities it seeks to represent.

What happens if, instead of reiterating, for example, the dominant mode of writing autobiographically, perhaps through the genre of the memoir, one commences a programme of citation and reiteration that starts to build new discourse? Responding to this question, Anna Poletti, in examining Jonathan Caouette's montaged autobiographical documentary *Tarnation* (2003), reads his use of the collage form as a particular queer practice. She argues that:

> Homemade life narrative texts by queer subjects that use collage present a compelling counterexample to the prioritizing of intelligibility and recognition promised by the citation of the discourse of memoir. These texts, instead, attempt a periperformative response to the normative formal techniques

associated with memoir and its owner to bring into being a self and life that [complicate] normative values associated with living and identity.[70]

Developing Eve Kosofsky Sedgwick's notion of the *periperformative*, which in turn is a development of Butler's concept of *performativity*, Poletti attributes to Caouette's film its potential to critique the performative power of life-writing while nevertheless seeking to represent the lived experience of its author.[71] Its collage aesthetics can be read as a practice that can provide a 'periperformative' revision of the documentary memoir form.

Jarman's writing has been described as 'a kind of critical collage that is more familiar from American experimental writing'.[72] Indeed, Ellis describes *Chroma* as 'an autobiographical experiment for a subject-in-process', using Kristeva's term, formed from methods reprised across the journals published as *Modern Nature* and the scrapbook-polemic *At Your Own Risk*, all of which use collage as a means not only to construct life narrative, but also to speak back to the cultural forms within which the narrative exists.[73] My work adds an important perceptual layer to Poletti's analysis, viewing the way Jarman uses collage as a queer practice of survival – across his work but most prominently in his writing – that also seeks to change the terms of his representation by 'cobbling together ways to attach to the world that cannot be subsumed into an identity or bionarrative'.[74]

At the beginning of *Mortal Embrace*, Emmanuel Dreuilhe's book of highly literary life-writing about his experiences of HIV/AIDS, he seeks to explain his intentions for his writing's form:

> This diary is a singular experience, but I have tried to present, in the manner of David Hockney's photographic montages, a complete series of images of the same sickroom: that mental room which now forms the confined universe of people with AIDS, a room we will leave only to die. All those snapshots with overlapping perspectives offer views that vary according to the day and mood. Here and there a detail might be arbitrarily enlarged, out of proportion to the other elements of the picture, because our perception of our own condition is uneven and discontinuous.[75]

Dreuilhe seeks to provide a rationale, perhaps, for the repetitious and fragmentary nature of his life-writing. The accumulated juxtaposition of 'overlapping perspectives' is a specific practice intended to communicate the 'uneven and discontinuous' nature of his subjectivity over time. This passage speaks to elements of Jarman's own *montage* or *collage* process. David Hockney's photographic montages provide a useful touchstone: they shatter his perception of a particular scene into an image comprised of different angles and sections that, when composed, seem at times to be more real than one unified image. This is because the montages echo the physical process in which one's eyes range over a scene, focusing on different points, then one's brain unifies the information it receives. In breaking down each image, Hockney attempts to represent our disunified perceptions – and perhaps subjectivities – to present a postmodern collage demonstrating the impossibility of a unified subjectivity yet nevertheless providing us with the advantages of a compound viewpoint.

Jarman's use of collage is similarly disunified, put to different purposes at different times. Although the overtly political nature of some of his writing is clear (the polemic *At Your Own Risk*, in particular), some of his work uses collage and citation in more allusive ways. Evaluating Cy Twombly's use of poetry in his art, Mary Jacobus writes, 'Twombly practices the poetics of incompleteness, drawing on the survivals and fragments of the past, and allowing the reader to project meaning onto textual *lacunae* and gaps'.[76] In collaging gestures and citations on the canvas, through the poetic quotation and allusion that are fundamental to his visual practice, Jacobus argues that he 'becomes the unstable image of his verbal self-representation, dissolved in the act of self-inscription'.[77] Similarly, Jarman's self-making through collage allows for disunity not only within a work, but also between methods. His self-making through text, particularly in the late paintings collected in *Queer* and *Evil Queen*, uses fragmentary gestures, repeated words and juxtaposed concepts to delineate a self that encourages its viewers to collaborate in the process of its construction, projecting their understandings of his meaning into 'textual *lacunae* and gaps'.

Chapter outline

Luminous presence examines Jarman's books in broadly chronological order, allowing that some works were created simultaneously, in particular alongside the late journals. This arrangement tells the story of his developing experimentation with self-representation from his early chapbook of poetry to the 'whirlwind of projects' he undertook between his diagnosis as HIV-positive in December 1986 and his death in February 1994, 'as he attempted to squeeze decades of work into a handful of years'.[78]

Chapter 1 explores Jarman's first book *A finger in the fishes mouth*, a chapbook containing poems dating back to his student years. It considers the meanings of the book's postcard-poem form and reflects on his understanding of history, conceived of as existing in a perpetual present, as well as the book's coded autobiographical content. Next, Chapter 2 offers a reading of his first extended autobiographical text, *Dancing Ledge*, in which he sought to understand the links between his personal and professional lives. He writes about his childhood and coming-out narrative alongside a series of rich anecdotes. Giving far less of an internal world than his later texts, *Dancing Ledge* is a fascinating, partial self-portrait composed using the collaborative methods that allowed him to write at a furious pace. Chapter 3 offers a reading of Jarman's playful engagement with Caravaggio's self-portraits in *Derek Jarman's Caravaggio*. He revises some of the autobiographical meanings presented by Caravaggio in order to make the historical figure's dramatic work speak to issues of queer representation in the early 1980s. As a consequence, the project marks a turning point in his work, where his experimentation with self-representation took on clearly political intent. Chapter 4 explores similar themes in relation to Jarman's interest in Pier Paolo Pasolini: he is cast as Pasolini in a short film, *Ostia*, about the last evening of the poet-filmmaker's life, ending with his brutal homophobic and possibly politically motivated murder, transferred to a setting of London in the mid-1980s. Chapter 5 investigates Jarman's collaborative writing technique in *Kicking the Pricks*, which is created using a method similar to that used for *Dancing Ledge*. It also examines several pivotal moments in Jarman's life as they are relayed in this book: his diagnosis as HIV-positive, and the reflective re-evaluation of his relationship with both of his parents, made possible by the death of his father.

Luminous presence continues in Chapter 6 by relating Jarman's life-writing to his self-representations in films through two experimental feature films: *The Last of England* and *The Garden*. These experimental works act as a queer practice of survival, building narrative and providing political contestation through juxtaposition, changing perception through the correct combination of often highly personal images. This technique of commingling images becomes important for Jarman, his audiences and his readership, at times reactivating or appropriating discourses from sources as diverse as medieval poetry and images of domesticity in post-war Britain. The discussion of *The Garden* introduces the thematic urgency of the physical effects of HIV/AIDS on Jarman's body and on his self-representations.

In the next three chapters, the pivotal themes of all Jarman's later work emerge: how the HIV/AIDS crisis affects his understanding of his body, his need for individuation and for community, and to bear witness. Chapter 7 explores Jarman's interiority in *Modern Nature*, as he uses flowers and plants as symbols that evoke his personal history, as well as a collective history of queer desire, alongside his discussion of the horrific personal impact of HIV/AIDS. Chapter 8 on *Queer Edward II* examines how Jarman invokes the figure of the queer child along with activist slogans and autobiographical fragments to create an unusual, imaginative activist text. Chapter 9 looks at how Jarman constructs the text *At Your Own Risk* in the context of the AIDS epidemic and his own HIV-positive status, using his own history alongside the personal histories of others to mark out a newly visible space for himself and queer communities in an often homophobic culture.

Although these texts were produced over the same period (1989–91), they create very different effects with autobiographical material. What they have in common is their use of different kinds of collage aesthetics to create activist work.

The final three chapters of *Luminous presence* attend to Jarman's final works, exploring questions of voice and collaboration, an ethics of bearing witness in the face of trauma and loss, and the therapeutic possibilities of abstraction. Chapter 10 examines Jarman's late diaries, *Smiling in Slow Motion*, collected posthumously by Keith Collins. Here, we explore his increasingly fragmented documentation of his life and influences, and the changing ways in which he responds to and refutes stereotypical portrayals of HIV/AIDS. Next, Chapter 11 thinks through Jarman's creative use of colour as a queer strategy for creating history in the midst of crisis in the film and accompanying book of poetry, *Blue*, and the book *Chroma*. Chapter 12 investigates the collaborative project at work in *Derek Jarman's Garden*. We think about the garden as a memorial and about Jarman's gardening as a therapeutic practice via Howard Sooley's photographs of Jarman, images of the Dungeness garden that so many friends had worked on and some of Jarman's very last writing.

Jarman's influence

Jarman has been enormously influential for so many of us. His magnetic public persona and incisive queer work across media provided what Martin Fletcher described as 'welcome thunderflashes of dissent' amid the conservatism of the 1980s and early 1990s.[79] His ground-breaking, idiosyncratic work obsessed me as a queer teenager, and it continues to inspire new queer generations, as well as socially engaged art-house audiences and filmmakers. More than this, Jarman continues to inspire a committed following: he had an infectious and inclusive drive to create work that involves everybody who seeks it out. By using his own life-story within his work, he demonstrated the particular urgency and relevance of every queer life, encouraging solidarity, community and a productive anger that could be channelled into queer activism. His reach was immense: through the period I have been researching this book, I have met so many people whose lives have been touched by Jarman's creativity and his spirit. More people than I can count have shared anecdotes about times when he touched their lives, often by providing opportunities for them that otherwise wouldn't have existed. The 2020 ArtFund campaign to preserve Prospect Cottage raised £3.5 million to conserve and maintain the building, its contents and garden. It is the largest campaign in ArtFund's history, and a testament to Jarman's reach and importance. His legacy has been one of illumination (see Plate 1).

For me, writing about Jarman is a mark of solidarity with the previous generation of queer people who lived through that wicked time and an elegy for those who did not survive. It is through the determination and strength of those LGBTQ+ activists, and the critical cultural work by Jarman and many others, that the Britain we live in today has been in many ways transformed. This book is a commitment to the process of rehabilitation and education that was key to Jarman's life and work. The skill and variety with which he engaged his diverse audiences have only just begun to be fully explored. In particular, his autobiographical writing, along with the fascinating sketchbook-journals that contains so many of the diary entries that would later appear in press, deserves sustained attention. This book shows that Jarman's self-representations provide a critical means through which to understand his pioneering contribution to the cultural history of HIV/AIDS, as well as to queer representation more generally. His life-writing has enduring relevance: it is a testament to optimism and belief in community in a time of crisis, it provides a demonstration of the power of politically engaged literature and art to speak out against inequalities, and it is a unique body of work that is committed to experimentation in its sustained engagements with self-representation.

One of Jarman's most manifest traits is the generosity with which he shared his own life. His diaries are the crystallisation of this openness: his sustained belief in the absolute importance of talking candidly about his experiences of childhood, sex, love, cruising, friendship, community, homophobia and HIV/AIDS. He did this not because he believed his own experiences to be of particular importance, but because to do so was a political response to a life lived in a country that remained inhospitable and homophobic over every decade of his life. His status as a famous film director allowed him a platform and an audience. By naming the realities of one queer life, Jarman added to the evidence of experience and testimonies of voices previously silenced. Although a variety of post-1967 and post-Stonewall projects from both within and outside of the academy focused on rehabilitating the queer context of historical lives that had been hitherto suppressed, Jarman not only does this with his own life and with the lives of others, but goes further. He is confrontational, sometimes sharing challenging realities, and engages with contentious areas of queer experience. He demands that normative moralities do not come into it. Jarman embodies the US direct action group Queer Nation's famous slogan: 'We're here! We're Queer! Get used to it!'[80]

Notes

1 Derek Jarman, *Modern Nature: The Journals of Derek Jarman* (London: Vintage, 1991), p. 20. Further references are given within the text.
2 Derek Jarman, *Chroma: A Book of Colour – June '93* (London: Vintage, 1994), p. 151. Further references are given within the text.
3 Derek Jarman, *At Your Own Risk: A Saint's Testament* (London: Vintage, 1992), p. 30. Further references are given within the text.
4 The friend Jarman refers to is the theatre critic Nicholas de Jongh, who would go on to slip Jarman's HIV-positive status into an article in the *Guardian*, upon Jarman's request, on 22 October 1987.
5 Jarman was 25 years old by the time that sex acts between men were partially decriminalised in England and Wales as part of the Sexual Offences Act of 1967. For a social history of homosexuality until Jarman was 35, see Jeffrey Weeks, *Coming Out: Homosexual Politics in Britain, from the Nineteenth Century to the Present* (London: Quartet, 1977). Statistics for the rise in the number of arrests for sodomy, gross indecency and indecent assault throughout the 1940s and 1950s can be found on page 158. For a history of homosexuality in Britain from the beginning of the First World War until after Jarman's, death, see chapters 5 and 6 by Matt Cook in *A Gay History of Britain: Love and Sex Between Men Since the Middle Ages*, ed. Matt Cook (Oxford and Westport, CT: Greenwood World Publishing, 2007), pp. 145–214; see also Hugh David, *On Queer Street: A Social History of British Homosexuality, 1895–1995* (London: HarperCollins, 1997). For a detailed account of sexual cultures in London up until the release of the Wolfenden Report in 1957, see Matt Houlbrook, *Queer London: Perils and Pleasures in the Sexual Metropolis, 1918–1957* (Chicago: University of Chicago Press, 2005).
6 Paul de Man, 'Autobiography as De-Facement', *MLN*, 94.9 (1979), 919–30 (p. 925).
7 See Sarah Brophy, *Witnessing AIDS: Writing, Testimony, and the Work of Mourning* (Toronto: University of Toronto Press, 2004), pp. 29–78.
8 For a history of the AIDS crisis in Britain, see Simon Garfield, *The End of Innocence: Britain in the Time of AIDS* (London: Faber, 1995).
9 'Face to Face: Derek Jarman, with Jeremy Isaacs', *Face to Face*, BBC, 15 March 1993.
10 Joan W. Scott, 'The Evidence of Experience', *Critical Inquiry* 17.4 (1991), 773–97 (p. 780).
11 Eve Kosofsky Sedgwick, *Epistemology of the Closet* (Berkeley: University of California Press, 1990), p. 43.
12 Simon Watney, 'The Spectacle of AIDS', in *AIDS: Cultural Analysis/Cultural Activism*, ed. Douglas Crimp (Cambridge, MA: MIT Press, 1987), pp. 71–86 (p. 77).
13 Legislative initiative 'Clause 28' was reintroduced in December 1987 (and passed into law as Section 28 in May 1988). It prohibited local authorities from 'promoting homosexuality by teaching or by publishing material', including in

schools. 'Section 28: Prohibition on Promoting Homosexuality by Teaching or by Publishing Material', *Local Government Act 1988*, www.legislation.gov.uk/ukpga/1988/9/section/28/enacted (accessed 4 December 2017). For a detailed discussion of Section 28, see Anna Marie Smith, *New Right Discourse on Race and Sexuality: Britain, 1968–1990* (Cambridge and New York: Cambridge University Press, 2008), 183–239. For Jarman's response to the legislation, see Brophy, *Witnessing AIDS*, p. 61. Jarman also prints it in full in *At Your Own Risk*, pp. 127–8.
14 L. P. Hartley, *The Go-Between* (London: Penguin Books, 1958), p. 7. After all, Hartley would only become open about his sexuality towards the end of his life.
15 Derek Jarman, Terry Eagleton and Ken Butler, *Wittgenstein: The Terry Eagleton Script, The Derek Jarman Film* (London: British Film Institute, 1993), p. 64. Further references are given in text.
16 Brophy, *Witnessing AIDS*, pp. 33–4.
17 José Esteban Muñoz, *Cruising Utopia: The Then and There of Queer Futurity* (New York: New York University Press, 2009), p. 1.
18 Ibid.
19 Ibid.
20 For an account of the history of the slogan, see Simon Watney, *Imagine Hope: AIDS and Gay Identity* (London: Routledge, 2000), p. 101.
21 Andrew Moor, 'Spirit and Matter: Romantic Mythologies in the Films of Derek Jarman', in *Territories of Desire in Queer Culture: Refiguring Contemporary Boundaries*, eds. David Alderson and Linda Anderson (Manchester: Manchester University Press, 2000), pp. 49–67 (p. 50).
22 *Ostia*, dir. Julian Cole (Royal College of Art, 1987), 02:17–02:25.
23 See www.jarman2014.org for full details of the commemorative events that took place in 2014.
24 *Modern Nature*, *Smiling in Slow Motion*, *Chroma* and *At Your Own Risk* were reissued with new introductions in 2018–19.
25 'Derek Jarman: PROTEST!', curated by Seán Kissane, was displayed at IMMA in Dublin (November 2019 to February 2020) and at the time of this book going to press, is planned at Manchester Art Gallery (December 2021 to April 2022). The exhibition is accompanied by the book *Derek Jarman: PROTEST!*, eds. Seán Kissane and Karim Rehmani-White (London: Thames and Hudson, 2020).
26 Catherine Silverstone, 'Remembering Derek Jarman: Death, Legacy, and Friendship', *Shakespeare Bulletin*, 32.3 (2014), 451–70 (p. 453).
27 Derek Jarman, *Dancing Ledge* (London: Quartet Books, 1984; repr. 1991), preface. Further references are given within the text. There are several published books that this book does not examine in detail. First, his film scripts, six of which are collected in *Up In The Air* (1996). Second, *War Requiem* (1989), a slim volume published alongside the film *War Requiem*, contains Britten's libretto, Jarman's visualisations of the libretto, and his commentary about trying to marry images to Britten's piece. The text is discussed briefly in relation to *Queer Edward II*, but this book does not examine it in detail because its life-writing content is very

limited. *Luminous presence* also does not look in detail at the book released alongside the biopic *Wittgenstein* (1993), *Wittgenstein: The Terry Eagleton Script, The Derek Jarman Film* (1993), which contains both Terry Eagleton's and Jarman's scripts. It contains only a brief introductory essay, and the script is presented without accompanying notes, unlike *Derek Jarman's Caravaggio* or *Queer Edward II*.

28 The text of *Blue* is contained within *Chroma* but is also published separately as a special volume of poetry that formed the soundtrack to the film of the same name.

29 Although edited by Keith Collins and published posthumously, *Smiling in Slow Motion* was always intended for publication, and the publication deal had been arranged well in advance of Jarman's death.

30 Jarman prepared the text for the book with this publication deal in mind and was present during Howard Sooley's photography of the garden, although the text was edited and published posthumously.

31 Jarman also appears in others' films. These include: *Nighthawks*, dir. Ron Peck (Nashburgh, 1978), *Ostia* (1987), *Prick Up Your Ears*, dir. Stephen Frears (Curzon Artificial Eye, 1987) and *The Clearing*, dir. Alexis Bistikas (1993). He also appears in many of his Super 8s from the 1970s and 1980s.

32 Sidonie Smith and Julia Watson, *Reading Autobiography: A Guide for Interpreting Life Narratives* (Minneapolis: University of Minnesota Press, 2010), p. 4.

33 Zachary Leader, 'Introduction', in *On Life-Writing*, ed. Zachary Leader (Oxford: Oxford University Press, 2015), pp. 1–6 (p. 1).

34 Virginia Woolf, 'A Sketch of the Past' (1939), in *Moments Of Being: Autobiographical Writings*, ed. Jeanne Schulkind (San Diego, CA: Harcourt Brace, 1985), pp. 61–159 (p. 80).

35 For further discussions of the expanded autobiographical signature or trace, see Jacques Derrida, *The Ear of the Other: Otobiography, Transference, Translation: Texts and Discussions with Jacques Derrida*, ed. Christie McDonald, trans. Peggy Kamuf and Avital Ronell (Lincoln: University of Nebraska Press, 1988), p. 45; Julia Kristeva, *Black Sun: Melancholia and Depression*, trans. Leon S. Roudiez (New York: Columbia University Press, 1989), p. 129; Hélène Cixous, *Hélène Cixous: Rootprints: Memory and Life Writing*, ed. Mireille Calle-Gruber, trans. Eric Prenowitz, first English edn (London: Routledge, 1997), pp. 95–6; Sarah Brophy and Janice Hladki, 'Visual Autobiography in the Frame: Critical Embodiment and Cultural Pedagogy', in *Embodied Politics in Visual Autobiography*, eds. Sarah Brophy and Janice Hladki (Toronto: University of Toronto Press, 2014), pp. 3–30.

36 Michel de Certeau, *The Practice of Everyday Life*, trans. Steven Rendall (Berkeley: University of California Press, 1988), p. 186.

37 Sidonie Smith and Julia Watson, 'Introduction', in *Getting a Life: The Everyday Uses of Autobiography*, eds. Sidonie Smith and Julia Watson (Minneapolis: University of Minnesota Press, 1996), pp. 1–24 (p. 3).

38 'Our society has become a recited society, in three senses: it is defined by *stories* [...], by *citations* of stories, and by the interminable *recitation* of stories.' De Certeau, *Everyday Life*, p. 186.

39 Smith and Watson, 'Introduction', p. 9.
40 Judith Butler, *Giving an Account of Oneself* (New York: Fordham University Press, 2005), p. 8.
41 See G. Thomas Couser, *Recovering Bodies: Illness, Disability and Life-Writing* (Madison: University of Wisconsin Press, 1997); Susanna Egan, *Mirror Talk: Genres of Crisis in Contemporary Autobiography* (Chapel Hill and London: University of North Carolina Press, 1999).
42 See Leigh Gilmore, *The Limits of Autobiography: Trauma and Testimony* (Ithaca, NY: Cornell University Press, 2001).
43 See Sarah Brouillette, *Literature and the Creative Economy* (Stanford, CA: Stanford University Press, 2017).
44 There were also several celebrity autobiographies by figures such as Noel Coward, John Gielgud and Kenneth Williams, which mainly glossed over matters of sexuality.
45 Alan Hollinghurst, 'Alan Hollinghurst on Edmund White's Gay Classic A Boy's Own Story', *Guardian*, 10 June 2016, www.theguardian.com/books/2016/jun/10/edmund-white-a-boys-own-story-rereading-gay-literature (accessed 12 November 2017).
46 In conversation, 1 September 2017, Chelsea, NY. Although one could argue that this is still true, there has been a trend towards confessional memoirs since the early 2000s – for example, narratives from queer or trans people, sex workers, those experiencing addiction, or physical or mental illness, or those confronting grief.
47 *Square Peg* no. 4 (1984), quoted in Tony Peake, *Derek Jarman* (London: Little Brown, 1999), p. 321.
48 Paul A. Robinson, *Gay Lives: Homosexual Autobiography from John Addington Symonds to Paul Monette* (Chicago: University of Chicago Press, 1999), p. 66.
49 See *Dancing Ledge*, p. 54.
50 In 1996, new combination therapies involving protease inhibitors were introduced at the XI International AIDS Conference in Vancouver. See special issue of *Science* on AIDS: *Science*, 272.5270 (1996), 1858–962.
51 Couser, *Recovering Bodies*, p. 92. For a discussion of memoirs written by sisters, parents, and (ex-)wives, see pp. 113–42.
52 Mark Edmundson, 'Taking Leave', *London Review of Books*, 11.5 (1989) 22–3 (p. 22).
53 See Jean-Pierre Boule, *Herve Guibert: Voices of the Self* (Liverpool: Liverpool University Press, 1999); Ralph Sarkonak, *Angelic Echoes: Hervé Guibert and Company* (Toronto: University of Toronto, 2017).
54 Richard Maguire, 'The Relics of St David Wojnarowicz: The Autobiography of a Mythmaker', in *Life Writing: Essays on Autobiography, Biography and Literature*, ed. Richard Bradford (Basingstoke: Palgrave Macmillan, 2010), pp. 247–68 (p. 249).
55 Eric Waggoner, '"This Killing Machine Called America": Narrative of the Body in David Wojnarowicz's *Close to the Knives*', *a/b: Auto/Biography Studies*, 15.2 (2000), 171–92 (p. 172).

56 Paul Monette, *Becoming a Man: Half a Life Story* (New York: Harcourt Brace Jovanovich, 1992), p. 2.
57 See Cindy Patton, *Inventing AIDS* (London: Routledge, 1990), p. 130; and Couser, *Recovering Bodies*, p. 170.
58 Brophy, *Witnessing AIDS*, p. 12.
59 Ross Chambers, *Facing It: AIDS Diaries and the Death of the Author* (Ann Arbor: University of Michigan Press, 1998), p. 7.
60 Dori Laub, 'Bearing Witness or the Vicissitudes of Listening', in *Testimony: Crises of Witnessing in Literature, Psychoanalysis, and History*, eds. Shoshana Felman and Dori Laub (New York: Routledge, 1992), pp. 57–74 (p. 58).
61 Amelia Jones, *Body Art/Performing the Subject* (Minneapolis: University of Minnesota Press, 1998), p. 18. She is writing about performance art, but her analysis is usefully applied to Jarman's multi-disciplinary context.
62 Ibid, p. 18.
63 Walter Benjamin, *The Arcades Project*, trans. Howard Eiland and Kevin McLaughlin (Cambridge, MA: Harvard University Press, 2002), p. 460.
64 Donald B. Kuspit, 'Collage: The Organizing Principle of Art in the Age of the Relativity of Art', in *Relativism in the Arts*, ed. Betty Jean Craige (Athens: University of Georgia Press, 1983), pp. 123–47 (p. 123).
65 Bartholomew Brinkman, 'Scrapping Modernism: Marianne Moore and the Making of the Modern Collage Poem', *Modernism/Modernity*, 18.1 (2011), 43–66 (p. 47).
66 Marjorie Perloff, *The Futurist Moment: Avant-Garde, Avant Guerre, and the Language of Rupture* (Chicago: University of Chicago Press, 1986), p. xviii.
67 Anna Poletti, 'Periperformative Life Narrative: Queer Collages', *GLQ: A Journal of Lesbian and Gay Studies*, 22.3 (2016), 359–79 (p. 362).
68 Thomas P. Brockelman, *The Frame and the Mirror: On Collage and the Postmodern* (Evanston, IL: Northwestern University Press, 2001), p. 2.
69 Judith Butler, 'Critically Queer', *GLQ: A Journal of Lesbian and Gay Studies*, 1.1 (1993), 17–32 (p. 17).
70 Poletti, 'Periperformative Life Narrative: Queer Collages', p. 368.
71 Eve Kosofsky Sedgwick, *Touching Feeling* (Durham, NC: Duke University Press, 2003). Her concept of the *periperformative* is developed in the chapter 'Around the Periperformative: Periperformative Vicinities in Nineteenth-Century Narrative', pp. 67–91.
72 Steven Dillon, *Derek Jarman and Lyric Film: The Mirror and the Sea* (Austin: University of Texas Press, 2004), p. 229.
73 Jim Ellis, *Derek Jarman's Angelic Conversations* (Minneapolis: University of Minnesota Press, 2009), p. 234.
74 Poletti, 'Periperformative Life Narrative: Queer Collages', p. 376.
75 Emmanuel Dreuilhe, *Mortal Embrace: Living with AIDS* (1987), trans. Linda Coverdale (New York: Hill and Wang, 1988), p. 5.
76 Mary Jacobus, *Reading Cy Twombly: Poetry in Paint* (Princeton, NJ: Princeton University Press, 2016), p. 4.
77 Ibid., p. 201.

78 Olivia Laing, 'Introduction', in *Modern Nature: The Journals of Derek Jarman* (1991), by Derek Jarman (London: Vintage Classics, 2018), pp. vii–xiii (p. xi).
79 Martin Fletcher, 'Bombs of Bitterness – *At Your Own Risk: A Saint's Testament* by Derek Jarman', *New Statesman & Society*, 5.202 (1992), 38.
80 The slogan was also taken up by British direct action group OutRage!, set up in part by Jarman's friend Simon Watney. For an account of OutRage! demonstrators taking part in Jarman's film *Edward II* (1991), see Ian Lucas, *OutRage! An Oral History* (London: Cassell, 1998), pp. 58–60.

1

'The porter into forgotten landscapes':
A finger in the fishes mouth

'Poetry runs like a golden thread through all his life', said Jarman's biographer Tony Peake at an event at the London Review Bookshop to mark the twentieth anniversary of Jarman's death.[1] The poetic sources for many of his films are self-evident: William Shakespeare in *The Angelic Conversation* and *The Tempest*, Christopher Marlowe in *Edward II*, and Wilfred Owen in *War Requiem*. *The Last of England* contains many fragmented references to poetry, for example to work by Chaucer, Dante, T. S. Eliot, and Allen Ginsberg. His notebooks, or artist's workbooks, are filled with poems alongside collages, diary entries, plans for projects, calligraphy, drawings and objects. His published writing is also interspersed with his own poems, and his final film, *Blue*, comprises a poetic monologue of his own devising. Yet aside from the script of the film, *Blue: Text of a Film* (1994), which was published posthumously, Jarman published just one volume of poetry.

Jarman's first book was published when he was 30 years old: *A finger in the fishes mouth* (1972), a slender chapbook containing thirty-two poems. A friend, Michael Pinney of the Bettiscombe Press (a small press based in Bettiscombe, near Bridport, Dorset), had offered to publish a volume of the poems Jarman had written in his early twenties. Each spread in the book pairs a poem on the recto with a postcard from his personal collection on the verso, colour-washed in acid-green. Jarman houses the collection inside a shimmering silver cover bearing a print of Wilhelm von Gloeden's photograph 'Boy with Flying Fish' (c. 1905). Though the poems in the collection range in style, they are brief, sparse, and hermetic. For the most part, they are inspired by travel or inward reflection. They give off a sense of quietness and reticence, communicated through their well-wrought minimalism. In this way, they far more readily display the influence of Robert Creeley than of Jarman's university-era heroes Allen Ginsberg and William Burroughs.

The poems are quite succinct, ranging from three lines to thirty-six, save for the longer 'Words Written Without Any Stopping', which is reproduced in two columns so as to fit on one page. They are varied formally, most in free verse with short line lengths of just a few words: 'November' is nineteen

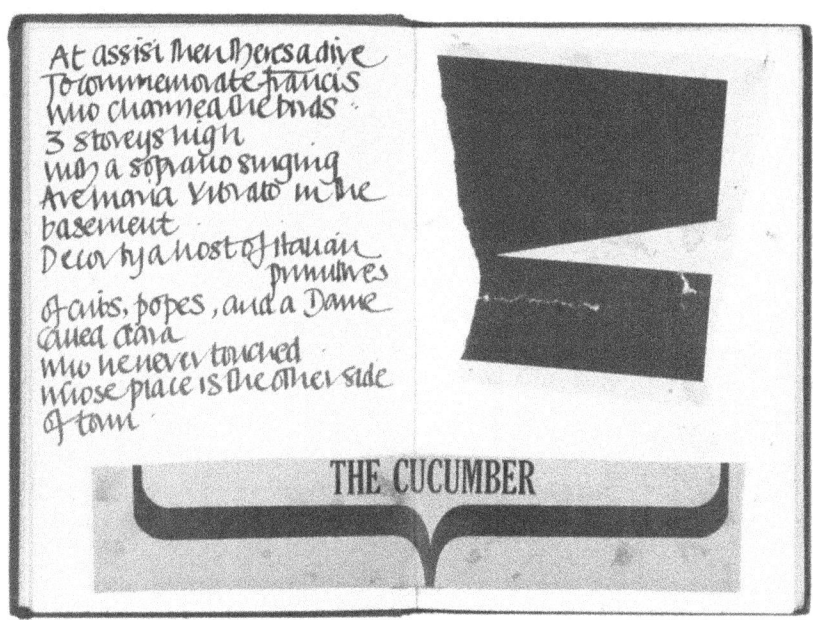

Figure 2 An early version of Jarman's 'Assisi' from 'untitled sketchbook', 1964. The poem appears as part of a collage that juxtaposes his poetry in careful calligraphy with found materials and carefully torn monochrome blocks, and dates from his time at the Slade. The line breaks are arranged differently from the 1972 version (the content remains the same); here, the words are arranged so as to fit into the visual scheme.

words in total, 'Poem I 1965' uses between one and four words per line. In an unusual more formal note, 'Fargo 64' is a loosely constructed ballade in which the second and third stanzas are a line shorter than the last, and the refrain 'for Jesus is right' is abandoned in the final stanza (*A finger*, 6).

Jarman often situates the poems in places he had travelled to: the Greek islands, San Francisco, New York, Calgary, Assisi, and Venice. Some, such as 'The Devil Old Junk Man' and 'A Victorian Poem', do not make their location overt, yet still seem to depict scenes from Jarman's travels. Others represent an imaginative journey not only to the old world, signalled by Greece and Italy, or the new, signalled by North America, but also back in time: Jarman's narrator acts as 'the porter / into forgotten landscapes' (*A finger*, 29). Looking towards space, 'Moon' riffs on different associations of the satellite, prefiguring the approach of collecting associations Jarman would develop throughout his career – for plants in *Modern Nature*, and for colours in *Chroma*.

The postcard images Jarman chose to accompany the peripatetic poems depict a range of topics: touristic, banal, historical, modern, religious and unusual. They originate from dispersed historical periods. That they have all been reproduced in the same green colour-wash adds a level of continuity to the collection. They depict a variety of geographical locations: two rowing boats upon a lake within a large cave, location unmarked; Thessalonika, Greece; Hoylake, Merseyside; Alexandria; A chief from the Wild West; Washington, DC; The First National Bank Building in Detroit, Michigan. A lot of them are difficult to make out. There are different modes: one image shows a couple looking out over the water at night, another shows Dante and Beatrice. There is an unmarked photograph of rock climbers, and one of society people in what looks like the main hall of a glamorous hotel. Together, they form a disparate collection of 'mementoes from places he visited and places he would have liked to visit'.[2]

The images sit in productive contrast to the texts they are paired with, at times posing 'extraordinary interpretative problems'.[3] In his satirical book *The Post Card: From Socrates to Freud and Beyond*, Jacques Derrida explains that 'What I prefer, about postcards, is that one does not know [...] what is the most important, the picture or the text'.[4] The potential for upsetting the hierarchy between the writer's text and the images chosen may have appealed to Jarman. The book is similarly constructed to Thom Gunn's collection *Positives* (1966), where the poetry is accompanied by photography by Ander Gunn, or the collaboration between Ted Hughes and the photographer Fay Godwin, whose collection *Remains of Elmet* (1979) is similarly arranged. Differently, Jarman controls the images chosen, which are selected from disparate sources.

Introducing the book's theme of journeying, the opening piece, idiosyncratically titled 'Poem II', understands travel as a temporal voyage undertaken both within the self and into history. We read of the poem's narrator:

> Now I am sailing on this rocking chair
> back
> back
> to where tomorrow
> washes the pavilions of today.
>
> (*A finger*, 1)

Time and history are conceived of in palimpsest, each era accessible to the poem's narrator – prefiguring the montage approach to time we will see throughout Jarman's films. However, history is accessible only dimly and impressionistically, as if through an old photograph or postcard. The image that accompanies the opening piece shows a large sea cave lit from the rear of the scene through a small opening in the rock. Two rowing boats sit in the water; their occupants are hard to make out, yet they seem to be dressed in period costume and face away from the image's viewers towards the back of the cave. They seem distant from us in time. The 'I' in 'Poem II' remains subtly unlocalised: we see from the narrator's perspective, but we gain little sense of the narrator himself. In this sense, the poem acts as a kind of manifesto for the collection.

Many of the poems contain the self-referent 'I', appearing to refer to a unified narrator across the collection. Yet the narrator remains abstracted and diffuse. As Jarman told Dom Sylvester Houédard of the collection: 'this is by the way autobiographical, although deeply buried'.[5] Although the narrator appears to be Jarman, he records his impressions of the world and of history, rarely looking inwards. For example, the opening lines of 'Patmos – Delos', 'I left blue flowers / by the phalloi of Dionysus' (*A finger*, 2), point away from the self towards the regarded objects. It is only through the narrator's act of leaving an offering that we gain a sense of his internal world. Similarly, two instances in 'From Gypsy Mar 1 66': 'I had a dream / through the mirror of the morning' and 'I had a dream / in the dawn light' (*A finger*, 3). The dreamer is effaced in contrast to the stark bright image of the external world. Dillon notes that 'Most titles are place-names or dates, which gives the flavor of a diary or a journal': the book gives us glimpses from an enigmatic travel diary.[6]

Nevertheless, the poetry is underpinned by Jarman's experiences. The year 1964 recurs in the poems' titles, and Jarman saw this year as momentous. It was 'the year of his first affair', explains Peake: he met his first lover Ron Wright early in the year, and therefore finally came out as gay, an event detailed in *Dancing Ledge* (and which I discuss in Chapter 2).[7] They travelled together to Italy that Easter and met up again in the summer when Jarman travelled to America for the first time. He spent several weeks with Ron in Calgary, Canada, before making a pilgrimage to the City Lights Bookstore in San Francisco, home of the Beats. He then started his second degree in art at the Slade and quickly became a part of London's gay art milieu. His travels through both Italy and the US feature prominently in *A finger in the fishes mouth*. New York seems full of promise in 'Manhattan Lower East Side', where a new generation is 'singing a new world song' among the 'wailing [...] sirens' (*A finger*, 10). He is captivated by his travels 'Through the billboard promised land', a phrase he repeats throughout the book and places on its back cover.[8] There he found that the cities 'composed of promises' (*A finger*, 10) he found in America sit in contrast to the heritage industry he found in Venice and Assisi, where 'there's a dive / to commemorate Francis / [...] / three stories high' (*A finger*, 13; see Figure 2).

To illustrate how some of Jarman's work is underpinned by his past, I will focus on the earliest composition in the volume, 'Poem I', which appears not as the first piece but towards the end of the collection. Peake informs us that this brief poem was written to celebrate meeting Ron Wright:[9]

> POEM I
>
> In the common silence
> of the world
> The white poppies of
> my love are dancing

(*A finger*, 30)

Jarman conjures a fleeting image like a moving postcard: we can imagine the flowers 'dancing' in the breeze, perhaps in the hushed haze of the summer heat. It is a quiet image, made so by its spare language and the 'common silence' it evokes, and it encourages its readers to pause for a moment to visualise the metaphor.

Jarman reprints 'Poem I' in *Dancing Ledge*. He describes the 'idyllic few weeks' (*Dancing Ledge*, p. 64) he spent living with Ron in a basement room in Calgary, where 'Outside our windows Ron's Russian neighbours cultivated opium poppies which they picked every morning to make their opium tea' (*Dancing Ledge*, p. 64). Michael Charlesworth comments of Jarman's metaphor that 'this use seems to make perfect sense since the gardening metaphor blends with that of love as an opiate'.[10] However, the white poppy, as opposed to the red, is a symbol of peace rather than remembrance, a distinction that – uncharacteristically for Jarman – he does not dwell on. Jarman writes about scarlet poppies frequently throughout his diaries: references to the flower are littered throughout *Modern Nature*, where wild poppies grow outside his windows at Prospect Cottage. He muses, 'Poppies have sprung up in many of my films: *Imagining October*, *Caravaggio*, *The Last of England* and *War Requiem*' (*Modern Nature*, p. 8), before including a roughly sketched poem titled 'Scarlet Poppies' where he points to their origins – 'A flower of cornfield and wasteland' (*Modern Nature*, p. 8) – and their medicinal properties – 'Bringer of dreams / And sweet forgetfulness' (*Modern Nature*, p. 9).[11]

The poem in the original collection is brief, its meaning evocative but elusive. But once the extra information about its origins is provided following the publication of *Dancing Ledge*, it is allowed more autobiographical resonance. Jarman thereby alerts us to the hidden autobiographical origins alive in the poetry, that we can share only if we are given the tools to decode them.

The poetry sits on a double-page spread with a characteristically enigmatic choice of postcard (see Figure 3). The image is of an elderly Henri Matisse, whom we have to identify ourselves.[12] Whereas in Jarman's later work,

POEM I

in the common silence
of the world
the white poppies of
my love are dancing

Figure 3 *A finger in the fishes mouth*, poem no. 30. The page spread shows a reproduction of a postcard of the elderly Matisse washed in acid green (verso) and 'Poem I' (recto).

images and words often work in an associative way, building meanings through productive and unexpected juxtapositions, in this instance it would be hard to unpack what he might have had in mind if one had been unable to identify the elderly man. Additionally, the image unsettles our understanding of the poem's narrator and the book's author as unified. Perhaps Jarman chose Matisse as he had painted several famous images of poppies – including the still life 'Poppies' (1919) and the bold cut-out print 'The Wild Poppies' (1953) in the year before his death. Or perhaps we are intended to read the poem as a statement that belongs with the older man here depicted. Or maybe the image might not be intended to add any meaning in particular to the text, other than whatever associations the book's readers bring to it, for example, that the spots on the card evoke the heads of flowers. It might represent a private meaning for Jarman, or it might not. The image and text exist on the page in a 'contrasting relationship that is inconclusive'.[13]

The most striking image in the collection is the one that does not sit in relationship with a poem: the image from which the collection takes its name and which is reproduced on its shimmering silver cover underneath Jarman's distinctive, calligraphic signature. In the middle of the page, there is an image of an adolescent boy, naked but for a wide-brimmed straw hat. His head at an angle to the camera, he looks out of the corner of one eye at the photographer, and thence out from the picture frame at the viewer, with a mixture of wariness and cheek. His smile looks forced, as if he has held it for a long time. In his left hand, he holds up a fish with beautiful wings affixed to its lumpen body. He has placed the tip of his right index finger inside its mouth. The photograph was taken by the eccentric Austrian Wilhelm von Gloeden (1856–1931), who is renowned for his pastoral nudes of Sicilian boys in classical poses. The image is part of a number of homoerotic images, taken of boys aged between 10 and 20, that are more sexually suggestive, because of the models' pose and eye contact with the photographer and the eventual viewers. There are several versions of 'Boy with Flying Fish' (c. 1905), the composition of at least one of which extends lower.

Jarman's choice of this image announces the queerness of its author and of its collection, though this is not often followed through in its contents, which are oblique and quite reticent for the period – far removed from the open, formally relaxed, confessional modes of poets he admired such as William Burroughs or Allen Ginsberg. Jarman gestures to the history of queer desire by placing the offering of 'blue flowers' by the phallic statues at Delos (*A finger*, 2) and mentions 'the white poppies / of my love' (*A finger*, 30), yet goes no further. The choice of the von Gloeden image speaks to Jarman's interest in the history of queer experience and of queer childhood and could be seen as a first, irreverent marker of this preoccupation. It prefigures the discussions of adolescent sexuality that Jarman returns to in *At Your Own Risk* and *Queer Edward II* (see the discussions in chapters 8 and 9, respectively): the framing of the image looks forward to one of the out-takes of the child Jody Graber from *Edward II*, published in *Queer Edward II*, that I analyse in Chapter 9. Yet by choosing to showcase his poetry in relation to von Gloeden, Jarman is linking his perspective to a disconcerting precedent.

Reception and afterlives

The reception of *A finger in the fishes mouth* was limited: Peake relates that 'After a poorly attended reading and a valiant but doomed attempt by Pinney's niece to subscribe it in university bookshops up and down the country, it [...] more or less vanish[ed] from view'.[14] Jarman later dismissed it as a piece of juvenilia: Collins reports Jarman as exclaiming, 'Don't read that, it's puerile rubbish', when Collins unwittingly picked it from the bookshelves in the Phoenix House flat.[15] Indeed, Colin MacCabe points out that Jarman 'apparently took efforts to destroy all known copies for reasons that are not clear'.[16] According to Peake, only a handful of copies remained:

a worn, delicate book held by the British Library, Jarman's sole personal copy, and two others held by friends.[17]

However, this rare volume was reprinted in 2014. After discovering the book in the British Library, writer and activist So Mayer had resolved to bring it to a wider audience. They partnered with small art-house publishers Test Centre to publish it in a facsimile edition that faithfully reproduces the volume's dazzling silver cover and grammatical eccentricities. The London Review Bookshop held a special event as part of *Jarman2014*, to commemorate the twentieth anniversary of his death.[18] On the anniversary, Wednesday 19 February, Mayer spoke along with Keith Collins, Jarman's biographer Tony Peake and the writer Ali Smith. The entire collection was read aloud: the guest speakers and members of the audience took it in turns to describe the green-tinted postcard on the verso before reading the facing poetry aloud. In this way, the image was entwined with the text with which it has been juxtaposed. The effect was curious: the images were improvised into a verbal translation by each reader, which the audience listened to along with the designated words of the poetry. The slippage here between image and text was more pronounced than when one reads the poetry as a solitary pursuit; the border between images and words collapsed in our imaginations as we listened.

To date, the book has received scant critical attention. It has broadly been considered juvenilia and it remained almost inaccessible until its republication in 2014. Dillon, however, provides an extended reading of the poems, predominantly to demonstrate how the book is a precursor 'to the way poetic language is juxtaposed with visual imagery in his more mature cinema'.[19] Michael Charlesworth provides a brief reading of two of the poems, pointing to the way the volume 'announces a bundle of Derek's themes, some continuing throughout his life'.[20] Robert Mills traces one of these themes – Jarman's interest in the figure of the Wandering Jew – back to some lines in a notebook from Jarman's time at the Slade, which would later be reprinted as 'Poem for Coleridge July 64' in *A finger in the fishes mouth*.[21] Jarman is here engaging with William Wordsworth's poem in the 1800 edition of *Lyrical Ballads* 'Song for the Wandering Jew', thought by Heidi Thomson to be a deflected address to Coleridge as the embodiment of the Wandering Jew.[22]

However, although Jarman considered the volume immature, it provides a fascinating insight into the developing artistic interests of the young Jarman: it shows a direction and a focus not taken. However, his poetry features throughout his career – his poems are used as voiceovers to films including *The Last of England*, *The Garden* and *Blue*, and poetry features as interludes throughout his life-writing in books such as *Modern Nature*, *Chroma* and

Derek Jarman's Garden. It is also an important step in the development of his artistic practice of using his life as material. As mentioned earlier, Jarman considered the collection 'autobiographical, although deeply buried'.[23] There is a transformation between the way Jarman uses his memories and experiences in 1972 and in his first book of autobiographical writing, *Dancing Ledge*, published 12 years later.

Notes

1 Gareth Evans et al., '*A Finger in the Fishes Mouth:* The Legacy of Derek Jarman', audio podcast, London Review Bookshop, 19 February 2014, www.londonreviewbookshop.co.uk/events/past/2014/2/a-finger-in-the-fishes-mouth-the-legacy-of-derek-jarman (accessed 1 May 2021). The chapter title quotes Derek Jarman, *A finger in the fishes mouth* (Bettiscombe, Dorset: Bettiscombe Press, 1972; repr. London: Test Centre, 2014), poem no. 29. Further references are given within the text as *A finger*. The chapbook is unpaginated so I refer to the poems by number.
2 Scott Morris, 'A Finger in the Fishes Mouth: The Legacy of Derek Jarman', *The Literateur*, http://literateur.com/a-finger-in-the-fishes-mouth-the-legacy-of-derek-jarman (accessed 9 August 2017).
3 Michael Charlesworth, *Derek Jarman*, Critical Lives (London: Reaktion Books, 2011), p. 52.
4 Jacques Derrida, *The Post Card: From Socrates to Freud and Beyond*, trans. Alan Bass (Chicago: University of Chicago Press, 1987), p. 13.
5 Quoted in Evans et al., 'The Legacy of Derek Jarman'.
6 Dillon, *Derek Jarman and Lyric Film*, p. 37.
7 Evans et al., 'The Legacy of Derek Jarman'.
8 The phrase is repeated in 'Poem for Coleridge July 64' (*A finger*, 11) and 'From Gypsy Mar 1 66' (*A finger*, 3), and on the back cover.
9 Evans et al., 'The Legacy of Derek Jarman'.
10 Charlesworth, *Derek Jarman*, p. 52.
11 Jarman also uses the poem in the draft script for the unrealised 'Dr John Dee and the Art of Mirrors' (BFI Archive, main listing, box 3, item 1b). Thus he demonstrates the way he used inspiration from his own life and autobiographical fragments to inform his art in completely different contexts.
12 Identified by Charlesworth, *Derek Jarman*, p. 52.
13 Dillon, *Derek Jarman and Lyric Film*, p. 36.
14 Peake, *Derek Jarman*, p. 178.
15 Evans et al., '*A Finger in the Fishes Mouth*'.
16 Colin MacCabe, '20 Years after His Death, We Still Know so Little of Derek Jarman', *New Statesman*, 20 February 2014, www.newstatesman.com/art-and-design/2014/02/20-years-after-his-death-we-still-know-so-little-derek-jarman (accessed 10 September 2017).

17 There may be several further copies available in libraries and personal collections across the world. For example, there is an original copy in Yale University's Beinecke Rare Book & Manuscript Library.
18 I summarise details of *Jarman2014* in the introduction to this book. Full listings can be found at: www.jarman2014.org.
19 Dillon, *Derek Jarman and Lyric Film*, p. 35.
20 Charlesworth, *Derek Jarman*, p. 54.
21 See Robert Mills, *Derek Jarman's Medieval Modern* (Cambridge: D. S. Brewer, 2018), p. 140.
22 See Heidi Thomson, 'Wordsworth's "Song for the Wandering Jew" as a Poem for Coleridge', *Romanticism*, 21.1 (2015), 37–47.
23 Quoted in Evans et al., 'A Finger in the Fishes Mouth'.

2

Dancing Ledge: 'An autobiography at forty'

Derek was a great lover of the English countryside and he knew a lot about it and he liked to read and study the history of the countryside and we went to places he'd been in his childhood like Dancing Ledge, we went to Dorset and we filmed and we went down to the sea to the cliffs and I said to him, so Derek this is Dancing Ledge and he said oh no, no this is Winspit and I said where is Dancing Ledge then? And he pointed to the end of the bay about a mile and a half away as it stuck out in the sea to the left and said there, over there, that's Dancing Ledge. And I said well when are we going there and he says we're not, I've never been there and I said well why did you call your book Dancing Ledge? And he said well I couldn't very well call it Winspit, could I?

(James Mackay)[1]

In 1970, Jarman acquired a Super 8 camera and started to film aspects of his own life: his friends and lovers, and the parties held in the beautiful warehouse spaces he lived in throughout the decade.[2] As Laurence Normand notes, in doing so he 'discovered the autobiographical subject that was to become the driving force of all his subsequent films and books'.[3] It would be just over a decade before Jarman sought to deepen his written engagement with this 'autobiographical subject' in his first book of life-writing, *Dancing Ledge* (1984). In contrast to the 'deeply buried' autobiographical subject in his early volume of poetry, *A finger in the fishes mouth*, he brings his memories and experiences to the fore in *Dancing Ledge*.[4]

As a first autobiographical text, *Dancing Ledge* covers the kinds of experiences one might expect: narratives about boyhood, adolescence and coming of age. The book can also be read as 'the gay equivalent of the *Bildungsroman*': it describes the challenges of growing up as a gay child and the pivotal period in which Jarman came out and was initiated into both the gay community of 1960s London and the interconnected worlds of art, ballet, theatre and film, where Jarman's career developed rapidly.[5] The memoir is characterised by the range of striking anecdotes that Jarman shares about his family and wide acquaintance. However, it is conspicuous

Dancing Ledge: 'An autobiography at forty'

Figure 4 Jarman in front of one of the GBH series of paintings shown at his exhibition at the ICA, 1984, photographed for the cover of *Performance Magazine*.

how little of an internal world we are given. Aside from the brief instance in which Jarman's fateful first encounter with his first love, Ron, leads to his violent destruction of his own paintings, Jarman chooses to share self-representations with limited interiority.

Instead, Jarman's intention was to share an account of a gay life framed as a success story – despite the difficulties he encounters in his career, he relates episodes that combine to produce an image of him as a Bohemian artist, with enchanting and unusual friends, and the freedom to pursue experimental projects that interested him. The glamour of *Dancing Ledge* stands in stark contrast to the tone of the life-writing that would follow as the 1980s continued.

The background to *Dancing Ledge*

In his preface to the 1991 edition, Jarman comments that 'what started as a book on the frustration of funding led to the writing of an autobiography at forty' (*Dancing Ledge*, n. p. Figure 4 is a portrait of Jarman at around the time of the book's publication). Following the release of *The Tempest* (1979), his film career came to an unexpected halt. Despite having released three features that had attracted much attention, he struggled to procure funding for his next planned feature, about the life of Caravaggio. He was stuck in a frustrating cycle involving a number of script re-writes and changes to the main personnel involved in the endeavour. However, the unwelcome break provided the opportunity for him to take up painting again with seriousness for the first time in a decade, working on a series of paintings in 1981 and 1982 initially drawing on seventeenth-century hermeticism then moving on to use 'gold [leaf] as ground' (*Dancing Ledge*, p. 229) to create work 'based on nineteenth-century photographs of the male nude mixed with sexual and religious iconography' (*Dancing Ledge*, p. 229). These works would go on to be exhibited as 'After the Final Academy' (1982) at the Edward Totah Gallery in London's Covent Garden. The exhibition, in Jarman's words, 'went off like a damp squib' (*Dancing Ledge*, p. 228), to his intense disappointment. However, this work served to solidify his split career not only as a filmmaker, but as an artist too. During this period, he also continued to produce experimental Super 8 films that seemed to bridge a gap between ideas of the moving image and painting.

A month after the limp reception of the 'After the Final Academy' show, Jarman found himself sitting down in a hotel room in Rome starting to write the book that would become *Dancing Ledge*. He uses the text to demonstrate the links between all the aspects of his diverse creative life. In an interview in *Square Peg*, he commented that he had wanted to 'tie up' the 'connections between painting and film' and between his features and Super 8s, which were 'as much a centre of my life as the feature films and painting'.[6] The catalyst was a further disappointment regarding progress on the Caravaggio film: Jarman had travelled to Rome with his producer, Nicholas Ward Jackson, to finalise funding for *Caravaggio*, and had expected to have the contracts signed swiftly by the Italian co-producers. This did not happen and when Jarman's frustrations mounted and he found himself with very little to occupy him, Ward Jackson suggested he 'write it out' (*Dancing Ledge*, preface). Peake describes the writing process:

> From January to April 1983, he wrote furiously, at the kind of speed he liked to paint, and with equal ease, treating the major events and people in his life section by section until he had amassed a vast jumble of pieces. These he then had typed. He called this 'diary after the event' *Jigsaw*, a reference to the haphazard nature of the material and the fact that frequently the pieces fitted together in a synchronistic fashion suggestive of the most Jungian of jigsaws.[7]

Dancing Ledge: *'An autobiography at forty'* 43

Although the text that would become *Dancing Ledge* comprises Jarman's first major written work for publication, he had of course written extensively: scripts, poetry and some early journals. He borrowed the collaborative approach he had found so fruitful working on film for this writing project: early in the summer of 1983, Jarman enlisted the help of a former lover, a young man called Shaun Allen, who was just finishing his English degree at Oxford. He was called upon to help edit and shape this 'vast jumble of pieces'. Allen's assistance enabled him to work at a pace that would have been challenging to maintain alone: he provided a sounding board for ideas and a vital second opinion. Working collaboratively, they first attempted to group the material by its theme. Failing, they took a broadly chronological approach instead, resulting in a text that to some extent provides coherently arranged narrative chunks that explain Jarman's childhood, coming out, and early career. Their flexible approach shows that Jarman considered the structure of his life-writing to be adaptable and provisional. However, they still allowed the synchronistic approach they'd initially been aiming for to shine through in places: the text is not always chronological, and at times juxtaposes episodes years apart that nonetheless are intended to inform one another.

'My Queerlife': A characterisation of *Dancing Ledge*

Described in the preface as 'my Queerlife' (*Dancing Ledge*, preface), *Dancing Ledge* is Jarman's most sustained, traditionally structured piece of long-form life-writing. Ellis describes the text as 'a provocative blend of personal history, family mythology, social history, diary, and artistic reflection'.[8] Like Jarman's later book *Kicking the Pricks* (1987), *Dancing Ledge* ranges over his childhood, experience in the film industry and gay identity, aspects of his life that are illustrated with eighty-eight black-and-white photographs. They include images of Jarman at different ages, of his art, his friends, stage designs and production photographs from his films. Jarman divides the book into twelve sections, the first ten of which are of a similar length (around twenty-five pages), and the final two comprise brief closing remarks. Each section loosely covers a particular period in Jarman's life: although the anecdotes range around in time in each section, the accounts are broadly chronological from the second section onwards. Within each section, short, subtitled passages describe incidents and memories in a few paragraphs.

Jarman commences with a fragmented account of the Caravaggio project titled 'The Rough Cut', which ranges across the issues he faced finding funding to reflections on the violence and intensity of Caravaggio's work and life. Rome, Jarman's location as he writes, sparks memories from earlier trips to Italy: the account describes one of his earliest memories on the banks of the Lago Maggiore as a four-year-old, listening to the sound of swallows – *'itys itys itys'* (*Dancing Ledge*, p. 16) – a precious refrain that will be found throughout his books. The account sweeps forward 25 years to a titillating story from 1971 about the priest guarding the San Servolo asylum in Venice. In this, the least chronological of the sections, Jarman focuses on sharing his relationship to the Caravaggio project, using juxtaposition to construct his account.

In the second section, 'Painting it Out', Jarman gives an account of his childhood, including the scarring event at Hordle House, his preparatory school, in which he is discovered sharing a bed with another boy (I relate this incident in the section titled '"SEX AT NINE": Polarising childhood' in Chapter 9). From this section onwards, he retains a predominantly chronological structure for his account. In the next section, 'The Thaw', Jarman describes both his student years, in which he comes to terms with his sexuality, and also his impressions of the London art scene and gay milieu of the 1960s.

In 'The Most Beautiful Room in London', he examines his early career – his set design for opera and ballet, and his work devising the enormous all-white sets for Ken Russell's *The Devils* (1971) and designing *Savage Messiah* (1972). He then gives an account of the making of his first three feature films, the independently made *Sebastiane* (1976), *Jubilee* (1978) and *The Tempest* (1979). The penultimate section, 'An Inventory' (*Dancing Ledge*, pp. 250–1), gives a stark register of his life in material terms at the time of writing: a small rented flat, debts and no stable income, but nonetheless cupboards 'full of paintings by friends' (*Dancing Ledge*, p. 250) and piles of scripts relating to Jarman's film projects that point to the richness of his world, conjuring an impression of the traditional Bohemian romance of an artist's life.

Jarman ends the text with an epilogue originally intended to comprise the end of *Jubilee*, in which Elizabeth I and John Dee walk along the Dorset coastal path under a darkening sky, signifying a journey into a future full of foreboding. A phoenix speaks to them. It cries, 'COME AWAY' (*Dancing Ledge*, p. 253), inciting them to leave the land. Here, autobiographical narrative is transposed into utopian fantasy, pointing to a potential regeneration that seems wider than purely personal.

The story behind the title of the book, *Dancing Ledge*, is typical of the purposeful creative licence that characterises Jarman's approach to sharing details from his life. In the epigraph to this chapter, I quote Jarman's long-time producer James Mackay who, in an interview with Andy Kimpton-Nye, recalls a visit to Dorset to do some filming some time after the publication of the book, which had been named after 'Dancing Ledge', a specific rock formation on the coastline. The name situates the text in a geographic location that he had at some point informed Mackay that he had visited as a child. He had returned in the 1970s to film the final scene of *Jubilee* described above, in which Elizabeth and John Dee walk along the Dorset cliff path. The personal history of the place – that it is connected not only to his childhood but also to his mature filmic output – is layered with the connotations of the name itself, which are appropriately evocative in relation to Jarman's own life.

The place name 'Dancing Ledge' is a metaphor for two critically intertwined elements of his life. Firstly, it describes the precariousness of his life as a filmmaker, doing his best to keep creating work in spite of the real possibility that by doing so, he might fall off the ledge, metaphorically speaking. The second connotation is of the fragility of the hard-won joys of his gay life: the place name recalls a phrase he would return to almost a decade later in *At Your Own Risk*, when he refers to himself and other people suffering from AIDS-related illnesses as follows: 'We are the 11,000 angels dancing on the head of a pin' (*Dancing Ledge*, p. 4).[9] Mackay relates the anecdote with humour, pointing out that the Dancing Ledge of Jarman's imagination is actually a place called 'Winspit', its name far less usefully evocative. The anecdote quoted above demonstrates Jarman's engagement with the spirit of a thing, rather than what he might have seen as pedantic detail. In the end, we are left with the images, the films and the texts that comprise Jarman's life output: in instances such as these, he alters the minutiae of the facts of his life to create a more representative impression of his world.

The narrating 'I' in *Dancing Ledge* is a prominent figure in his world who, from the outset, describes a fashionable, well-connected milieu: an early photograph depicts Jordan, actress and icon of 1970s London punk subculture, with David Bowie at Cannes promoting *Jubilee* (*Dancing Ledge*, p. 12); he relates tussles with the *Telegraph* and Channel Four over the showing of his films (*Dancing Ledge*, p. 10). His class is always apparent: the series of public schools that he attended, his relatives' involvement with empire, the comfort he feels engaging with the Classics at university, his easy access to the beau monde of 1960s London. The first entry in the book takes place during a Christmas spent in Tuscany. It describes an amusing misunderstanding over whether the dog belonging to 'the maid' had just died in a hunting incident – 'Shot […] like the butcher last year' – or down to simple old age. Apparently the 'traditional Saint Stephen's Day massacre' had caused 'a heart attack' (*Dancing Ledge*, p. 9). The tone that emerges through the narrative voice is that of someone self-assured and straightforward, with a sense of authority. It is the voice of an educated, confident man, who delights in the ridiculous. Despite the career setbacks *Dancing*

Ledge describes, the narrator is someone comfortably aware of his own magnetism, creative powers and place in his social world.

Curiously, there is not a significant difference between the narrating 'I' and the narrated 'I'. The text is structured in a disjointed way, but the person it describes appears to have a unified subjectivity, even when the narrated 'I' was a young boy. That the text is a partially constructed 'jigsaw' points more to the fact that Jarman avoids writing about the parts of his life that didn't strike him as being of particular interest at the time of writing.[10] However, at this stage in his life, the term 'jigsaw' is apt: his autobiographical writing involves writing out all the different parts and then reassembling them, while aware that these parts all add up to a whole.

In *Dancing Ledge*, Jarman rarely focuses on particular ways of remembering, via symbols or objects, such as flowers, colours or quotations from his reading, as he would go on to in *Modern Nature* and other later texts. The anger and the darkness that are characteristic of his later works are absent, as is a consistent sense of emotionally engaged interiority. Even when Jarman describes going through a terrible time as a boy or young man, he describes the experiences in a predominantly practical way. Aged 14, he comments: 'I feel threatened, isolated, and friendless – I'm hopeless at all the communal activities, particularly ball games. And so I take refuge in the art house, where there is an old coke stove' (*Dancing Ledge*, p. 51). Here, he associates negative feelings with alienation from team sports, yet instead of lingering further on how 'threatened' he feels, he swiftly moves on to the actions he took instead. The section on his art master and the sanctuary of the art school is far longer. This stands in contrast to *Modern Nature*, in which Jarman describes emotional events more fully. Describing a hurricane, he shares his emotions as the night unfolds. Interspersed with the action, he writes that 'The first dull waves of panic washed over me', then finds himself 'Feeling cold and nauseous' (*Modern Nature*, p. 19). His choice to keep his earlier writing in *Dancing Ledge* condensed and focused on action ensures even darker moments seem secondary to an overall narrative of personal and artistic growth.

On genre

Jarman describes *Dancing Ledge* as an 'autobiography' (*Dancing Ledge*, preface) rather than any other term – a memoir or journal, for example. In this first book, he relates an account of his life from his family background and early childhood to the present in which he was writing. In doing so, he produces a text that fits Lejeune's widely quoted general definition of an autobiography: 'A retrospective prose narrative produced by a real person concerning his own existence, focusing on his individual life, in particular on the development of his personality'.[11] The text moves between micro-stories to construct an impression of his world, which is a technique he would reuse in *Kicking the Pricks*. He assumes, in Smith and Watson's words, 'the role of the *bricoleur* who takes up bits and pieces of the identities and narrative forms available and, by disjoining and joining them in excessive ways, creates a history of the subject at a precise point in time and space'.[12] Dillon comments that the text is 'built out of nonnarrative blocks': it tends towards chronological organisation, but isn't bound by this structure and breaks it whenever it makes more thematic sense to do so.[13] In particular, he regularly splices snatches from his contemporary life with recollections from his early years, as in the example given above where he juxtaposes his early sexuality at Lago Maggiore with an experience as an adult at San Servolo. In doing so, he presents a vivid account of the 'development of his personality' that builds narrative not through a straightforward chronology but by using a different aesthetic. The careful juxtaposition of these 'blocks' of text to draw out important themes: the influence of a repressive English childhood, the intertwined development of his sexuality and creative work, and influential friendships, under a backdrop of the prevalence of homophobia in Britain.

The idiosyncratic structure of the text wasn't always happily received. Peake comments that *Dancing Ledge* 'dart[s] between the professional and the personal in a seemingly haphazard fashion'.[14] Indeed, Tom Phillips, writing for the *TLS*, described reading *Dancing Ledge* as 'a maddening experience, akin to watching a set of muddled rushes in a viewing room double-booked by the British Film Institute and *Gay News*'.[15] The technique Phillips objects to was not chosen for its haphazard nature: it is a formal tool employed by Jarman to demonstrate that his personal life and his work for the stage, in film and in art are indistinguishable: his life is his art, and vice versa. I wonder whether it is now harder, 34 years on, to recapture a sense of *Dancing Ledge* as a 'maddening' cut-up: Jarman's formal decision to create meaning through partial stories and juxtaposition is echoed in some excellent recent accounts such as, for example, Maggie Nelson's *The Argonauts* (2015) and Claudia Rankine's *Citizen* (2014).

Written in his early middle age, *Dancing Ledge* could be thought of more specifically as an autobiographical Bildungsroman, charting the development of its author's personality until maturity. The Bildungsroman, or 'apprenticeship novel', as C. Hugh Holman summarises, 'recounts the youth and young adulthood of a sensitive protagonist who is attempting to learn the nature of the world, discover its meaning and pattern, and acquire a philosophy of life and "the art of living"'.[16] We are accustomed to thinking of texts such as Johann Wolfgang von Goethe's *Wilhelm Meister's Apprenticeship*

(1795–96) in these terms, as well as Charles Dickens's *Great Expectations* (1861) or Mark Twain's *The Adventures of Huckleberry Finn* (1884). Common to these texts is the development of the narrator-protagonist's character, involving a measurable change in perspective and moral or philosophical outlook by its conclusion. Jarman would have studied canonical texts such as these through his schooling and university education at King's College London.

However, Smith and Watson point out that the Bildungsroman form has more recently been a useful one outside of fiction for 'women and other disenfranchised persons' because it provides a structured way of narrating a life-story to 'consolidate a sense of emerging identity and an increased place in public life'.[17] Indeed, 'the gay equivalent of the *Bildungsroman*' is the coming-out story, often described in novel form.[18] The narrative often takes the form of 'gradual and eventual self-empowerment, the first step of which involves negotiating a way to grow up in spite of, or by somehow sidestepping, parental power and its related instruments of discipline'.[19] Jarman's text does not translate his experiences into autobiographical fiction as, for example, Edmund White does in his two connected autobiographical novels, *A Boy's Own Story* (1982) and *The Beautiful Room is Empty* (1988). Indeed, he does away with providing a coherent narrative. Yet the form is similar: an exploration of Jarman's boyhood, adolescence, and coming of age and coming out, involving initiation into both the gay community of 1960s London and the interconnected worlds of art, ballet, theatre and film.

Meeting Ron Wright: the coming-out narrative in *Dancing Ledge*

A vital part of the process of self-construction, whether one writes autobiographically or not, is the way one tells the story of one's origins, including the ways one has dealt with alienation from the culture in which one is embedded. Ken Plummer argues that the stories one tells about oneself –for those with non-normative sexual identities, coming-out narratives in particular – form the 'bases of identity', and 'provide tropes for making sense of the past'.[20] Colm Tóibín, writing in the early twenty-first century but looking back to the pasts of queer icons including Oscar Wilde and Pedro Almodóvar, comments that 'Gay people [...] grow up alone; there is no history'.[21] As a result of this lack of access to history, he believes that 'the discovery of a history and a heritage has to be made by each individual as part of the road to freedom, or at least knowledge'.[22] Although this is not always now true in the UK, particularly in urban centres, it is certainly the way Jarman conceived of the experience he had had: if one was an adolescent before the mainstreaming of gay (though rarely lesbian or bisexual) characters on television in the late 1990s, or even educated before the repeal of Section 28, the lack of an easily accessible and visible gay culture could cause acute anxiety.[23] Adrienne Rich has written poignantly about this absence: 'When those who have the power to name and to socially construct reality [...] describe the world and you are not in it, there is a moment of psychic disequilibrium, as if you looked in the mirror and saw nothing'.[24]

A large part of Jarman's self-representational project was to work to prevent this sense of alienation in others through the publication of his own experiences growing up. Looking back at his serial autobiographical production in *At Your Own Risk*, Jarman explains that he 'wrote autobiography' because 'THE ABSENCE OF THE PAST WAS A TERROR' (*At Your Own Risk*, p. 30) – a sentiment I analyse in the introduction of this book. The lack of a gay past for Jarman and others of his generation is linked to the critical coming-out moment or moments, and the narratives constructed about this or these events and their afterlives. Writing and publishing coming-out narratives is an attempt to provide something of 'a history and a heritage' for the next generation of queer adolescents as well as a way to create community through a commonality of experience.[25] *Dancing Ledge* is not only the most traditionally autobiographical of his texts, but the one in which his lived experience is told and understood around the pivotal point of his coming-out story which, in later works, would be re-told and re-formed to different ends.

Jarman relates the 'crisis' (*At Your Own Risk*, p. 43) of his first adult affair in *Dancing Ledge*, which would be the catalyst for his coming out. In a passage titled 'March 1964. Camden' (*Dancing Ledge*, p. 62), Jarman describes a scene that opens with him lying 'in the dark with [his] heart pounding'. Another person speaks: 'Then Ron said, "Why don't you come over to my bed, it's really cold in here"'. Jarman obliges, describing the way that they 'stared at each other for ever in the darkness', and that 'Each time [Jarman] touched him it was like an electric shock'. However, in the morning, Jarman woke to find that 'Ron [had] slipped out of the house'. Jarman's housemates did not have the number of the place where Ron was staying, so 'the roof of the world caved in'. Jarman went about a distracted day at the Slade, before hurrying back to the Camden house, where there had been no news from Ron. 'By six o'clock some dark force overwhelmed me', Jarman writes, 'I seized Brenda's dressmaking scissors and in a blank frenzy hacked my paintings which hung on the living-room wall into shreds' (*Dancing Ledge*, p. 62).

The passage is sparing in its detail: we are not here told who Ron is, or what events have led to the scene that Jarman describes. The previous passage focuses on a different topic: how young English artists, faced with the dreariness of post-war England, looked longingly across the Atlantic to the American dream of brash commercialisation and plenty, as well as imagining America as a sexually liberated elsewhere. It doesn't lead on to this particular memory. We are given the date ('March 1964') and location ('Camden') in the title, plus just enough detail to allow us to picture the scene unfolding. In this respect, it is much like a poem. By mentioning their mutual gaze and the electricity he felt when he touched Ron, one would assume that this passage is a diffident relation of his first adult sexual encounter, which he shies away from naming more directly. In fact, we later discover (from the story's retelling in *At Your Own Risk*) that this was not to happen until Ron was found the following evening. He encourages his readers to make assumptions about the story's implied content because the shorthand provides a cleaner story: he does away with the messiness and incompleteness of real life in order to get to the important part of the story.

The most striking part of the story is that this rupture is one of the rare moments in the text where Jarman shares his emotional world. We gain a rich visual impression of the scene, as if we were watching Jarman replaying it on film. Although to some extent the sense of Jarman as a spectator within his own life is explained by the generic implications of writing a 'diary after the event', the descriptive choices he makes are considered.[26] His actions display an extreme reaction to losing Ron. Pain is understood as a structural collapse: it is 'the roof of the world [that] caved in' (*Dancing Ledge*, p. 62). The anguish he experiences is figured as 'some dark force', which in its unspecificity describes an emotion that is experienced as almost alien. The unfamiliar 'force' leads him to a violent and symbolically resonant act: he 'hacked [his] paintings which hung on the living-room wall into shreds' (*Dancing Ledge*, p. 62). He then writes, 'Roger, who was also in tears by now, took hold of the scissors, imagining I was about to turn them on myself' (*Dancing Ledge*, pp. 62–3). This is a specific example of his perception that there were no boundaries between his life and his art. Having been abandoned, he seeks to attack himself: he turns his anger and grief towards his art. The transposition of the canvas for his own skin can be read as a form of externalised self-harm. One might connect this scene to a well-known literary use of a knife to destroy a painting: Oscar Wilde's Dorian Gray slashes his portrait with the knife he used to kill Basil Hallward, in a similar bid to harm himself.[27]

The passage foreshadows Jarman's repeated use of a technique in his writing that imbues the images he chooses with transformative potential: they become a repository of multiple meanings, connecting events in Jarman's past to a wider queer past. He uses particular objects or ideas – in this case, a pair of scissors – to collect the richness and variety of meanings connected with them and deploy them for his own purposes. Here, he performs the role of Claude Lévi-Strauss's 'bricoleur': he uses whatever is at hand (in this case, a pivotal memory and a meaningful object) and makes something new from it.[28] In *The Savage Mind*, Lévi-Strauss connects two strands that would later become important for Jarman: 'Mythical thought appears to be an intellectual form of "bricolage"'.[29] Jarman demonstrates an imperative throughout his work to use meaningful, mythically resonant objects to create new combinations, and this example in *Dancing Ledge* develops a method we have seen in his early poetry printed in *A finger in the fishes mouth*.

The incident appears to be told in isolation, but acts as a watershed moment. After his friends pledge to find Ron, the passage ends. Jarman focuses solely on the moments and events that seemed most critical, leaving aside transitions or explanatory passages that he did not feel added anything to a sense of who he was becoming. The subsequent passage sees Jarman's gaze flickering forwards three months to his first trip to New York and onwards to Calgary to visit Ron. He describes his arrival in New York and entry into a gay world: he is staying at a mission in Greenwich Village where 'all the priests were after me, all of them unbelievably forward' (*Dancing Ledge*, p. 63). On his return from America, 'Life was to change for ever' as he 'discovered [his] first gay pub' (*Dancing Ledge*, p. 67) in London, and entered a new phase of his life. The experience of first meeting Ron Wright is placed just before the chapter titled 'The Thaw', which foregrounds his flourishing in a new, gay world following his difficulty coming out. Pitted against the restriction and repression of Jarman's school years and the resultant freeze that placed on his first three years of adulthood, it describes, using Ken Plummer's model of the typical coming-out narrative in *Telling Sexual Stories*, the transformation from a childhood of 'suffering' and 'surviving' into an adulthood that is able to 'surpass' these initial challenges.[30] Using the metaphor of a melting frost, Jarman encourages us to understand his coming out in terms of the seasons: winter is followed by the spring and then the summer – a process of positive progression, growth and warmth.

'Other people's mythologies'

Jarman's 'autobiography' (*Dancing Ledge*, preface)[31] is not only the story of his own development. It is also a portrait of his friends. His account juxtaposes critical moments in his 'Queerlife' (*Dancing Ledge*, preface) with the worlds he was part of. *Dancing Ledge* is heavily populated with vivid accounts of his friends, acquaintances and colleagues. It gives an account that is at times a gossip-filled portrait of a particular moment in several overlapping worlds: the 1960s and 1970s gay scene, and the art, film and ballet worlds. It gives younger gay male readers of the time of its publication a sense of an available, glamorous milieu. The second image in the book is of 'Jordan with David Bowie at Cannes, 1978' (*Dancing Ledge*, p. 12), where Jarman and Jordan had been promoting *Jubilee*. Jarman weaves between portraits of David Hockney, Ossie Clarke and Patrick Procktor, who also went to the Slade, his encounters at the Royal Ballet with Rudolf Nureyev, who 'was a law unto himself' (*Dancing Ledge*, p. 86), and anecdotes about working with director Ken Russell. He includes comments on many famous gay men, including Allen Ginsberg, William Burroughs and Pier Paolo Pasolini, whom Jarman saw as heroes of a kind. He provides fascinating extended accounts of his unusual friend Anthony Harwood and the eccentric elderly Francis Rose, a friend of Gertrude Stein. The diaries collected in *Modern Nature* and *Smiling in Slow Motion* contain vignettes of friends or small obituaries of those who had died from AIDS-related illnesses, but the longest accounts of others are found in *Dancing Ledge*. The inclusion of fascinating stories from the lives of his friends has the effect of tempering the autobiographical account with the sense of a countercultural, gay, celebrity memoir.

For example, Harwood receives extended attention on several occasions. Jarman sketches a character of unusual style and shimmering appeal: 'He always dressed immaculately, if eccentrically, in silver wind jackets, black polo-necks, velvet breeches and court shoes with diamond buckles' (*Dancing Ledge*, p. 78). Harwood maintained a peculiar and glamorous lifestyle, which Jarman relates with entertainment:

> Anthony lived an itinerant gypsy life with his Georgian wife, Princess Nina – travelling across Europe from one hotel to another. In London, which he considered home, he kept a flat in the block above Sloane Square tube station, where he retired in the daytime to write his plays, before cooking Nina supper, which he would take to her hotel in a plastic carrier bag.
>
> (*Dancing Ledge*, p. 78)

By including the detail of the incongruous 'plastic carrier bag' that marks their singular domestic arrangement, Jarman provides an effective, humorous portrait of the chic veneer of their lives, especially when slumming it. After setting the scene, Jarman commences a series of unlikely and alarming anecdotes about the pair: Nina's bejewelled exterior yet unwillingness to part with cash, Harwood's paralysis through poliomyelitis then miraculous recovery at the hands of a holy man in the Himalayan foothills and a painful attempt at an escape from Nina, who then set a private detective to follow Harwood and his friends for a month. Not printed in *Dancing Ledge* but raised by Tony Peake in *Derek Jarman* were the rumours about the untimely death of Nina's second husband, then Harwood's employer, a descendant of Arthur Conan Doyle, whose demise left the pair in receipt of one-third of the Conan Doyle estate.[32]

It is noticeable that Jarman first chooses to characterise his friend by relating a particularly capricious tale from Anthony's childhood:

> Seizing the family's white Persian cat, Alex, he climbed gingerly to the top of the house and threw him out of the highest attic window. Then he rushed downstairs to retrieve the shaken and angry tom. Before it could escape his clutches, Anthony had whisked it away, breathless with excitement and fear that he might be caught; he hurled himself back upstairs before hurling Alex through the window a second time.
>
> (*Dancing Ledge*, p. 38)

The little boy is shown to be keen to test out the theory that a cat has nine lives, which he had heard at school, but heartless about the potential that the experiment might end badly for the poor cat. The story is told like a dinner-party anecdote: careful details, such as the expensive breed of the pet, set a scene of wealth. The boy Anthony's actions are described with precise verbs: he 'climbed gingerly', he 'whisked', he 'hurled', he was 'breathless with excitement and fear' (*Dancing Ledge*, p. 38). One is able to imagine the scene with awful clarity. Precision coupled with the content – the tale reveals a level of sociopathy, cruelty or perhaps ruthless curiosity in the child – gives the anecdote its humour.

In *Dancing Ledge*, Jarman does not directly discuss the manner of friendship he shared with Harwood, whom Peake describes as a 'friend and mentor' and a 'father figure' in his biography.[33] Instead, we are given brief glimpses in *Dancing Ledge* that demonstrate the closeness of their relationship. For example, Jarman lived in the Sloane Square flat while Harwood was away. In a summary of his life around his thirty-second birthday, Jarman mentions, 'With Anthony paying the rent at Sloane Square it should be easy to get by until I go to NYC' (*Dancing Ledge*, p. 134). In *Dancing Ledge*, Jarman rarely ruminates in any detail on the qualities of his close friendships, his lovers or other more personal topics. Of his relationships with others, including the young photographer Gerald Incandela, we likewise only receive glimpses. Although Incandela is a regular presence in the book in anecdotes relating to the early 1970s, it is not until we hear that 'Gerald left [Jarman's birthday party] in tears' (*Dancing Ledge*, p. 134) that we might consider there may be more to their relationship. All of that, Jarman glosses over: personal details such as boyfriends are not consistently shared. As an autobiography, it provides less information about personal topics than we might expect. Perhaps the focus on action and anecdote over emotion is typical of a man of his generation – at least until his life took a much more serious turn when he decided the time was right to take the test and was diagnosed seropositive in December 1986.

I am struck throughout these episodes by Jarman's verve, curiosity and insistence on reveling in the most unusual stories he can find. There is a sense in which he is using his autobiography to show us how bizarre and wonderful the world can be. Jarman mentions how, throughout the late 1960s, 'experienced mentors' within the 'gay art world' would 'spice up the evening with delicious gossip' and 'relate tales of chance and magical encounters' (*Dancing Ledge*, p. 95). *Dancing Ledge* sees Jarman taking up a similar role.

'Visible Manifestations': the first news of AIDS

To any reader coming to the text more than a year or two after its publication, one of the most striking things about *Dancing Ledge* is its lightness or even frivolity.[34] Despite their lack of money, the world of Jarman and his friends in the 1970s that he describes in the book involves large artist's warehouses on the river, giving them the space to make art and to have large parties like Andrew Logan's outrageous Alternative Miss World competitions.[35] Jarman regularly visited Europe and America, and counted many unusual and famous people among his friends. Harwood's patronage kept him housed during challenging periods. Towards the end of that decade, he describes the success of three consecutive feature films. As Jarman was writing at the start of the 1980s, although he was frustrated by a lack of funding and by the tortuous hiatus in a critical part of his career, he was still relatively trouble-free. This accounts for the writing in this autobiographical account being, in many ways, a way of recording the glamour of the stories from his youth – and entertaining anecdotes from his youthful acquaintance. There is also a sense that Jarman wanted to give a gay life the shape of a success story, especially as he saw so few accounts of openly gay lives in publication. There is no particular urgency to the stories' telling: they came into being because Jarman found himself with time on his hands to devote to the project.

One particular moment stands out as indicative of its time: Jarman's account of the summer of 1974, which he spent in New York. Jarman writes of his summer spent staying in 'an empty roach-infested loft with an escaped python in SoHo' (*Dancing Ledge*, p. 137), which enabled him to film the final section of *In the Shadow of the Sun* at Fire Island, and spend time cruising the piers and bathhouses of New York. He describes the 'angel dust eye[d]' dealers at the Continental Baths, who 'fuel the dynamo which keeps the baths dancing' (*Dancing Ledge*, p. 135).[36] After a night at the baths, the next morning the 'carefree boys of the night return home to empty apartments where the roaches can be heard clattering through a week's washing up' (*Dancing Ledge*, p. 136). It recalls the hedonism, impoverishment and ideological freedom in Andrew Holleran's *Dancer from the Dance*: 'We lived', says the narrator, 'on certain chords in a song, and the proximity of another individual dancing beside you, taking communion from the same hand, soaked in sweat, stroked by the same tambourines'.[37] Although the pleasures of the city came at a cost, its freedoms and fascinations were equal to the sometimes sordid challenges of roaches and other results of staying there with very little money.

During the period of the text's composition (summer 1982 to spring 1983), many people on this side of the Atlantic had only somewhat begun to respond to the seriousness of the first news of what would come to be known as HIV/AIDS from the US. As a consequence, this particular project did not contain the same register of thanatographic urgency that would follow in all Jarman's later work. However, reports from the US had started to trickle through: 121 people had died by the end of 1981, and Larry Kramer had set up Gay Men's Health Crisis in January 1982. However, news was slow. In July 1983, Terry Higgins became one of the first people to die in the UK, and what was to become the Terence Higgins Trust was set up in November 1983. By the end of the same year, avant-garde US singer Klaus Nomi had died. Jarman mentions the virus in *Dancing Ledge*, but only once – and buried towards the end of the book:

> Now, from out of the blue comes the Antidote that has thrown all of this into confusion. AIDS. Everyone has an opinion. It casts a shadow, if even for a moment, across any encounter. Some have retired; others, with uncertain bravado, refuse to change. [...] the immediate effect has been to clear the bath-houses and visibly thin the boys of the night. [...] I decide I'm in the firing-line and make an adjustment – prepare myself for the worst – decide on decent caution rather than celibacy, and worry a little about my friends. Times change.
>
> (*Dancing Ledge*, pp. 239–40)

The section feels as if it has been added in as an afterthought, soon before publication. Its mood is not evident in the rest of the text. Although Jarman is well aware that he is 'in the firing-line', as he terms it, the sense of unease is limited to its expression within this passage.

As a first autobiographical text, *Dancing Ledge* engages with experiences and memories one might expect: childhood injuries, a first love, notable trips abroad and the entertaining anecdotes about acquaintances that give life to the memoir. However, it is conspicuous how little of an internal world we are given. Aside from the brief instance in which Jarman's first meeting with his first love Ron leads to a dark episode, Jarman's self-representations are light and exterior. Of *Dancing Ledge*, Ellis explains that 'It is less interested in outlining the private, interior world of its subject than in exploring the mutual interpenetrations of self and world'.[38] Jarman sometimes reduces critical moments in his life: the explanations that might provide background to the narrative sections are brief or missing, ridding the text of much of the tediousness and banality of the complexity of our everyday lives, with its messiness and narrative cul-de-sacs. Instead, Jarman favours dream-like cyphers, which communicate more meaning the more one knows about his life and work. The glamour of *Dancing Ledge* stands in contrast to the texts that would follow: *Kicking the Pricks*, which develops much of the content of *Dancing Ledge* and returns to much of the same subject matter, the diaries collected in *Modern Nature*, and the posthumous works *Derek Jarman's Garden* and *Smiling in Slow Motion*. *Dancing Ledge* is a fascinating early portrait of some sides of Jarman's personality, career and social world before his life was to change forever.

Notes

1. James Mackay interviewed by Andy Kimpton-Nye, *400blows*, www.400blows.co.uk (accessed 28 January 2012). The quote in the chapter title is taken from the preface to *Dancing Ledge*.
2. For a list of Jarman's Super 8s within a full filmography, see Peake, *Derek Jarman*, pp. 573–87. Many stills from the Super 8s are printed in James Mackay, *Derek Jarman: Super 8* (London: Thames and Hudson, 2014).
3. Laurence Normand, 'Jarman, Derek' in *The Gay and Lesbian Literary Heritage: A Reader's Companion to the Writers and Their Works, from Antiquity to the Present*, ed. Claude J. Summers (New York: Routledge, 2002), pp. 405–6 (p. 405).
4. Quoted in Evans et al., '*A Finger in the Fishes Mouth*'.
5. Gregory Woods, *A History of Gay Literature: The Male Tradition* (New Haven, CT: Yale University Press, 1998), p. 346.
6. *Square Peg* no. 4 (1984). Quoted in Peake, *Derek Jarman*, p. 320.
7. Peake, *Derek Jarman*, p. 321.
8. Ellis, *Angelic Conversations*, p. 90.
9. Jarman is here likely to be referring to the number of people living with AIDS (rather than diagnosed as HIV-positive, or the number of deaths caused by AIDS-related illnesses) at the time of writing. Jarman here references the early modern dismissal of medieval scholasticism, which seeks to devalue earlier work by insinuating that it discusses irrelevant points of logic such as, for example, the question of how many angels can dance on the head of a pin, punning on 'needless points'.
10. Peake, *Derek Jarman*, p. 321.

11 Philippe Lejeune, 'The Autobiographical Contract', trans. R. Carter, in *French Literary Theory Today*, ed. Tzvetan Todorov (Cambridge: Cambridge University Press, 1982), pp. 192–222 (p. 193).
12 Smith and Watson, 'Introduction', p. 15.
13 Dillon, *Derek Jarman and Lyric Film*, p. 228.
14 Peake, *Derek Jarman*, p. 398.
15 Tom Phillips, 'Down among the Rushes: *Dancing Ledge* by Derek Jarman', *Times Literary Supplement*, 4227 (6 April 1984), 367.
16 C. Hugh Holman, *A Handbook to Literature*, based on the original edn by William Flint Thrall and Addison Hibbard, 4th edn (Indianapolis, IN: Bobbs-Merrill, 1980), p. 33.
17 Smith and Watson, *Reading Autobiography*, p. 189.
18 Woods, *A History of Gay Literature*, p. 346.
19 Ibid.
20 Ken Plummer, *Telling Sexual Stories: Power, Change and Social Worlds* (London and New York: Routledge, 1994), p. 18.
21 Colm Tóibín, *Love in a Dark Time: Gay Lives from Wilde to Almodovar* (New York: Scribner, 2002), p. 9.
22 Ibid.
23 Section 28 was repealed on 21 June 2000 in Scotland by the Ethical Standards in Public Life etc. (Scotland) Act 2000, and on 18 November 2003 in the rest of the United Kingdom by Section 122 of the Local Government Act 2003.
24 Adrienne Rich, 'Invisibility in Academe', in *Blood, Bread, and Poetry: Selected Prose 1979–1985* (New York: Norton, 1986), pp. 198–201 (p. 199).
25 Tóibín, *Love in a Dark Time*, p. 9.
26 Jarman quoted in Peake, *Derek Jarman*, p. 321.
27 Oscar Wilde, *The Picture of Dorian Gray* (1891; repr. London: Penguin Popular Classics, 1994), p. 255.
28 Claude Lévi-Strauss, *The Savage Mind*, trans. George Weidenfeld & Nicolson (London: Weidenfeld & Nicolson, 1966), p. 16.
29 Ibid., p. 21.
30 Plummer, *Telling Sexual Stories*, p. 16.
31 The quote in the subheading is from *Dancing Ledge*, p. 38.
32 See Peake, *Derek Jarman*, p. 121.
33 Ibid, pp. 233–4.
34 The quote in the subheading is from *Dancing Ledge*, p. 238.
35 Andrew Logan's Alternative Miss World competitions are the subject of the documentary *The British Guide to Showing Off*, dir. Jes Benstock (Living Cinema, 2011).
36 Continental Baths was a gay bathhouse and hub for queer culture, music and dancing in the basement of the Ansonia hotel, New York, from 1968–76.
37 Andrew Holleran, *Dancer from the Dance* (New York: William Morrow, 1978; repr. New York: Perennial, 2001), p. 112.
38 Ellis, *Angelic Conversations*, pp. 90–1.

3

Derek Jarman's Caravaggio: 'Reading between the lines of history'

Derek Jarman's approach to the past was always provisional and always collage-based: he quickly gathered together different materials and subject matters and by doing so, created polyvalent, multi-layered works aimed at understanding and expanding the relationship between the past and present, and in particular articulating new ways in which we might understand how, in Jim Ellis's words, 'history inhabits and informs the present'.[1] Jarman, in his earliest feature films *Jubilee* and *The Tempest*, uses the moment of the English Renaissance in order to interrogate and satirise contemporary ideas of Englishness and the nation. Yet to understand his later sharply focused political engagement with our queer past, we might return instead to his work on the life of the Renaissance artist Michele Angelo Merigi da Caravaggio, a project that had its genesis at the end of the 1970s. Jarman had intense difficulty obtaining the financing necessary for this, his next planned feature film, and he struggled over a period of years to arrange for the funding required while writing and re-writing scripts with a number of collaborators. He eventually made *Caravaggio* in 1985, and it was released early the following year.

A lavishly illustrated book titled *Derek Jarman's Caravaggio* (1986) was published alongside the release of the film. It is the first example of the books that Jarman released alongside his films, starting a practice that would be maintained for the rest of his career. Like the later books *War Requiem* (1989) and *Wittgenstein: The Terry Eagleton Script, the Derek Jarman Film* (1993), it contains a version of the script for the film, yet unlike those books, various different kinds of text are included: the script itself is interspersed with information about the making of the film and Jarman's reflections on Caravaggio's life and art, and on his own career. Jarman inserts autobiographical musings alongside the script itself, much as he does in the later *Queer Edward II* (1991). In another font, quotations from contemporaries and near-contemporaries of Caravaggio provide multiple accounts of his life and personality. The book is slightly short of A4 in size and reaches

136 pages. Although it is lavishly illustrated with photographs, it is a less expensive production than an art monograph.

The text of *Derek Jarman's Caravaggio* acts as an addition to *Caravaggio* by expanding on its contents, laying out Jarman's approach to the biography of the painter, in which Jarman recreated Caravaggio's paintings as tableaux vivants through which to create a narrative of his life. At times, the technique works overtly to tie Jarman's own life to the life of the Renaissance painter. In other instances, Jarman uses more oblique methods to comment on Caravaggio's self-representations. The book combines different kinds of text with photographs taken during production by Gerald Incandela. The photographs are predominantly black and white production stills and shots of the crew, with a small number of rich colour photographs also included. Incandela has painted over part of several of the photographs, transforming them into mixed-media artworks. His technique has the effect of breaking down the boundaries between life (as captured in photography) and art (as signalled through the use of paint). In sum, the book comprises a collage of different views and media that provides perspectives not only on Caravaggio, but on Jarman too.

This chapter contains analyses of several elements of the Caravaggio project. It begins with a summary of Jarman's deeply personal use of the past that acts as a means of finding and linking queer forebears to his own experience. He uses the text to advance what would become a refrain throughout the rest of his career: intermingling alternative queer histories with contemporary political contestation. Jarman placed his historical project in productive relation to Caravaggio's own iconoclastic historical project, in which the painter overlaid biblical and classical scenes with private meaning from his own life. Jarman playfully engaged with Caravaggio's dismembered self-portraits in *Derek Jarman's Caravaggio*, speculating about the autobiographical meanings found within these grisly images. He revisits the self-portraits as a means to claim them – and the choreographed stagings of Caravaggio's personal life they depict – for his own uses. Jarman also makes use of the Christ-figure from Caravaggio's famous *The Incredulity of Saint Thomas*, inserting Caravaggio's features into the role of Christ in his own composition, as a means to explore the well-trodden trope of queer martyrdom, highlighting his anger at the suffering that queer experience too often involved. I also investigate how Jarman uses his own body in the film, where he appears in a brief cameo as a cardinal. The moment could easily be missed in the film but is recreated in several rich colour plates in *Derek Jarman's Caravaggio*.

Throughout the chapter, I follow Jarman's preoccupation with looking, which is recorded in the book. Jarman highlights the links between Caravaggio's self-portraits, his subjects and the subjects' audiences; Jarman's role as both director and painter; and the viewers of both paintings and film. Each looks towards another: at himself, at his subjects, or out from the picture plane at his audiences. Critically, *Derek Jarman's Caravaggio* highlights self-representational acts that are fleeting in the film – Caravaggio's self-portraits, as well as Jarman's own self-conscious engagement with his role as painter and director – allowing readers the time to engage with them and absorb their meaning. Most importantly, Jarman uses collage as a technique throughout the book to emphasise the way the film, like any other version of the painter's life, is just one possible construction or reading. Rather than viewing the film as a finished product, I argue that the publication of *Derek Jarman's Caravaggio* demonstrates that Jarman's work on Caravaggio's life should be seen as a queer history project, the process of which is at least as important as the final product of the film *Caravaggio*.

Jarman was always invested in what Carolyn Dinshaw has summarised as 'a queer desire for history': he was driven to insist upon a queer past (using the terms of the present) and thereby forge community across time.[2] Yet he also, in doing this, displays a desire to enable different kinds of connections across time and different – or queer – conceptions of time that enable ways of being historical that exceed linear time. For Elizabeth Freeman, engaging with queer temporalities involves 'mining the present for signs of undetonated energy from past revolutions', and it is this drive, which we see in *Derek Jarman's Caravaggio*, that this chapter unpacks.[3]

Jarman's use of the past: Caravaggio

The choice of Caravaggio as a subject was not originally Jarman's, but that of his producer Nicholas Ward-Jackson, yet the artist was an appropriate pick for Jarman. In his 1992 polemic *At Your Own Risk*, Jarman described the deeply personal nature that his queer history project had always taken. Speaking of his self-education in the early 1960s while he was at King's College London, he comments 'I began to read between the lines of history. The hunt was on for forebears who validated my existence' (*At Your Own Risk*, p. 46). Caravaggio was just one of a list of queer forefathers from this period in Europe, who, throughout his career, Jarman explored and made use of.[4] He asks, 'Was Western civilization Queer? The Renaissance certainly was. Lorenzo di Medici, Michelangelo, Leonardo, Botticelli, Rosso, Pontormo, Caravaggio, Shakespeare, Marlowe, Bacon' (*At Your Own Risk*, p. 46). Jarman claims these artists, writers and polymaths for a queer tradition of which he is the latest part.[5] Aebischer summarises aptly: 'The point is not historical accuracy, but a politically motivated need to insist on the contribution formulations of queer desire have made to Western civilisation'.[6]

Caravaggio holds a reputation as a dashing troublemaker, a man said by his contemporaries to be 'a quarrelsome individual', and 'a pernicious poison who did a little good but much harm'.[7] Indeed, Leo Bersani makes purposeful anachronistic use of twentieth-century *enfant terrible* Jean Genet, branding Caravaggio 'that Genet-type outlaw'.[8] Jarman makes plain his interest in the painter in *Derek Jarman's Caravaggio*:

> Caravaggio was the first to take a bottle of paint-stripper to the Renaissance. He burnt away decorum and the ideal, splattered the clear clean colours of Mannerism with his lamp-blacks, knocked the saints out of the sky and onto the streets, stole and smelted their haloes. This wild youth with his pagan obsession was to end high on the altars of Rome – the fate of successive avant-gardes. (p. 44)

Jarman named a technique here that also became his own: he too takes 'a bottle of paint-stripper' to his subject matter, paring it back to its base components in order to make something direct and useful in his contemporary moment. Genevieve Warwick explains that Caravaggio 'conceived of his subject as a performance of history staged in the present. [...] Caravaggio demonstrated the relevance of the past to his contemporaries by enacting it within the framework of the present'.[9] Ellis links Jarman's technique to the painter's: 'Jarman figures Caravaggio in the same way that Caravaggio remakes his historical subjects, making them embody the relation between two historical moments'.[10] Jarman shares his approach to the past with the painter. When Jarman writes 'I am obsessed by the interpretation of the past' (*Derek Jarman's Caravaggio*, p. 44), he is pointing to his preoccupation not with the past itself, but with its 'interpretation', or in other words, the past as seen through the lens of the present. As Jarman wrote in his final diary, 'It is not possible to look at works through the eyes of the past, only the present, and no one coming to Michelangelo or Shakespeare should ignore this unveiling'.[11]

Caravaggio's self-representations: *Bacchino Malato*

In addition to finding in Caravaggio a way of working with the past that he admired and perhaps emulated, Jarman developed an interest in Caravaggio's self-representations. The artist's self-portraits often use mythmaking strategies that bear further analysis because they are strategies taken up by Jarman in his own work. Caravaggio's work was often highly self-referential: he would sometimes give his own features to a character in the religious or classical scenes that he painted, and, like Jarman, would generally work with a group of collaborators who modelled for him and were involved in

7

IN HOSPITAL. A FATEFUL MEETING

"He was struck by sickness and, being without money, was obliged to enter the hospital of the Consolazione, where during his convalescence he made many pictures for the prior."

MANCINI

VOICE-OVER
Michele paid for his wild life by spending the summer in hospital with jaundice, where he painted his hangover with which he christened 'The Sick Bacchus': in it he is pea-green and twined with ivy leaves. One afternoon the Cardinal Del Monte — patron of the hospital, ambassador of the Medici, arch-priest of the basilica and also, as luck would have it, president of the painters' academy of St Luke — made a visit to wash the feet of the sick as a penance. The look the old cardinal gave Michele fooled no one. He smiled sweetly and said, as he studied the painting with the aid of his pince-nez.

DEL MONTE
Why did you paint the flesh so green?

MICHELE
I've been ill all summer, Excellency.
It's true to life.

DEL MONTE
And art?

MICHELE
It doesn't pretend to be art.

DEL MONTE
I see. A most interesting idea.
What is your name?

MICHELE
Michelangelo da Caravaggio. Excellency.

DEL MONTE
Michelangelo? Michelangelo!

VOICE-OVER
And he left the room clutching the dagger which Michele loved above all else, even the blood-red cinnabar. The rich never take their pleasures simply. Dukes and duchesses, cardinals and even popes, all of them conspire to guard each other's exemplary lives whilst dreaming of sodomizing the poor like dogs on heat.

The Sick Bacchus

Figure 5 Spread from *Derek Jarman's Caravaggio* showing a production still by Gerald Incandela of the young Caravaggio (Dexter Fletcher) in a hospital bed, with the *Bacchino Malato* resting on the wall behind him (verso). The script relating to the production shot is reproduced, along with a quotation from Giulio Mancini (1559–1630), whose *Considerazione* is one of the earliest sources for biographical information about Caravaggio. Caravaggio's *Bacchino Malato* (c. 1593–94) is also reproduced in black and white (recto).

his own life. These methods ensured his painting acted as a kind of autobiographical practice, or, as David Stone contends, show him to have created a 'mythical self [...] which critics have often mistaken for autobiography'.[12] Like Jarman, Caravaggio demands we acknowledge the inseparability of life and art.

In an early self-portrait, Caravaggio uses his own boy-like features for his *Bacchino Malato*, or *Young Sick Bacchus* (c. 1593–94), the god of unrestrained consumption and ritual madness, sick with surfeit. Bacchus was sometimes figured as either androgynous or effeminate: Walter Otto finds examples of him being described as 'man-womanish' in classical literature.[13] He is described as 'the womanly one' by Aeschylus and as 'the womanly stranger' in Euripides' *The Bacchae*.[14] Bersani reads the self-portrait as an 'erotic tease' which provides a 'come-on' tempered by ambiguity.[15] The young Caravaggio poses coyly: he wears an open expression on his face and his bare shoulder is enticingly angled towards the painting's viewers, yet his body is shrouded loosely in material and is facing away from viewers, in a gesture that 'is at once exhibitionist and self-concealing'.[16] The boy is also depicted with greenish skin, showing his sickness, adding what Bersani and Dutoit describe as 'a repellent and repelling note to the provocation'.[17]

Caravaggio takes on an intriguing pose in this early painting that offers viewers the opportunity to interpret it in tendentious ways: he becomes the vision of the onlooker's downfall, simultaneously showing an initial attraction and ensuing catastrophe that will result if one gives in to one's urges. Yet he is an ambiguous character in another way: he trades on an androgynous gender presentation to attract his disciples, providing an opportunity for a contemporary viewer to read the pose as a commentary on sexuality. However, the Bacchus is a choreographed pose, which complicates the autobiographical significance of this work.

Jarman uses the painting as a plot device in *Caravaggio*, which he expands upon in *Derek Jarman's Caravaggio*. Early in Jarman's film, the older Michele states in a voiceover that 'I painted myself as Bacchus and took on his fate, a wild orgiastic dismemberment' (*Caravaggio* 00:10:42; *Derek Jarman's Caravaggio*, p. 21). Although the older man comments on the self-representation as being a role he took on, the younger Caravaggio is depicted as fully invested in the role. In the same scene, a reproduction of *Bacchino Malato* created by Christopher Hobbs is shown leaning against a wall in the film (*Caravaggio*, 00:11:01), prompting a discussion of the painting between the Cardinal Del Monte and the young Michele:

DEL MONTE
Why did you paint the flesh so green?

MICHELE
I've been ill all summer, Excellency.
It's true to life.
DEL MONTE
And art?
MICHELE
It isn't art.[18]

Jarman here guides us to a particular interpretation of the self-portrait: while enacting the role of Bacchus as he poses for his own painting, the young artist becomes Bacchus. Or rather, Bacchus becomes the young artist: the real subject becomes indistinguishable from the mythic origins that inspired the painting. Although sources from this period are inconclusive, they agree that at one point as a young man, Caravaggio fell extremely ill and spent six months in the hospital of Santa Maria della Consolazione. This painting is in part, an autobiographical record of the physical effects of the sickness. The scene is presented in *Derek Jarman's Caravaggio*, though with Michele's last line altered to 'It doesn't pretend to be art' (p. 25, see Figure 5), rather than the simpler 'It isn't art' of the film. Jarman has Michele declare the painting's lack of pretence, focusing on his interest in depicting life without regard for aesthetics, and scorn for the practice of elevating life to art. Of course, this could also be a pose, but it gives a good indication of how Jarman wishes us to understand Caravaggio's self-representational gesture here. It also shows a darker sense of what goes into artistic creation than in *Dancing Ledge*.

Caravaggio's self-representations: *David with the Head of Goliath*

In a second major self-portrait, Caravaggio uses his own features to disquieting effect in a graphic depiction of the David and Goliath story. In one of his engagements with the biblical story, titled *David with the Head of Goliath* (c. 1605–10) and held in the Galleria Borghese, Caravaggio paints his own features onto the dismembered head of the vanquished giant.[19] The intense drama of the scene in the painting is aided by the young David's stance: he holds Goliath's severed head by its hair, its blood pours from the torn flesh at its neck. There is a scholarly consensus that Goliath's features belong to Caravaggio, derived from a comparison of the painting with the famous portrait of Caravaggio by Ottavio Leoni (c. 1621). To a contemporary viewer, this self-depiction seems striking. Why would Caravaggio have used his own features on Goliath? To understand this pose, one might consider who he is depicting himself as being vanquished by. There are two competing readings that comment on the identity of David. In the first, David, whose

Figure 6 Cover image of *Derek Jarman's Caravaggio*. The young Caravaggio (Dexter Fletcher) here grasps the severed head of the older Caravaggio (Nigel Terry) in Jarman's tableau.

expression contains more sadness than delight in conquering his adversary, betrays 'an unusual psychological bond' between the two.[20] The figure is thought to hold the features of a former studio boy, Cecco del Caravaggio, 'il suo Caravaggino', who had been his lover.[21] In this version, one can read the painting as Caravaggio's statement of being slain by desire for the younger man. In the second interpretation of David's identity, David's features are thought in fact to be Caravaggio's own, as a younger man. In this version, the double self-portrait of 'self-mutilation' perhaps indicates Caravaggio's acceptance that the behaviour of his youthful self has curtailed his life as a man.[22] In both versions, Caravaggio uses a familiar religious subject to reflect on his own life (and perhaps relationships).[23]

David Stone describes Caravaggio's self-portraits as 'demonstrations of the artist's fierce competitiveness and quest for originality'.[24] Yet his painting of his severed head in this instance has a curious parallel with the self-portraits of another figure included in Jarman's list of queer figures from the Renaissance (*At Your Own Risk*, p. 46), the painter Michelangelo, found in the frescoes of the Sistine Chapel and made up to a century earlier (ceiling: 1508–12; *The Last Judgement*: 1536–41). Strikingly, Michelangelo uses his own features on the decapitated head of Holofernes in the *Judith and Holofernes* lunette on the Sistine ceiling, placing himself in the role of the lecherous Assyrian general whose desire for Judith was the weakness that led to his death: he allowed her to enter his tent when he was unguarded, whereupon she killed him before he could destroy the city of Bethulia, her home. In this role, Michelangelo becomes the warmonger destroyed by his own (heterosexual) lust. In a second, later self-portrait within *The Last Judgement* (1536–41), Michelangelo again depicts himself in a mutilated form, this time as St Bartholemew's flayed skin, held by the saint as the symbol of his martyrdom in a pose described by Laura Camille Agoston as 'simultaneously self-aggrandizing and self-annihilating'.[25]

In the context of these examples from Michelangelo's work, Caravaggio's own grisly self-representational pose as Goliath seems to be not extraordinary but instead an example of how he borrowed techniques not only from distant spiritual narratives and classical myth, but also from his more recent cultural history. Agoston has written at length about the convention in Italian Renaissance and Baroque painting of artists making self-portraits where their features are placed onto the severed heads of Holofernes, Goliath or John the Baptist. She observes that 'the biblical narrative is coded with private, autobiographical significance, while the faces of Judith, David, or Salome also take on a specificity known only to the artist and his circle as portraits of former lovers'.[26] These narratives of inversion, where the weaker (the smaller David, the female Judith or Salome) subdues the stronger, seem to depict the artist as the rightly defeated victim. Yet they are always ambiguous: they demonstrate the artist's power to transform myth and biblical narrative into personal history. By preserving references to one's life in paint, one can enact 'durable commemoration and oblique revenge'.[27]

Jarman takes up the ambiguous backstory to *David with the Head of Goliath* (1605–10) most visibly in the book rather than the film *Caravaggio*. On the front cover of *Derek Jarman's Caravaggio*, a hybrid photograph with hand-painted areas shows Jarman's tableau recreation of the setting for Caravaggio's *David with the Head of Goliath* (see Figure 6). In this version, Goliath has the features of Nigel Terry, the actor who plays Michele Caravaggio in the film. The teenager holding the head of the vanquished Goliath aloft is Dexter Fletcher, the actor who plays the young Caravaggio in the film. His younger self holds the older self's decapitated head aloft, as it drips blood. By placing a double self-portrait on the front cover of the book, Jarman frames the Caravaggio project with an image that explores Caravaggio's biography through the painter's own autobiographical project.

In this case, Jarman privileges a reading where the painter depicts the actions of his younger self annihilating the older man.

Yet Jarman includes another version of the scene in the book. On a spread that focuses on Caravaggio's self-portraits, Jarman includes another full-size photograph of *David with the Head of Goliath* (*Derek Jarman's Caravaggio*, p. 49) recreated as a tableau vivant (see Figure 7). In this version, the image captured is different from the one on the cover. The young boy this time is not the young Caravaggio (played by Dexter Fletcher), but another adolescent boy. The photograph has, like the front cover, been partly painted over, the black watercolour paint giving the piece a dream-like quality. Jarman's text on the opposite page is ambiguous. He comments:

> Six years before, when he painted *The Martyrdom of St Matthew*, he included his own self-portrait, staring wistfully over his shoulder at a beautiful naked youth. [...] This painting and *David with the Head of Goliath* – another self-portrait, in which a tough street boy holds Caravaggio's severed head – show martyrdom at the hands of youth. (*Derek Jarman's Caravaggio*, p. 48)

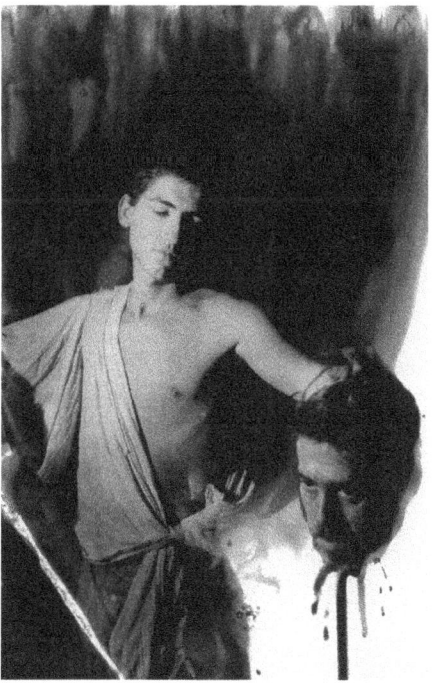

Figure 7 Jarman includes another full-size photograph of *David with the Head of Goliath* in *Derek Jarman's Caravaggio*, in which the severed head of the older Caravaggio (Nigel Terry) is held aloft by a youth (p. 49).

In a way, it doesn't matter whether the 'youth' Jarman here refers to is the painter's younger self or another young man. Both versions of the painting's sitters' identities coexist: Caravaggio's posed self-destruction, as well as his demise at the hands of a young lover. The variant tableaux provide a lens through which to understand not necessarily the events in the film but Jarman's understanding and engagement with Caravaggio's autobiographical play. Jarman engaged with multiple versions of Caravaggio's life: those readings encouraged by Caravaggio himself, his contemporaries in Italy and his afterlives in cultural history.[28] His own reading allowed for multiple versions to coexist and *Derek Jarman's Caravaggio* provides a record of the working process.

Neither tableau appears as a scene in the film. The inexact match between the contents of the film and the contents of the book shows us one way to understand Jarman's working practice. This example demonstrates that the book is not simply a printed illustration of the contents of the film. Instead, it is an extension of its subject matter, showing far more not only of the filming on set, but of the collaborative working processes that informed the film's direction. The project is not simply about the finished result of the film release, although that was a huge relief after so many years' hiatus, but about the collaborative process of exploring then re-enacting the painter's history.

Caravaggio, Christ and Jarman taking things further

On the double-page spread dedicated to self-portraits in *Derek Jarman's Caravaggio*, Jarman comments on a further self-portrait, which is subtly featured in *The Martyrdom of Saint Matthew* (1599–1600), installed in the San Luigi dei Francesi, Rome. The famous painting features an image of the saint being murdered by a soldier sent by the king of Ethiopia, to repay him for rebuking the king for his lust for his own niece, a nun. The young soldier, or murderer, is situated at the centre of the image, his muscles made more prominent by the direction of the light on his unclothed body. As Jarman describes him, 'A murderer, who [Caravaggio] has painted triumphantly' (*Derek Jarman's Caravaggio*, p. 48). A face, again recognisable from the Ottavio Leoni portrait of Caravaggio, looks askance at the scene from the background, perhaps 'a saddened bystander' or, given a queer reading, a portrait of the artist throwing a backwards glance at the beautiful soldier, perhaps claiming a relation of unrequited desire.[29] Jarman gives a queer reading to the painting in his earlier autobiography, *Dancing Ledge*. He includes the following commentary on the painting:

> Michele gazes wistfully at the hero slaying the saint. It is a look no one can understand unless he has stood till 5 a.m. in a gay bar hoping to be fucked

by that hero. The gaze of the passive homosexual at the object of his desire, he waits to be chosen, he cannot make the choice. (*Dancing Ledge*, p. 22)

The passage demonstrates the direct way Jarman makes a reading of the past in the terms of the present: the mention of the gay bar helps contextualise the onlooker's gaze, yet once again, we receive a hint of darker impulses than hedonism.

Jarman recognises that 'it's difficult to know how the seventeenth century understood physical homosexuality' (*Dancing Ledge*, p. 21), in a nod towards the first volume of Michel Foucault's *The History of Sexuality* (1976), but the point is not historical accuracy but instead recognising and drawing out a lineage of queer forefathers. In Jarman's film, Ranuccio (Sean Bean) poses as Saint Matthew's killer in the tableau for the painting. Jarman thereby invites us to understand the painting in terms of Michele's unrequited passion for Ranuccio.

In *Derek Jarman's Caravaggio*, Jarman makes explicit the ways in which he uses Caravaggio's paintings as a framing device with which to construct a narrative of Caravaggio's life. In the above example, Jarman makes clear his intent to use *The Martyrdom of Saint Matthew* to highlight the unequal desire between Caravaggio and Ranuccio. He names the implied relation in the tableau shown in the film. But in another spread in *Derek Jarman's Caravaggio*, Jarman goes further still. He uses the actor who plays Caravaggio in the film (Nigel Terry) to extend the legend of the historical Caravaggio in a playful way. In a pastiche of a famous painting hung in the gallery at Sanssouci, Potsdam, Jarman places the real (as opposed to posed) Caravaggio into a self-representational role within one of his paintings that Caravaggio did not take on himself. A grainy reproduction of Caravaggio's intense, voyeuristic *The Incredulity of Saint Thomas* (1601–02), shows a religious scene following Christ's resurrection. According to the Gospel of Saint John, Christ appeared to his disciples after his resurrection and showed them his wounds in order to prove that he had truly risen from the dead. Saint Thomas was absent, yet when the others told him that they had seen Christ, he would not believe them. Saint Thomas is reported as saying, 'Except I shall see in his hands the print of the nails, and put my finger into the print of the nails, and thrust my hand into his side, I will not believe'.[30] Caravaggio's painting depicts the risen Christ forcing Saint Thomas to penetrate the wound on his side with a finger (reproduced in *Derek Jarman's Caravaggio*, p. 60), as two other apostles look on. On the opposite page, a production shot from the film shows Caravaggio (Nigel Terry) drawing the hand of Davide (Garry Cooper) towards him and into the wound on his side, the result of a knife fight with Ranuccio (Sean Bean), with whom he is in love (see Figure 8).

Jarman uses Caravaggio's paintings as a framing device that helps him structure a film that looks to the art to provide a creative biography of the

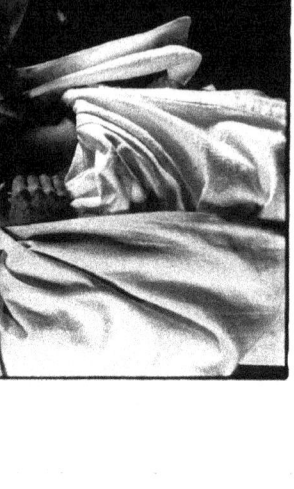

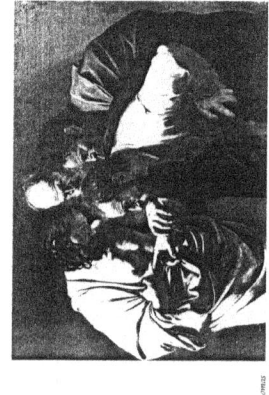

Figure 8 Spread from *Derek Jarman's Caravaggio* showing the relevant section from the script, a quotation from the art theoretician Carel van Mander (1548–1606) and a black-and-white reproduction of Caravaggio's *The Incredulity of Saint Thomas* (verso). Jarman's recreation of *The Incredulity of Saint Thomas* is captured on the recto in a production still by Gerald Incandela.

life. In this instance, Jarman provides a reading that extends Caravaggio's own self-myth-making: the character of Caravaggio in the film becomes a living enactment of the historical Caravaggio's painting. Jarman thereby places even more weight on a reading of Caravaggio's paintings as an autobiographical practice than Caravaggio did. But he is also doing something else simultaneously: alongside his commentary on the practice of 'Life as art', Jarman is creating a symbolically resonant image.[31] By depicting Caravaggio in a choreographed pose as the risen Christ, Jarman is depicting the painter in the role of queer martyr. Indeed, Jarman makes use of Christ at other moments in his work: this particular moment in Christ's passion is a motif that is reprised in *The Garden* (1990), in which the older Christ (played by Roger Cook) opens his garments to display his wound to the camera, pointing to a history of gay suffering at the hands of homophobic persecution. *The Incredulity of Saint Thomas* is a painting that particularly lends itself to re-appropriation by a gay audience: the original painting is a startling erotic scene depicting an intense exchange involving material penetration between men. Neil Bartlett also uses the painting in his novel *Skin Lane* (2007): the protagonist, Mr F, whose trade as a furrier makes him a relic from an older world, visits the National Gallery in 1967 where he comes across the painting. Bartlett uses the painting as part of a code of urban gay culture that Mr F slowly becomes aware of. By recreating the painting as a tableau in both *Caravaggio* and *Derek Jarman's Caravaggio*, Jarman, in Ellis's words, 'claims Caravaggio for a gay historical tradition, putting his sexuality at the center of his artistic genius'.[32]

Jarman in *Caravaggio*

Jarman aligns himself with Caravaggio by creating an oblique self-portrait in the film, which is carefully documented in two rich, coloured plates printed in *Derek Jarman's Caravaggio* (see Plate 2 for one of these). In what is Jarman's first physical appearance in one of his own feature-length films, he appears in a cameo role as a cardinal towards the end of *Caravaggio*, dressed in incarnadine robes. He is present and silent throughout the scene (depicted in *Derek Jarman's Caravaggio*, p. 120) in which a camp Pope Paul V (Jack Birkett) gives an audience to Michele Caravaggio. They negotiate the painting of a portrait in exchange for the release of Ranuccio, who had been erroneously jailed for murdering the prostitute Lena (the real culprit was the Pope's nephew, Scipione Borghese). The scene cuts to Jarman, who dips an aspergillum into a golden bowl filled with water, then sprinkles the water over some objects on a table. In the script, Jarman is mentioned in the scene's directions as follows: '*A cardinal takes a holy water sprinkler and silently blesses the immaculate paints and blank white canvas that have been prepared for the portrait sitting*' (*Derek Jarman's Caravaggio*, p. 120). Jarman never looks at the camera or at the other characters, but takes on a quiet and ritualistic role. The cameo in *Caravaggio* is brief and unobtrusive. An audience might not notice his appearance, taking place as it does in a tense scene between Michele and the Pope. However, that the images of Jarman posing as the silent cardinal are reproduced in *Derek Jarman's Caravaggio* in rich colour plates signals that Jarman wanted the self-representation to be remembered.

Jarman playfully demonstrates his own identification with Caravaggio through this indirect means: he uses the painter's own methods, mimicking the way Caravaggio used other figures to symbolise certain aspects of himself, rather than being more direct. By posing as a cardinal in the film, Jarman may have been gesturing towards his role as film director. We watch the cardinal undertake the almost spiritual preparation that underpins the making of a painting. Jarman ritualistically blesses the tools that will be used by the artist rather than seeking to show control of exactly what occurs. This mirrors Jarman's approach to filmmaking, in which the actors are encouraged to bring their own interpretation and autonomy onto set. He places himself as an oblique observer who doesn't even look directly at the events taking place, let alone being part of the action, perhaps overdoing the sense of himself as being at a remove from the action of the film.

Curiously, Jarman places himself in a role that notably does not involve a preoccupation with looking: Caravaggio's self-portraits always involve significant glances, as detailed above, and Jarman appears in other films in roles that always prioritise the ways in which he looks at his surroundings. In Chapter 6, for example, I analyse how he frames his own role as director in *The Last of England* through repeated appearances wielding a movie camera, looking at the world within his film through the remove of the recording equipment. In the earlier film *Nighthawks* (dir. Ron Peck, 1978), Jarman has an extended cameo role in the background of a gay disco scene, where he leans languidly against a wall, casually smoking, very handsome, observing the scene – in his own words, he makes 'a very creditable cruiser' (*Dancing Ledge*, p. 230).[33] In the cameo role in *Nighthawks*, Jarman remains at a distance from the action of the film: by looking, however, he is able to choose how and when to act, and with whom. Similarly, Jarman also features in a cameo role in Stephen Frears's biographical film about the life and violent death of Joe Orton and his relationship with Kenneth Halliwell, *Prick Up Your Ears* (1987), filmed not long after the release of *Caravaggio*. Jarman briefly plays the part of his university friend, the artist Patrick Procktor, who he knew from their time at the Slade School of Fine Art. As Procktor, Jarman paints a portrait of the naked Joe Orton for a commission undertaken in 1967 that would appear as a Royal Court programme insert.

He again features in a role as an observer: similar to the cardinal in *Caravaggio*, he is present during the action of the film yet not truly a part of it. As a painter in *Prick Up Your Ears*, he creates something new by looking carefully at his subject, but he tries to avoid being a subject himself.

In the cameos in Ron Peck's and Stephen Frears's films, Jarman is called on to represent an aspect of London's gay scene. In the first, he enacts an aspect of his own character: a hallmark of London's gay nightlife during a certain period, comfortable passing the time in bars, which the film's protagonist is not able to do. In the second, he is called on to represent London's gay art scene in late 1960s Islington by taking on the role of his friend Procktor. Yet in the cameo in *Caravaggio*, we see a different kind of self-representation: he is physically present for the exchange between the painter and the pope, but demurs his role as witness to the scene. He appears to be presenting a quieter, more serious aspect of himself, perhaps reminiscent of his personality during his time as a student at King's College London. If anything, the role draws attention to Jarman's interest in temporal displacements, where several temporalities co-exist at any given time. In this light, the self-representation shows Jarman in costume as part of an institution, the Catholic Church, whose existence in the present is steeped in the histories from Renaissance Rome, as well as showing the then-present Jarman make a commentary on both his own role as painter and film director, and his identification with Caravaggio, as he blesses the means of artistic production.

In a reading of Caravaggio's self-portraits, Bersani draws out the artist's use of his body as a 'relational term' in his art: 'The activity of Caravaggio's body in the work of his painting is figured in his painting by his occasional presence as a witness. [...] In this art, the communication of forms takes place, ultimately, as the artist's painted recognition of himself'.[34] Bersani focuses primarily on the work acting as a kind of mirror, bearing 'witness' not only to the events depicted in the paintings Caravaggio appears in, but also to the very act of painting itself. The movement of Caravaggio's body is recorded in the traces of paint he places on the canvas, but to ensure these traces cannot be misunderstood as somehow removed from the acts of the body that has made them, his body's presence is made yet more visible through the depiction of its likeness. Jarman echoes Caravaggio's interest in the 'communication of forms' by making visible his own body present in the events of the film, underlining his identification with the painter.

Derek Jarman's project

Caravaggio shows himself to be a 'deft mythologiser of his own life' in the self-portraits I have detailed above, a description that Tony Peake uses of Jarman.[35] He takes on choreographed poses in his self-representations that mean they acquire myth-like properties. In *Bacchino Malato*, he makes a playful commentary on desire. In his self-portrait as Goliath, and perhaps as David too, he raises the events of his own life to the status of the biblical story, as he poses as the vanquished lover. In *The Martyrdom of Saint Matthew* he becomes a bystander rather than a subject, perhaps making a playful comment on the purported role of the painter as an observer in translating ideas or events into art. Jarman demonstrates enthusiasm for Caravaggio's willingness to depict the body as fragmented, multiple, mutilated or sickening. In *The Martyrdom of Saint Matthew*, he even flirts with the body becoming irrelevant: an inconspicuous observer not tied to the action. Jarman borrows from the artist the technique of playing with ambiguity and inverted or perhaps unexpected power structures as a means by which to take on historical narratives and make them relevant to the present.

In an article subtitled 'Why Caravaggio's painting is even more exciting than his biography', Keith Christiansen, the Metropolitan Museum of Art chairman of European Painting, doesn't find much to love in Jarman's film. He states that Jarman has simply provided a useful introduction to some of the 'common assumptions' about the artist, whose 'impetuous, defiant, and often violent life has created a fascinating but distorting lens for the understanding of his works'.[36] He considers Jarman's portrayal to be a 'cliché' – 'Caravaggio as an archetype of the modern artist' – and understands the film as staging a clash between temporalities in its treatment of the interrelated nature of love (same sex), violence and art – 'Rome circa 1595 meets New York circa 1985'.[37] His criticisms are valid, but only if one was looking to Jarman's treatment of Caravaggio for a historically faithful education. Likewise, Jarman's focus on *Caravaggio's* general reception makes him vulnerable to Christiansen's charge that the film is clichéd. However, Jarman might reply that the terms by which the film has been judged here are wide of the mark.

Jarman's engagement with the Caravaggio project is clear on this front. *Derek Jarman's Caravaggio* is a collage that emphasises the degree to which the film, like any other version of Caravaggio's life, is a construction. For Jarman, claiming a stake in Caravaggio's history by creating a portrait of the painter through his paintings in the film, then chronicling the interchangeable nature of Caravaggio's art and life in *Derek Jarman's Caravaggio*, is a way to claim the painter for a queer lineage. Questions of historical accuracy do still count, yet Jarman might respond that the queer content of much of the official record has been excised, so cannot be relied upon to provide a faithful account. He isn't seeking to provide a biographical film in *Caravaggio* per se, but instead to do queer work by laying claim to his sexuality through an engagement with his chaotic, violent life. As a result, his interest does focus on his homosexuality, and events in his life where his sexuality is closest to the surface. He uses Caravaggio very much from the standpoint of the then present: his interest lies in the *interpretation* of Caravaggio's life – and associated self-representations, not necessarily in the life itself. Where Keith Christiansen states that he sees 1985 New York in the film, his reading is surely far more of a compliment than he had intended. Ellis, whose work on Jarman focuses on his 'ongoing and shifting engagement with historical material', primarily material from the early modern period, conceives of Jarman's work as a whole as a 'project of responding to the challenges of his own time'. He summarises an important point that I return to throughout this book: Jarman felt that 'By remaking the past, he was remaking the present, and allowing for the invention of new possibilities for living'.[38]

Although revisiting the past was a preoccupation for Jarman throughout his career, to do so did not always mean the same thing. Between the release of his first feature film *Sebastiane* and the release of *Caravaggio* and *Derek Jarman's Caravaggio*, the terrain had shifted. The making of *Caravaggio* came at a time when mainstream society's thinking about sexual minorities was rapidly changing in response to increasingly hysterical media portraits of HIV/AIDS. A project that had been conceived of during a period of relative positivity for queer people, in terms of the political landscape, finally came into being at a stark turning point. Although scholarly consensus is, as Ellis notes, that '*Caravaggio* was his last work of art not to be marked in some way by the epidemic', this is not entirely true to its contexts.[39] Its origins, certainly, predate the epidemic, as do many of the script versions produced before its final form. However, it was filmed in 1985, so it is a stretch to consider the work unmarked by the contexts in the gay world – New York in particular, but London, too – simply because Jarman had delayed his own testing 'for as long as was decently possible', which he put off until the end of the year in which *Caravaggio* was released.[40]

Instead, the double release of *Caravaggio* and *Derek Jarman's Caravaggio* marks a turning point in Jarman's career. For the first time, he makes his working processes visible to his publics by publishing *Derek Jarman's Caravaggio* alongside the film, a technique he would use again to great effect in the later *Queer Edward II*. The visibility includes making use of the traces of the process recorded in the large, black sketchbooks Jarman kept throughout his career to produce the collage book. The newly visible approach makes clear Jarman's engagement in the process of making a particular work, rather than its finished product. Jarman privileges the energy and delight that comes from the working process, claiming the process – the project – as the main point. I consider that Jarman's work here sees the process as indistinguishable from the product: the final product includes the self-consciously visible marks of its creation. Jarman insists on Caravaggio as a model for what Dominique Viart calls 'the surrealist determination not to separate life from art, but to treat life as a work of art and vice versa'.[41] His detailed, recurrent engagement with Caravaggio's self-representations and associated 'self-implication' marks the beginning of a new chapter in Jarman's engagement with material from his own life. He insisted on the possibilities and uncertainties of queer temporalities as a means to unsettle and contest the politics of the contemporary that both threatened and circumscribed queer existence with increasing urgency as the 1980s wore on.

Notes

1 Ellis, *Angelic Conversations*, p. viii. The quote in the title of this chapter is from *At Your Own Risk*, p. 46.
2 Carolyn Dinshaw et al., 'Theorizing Queer Temporalities Roundtable', *GLQ: Journal of Lesbian and Gay Studies*, 13.2–3 (2007), 177–95 (p. 178).
3 Elizabeth Freeman, *Time Binds: Queer Temporalities, Queer Histories* (Durham, NC and London: Duke University Press, 2010), p. xvi.
4 For a summary of scholarly interpretations of Caravaggio's sexuality, see Leo Bersani and Ulysse Dutoit, *Caravaggio's Secrets* (Cambridge, MA: MIT Press, 2001), pp. 9–11. Bersani and Dutoit point out the tendentious nature of some of the early criticism advocating for Caravaggio's homosexuality, especially Donald Posner's essay, Donald Posner, 'Caravaggio's Homo-Erotic Early Works', *Art Quarterly*, 34 (1971), 301–24; and Michael Kitson, *The Complete Paintings of Caravaggio* (New York: Henry N. Abrams, 1967). Bersani and Dutoit note that 'distinguished scholar Howard Hibbard remains sensibly neutral on the subject' (*Caravaggio's Secrets*, p. 10). Further accounts can be found in Ellis, *Angelic Conversations*, p. 114; Andrew Graham-Dixon, *Caravaggio: A Life Sacred and Profane* (London: Penguin, 2011), p. 4.
5 For an account of the history of reclaiming the queer past through lists of queer forebears, see Woods, *A History of Gay Literature*, pp. 3–6. Woods traces the approach back to around 1870, to 'bookish homosexuals' (p. 3) who were, for example, students of Walter Pater at Oxford.
6 Pascale Aebischer, *Screening Early Modern Drama: Beyond Shakespeare* (Cambridge and New York: Cambridge University Press, 2013), pp. 30–1.
7 Quoted in Derek Jarman, *Derek Jarman's Caravaggio: The Complete Film Script and Commentaries* (London: Thames and Hudson, 1986), p. 44 (Baglione) and p. 58 (unattributed). Further references are given within the text. References to the film, *Caravaggio* (British Film Institute, 1986), are also given in the text.
8 Leo Bersani, *Is the Rectum a Grave?: And Other Essays* (Chicago: University of Chicago Press, 2009), p. 35.
9 'Genevieve Warwick, 'Introduction: Caravaggio in History', *Caravaggio: Realism, Rebellion, Reception*, ed. Genevieve Warwick (Newark: University of Delaware Press, 2006), pp. 13–22 (p. 19).

10 Ellis, *Angelic Conversations*, p. 117.
11 Derek Jarman, *Smiling in Slow Motion*, ed. Keith Collins (London: Century, 2000), p. 176. Further references are given within the text.
12 David Stone, 'Self and Myth in Caravaggio's "David and Goliath"', in *Caravaggio: Realism, Rebellion, Reception*, ed. Genevieve Warwick (Newark: University of Delaware Press, 2006), pp. 36–46 (p. 36).
13 Walter Friedrich Otto, *Dionysus: Myth and Cult* (Bloomington: Indiana University Press, 1965), p. 176.
14 Both quoted in Otto, p. 176.
15 Bersani, *Is the Rectum a Grave?*, p. 35; Bersani and Dutoit, *Caravaggio's Secrets*, p. 3.
16 Bersani and Dutoit, *Caravaggio's Secrets*, p. 3.
17 Ibid.
18 *Caravaggio*, 00:11:45–00:12:02.
19 I refer to the version held in Galleria Borghese, Rome, formerly in the collection of Scipione Borghese. Caravaggio also painted two other versions: *David with the Head of Goliath* (1607) held in the Kunsthistorisches Museum, Vienna, and the early 'David and Goliath' (c. 1599) held in the Prado, Madrid. Neither of these versions are self-portraits.
20 Catherine Puglisi, *Caravaggio* (London: Phaidon Press, 2000), p. 363.
21 Quoted in Puglisi, *Caravaggio*, p. 363. For an account of the gossip circulating throughout the seventeenth century and various unverifiable accounts, see Puglisi, *Caravaggio*, p. 363.
22 Stone, 'Self and Myth', p. 41.
23 For an analysis of the painting as self-mutilation, see Stone, 'Self and Myth', p. 41; Alfred Moir, *Caravaggio* (New York: Harry N. Abrams, 1989), p. 116.
24 Stone, 'Self and Myth', p. 43.
25 Laura Camille Agoston, 'Sonnet, Sculpture, Death: The Mediums of Michaelangelo's Self-Imaging', *Art History*, 20.4 (1997), 534–55 (p. 546).
26 Ibid.
27 Ibid., p. 548.
28 Psychological analyses from the 1970s of Caravaggio's self-portrait as Goliath (rather than as a double self-portrait) and as 'Medusa' (1597) read a castration complex into the self-representations that involve decapitation. See, for example: Laurie Schneider, 'Donatello and Caravaggio: the Iconography of Decapitation', *American Imago*, 33.1 (1976), 76–91.
29 Stone, 'Self and Myth', p. 43.
30 *The Bible*, Authorized King James Version with Apocrypha (Oxford: Oxford World Classics, 1998), John 20.25.
31 *Derek Jarman: Life as Art*, dir. Andy Kimpton-Nye (400Blows/VET, 2004).
32 Ellis, *Angelic Conversations*, p. 111.
33 See *Nighthawks*, 00:27:25–00:29:15.
34 Bersani, *Is the Rectum a Grave*, pp. 185–6.
35 Peake, *Derek Jarman*, p. 535. Matt Cook also explores the phrase in relation to Jarman in 'Wilde Lives: Derek Jarman and the Queer Eighties', in *Oscar Wilde*

and *Modern Culture: The Making of a Legend*, ed. Joseph Bristow (Athens: Ohio University Press, 2008), pp. 285–304 (p. 291).
36 Keith Christiansen, 'Low Life, High Art', *The New Republic*, 8 December 2010, https://newrepublic.com/article/79749/life-art-paintings-carvaggio (accessed 4 May 2021).
37 Ibid.
38 Ellis, *Angelic Conversations*, pp. x–xi.
39 Ibid., p. 133.
40 Jarman, Derek, *Kicking the Pricks* (first published as *The Last of England*, London: Constable, 1987; London: Vintage, 1996), p. 16. Further references are given within the text.
41 Dominique Viart, 'Programmes and Projects in the Contemporary Literary Field', in *The Art of the Project: Projects and Experiments in Modern French Culture*, eds. Michael Sheringham and Johnnie Gratton (New York: Berghahn Books, 2005), pp. 172–87 (p. 177).

4

Becoming Pasolini: Derek Jarman in *Ostia*

'Had Caravaggio been reincarnated in this century it would have been as a film-maker, Pasolini', Jarman writes in *Dancing Ledge* (p. 40). He considers Caravaggio 'the most homosexual of painters, in the way that Pasolini became the most homosexual of film-makers' (*Dancing Ledge*, p. 40). Jarman's identification with Caravaggio is exceeded by his identification with gay filmmaker, poet, essayist, social commentator and radical Pier Paolo Pasolini.[1] Indeed, Pasolini is an influence visible in Jarman's films, almost all of which are indebted to his work, from his first feature *Sebastiane*, which recalls *The Gospel According to St Matthew*, to his last film *Blue*, which is indebted to *Teorema*.[2] His interest in Caravaggio overlaps with his interest in Pasolini. Though born just over 350 years apart, the two Italians have in common their iconoclasm, their interest in depicting struggles or otherwise difficult subject matter and, perhaps, their homosexuality. Jarman felt an affinity with these characteristics in both men. During the lengthy period that Jarman was working on the various Caravaggio scripts, he also produced an outline proposal for a film about the last days of Pasolini titled *The Assassination of P. P. P. in the Garden of Earthly Delights*.[3] This chapter analyses a particular moment in Jarman's life-long interest in Pasolini – his unrealised project, and his appearance in the lead role in Julian Cole's short film about the death of Pasolini, *Ostia* (1987).

This chapter also tracks a move in Jarman's engagement with self-representation. His self-representations across media shift in 1986–87 from a preoccupation with looking – as a witness, as a play on his role as filmmaker, as a cruising man – to a commitment to action. In the shift between *Caravaggio* and *Derek Jarman's Caravaggio* and Jarman's next projects, including *The Last of England* and *Kicking the Pricks*, Jarman transitions from an aesthetic engagement with cultural politics through visual methods including representations of different kinds of gaze, to a much more active, embodied engagement with activism to battle homophobic feeling, legislation and media responses. Although Caravaggio was deeply physical – and often violent – Jarman's self-representation in relation to him was markedly quiet. However, his reaction to his queer forefathers seems to shift at the point of the Caravaggio project's fruition.

With *Caravaggio* almost ready to be launched at the start of 1986, and well before filming for *The Last of England* was to start in the summer, Jarman was finally able to move on to other projects. At the year's start, he had intended to take forward some existing plans, including developing the Pasolini outline, *P. P. P. in the Garden of Earthly Delights*. The synopsis presents a series of isolated scenes: the set for the final scene from *Salò, or the 120 Days of Sodom* (1975), an expensive restaurant, a night scene in which Pasolini is cruising by a railway station, a cheap diner and an area of scrubland where Pasolini is killed by the rent boy he had picked up. The background to the film juxtaposes the final events in the director's life with a prism of references to his cinematic work, as well as to the paintings of Hieronymus Bosch. Although Jarman's Pasolini project did not come to fruition, he found himself taking part that spring in a short film about Pasolini's death, with much the same plot as his own. Julian Cole, a friend of his and a student at the Royal College of Art, had discussed his idea for his graduate film with Jarman, and it was Jarman himself who suggested that he play the lead role. The result, *Ostia*, is a short film that reconstructs the events leading up to Pasolini's murder, relocated from Rome and Ostia to 1980s London. Jarman plays the 53-year-old filmmaker, cruising in his car, watching younger men spill out from a gay club into a side street, before picking up a young man (David Dipnall) on a deserted street next to the canal in Cambridge Heath. It becomes apparent that the man is not, in fact, a queer youth, but is acting as bait to draw Pasolini into the hands of a criminally violent and homophobic gang. The pair travel through the city, and eat in a café, talking at times antagonistically (see figures 9 and 10). They eventually reach a deserted beach where they grapple, before the younger man hits him with a rock. The gang arrives and bludgeons the unconscious Pasolini to death. Cole chooses to present as fact the convincing theories that Pasolini's death wasn't an accident of cruising, but a political plot.

Ostia forms the one notable instance in which Jarman acted in a traditional part with dialogue, involving a straightforward narrative and what might be understood as character acting. Jarman mentions little about the performance in his published writing. In *Kicking the Pricks*, he simply writes that 'Getting murdered and buried in freezing mud at 4 am as an uncertain sun came up was gruelling' (p. 239), though he adds that he had brought his Super 8 camera to the shoot. Highlighting the interconnectedness of his working practice, he writes: 'one shot from that day, my shadow racing across the sand, ended up in *The Last of England*' (p. 239). Though he made limited mention of the film in his published writing, the role is significant in an understanding of Jarman's shifting self-representations because of Jarman's deep identification with Pasolini.

Becoming Pasolini: Derek Jarman in Ostia

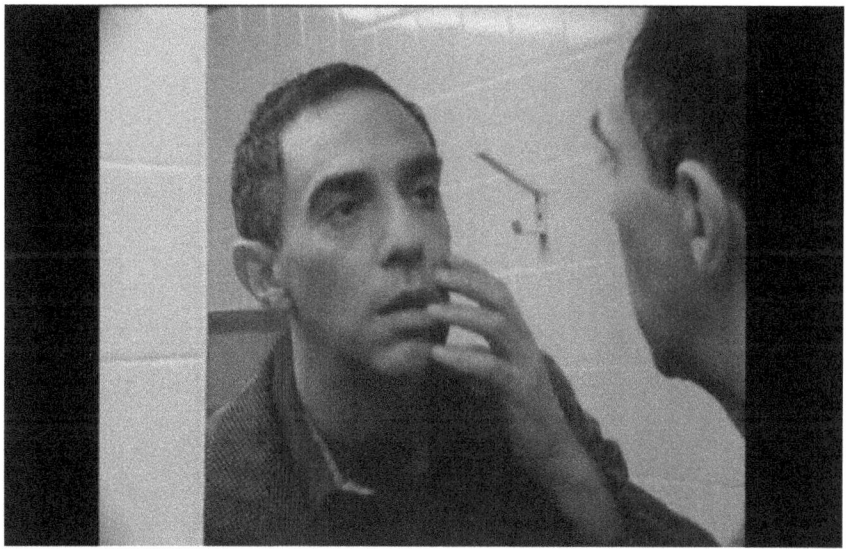

Figure 9 Pier Paolo Pasolini (Jarman) in *Ostia*.

Figure 10 Pasolini (Jarman) and Pino Pelosi (David Dipnall) in *Ostia*.

Pasolini, twenty years Jarman's senior, had a life that in many ways paralleled – or perhaps foreshadowed – Jarman's. He came from a similar family background to Jarman: he had a middle-class upbringing under the shadow of an authoritarian military father, but a loving relationship with his mother. Pasolini's career saw him work across a range of artistic media: he gained critical acclaim as a novelist and poet before he commenced his film career, and he was a political activist, public intellectual and essayist.[4] He followed eclectic interests in his reading and thinking, pronouncing passionately on a variety of subjects and demonstrating unconcern about revising or contradicting earlier opinions – Ellis comments that the two filmmakers were 'passionate if muddy thinkers'.[5] His films developed from neo-realism to more Brechtian techniques, and he moved from using modern settings to historical and mythic ones. Pasolini was a notorious public figure with unorthodox left-wing politics whose films were the cause of public controversy and subject to government scrutiny. He was controversial in parts of the gay community (and far more than simply controversial for the general public) for his desire for young rough trade. In *Kicking the Pricks*, Jarman dwells on the similarities between them. He comments that 'Pier Paolo's enemies saw him as a radical, but in fact he fought for traditional values' and 'I wonder if he would like my films; like his, they are made in an older tradition' (p. 81). Most noticeably, their strong public personae while they were alive tended to overshadow their films, meaning that their films' reception was often more about the director than the work.

'Throwing his body into the struggle': Casting Jarman as Pasolini

Jarman's body stands in directly for the body of his queer icon Pasolini in *Ostia*.[6] Jarman was interested in the filmmaking technique of superimposition, in which two different scenes are combined and made visible to the film's viewers at once. Peake comments that the technique is a metaphor for his artistic approach as a whole: 'fusing one concern with another [...] so that nothing is lost, everything is simultaneous'.[7] By acting in the role of someone he admires and indeed emulates, Jarman gives us a similar sense of palimpsestic identity.

By substituting figurehead for figurehead, Cole presents us not only with a witty conceit but also with a vision of Jarman's persona yoked in a literal way to recent queer history. The film enacts Jarman's way of doing queer history, which involves using himself in relation to the history of queer experience: Pasolini's story is brought to bear on Jarman's present. The biographical portrayal of the rumoured circumstances around Pasolini's death is also simultaneously a statement about the contemporary world around Jarman and the gay scene more widely. The soundtrack prominently features industrial music pioneers Test Dept, known for their political anger and anti-Thatcherite sensibility.[8] The mood evoked by the dislocating sounds and the barren urban setting of Tower Hamlets links the film to the particular political circumstances of London in the late 1980s, under a government that at times found the homophobia of its population politically expedient.

In the previous chapter, on *Derek Jarman's Caravaggio*, I mentioned two cameo roles in which Jarman's body is used to signify aspects of London's gay scene at a certain moment. In *Nighthawks*, he is very much a part of 1970s gay nightlife: confident, easygoing, a regular presence. In *Prick Up Your Ears*, he acts as a relic of the gay milieu within the 1960s London art scene that included David Hockney and Ossie Clarke. But in *Ostia*, Jarman's body is used to draw an ambivalent portrait of a middle-aged man aware that he is ageing, and whose diminishing sexual power is pointed to by the young men who populate the gay bar he pulls up outside. He is mocked by the younger man he picks up: 'you're like every other fucking old queen' (*Ostia*, 17:59–18:02). This could be read as a kind of autobiographical statement about the anxieties of ageing, leading – as Jarman puts it in relation to Caravaggio's self-portrait as the head of Goliath – to 'martyrdom at the hands of youth' (*Derek Jarman's Caravaggio*, p. 48). Jarman plays the role of a man unwittingly forced by his sexuality into a place of danger and vulnerability, ultimately resulting in his death.

The lure and gang violence depicted in the film represent the rumours surrounding the murder eleven years earlier: although the official record states that Pasolini was murdered by a rent boy alone, other suspicious circumstances surrounding the death were ignored. Pasolini was a dissident who was highly vocal about the state's corruption, neo-fascist links and collusion with the Mafia. Many on the left believed that political, perhaps even state-linked opponents, had arranged his death. Cole's film gives credence to the unofficial accounts of the poet-director's murder, giving Jarman a role in which he works to reinscribe a counter-history to the official record, in which the murder's complexity and political overtones are not excised.[9]

However, the film addresses more than this: throughout the film, Jarman reads Pasolini's poetry, adding a lyricism to the film that, juxtaposed with a brutal narrative of not only homophobic but also politically motivated murder, echoes Jarman's own autobiographical approach in *The Last of England* and *The Garden* (which I discuss in Chapter 6). Both filmmakers insist on the inseparability of art from the personal and the political. The poems also elevate the narrative from a possible interpretation as a sordid, dispiriting account of the poet's downfall. This role marks a definitive shift from Jarman's presence in *Caravaggio* as a careful onlooker, watching the negotiations between the actors of the narrative. At the beginning of *Ostia*, Jarman/Pasolini appears on television, wearing a suit. He says, 'Being a poet because life is expressed only with itself, I'd like to express myself with examples, to throw my body into the struggle' (*Ostia*, 02:17–02:25). Pasolini's well-documented desire for rough trade, which was viewed ambivalently by his peers, becomes part of the 'struggle'. Jarman's performance in this role is an instance in his wider use of his self-representations to reinforce a political refusal to excise the controversial aspects of some people's queer experience. He here demonstrates his political interest in undoing the 'gay is good' narrative that had gained prevalence in the post-Stonewall years to contribute to a more varied depiction of queer lives and a confrontational, rights-based rather than conciliatory approach. This approach is echoed in his accounts of seeking utopia of a kind while cruising on Hampstead Heath in the final years of his life, as recorded in *Modern Nature*, *At Your Own Risk* and *Smiling in Slow Motion*.

To 'throw [one's] body into the struggle' (*Ostia*, 02:17–02:25) was an important sentiment for Pasolini, who had co-opted the memorable slogan from the 1960s American Black Panthers, some of whom he met during a visit to Harlem.[10] Jarman, like other followers of Pasolini such as the queer performance artist Raimund Hoghe, has taken up the phrase to talk about his embodied experiences and his resistance from marginal positions.[11] Pasolini uses the phrase in the verse script *Bestemmia* (*Blasphemy*) (1962–67), which occupied Pasolini's imagination for five years but was never produced as a film. The slogan becomes the protagonist Bestemmia's motto, eventually causing him to become a revolutionary, bound to class warfare. Pasolini also uses the phrase in his poem 'Poet of Ashes', begun in 1966 but never published (alluding to the earlier poem 'Le cenere di Gramsci', 1957):

> ...nothing is worth as much as life.
> That's why I want only to live
> even while being a poet
> because life can express itself alone, too, with itself.
> I would like to express myself through examples.
> To throw my body into the struggle.[12]

The poem's narrator appears to be the poet himself: it seems to be a statement of his own artistic intent.

In *Ostia*, Jarman is not the director, but instead an actor contributing to someone else's artistic vision, however influenced by Jarman's project synopsis the film might be. However, Jarman was a highly recognisable figure throughout the 1980s and 1990s. This means that even as he takes on the role of another figure, he is making a creative decision to mix elements of their character and biography with his own. He cannot take part in the production of their biographies without overlaying them with his own interests and political concerns. David Gardner has commented that 'Jarman's autobiographical strategy not only emulates or alludes to those of Genet, Pasolini and Caravaggio, but also is projected over them, reinstigating the production of those other autobiographies to arrive at an entirely new meaning'.[13]

In this instance, by acting out the rumoured circumstances of the brutal murder, Jarman can be seen to be wholeheartedly taking up the lead from Pasolini by throwing his own body into the struggle to ensure queer histories are not lost, especially in instances where, as with Pasolini, justice is rumoured not to have been served. We might understand the incitement as critical for his political work.[14] Jarman's appearance in the film is not to further a battle for representation, but a quest for a truer depiction of Pasolini's murder. As Dillon notes, both 'Pasolini and Jarman repeatedly negotiate the expressive territory between "I" and community, between the individual suffering speaker and political activism'.[15] Speaking of Jarman's homage to Pasolini in *Sebastiane*, as well as his life-long engagement with a tradition of gay filmmaking, Ellis comments that 'This interest […] is associated with […] what would become the more central and pressing question of a gay ethics, and of our responsibilities to each other'.[16]

Notes

1 An identification noted by critics. See, for example, Ellis, *Angelic Conversations*, pp. 32–5; William Pencak, *The Films of Derek Jarman* (Jefferson, NC: McFarland, 2002), pp. 171–84; Dillon, *Derek Jarman and Lyric Film*, pp. 134–7; David Gardner, 'Perverse Law: Jarman as Gay Criminal Hero', in *By Angels Driven: The Films of Derek Jarman*, ed. Chris Lippard (Wiltshire: Flicks Books, 1996), pp. 31–64.
2 For a close reading of the ways Jarman uses Pasolini's work in *Sebastiane*, see Ellis, *Angelic Conversations*, pp. 32–5.
3 The outline in the Jarman Papers is undated, but a workbook relating to the project is dated August 1984. For brief information about the project, see Peake, *Derek Jarman*, p. 290. It would use elements from Hieronymus Bosch's *The Garden of Earthly Delights* (1503–15). The synopsis was published in a special issue of *Afterimage*, 'Derek Jarman … Of Angels and Apocalypse': Derek Jarman, 'P. P. P. in the Garden of Earthly Delights', *Afterimage*, 12 (Autumn 1985), 22–5.
4 For more detailed accounts of Pasolini's career, see Stefania Benini, *Pasolini: The Sacred Flesh* (Toronto: University of Toronto Press, 2015); Viola Brisolin, *Power and Subjectivity in the Late Works of Roland Barthes and Pier Paolo Pasolini* (Oxford: Peter Lang, 2011); *Pier Paolo Pasolini: Contemporary Perspectives*, eds. Patrick Rumble and Bart Testa (Toronto: University of Toronto Press, 1994); Enzo Siciliano, *Pasolini: A Biography*, trans. John Shepley (New York: Random House, 1982).
5 Ellis, *Angelic Conversations*, p. 32.
6 The quote in the subheading is from *Modern Nature*, p. 25.

7 Peake, *Derek Jarman*, p. 543.
8 Test Dept's EP *Shoulder to Shoulder* (1984) was recorded with the South Wales Striking Miners Choir. They performed together throughout the country at community events to raise money and awareness, which seems extraordinary looking back because Test Dept make avant-garde industrial noise.
9 Other notable artists, writers and musicians have returned to the events surrounding Pasolini's death. Kathy Acker's *My Death My Life by Pier Paolo Pasolini* (London: Pan, 1984; repr. in *Literal Madness*, New York: Grove, 1988), pp. 171–393 provides a fictional autobiography of the filmmaker in which he solves his own murder. Queer experimental avant-garde outfit Coil produced a long-form track titled 'Ostia (the Death of Pasolini)', which looks at the murder as a political act. Its refrain is: 'Killed to keep the world turning' (Coil, 'Ostia (the Death of Pasolini)', *Horse Rotorvator* [music track, cass] Perf. Stephen Thrower, Peter Christopherson and John Balance with Billy McGee, Some Bizzare Records, UK, 1986. 6mins 20secs). A more recent mainstream film depicting Pasolini's last days and murder, *Pasolini*, dir. Abel Ferrara (Capricci Films, 2014), stars Willem Dafoe.
10 See Adam Thirlwell, 'Reality Hunger: Pasolini's Seductive Utopian Vision', *Bookforum* (June/July/Aug 2014), www.bookforum.com/print/2102/pasolini-s-seductive-utopian-vision-13281 (accessed 12 June 2021).
11 See, for example, *Throwing the Body into the Fight: A Portrait of Raimund Hoghe*, ed. Mary Kate Connolly (Bristol: Intellect, 2013). Hoghe is quoted as saying: 'Pier Paolo Pasolini wrote of throwing the body into the fight. These words inspired me to go on stage' (p. 6). The incitement forms the title of one of Hoghe's solo performances.
12 Pasolini quoted in James Ivory, 'Pier Paolo Pasolini: A Life in Poetry', in *The Selected Poetry of Pier Paolo Pasolini: A Bilingual Edition*, by Pier Paolo Pasolini, ed. and trans. Stephen Sartarelli (Chicago: University of Chicago Press, 2014), pp. 1–58 (p. 8).
13 Gardner, 'Perverse Law', p. 34.
14 Another example of Jarman's use of the phrase is in relation to the work of the sculptor Eric Gill. On reading Fiona MacCarthy's 1989 biography of the sculptor, famous for making public Gill's incest and his sexual acts with his dog, Jarman commented in his diary that Gill 'attempted to fuse his art and life, throwing his body into the struggle' (*Modern Nature*, p. 25). Jarman does go on to call Gill 'eccentric, even silly', and mentions that the sculptor was 'at odds with the world around [him]' (*Modern Nature*, p. 25).
15 Dillon, *Derek Jarman and Lyric Film*, p. 14.
16 Ellis, *Angelic Conversations*, p. xix.

5

Kicking the Pricks: 'Forward into an uncertain future…'

Derek Jarman's next published book of life-writing, *Kicking the Pricks* (1987), is compiled from 'diary entries, interviews and notes for the script' (*Kicking the Pricks*, p. 9) of *The Last of England*.[1] His preface situates the text in its context and time. He links the book to the making of *The Last of England*, which, he tells us, 'started filming in August 1986' (p. 9). Its contents were mostly written in the weeks following the commencement of filming and it was intended to be a companion piece of a kind to the film. The book had been commissioned by Robin Baird-Smith (Constable), who had expressed interest in publishing 'a book of Jarman's thoughts and opinions, interlaced with autobiography'.[2] Jarman had taped some material with interviewer David Hirst earlier in 1986 for a proposed book on cinema and the theatre, and as his interest in that project had waned, the commission provided an opportunity for him to use the material they had produced. He combined this with further interviews with Michael O'Pray and others, along with excerpts from his diaries. The book also contains proposed voiceovers for *The Last of England*, some of which appear in the final film. He comments in his preface that *Kicking the Pricks* 'takes us on a journey back in time' (p. 9). The past it takes us back to is, of course, Jarman's past and we are invited, as readers, to accompany him there. But it also looks ahead: the inclusion of scenes from *The Last of England* looks 'forward into an uncertain future . . .' (p. 9).

Kicking the Pricks is Jarman's fourth published book and the second one that prioritises life-writing above other genres. *A finger in the fishes mouth*, the early chapbook of poetry, provides fleeting instances from a kind of travel diary, where the 'I' remains diffuse and hard to locate. *Derek Jarman's Caravaggio*, discussed in Chapter 4, places rich visual self-representations in productive contrast to those of the Renaissance painter. *Dancing Ledge*, which Jarman termed 'my Queerlife' (*Dancing Ledge*, preface), is the most clear precursor to *Kicking the Pricks*. Its subject matter – Jarman's childhood and relations with his family, his background, and his experiences in the film world – is further expanded as he returns to particular episodes, with a renewed honesty and engagement with the past. Similarly to his approach in *Dancing Ledge*, he offers a memoir of his career and relationships in the film world – not unlike Peter Hall's diaries about London's theatre world, *Peter Hall's Diaries: The Story of a Dramatic Battle* (1983). *Kicking the Pricks* constitutes Jarman rewriting his 'Queerlife', this time from a newly focused perspective. As Jarman wrote in an abandoned preface, 'The passing of four years creates a different view'.[3]

The 'different view' Jarman refers to has been created by three circumstances: first, the death of his father, second, the confirmation he was HIV-positive, and third, another term of Thatcher's government on the horizon. *Kicking the Pricks* is the first instance in Jarman's published work where he presents his experience as politically inflected, an approach that will remain marked in all his future life-writing. In previous works, Jarman viewed his life and art as entwined. With the intrusion of HIV/AIDS into so many of his friends' lives as well as into his own, his life and art remained interchangeable as before, but his life became sharply politicised. The result of the change is that Jarman's life-writing became even more visible as an ongoing project, recorded across personal journals and published books, that in each iteration intervenes in its contemporary political moment as an HIV/AIDS activist text.

Writing lives in collaboration

As with Jarman's films and his previous autobiographical text *Dancing Ledge*, *Kicking the Pricks* was produced in collaboration. This time, Keith Collins, whom he had recently met and become close to, helped him with the editing process. In Collins's new foreword to the reprinted edition (1996), he describes the part of the writing and editing process that took place in early 1987:

> Each day Derek would produce a handful of A4 pages illegibly handwritten in red Pentel: opinions; reminiscences; portraits of people and places; and audio-taped rambling interviews with friends and colleagues Derek had recorded that afternoon. Each night, as the production office wound down I would transcribe these tapes and writings; ending at midnight with a new sheaf of papers for Derek's corrections over chips and salt beef sandwiches in a nearby cafe. (*Kicking the Pricks*, preface)

Collins shows the importance of method for Jarman's autobiographical process. He uses a similar multimedia technique to that used in the construction of his films: he scribbled his own notes, portraits and memories, and also generated content in discussion with others. Collins's recollection also connects the work to Jarman's body: he draws attention to the 'illegibly handwritten' pages Jarman produced that were the result of self-reflection and the messy creative process. He also points out the everyday nature of the work: they would look through the day's work 'over chips and salt beef sandwiches' in a late-night café. Collins shares Jarman's working process, describing a period of busy, joint industry reaching late into the night. Collins's story of the production of this book of life-writing becomes a kind of memoir too, memorialising Jarman's frenetic way of working from the perspective of four years after his death. Jarman's approach is the opposite of the serious, solitary method one might assume is part of the creation of a work of autobiographical writing: Philippe Lejeune's definition of autobiographical writing, which assumes the unity of author, subject and narrator, is here disrupted. Lejeune distils his definition to the following: 'Retrospective prose narrative written by a real person concerning his own existence, where the focus is his individual life, in particular the story of his personality'.[4] In the case of *Kicking the Pricks*, although the main author is Jarman, he does not work alone, and the text might be thought to have multiple authors who help Jarman develop his self-representations. Of course, he remains the main actor in the collaboration, much like a film's director, but the approach is worth noting: the working method that Collins draws attention to in the preface highlights the constructed nature of the text, and, by extension, the partial, fragmentary and serial nature of autobiographical production that attempts to document a life in progress.

It is critical to his autobiographical process that he gained a sense of what he wanted to communicate through collaboration: conversation with other people and discussions regarding editing with Collins late each night. Partly, this technique may have been expedient – the particulars of our lives can be recovered through dialogue with others – but partly, the technique echoes the way that Jarman conceives of the self as not purely individual, or part of a large, interconnected social world, but also as one exemplary gay life-story. For Jarman, preparing a published book of life-writing is a similarly joint project to devising a film. By recording interviews, he is demonstrating that his life-writing should attempt to capture more than just the sum of one person's recollections. Different perspectives are crucial. He seeks out others who may be able to draw something different from him because of their particular connection to him. This approach perhaps recalls the method of the biographer rather than the autobiographer, who seeks out sources and conducts interviews with people close to the subject. The result combines a kind of oral history with the more individual, focused reflection from diary entries. This is an approach Jarman would further develop in later polemic *At Your Own Risk*, discussed in Chapter 8, which provides a history of homophobic Britain in relation to an individual instance of a queer life – Jarman's – affording one section to each decade in which he has been alive.

In a section of a transcribed interview in *Kicking the Pricks*, Jarman speaks of the collaborative, community-driven nature of *The Last of England*:

> I would never say I am making this film for an audience: that's very dishonest. It would be true to say I am making this film for myself with my collaborators, we are the community. I am the pivot who gathers the communal threads and creates the pattern, I pull some strands, leave others. The work is the end – whether it's appreciated or not by an audience is not important. The important thing is the creation of the work itself, not the finished product. This harnessing of everyone's creativity, so that when you call 'wrap' for the last time you can all feel the loss physically. Audiences are after the fact. (*Kicking the Pricks*, p. 197)

The passage is important both for Jarman's filmmaking and his life-writing. By claiming a lack of interest in 'the finished product', he lays a claim for the work's value being in its 'creation': the process or the project is the key. A perspective shared by Orson Welles, this appears to be a traditional romantic view of the artistic process. Exploring what it might mean in relation to life-writing has interesting consequences. If he views himself as 'the pivot who gathers the communal threads', he is trying to create a tapestry that is less concerned with the specific workings of an individual consciousness, focusing more on its social relevance. Ellis argues that, as a result, *Kicking the Pricks* cannot be viewed as autobiography: 'at most we could say that it uses autobiographical elements to push the reader toward a particular political awareness'.[5] The juxtaposition of the various kinds of collaborative material in the book is a way to encourage the ideological awareness of the readers. By claiming relative lack of interest in 'the finished product', producing swiftly made collage that at times gives the impression of a scrapbook, he indicates the necessity of getting the work out there with speed.

'Nothing to be afraid of? Are these words too brave?'

One of the early passages in *Kicking the Pricks* gives an account of the day of his HIV-positive diagnosis. Titled 'Nothing to be afraid of? Are these words too brave?' (*Kicking the Pricks*, p. 16), the way the scene unfolds is carefully composed. Although undated in this publication, we know from other sources that he received the news on 22 December 1986. In this account, Jarman represents himself as almost nonchalant as he received the diagnosis: 'The young doctor who told me this morning I was a carrier of the AIDS virus was visibly distressed. I smiled and told her not to worry, I had never liked Christmas' (*Kicking the Pricks*, p. 16). Daniel Humphrey argues that Jarman 'refused the impact of the bad news (by smiling at his test results)'.[6] However, that doesn't quite get to the heart of it: his quip uses black humour to diffuse the gravity of the news in that particular interpersonal dynamic. The patient–doctor relationship is almost inverted: he comforts the 'visibly distressed' doctor, rather than the other way round. After all, he comments, 'I thought it was inconceivable I could have avoided the virus, though I had avoided the test for as long as was decently possible' (*Kicking the Pricks*, p. 16).

Jarman writes, 'The sword of Damocles had taken a sideways swipe, but I was still sitting in the chair' (*Kicking the Pricks*, p. 17). Although Humphrey comments that Jarman 'felt he had already been killed [...] at the moment when his HIV status was confirmed by the doctor', this is not evidenced in Jarman's writing, where he signals his perseverance with grim, black humour. Humphrey considered that the meeting constituted 'a discursively produced death that Jarman had physically survived'.[7] Yet the event is not quite a death of a kind, but death's prediction or forewarning. Ellis comments that 'The diagnosis occasions a kind of grim rebirth through the knowledge of death, and the experience of social space has changed entirely'.[8] Ellis's reading seems to corroborate Jarman's words: 'As I joined the crowds at Oxford Street, I thought – could my perception of all this change, could I fall in love with it again as I did when I left home early in the 1960s?' (*Kicking the Pricks*, p. 17).

Jarman goes on to comment: 'I thought how fortunate to be forewarned so that one can wind one's life up in an orderly fashion. The finality of it seemed attractive' (*Kicking the Pricks*, p. 17). This statement reads as a camp response to an awful situation – yet the diagnosis provided Jarman with a purpose and a vigour that underlined all his work from then until his death, over seven years later. Along with Jarman's HIV diagnosis (and the increasing number of positive diagnoses among his friends, especially those in New York), came a new sense of history. *Kicking the Pricks* stages the beginning of Jarman's heightened awareness that, as Simon Watney has noted, HIV/AIDS brought a clear awareness that 'gay men are officially regarded, in our entirety, as a disposable constituency'.[9] Jarman had previously been politically engaged only patchily, but the diagnosis signalled the start of a firm commitment to activism, enacted in often unusual ways through the media he worked in – film, Super 8, paint, writing, gardening and occasional live art.

Kicking the Pricks was predominantly composed in the months leading up to the confirmation that Jarman was HIV-positive, though it was finished and edited early in 1987, following his diagnosis. Created at a turning point, it is not primarily about the virus, and the virus does not colour as much of its contents as one might expect. Later in the book, part of a conversation about the virus with an unnamed interviewer is printed, followed by a long poem titled 'Hope' that prefigures the later poetry dealing with AIDS (*Kicking the Pricks*, pp. 226–33). One of its lines raises the notion that Jarman is now living 'In Borrowed Time' (*Kicking the Pricks*, p. 232), which is a phrase Jarman would return to, and which was an early title for *Modern Nature*. Yet aside from these few pages, mention of the virus is infrequent.

Theorisations of AIDS writing and AIDS diaries by Ross Chambers (on the literal death of the author and the problematics of survivorhood), Timothy Murphy (on testimony) and Sarah Brophy (on unresolved grief) have helped my readings of Jarman's late diaries. Throughout chapters 7–12, I draw on scholarship that evaluates the significance of writing 'at the symptomatic state of AIDS', exploring its functions as testimony and elegy.[10] *Kicking the Pricks* is written in a resolutely heterogeneous style that disrupts the ability to read it as firmly part of the genre of 'AIDS writing'. The majority of 'AIDS writing' is by subjects who had begun to suffer the physical effects of illnesses associated with the virus, or by those close to HIV-positive subjects. Jonathan P. Watts connects Jarman's diagnosis to his renewed preoccupation with life-writing: 'Jarman's obsession began with this mid-life shock; the tremors worked retroactively into childhood, unearthing [...] structures, devices and archetypes, [and] layers of buried memories, earlier traumas'.[11] Jarman's diagnosis, along with the recent death of his father, prompts a shift in tone in his serial, dispersed autobiographical production. The shift is most clearly marked in relation to Jarman's re-evaluation of his family.

On the family

That Jarman returns to the same episodes over and over in his autobiographical production is well documented.[12] For the main, he puts incidents in his past to use in different ways, depending on context. He uses his life as material for his art, politically inflecting episodes to different ends depending on the purpose of the publication or artwork in question, some of which I discuss in Chapter 7 on *Modern Nature* and Chapter 9 on *At Your Own Risk*. However, if we look at a general trend between *Dancing Ledge* and *Kicking the Pricks*, the way he describes his parents, especially the impact of his father on the family, changes significantly. The passage that informs us of Jarman's HIV-positive diagnosis also provides readers with a piece of pivotal information. We hear that he had chosen to wear his much-loved 'dark black overcoat' for the appointment to get his results. He slips in the information that he also wore the overcoat at his father's funeral 'a few weeks ago' (*Kicking the Pricks*, p. 16), thereby communicating the death of his father, Lance Elworthy Jarman.

Now that his father was newly deceased, Jarman was freer to discuss his father's troubling behaviour and the effects it had on their family dynamic, and the death prompted a period of reflection and re-evaluation of his childhood. Indeed, he named the relationship with his father the book's 'central dynamo'.[13] We learn that Jarman's father had shadowed his childhood with rages, possibly the result of post-traumatic stress disorder following his time as a pilot during the Second World War, and that, in his old age, he had become a kleptomaniac.

The most notable difference between *Dancing Ledge* and *Kicking the Pricks* is that family details are not glossed over, and are depicted with far greater psychological insight. For example, after Jarman has finished reporting stories from his childhood years in *Dancing Ledge*, he rarely mentions his parents. The seriousness of an unexpected dated account comes as a surprise in the patchwork text:

> Friday 4 August 1978 – Halton: Late in the afternoon I sat with my sister, Gaye, at my mother's deathbed. She was totally lucid the whole time. Worried about her appearance, she asked for a mirror, had the photos of my nephews and nieces moved so she could see them, and asked me about Italy, where for the last three months I had been writing the first script for *Caravaggio*. (*Dancing Ledge*, p. 183)

Even this account is told with a surprisingly light touch: her touching vanity, her desire to see photographs of her grandchildren and her interest in Italy, where she had lived with her children thirty years previously. Jarman makes the link to that foundational period in his early childhood by using a simile to describe her last moments: 'My sister and I took one fragile hand each as her life fluttered away like the proverbial swallows' (*Dancing Ledge*, p. 184). The mention of swallows recalls the refrain in Jarman's printed life-writing and journals – 'itys itys itys' – the sound of the swallows that had so captivated him during his early childhood at the Villa Zuassa (*Dancing Ledge*, p. 16).[14] The whereabouts of his father at this point is not mentioned. He follows the scene of his mother's death with a comment that is left unexplored: '*I often wonder about the effect of Ma's eighteen years of illness, borne with such serenity, on myself and my sister*' (*Dancing Ledge*, p. 184), before giving us a portrait of her funeral, her forbearance, her practicality and light. But he does not detail what the effects of these long years of illness were. It is enough to leave that unstated. Nowhere else in the book is there much glimmer of the continued illness and decline of his mother: she is mostly absent past the point of childhood.

Distinct from his approach in *Dancing Ledge*, Jarman produces a more direct portrait in *Kicking the Pricks* of a self-effacing yet fun-loving woman of her generation determined never to let a 'shadow' (*Kicking the Pricks*, p. 126) of either her difficult marriage to an irascible man or the pains of a long illness cross their lives. Early in *Dancing Ledge*, Jarman describes his parents' wedding: 'They were a most glamorous couple. My father in his RAF uniform, my mother, her veil caught by the wind, holding some lily of the valley' (p. 38). Yet in *Kicking the Pricks*, Jarman comments on their later years: 'My aunt said she would have divorced him, but she had no independent income, she was trapped, but never showed it' (p. 126). An anecdote about the effects of long-term, high-volume drug use to manage her condition surfaces in both accounts almost verbatim, yet what is portrayed humorously in *Dancing Ledge* resurfaces with more considered context in *Kicking the Pricks*. In *Dancing Ledge*, Jarman recalls that 'One night she entertained some rather 'proper' friends – the editor of one of the dreaded popular dailies and his wife. She inadvertently poured salad cream over the strawberries', which she served with fanfare as they were 'the first strawberries of the summer' (p. 185). In *Kicking the Pricks*, the anecdote returns, yet he points out that 'The cortisone took its toll. She worried a little about her looks, and grew increasingly forgetful' (p. 126). He ends the anecdote about the strawberries with 'The drugs played tricks' (*Kicking the Pricks*, p. 126).

Jarman chooses two photographs of his mother to complement the text. In the first, she wears an elegant light cotton dress and looks away from the camera at a flowering shrub (*Kicking the Pricks*, p. 123). It is 1939: she is young, it appears to be summer – if the photograph was taken earlier than September, the United Kingdom had yet to declare war on Germany. She was a year from being married and three from having her first child. In the second, she is seated in another garden, wearing a glamorous Pakistani outfit and traditional bridal jewellery including a tikka at her hairline and a heavy neckpiece (*Kicking the Pricks*, p. 127). It was taken in Pakistan in 1953, when Jarman would have been 11, and may well not have been present at the time.

Jarman provides images that seem to document the autobiographical text they are placed with. Susan Sontag refers to photographs as 'something directly stencilled off the real, like a footprint or a death mask'.[15] For Roland Barthes in *Camera Lucida* 'The photograph is literally an emanation of the referent' (as we see in his own inclusion of photographs in *Roland Barthes par Roland Barthes*), and for Paul John Eakin, in *Touching the World: Reference in Autobiography* 'autobiography is nothing if not a referential art'.[16] This may be so, but the qualities of the images chosen do not quite seem to directly reflect the text. He chooses curious images: one that predates his birth, and one that likely depicted a scene he would not have seen first-hand as he was at boarding school in England. In *Light Writing & Life Writing: Photography in Autobiography*, Timothy Dow Adams comments that 'Photography may stimulate, inspire, or seem to document autobiography'. However, he continues: 'text and image complement, rather than supplement, each other; since reference is not secure in either, neither can compensate for lack of stability in the other'.[17] Betts exists in these images in a permanent state of youth, beauty, glamour, exoticism and, as a result, she seems out of reach. He chooses to remember his mother as an idealised feminine image, rather than as she would have appeared in her later years. I further examine Jarman's engagement with youthful images of his mother in Chapter 6, in the section titled 'Childhood and the home movies in *The Last of England*', linking them to Barthes' ruminations on old photographs of his recently deceased mother in *Camera Lucida*.

'The Terror in a Photo'

Jarman's father, who is barely mentioned in *Dancing Ledge*, is presented in palpably different terms in *Kicking the Pricks*.[18] Apart from a disastrous Christmas dinner involving an accident with the turkey where Jarman recalls that 'My father shouted at me' (*Dancing Ledge*, p. 43), he limits his discussion of his father's character to brief mentions of factual material such as his interest in art and his military career. In *Kicking the Pricks*, the portrait is very different. A section titled 'An inheritance' (*Kicking the Pricks*, pp. 115–23) revisits the story of his parents' meeting and wedding. This time, he mentions that his beloved grandmother Mimosa had not warmed to 'the handsome young squadron leader': 'the dislike was instinctual' (*Kicking the Pricks*, p. 118). Over the following years, Grandmother Mimosa 'protected' the young Derek 'with increasingly short temper from [his] father's outbursts, which grew more severe as the war continued' (*Kicking the Pricks*, p. 121). The older Jarman intervenes at this point to explain that 'Many years later the RAF psychiatrist told my sister that all the Pathfinders have severe psychiatric disorders', as 'the family became an extension of the war'. He uses a comic story to illustrate his father's displaced approach to civilian life: his father's method of driving to London. '40 miles an hour he went up the motorway and down Oxford Street', Jarman recalls, 'Perfect for the engine, he said' (*Kicking the Pricks*, p. 121). Of course, this is quite funny – if dangerous ('one moment we were crawling like a snail along a motorway, the next careering down some High Street'). Yet it is the element of steely, inflexible control that is disconcerting: Jarman writes that 'He demanded complete silence, and treated other travellers as the enemy' (*Kicking the Pricks*, p. 121). Jarman links his father's behaviour on the roads to his approach as a pilot, writing that 'He had the wartime reputation of never avoiding the flack: he just flew straight ahead steadily. I believe he terrified his crew' (*Kicking the Pricks*, p. 122). The fighter pilot's controlled response to the danger around the cockpit seems both to deny his humanity, at the same time as also appearing to be a traumatic symptom that instances his humanity.

Jarman includes a photograph of his father standing in the snow in a regulation great coat, dwarfed by the dark metal of his bomber plane, dated 1940 (*Kicking the Pricks*, p. 124). The passage opposite is titled 'The Terror in a Photo' (*Kicking the Pricks*, p. 125), and begins with a description of his father's strength and endurance into his late sixties. Jarman describes a hectoring man who bullied and blamed his children (in an earlier interview section, Jarman states that 'It is hard to forgive the belts and whips of my inheritance' (*Kicking the Pricks*, p. 107)). The passage does not mention a photograph, but is positioned next to the austere image of his father during the war, thereby creating meaning through juxtaposition. Like the image of his mother on the previous page, the photograph of his father shows the man before Jarman's birth. To return to Adams's statement that 'Photography may stimulate, inspire, or seem to document autobiography', the image's placement opposite the striking title 'The Terror in a Photo' implies that the image had perhaps stimulated or inspired the stark passage printed in the text.[19] If this is the case, the printed book can be interpreted as staging an encounter between Jarman and his memories of his past. Elizabeth Bruss argues that autobiography is 'an act rather than a form' and this example seems a case in point.[20]

Jarman also comments on his father's miserliness: 'He was determined to impose austerity', allowing 'no more than four inches in the bath, two sheets of toilet paper' (*Kicking the Pricks*, p. 122). The portrait of the father drilling restraint into his young children foretells the characteristics that would entrap him when he grew old. Jarman, surprisingly generously, comments, 'I regret him, poor soul, in his old age eating baked beans and boiled eggs; alone in his fortress home, leaving a miser's fortune that would have made my mother's life more bearable, especially the last 18 years during which she was dying of cancer' (*Kicking the Pricks*, p. 122). As in the case of Jarman's mother, he includes no later images of his ageing father.

'Forward into an uncertain future…': Derek Jarman's journals

In *Kicking the Pricks* and *The Last of England*, we see traces of the working method that underpinned Jarman's interdisciplinary projects: his journals.[21] His beautiful journals comprise an extended series of his most distinctive autobiographical trace.[22] Large, square, black albums from Venice are modified with gold leaf on their covers. Inside, their contents are various, but can be broadly categorised into an interconnected collection of memories and ideas. The journals are a physical manifestation of the utter inseparability of Jarman's life and art. Notes for scripts and plans for scenes in films jostle for space with mementos, photographs, personal phone numbers, pressed flowers, newspaper clippings and found objects. In a lyrical introduction to the recent selection of pages from the journals printed in *Derek Jarman's Sketchbooks*, Tilda Swinton describes their variety and value:

> Each of Derek's sketchbooks is as close a thing to manifest evidence of the inner workings of his head as I can imagine. They were the very battery of his creative process. [...] Way beyond a scrapbook, it was a movable brainbox: littered with pasted and drawn images, snatches of dialogue, scored revisions, the typed pages of his latest screen play draft, filigreed with the henna-like pattern of his brown or black hieroglyphic handwriting. Part talisman, part private confessional, wholly unmediated raw dreamscape, reliable invisible friend and booster jet.[23]

From 1987 onwards, long diary entries pepper the texts. The deeply personal nature of their contents is complemented by his drawings and instantly recognisable handwritten script. Swinton's description of the books as 'part talisman, part private confessional, wholly unmediated raw dreamscape' is particularly evocative, as is Stephen Farthing and Ed Webb-Ingall's description of them as 'sketchbooks' or even better, 'grimoires'.[24] When discussing the published works, the shadow of their rich origins in these journals is always behind them. What we receive in the printed autobiographical texts is a partial copy derived from the thinking and self-reflection contained in these personal journals. Farthing and Webb-Ingall refer to them as 'intentionally glamorous, but nonetheless deliberative, reflective work spaces, in which the recording and ordering of the past is as significant as the anticipation of the future'.[25] This helps us consider Jarman's published autobiographical texts as part of a wider life-writing project, using material from his life as art, but not hoping to arrive at a set destination or finished product.

In *Kicking the Pricks* and *The Last of England*, we see snippets of the working method that was fundamental to Jarman's interdisciplinary project. At the beginning of *The Last of England*, Jarman is filmed working late at night at his desk in Phoenix House (see figures 11 and 12). He hunches over his journals, one of which is opened to a visually arresting spread. He consults pages in one journal as he writes in a second. Finally, he plucks a small sprig from a vase on the desk and places it within the book, pressing the cutting flat as he closes the book. In Chapter 6, I discuss Jarman's use of his own body in the film as a framing device, where he takes on the role of the medieval dream poet or 'Prospero-like figure'.[26] In this chapter, I

98   *Luminous presence*

Figures 11 and 12 Jarman working at his journals in *The Last of England*.

linger on the contents of the journal that appears in *The Last of England*. In the page spreads that are shown in the film, we see an exercise in composition as well as in writing: the visual and written elements work in harmony. First, Jarman would prepare sections on the page by painting blocks of black oil paint. Of the process, Collins comments:

> The time and planning to do this beggars belief, but the results are worthwhile. The sketchbooks would be standing upright on the furniture with pages fanned as the lines of oil paint dried in the heat of a three-bar electric fire, filling the flat with the smell of warm paper and turpentine.[27]

Once the pages had dried, they were ready for Jarman's handwriting, often in shimmering gold ink. Farthing and Webb-Ingall write that Jarman's choice of method 'brought an element of grand opera to his private working space as he prepared his intimate, private world for a public audience'.[28] There is a disparity between the slow creation of these beautifully constructed workbooks and the hectic working process Collins describes taking part in as they later compiled content for inclusion in *Kicking the Pricks* then edited and revised its contents. This way of working results in a series of individual, treasured books that are distinct from the mass-produced published books that derive in part from the journals' contents.

On the spread shown in *The Last of England*, the verso contains enigmatic half-legible statements that form a brief prose-poem (see Plate 3). At the top and bottom of the page, Jarman places what seems to be a title of a kind: 'In other rooms', 'in other landscapes', recalling the title of Truman Capote's 1948 novel *Other Voices, Other Rooms*, which also deals with themes of alienation. The first lines of the prose-poem are 'I'll call you Johnny', referring to the protagonist in the first half of *The Last of England*, played by Spring, whom we see wander disconsolate and angry around a barren landscape. The next words, 'You are trapped in your world (Rotherhithe)', perhaps recalls the setting for some of the film: the barren area to the east of Central London along the Thames. The London scenes of the film were set in and around the Royal Victoria Docks and Spillers' hulking, decaying Millennium Mills in Newham (see Figure 13). Further lines are hidden in part by the vivid splash of yellow from a preserved sprig of Mimosa. A final line reads 'don't think I believe in my fictions'.

On the recto, a longer section of prose describes a broken suburban world. It is similar in tone to the voiceovers in *The Last of England*, and may have been intended as such. A version of this writing is printed in *Kicking the Pricks* in a section titled 'The Winds of Change', flanked on either side by an interview with Jarman on the subject of his father. Again, the writing for the film is juxtaposed with personal recollections about family – though more overtly than the insertion of the mimosa into the journal. The page spread in the journal recalls the feel of illuminated medieval manuscripts but its reproduction in *Kicking the Pricks* is stripped of its initial rich aesthetic setting. The result is that one gets a sense that the works should be appreciated in conjunction with one another, the film alongside the book, and both alongside the journal. The journal is the most personal – irreproducible and handmade – whereas the film and book are the public-facing parts of the project geared to provide social commentary.

The character Johnny links the verso to the world of the film, yet the sprig of Mimosa is a personal refrain that is more readily autobiographical. Autobiographical meaning is here suggested in a subtle way through the use of plants. Jarman's grandmother's nickname was Mimosa, after her

Figure 13 Jarman and others in front of Spillers' Millenium Mills during the filming of *The Last of England*.

favourite blossom. Collins comments that it was 'Derek's [favourite] too: we would often have bunches of it filling the flat with its scent of honey and hay. Derek would use sprigs of it as bookmarks'.[29] By placing the blossom in the book as he closes it, Jarman marks his place with an object that acts as a 'talisman' recalling his own past.[30] In the chapters on *Modern Nature*, *Smiling in Slow Motion* and *Derek Jarman's Garden*, I examine how Jarman uses plants' symbolic resonances, histories and uses in herbal medicine to create and extend autobiographical meaning in each of these books. He was often drawn to plants that not only held personal meaning for him, from his childhood, but also those that aligned his store of personal meanings with a history of plant lore. The mimosas of his childhood (*Acacia dealbata*) are not explored in *Kicking the Pricks* or the journal depicted in *The Last of England*: the physical plant stands alone as a marker of his past.[31] Swinton summarises the role of the journals in Jarman's creative process: 'When I think of describing his sketchbooks, it's hard not to reach for a horticultural analogy: the seedbed, the source, the germinator of the garden. They were generators for his work, the guardians of his inner eye, handmade and heart-started'.[32]

At the beginning of this chapter, I mentioned the abandoned foreword to *Kicking the Pricks* in which Jarman expressed why he had needed to write another autobiographical text so soon after *Dancing Ledge*: 'The passing of four years creates a different view', Jarman writes.[33] The loss of his father inflects the writing with a new candour about the circumstances of his childhood. The political landscape in Britain shadows the text: it was written in tandem with the creation of *The Last of England*, a desolate vision of a nation in crisis. But, most pressingly, the confirmation of Jarman's HIV-positive status leads to a change in emphasis in his life-writing. Lee Edelman argues that AIDS prompts 'a crisis in [...] the social shaping or articulation of subjectivities'.[34] In Jarman, the 'crisis' leads to a political move in which the 'articulation of [his] subjectivit[y]' becomes a critical means by which to advance greater social understanding both within the communities affected by HIV/AIDS and wider society.

In his preface to the second edition, Collins admits that 'I had always overlooked this volume, preferring the lyricism in *Modern Nature*' (n.p.). But on re-reading *Kicking the Pricks* in 1996 before it went to press under its originally intended title, he writes that he 'found in it poetry, terseness' and 'clarity' (preface, n.p.). It is important for the books that would follow: following his diagnosis 'He was keeping his diary on a more regular basis than ever before'.[35] The energies collected in *Kicking the Pricks* are followed by a succession of journals, diary entries and published books that continued to gather frequency and intensity until New Year's Day 1994, when Jarman made his final journal entry.

Notes

1 To make the book more clearly marketable as the companion piece to the film, *Kicking the Pricks* was initially retitled and published as *The Last of England*

in 1987, 'with some reluctance' (*Kicking the Pricks*, p. 9) on Jarman's part. It was republished under its originally intended title with a new foreword by Collins in 1996, and it is to this volume that I refer in this book. I use this title throughout, but with the original publication date, in order to clearly differentiate between the book *Kicking the Pricks/The Last of England* and the film *The Last of England*. The quote in the chapter title is from *Kicking the Pricks*, p. 9.
2 See Peake, *Derek Jarman*, p. 397 for an account.
3 Quoted in Peake, *Derek Jarman*, p. 398.
4 Philippe Lejeune, *On Autobiography*, ed. Paul John Eakin, trans. Katherine Leary (Minneapolis: University of Minnesota Press, 1989), p. 4.
5 Ellis, *Angelic Conversations*, p. 136.
6 Daniel Humphrey, 'Authorship, History and the Dialectic of Trauma: Derek Jarman's *The Last of England*', *Screen*, 44.2 (Summer 2003), 208–15 (p. 209).
7 Ibid.
8 Ellis, *Angelic Conversations*, p. 147.
9 Simon Watney, *Policing Desire: Pornography, AIDS and the Media* (London: Comedia, 1987), p. 137.
10 Chambers, *Facing It*, p. vii.
11 Jonathan P. Watts, 'Derek Jarman: Black Paintings at Wilkinson', Galleries Now, n.d., www.galleriesnow.net/shows/derek-jarman-black-paintings (accessed 12 October 2017).
12 See, for example, Charlesworth, *Derek Jarman*, p. 8.
13 Jarman papers, quoted by Peake, *Derek Jarman*, p. 398.
14 'Dancing Ledge' journal (1982), Box 17, *Derek Jarman's Papers*, BFI Archive (London); 'Borrowed Time' (n.p., Jarman Papers); the swallows that attempted to nest in the corner of his bedroom are mentioned in *Modern Nature*, p. 10.
15 Susan Sontag, *On Photography* (London: Penguin, 2008), p. 154.
16 Roland Barthes, *Camera Lucida: Reflections on Photography*, trans. Richard Howard (London: Vintage, 2000), p. 80; Paul John Eakin, *Touching the World: Reference in Autobiography* (Princeton, NJ: Princeton University Press, 1992), p. 3.
17 Timothy Dow Adams, *Light Writing & Life Writing: Photography in Autobiography* (Chapel Hill: University of North Carolina Press, 2000), p. xxi. For more analyses of the ways in which photography plays a significant role in written autobiographical narratives, incorporated as another mode of telling within the text, see Linda Haverty Rugg, *Picturing Ourselves: Photography and Autobiography* (Chicago: University of Chicago Press, 1997), and Marianne Hirsch, *Family Frames: Photography, Narrative and Postmemory* (Cambridge, MA: Harvard University Press, 1997).
18 The quote in the subheading is from *Kicking the Pricks*, p. 125.
19 Adams, *Light Writing*, p. xxi; *Kicking the Pricks*, p. 125; Adams, *Light Writing*, p. xxi.
20 Elizabeth W. Bruss, *Autobiographical Acts: The Changing Situation of a Literary Genre* (Baltimore, MD: Johns Hopkins University Press, 1976), p. 119.
21 The quote in the subheading is from *Kicking the Pricks*, p. 9.

22 The journals have recently attracted interest and sparked a series of exhibitions. Some of them were shown at PROTEST!, IMMA (2019–20). Selections were shown in three locations during *Jarman2014*: at the exhibition 'Pandemonium!' at King's Cultural Centre (curated by Mark Turner); selections were placed in a special display during the BFI festival of Jarman's films; and Chelsea Space showed a selection of the 'Blue' journals (curated by Donald Smith).
23 Tilda Swinton, 'Foreword', in *Derek Jarman's Sketchbooks*, eds. Stephen Farthing and Ed Webb-Ingall (London: Thames & Hudson, 2013), pp. 18–19 (p. 18).
24 Stephen Farthing and Ed Webb-Ingall, 'An Introduction to the Sketchbooks', in *Derek Jarman's Sketchbooks*, eds. Stephen Farthing and Ed Webb-Ingall (London: Thames and Hudson, 2013), pp. 24–7 (p. 24).
25 Ibid., p. 25.
26 Duncan Petric, 'Autobiography and British Art Cinema: The Films of Bill Douglas, Terence Davies and Derek Jarman', in *Biographie als religiöser und kultureller Text (Biography as a Religious and Cultural Text)*, ed. Andreas Schule (Munster: Lit Verlag, 2002), pp. 55–66 (p. 64).
27 Keith Collins, in *Derek Jarman's Sketchbooks*, eds. Stephen Farthing and Ed Webb-Ingall (London: Thames and Hudson, 2013), p. 129.
28 Farthing and Webb-Ingall, 'An Introduction to the Sketchbooks', p. 26.
29 Collins, in *Derek Jarman's Sketchbooks*, p. 116.
30 Swinton, Foreword', p. 18.
31 *Acacia dealbata*, the variety of mimosa Jarman preserves in his journals, is cultivated specifically as an ornamental plant, and is not known to have particular medicinal or cultural uses.
32 Swinton, 'Foreword', p. 19.
33 Quoted in Peake, *Derek Jarman*, p. 398.
34 Lee Edelman, *Homographesis: Essays in Gay Literary and Cultural Theory* (New York: Routledge, 1994), p. 96.
35 Peake, *Derek Jarman*, p. 397.

6

Self-projection in film: *The Last of England* and *The Garden*

The present dreams the past future

(Derek Jarman)[1]

L'homme qui revêt l'uniforme
de matelot n'obéit pas à la seule prudence

(Jean Genet, *Querelle de Brest*)[2]

By repeatedly invoking particular images and symbols, Jarman creates a transhistorical, allegorical form of self-representation that relies less on narrative than on suggestion. The previous chapters have explored his first forays into life-writing: the unlocalisable 'I' in his early collection of poems *A finger in the fishes mouth*, his most traditionally autobiographical text, *Dancing Ledge*, and the links he draws between his own life, a history of homophobia and the life of the painter in *Derek Jarman's Caravaggio*, as well as the cut-up technique he uses in *Kicking the Pricks*, the book of life-writing that was released alongside *The Last of England*. This chapter attends to another strand of his self-representational project: the ways in which he uses his own body on screen in the experimental films *The Last of England* (1987) and *The Garden* (1990). Both of these films construct meaning in unorthodox ways that avoid traditional narrative: through the use of montage, repeated images and symbols, and cultural reference. Autobiographical meaning is created through suggestion rather than from overt narrative.

In these two films, Jarman puts his compulsive magpie learning to use alongside material from his own life in his work to counter a homophobic post-war Britain. *The Last of England* comprises a visceral, deeply emotional response to the loss of culture and community after two terms of Thatcherism, set among the ruins of industrial Britain. *The Garden* loosely follows Christ's passion, played out by two gay lovers on the shingle at Dungeness, forming a commentary on a bitterly homophobic society and the devastation wrought by the HIV/AIDS crisis.

His experimental works are often non-narrative and at the same time determinedly political, attempting to use the hermetic technique of changing perception through the correct combination of significant images, often in a highly personal capacity. This technique of commingling images becomes important for Jarman, his audiences and his readership, a way of reactivating or appropriating discourses from diverse sources. Expressive artefacts, self-representations and symbols take up difficult, troubling and complex meanings, pointing to politically crucial counter-memories that he hopes have the potential to develop affective investment from his audiences and to create connections with others.

This chapter focuses on particular moments from the two films in which Jarman uses his body on screen. These self-representations comprise part of his wider life-writing project. Premised on the expanded concept of the autobiographical signature or trace, the term 'life-writing' encompasses every instance of cultural production that involves the representation of a body, relation of life stories or inscriptions that form a record of a life. For example, the representation of the body itself forms part of this category: the marks of ageing, trauma and illnesses upon it, and the symbolic functions it might enact at different times. Life-writing can also include the objects that, in their curation, communicate a life: personal effects, shopping lists, photographs or a library. This generic inclusiveness allows for a rich collection of source material, but it is also a political decision to prioritise a reading that delineates the nuanced, embodied politics Jarman enacts through his multiple roles.

The chapter begins by looking briefly at how Jarman intervenes in the genre of 'filmic autobiography' in *The Last of England*, arguing that he disrupts traditional and new conventions alike by producing a film that seems to be deeply personal, but contains few straightforwardly autobiographical details, to produce something that Rayns terms 'The "I-Movie"'.[3] It then investigates Jarman's use of his family's home movies in *The Last of England*: rather than using them to create a nostalgic sense of a safe, domestic past situated in his childhood, as some critics have suggested, he uses them to highlight the ambivalence of the post-war family structure. He points to what can be poisonous underneath a beautiful domestic veneer, using his family as an example.

The chapter then compares some motifs that recur in *The Last of England* and *The Garden*. Both films commence with sequences showing Jarman sitting at his desk, either working (as in *The Last of England*) or sleeping sprawled across his workbooks (as in *The Garden*), late into the night. His physical presence frames both films, setting them up as a contemporary re-imagining of medieval dream allegory, originating in the mind of the films' director. In *The Last of England*, I argue that, while this framing device makes the film appear autobiographical, it is a self-representational act in the character of the dream poet, the purpose of which is to enable his audience to collaborate in the sharp socio-political critique portrayed by the visions in the film. This role changes in *The Garden*, however, where the dream poet is shown asleep. As water drips down from the ceiling onto the sleeping Jarman, we are invited by a voiceover to read the film as 'a journey without direction' (*The Garden*, 01:45), a journey 'in search of [...] self' (01:54). The scene forms a contemporary representation of the Anglo-Saxon text *The Dream of the Rood*, in which I argue that Jarman situates himself as both the poet relating the vision of the cross and also as the cross itself. He does this in order to create a complex portrait firstly aligning himself with a history of suffering as a gay man, but also as a commentator on the suffering caused by the interrelated issues of HIV/AIDS, homophobia, and harmful government policy.

The chapter also briefly explores the symbolic function of the director as auteur, considering how he engages with this tradition in film by appearing on screen, camera in hand, in both films. The chapter ends with a link to the biographical context behind the making of *The Garden*, that extends the meaning of the dream poet to a direct commentary on Jarman's AIDS-related illnesses and resultant hospital stays during the post-production of the film.

Filmic autobiography and *The Last of England*

The Last of England is the first of Jarman's feature-length films to blend art with material from his own life. Jarman's physical presence frames the varied, dystopian sequences that make up the film. The first shot of the film, in black and white, reveals his worktable, which we look down on from above (see Figure 14). We find ourselves watching him work at the desk in the window of what some viewers might recognise as his Phoenix House studio flat on Charing Cross Road. He forms 'a Prospero-like figure', alone at night, idiosyncratically wearing a white sailor's hat as he writes and paints in his large journals (see Figure 15).[4] Before the film launches into what Annette Kuhn terms its 'dizzying phantasmagoria of memory fragments', Jarman provides a visual reminder that it is he, the director, who not only participates in the action of the film, but sparks off its visions and determines its events.[5]

The Last of England is built from brief snippets of film showing a variety of dystopian images that are juxtaposed with one another to build a sense of claustrophobia and desolation. Recalling Dziga Vertov's *Man with a*

The Last of England *and* The Garden

Figure 14 Jarman writes in his sketchbooks in *The Last of England*.

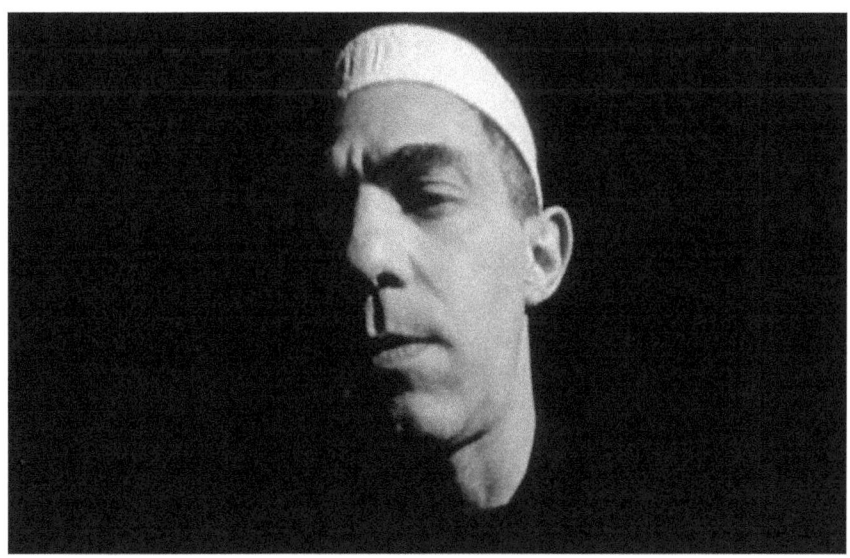

Figure 15 Jarman wearing a sailor's hat in *The Last of England*.

Movie Camera (1929), the fast-paced cuts between shots create a montage of images with which it is hard to keep pace.⁶ Some fragments are just a fraction of a second long, leaving visual traces in the mind, but not allowing time to be digested or interpreted. As similar images recur over longer sequences, one starts to build a sense of place and meaning. The film is a cry of anger and despair about 1980s Britain after two terms of Thatcherism: for Jarman, Thatcher stands for 'the fragmentation of society into rich and poor, haves and have-nots'.⁷ An experimental, non-narrative film, *The Last of England* comprises a visceral, deeply emotional response to the loss of culture and community. It is countercultural and wilfully obscure, with a powerful soundtrack.

The film includes a number of memorable performances. Dillon comments that of all Jarman's films, *The Last of England* is 'most readily seen as made out of performance art'.⁸ We watch a bare-chested punk dancing ballet to an industrial soundtrack in a setting of urban decay. Refugees stand on the docks, reminiscent of Ford Madox Brown's painting *The Last of England* depicting emigrants leaving England for a new life in Australia (1855). A man shoots up before violently destroying Michele Angelo Merigi da Caravaggio's painting *Amor Vincit Omnia* (1601) by the side of the docks. A destitute man, naked but for a ragged blanket, huddles near a fire in a dustbin and chews on a raw cauliflower. Two people, one wearing a military uniform, have sex on a mattress covered in a Union Jack. One is later executed by firing squad on the roof of the abandoned Millenium Mills in Silvertown. In its most famous scene, set outside on the docks, Tilda Swinton cuts off her wedding dress to the haunting vocals of avant-garde singer Diamanda Galás.⁹

As a contrast to these dystopian scenes, Jarman inserts another autobiographical element. He appears on screen as a young child in a range of home movies filmed by his father, Lance Elworthy Jarman, in the 1940s. Duncan Petrie has argued that 'The autobiographical elements play an important part in *The Last of England*'.¹⁰ Before proceeding with an analysis of Jarman's appearances on screen, it is important to distinguish between these 'autobiographical elements' and what might be understood more widely as 'filmic autobiography' in order to understand Jarman's interventions in context.¹¹ In her essay, 'Eye for I: Making and Unmaking Autobiography in Film' (1980), Elizabeth Bruss has written about some of the complexities of creating filmic autobiography. She contends that 'the unity of subjectivity and subject matter' – Philippe Lejeune's autobiographical pact on which classical autobiography depends – is impossible to deliver in film: 'the autobiographical self decomposes, schisms, into almost mutually exclusive elements of the person filmed (entirely visible; recorded and projected) and the person filming (entirely hidden; behind the camera eye)'.¹² Jarman seems to undermine her contention that the separate roles of camera-person and person-being-filmed must be distinct in *The Last of England*. He plays with his role in the action: at times, he is present on screen, at times, he is the camera man and at times, he is filmed holding a camera. He makes us unsure of what exactly his roles might be, refusing to be contained by any particular activity in the collaborative enterprise of making a film. However, he also avoids any gesture towards providing a fully fleshed out autobiographical self: this film uses self-representational acts to do something other than attempt autobiography proper, something Jarman has rarely been interested in (aside from in *Dancing Ledge*). His presence frames the action, so this chapter considers what 'signifying practices' are at work here.[13]

There is little sign of directly autobiographical detail in the film. As several critics have noted, the film was released at the juncture of two profound life events for Jarman: his father died in November 1986, and he finally tested for HIV and discovered he was HIV-positive the following month. Pressures from outside were also profound: rising negative attitudes towards homosexuality were at their peak around this time, and Lord Halsbury had first tabled the Local Government Act 1986 (Amendment) Bill earlier in the year, that, though it was defeated, paved the way for the amendment to the Local Government Act that would be passed in 1988 and was known as 'Section 28' (discussed in the introduction to this book). Jarman responds to the shaky terrain by describing the war he is engaged in as a director: 'The battle for a cinema which grows up and uses the direct experiences of the author like any other art form, and which stands up to the commissioning bodies and declares that experience is the basis for serious work' (*Kicking the Pricks*, p. 167). In doing so, he invites us to read elements of the film as 'direct experience', or perhaps, an imaginative response to these experiences conceived of obliquely.

Tony Rayns understands the film as an example in the tradition of the 'I-Movie', a genre that can be traced to Jean Cocteau's *The Blood of a Poet* (1932). He comments that 'The "I-Movie" has featured film-makers who place themselves at the centre of more-or-less fictional worlds in which the settings, characters and events are both an expression of the author's psyche and a distorted reflection of aspects of the real world'.[14] Another example is Kenneth Anger's *Fireworks* (1947), in which Anger appears, but not necessarily exactly as himself. Bruss analyses *Fireworks* in some detail: 'The mixture of real bodies and artificial members, actual settings and imaginary events, literal desires with figurative fulfillments is dizzying and skews our usual assumptions about the self-evidence of visual information and the coherence of the visible person'.[15] This summary gives a flavour of the tradition of queer cinema and self-representation that Jarman reworks by including his own body in *The Last of England*.

Childhood and the home movies in *The Last of England*

Aside from the physical presence of the director on screen, *The Last of England* is notable for its inclusion of a range of home movies belonging to Jarman's parents and grandparents on his mother's side. He includes sixteen segments, predominantly showing family scenes, many of which contain him as a young child. Eleven out of sixteen show the Jarman family in gorgeous colour: the first shows his mother Betts standing outside her house, attaching a rose to her clothing (*The Last of England*, 07:15), others show Jarman and his sister Gaye playing in a garden, racing across a meadow or picnicking with their mother (see Figure 16). They range in length from just a second (a single shot of Gaye as a child running across the grass towards the camera; *The Last of England*, 08:46), to more than half a minute (the six-year-old Jarman, Gaye and his mother playing with a ball in the garden of the RAF station in 1948 across five shots, starting at 25:09). He mentions the longest scene, which shows him playing with his mother and sister with the ominous sight of barbed wire in the background in his diaries: the scene depicts 'my sister Gaye, and myself playing with a ball on the lawns of RAF Abingdon where my father was Station Commander – I'm six years old, it's the summer of 1948' (*Kicking the Pricks*, p. 178). Later on in the film, a long section intercuts Jarman's father's camerawork

Figure 16 Jarman's mother and sister in the garden in front of their housing area at an RAF station. Home movie inserted into *The Last of England*.

with Jarman's own. Lance's sections include scenes from Pakistan, military scenes, cavalry and military receptions.

Justin Wyatt views the inclusion of personal material, in particular the home movies, as an important autobiographical intervention that speaks to his wider political project:

> By referencing his family's and his own past through home movies and published journals and then placing these materials against the elaborate and theatrical worlds within his films, Jarman is able to construct both a personal history and a history of gay life. Using home movies matched to fictional worlds and literary autobiography, Jarman can address issues related to the family, its institutional supports, and gay people.[16]

To some extent, Jarman constructs his own past by abutting this 'personal cinema' against the sequences created for the film.[17] Martin Frey agrees with Wyatt: 'Searching for a place called "home", these home movies called up memories of the bygone years of his early childhood, and – for brief moments – they became safe havens within precisely that past'.[18] In *Dancing Ledge*, Jarman recalls the status of home movies during his childhood: 'The "home movie" nights of my childhood were the most exciting. To watch Grandma Mimosa cutting up the Sunday chicken in 1929 seemed no less than a miracle' (*Dancing Ledge*, p. 114). He returns to the theme in *Kicking the Pricks*, where he quips: 'I think why I like The Wizard of Oz so much is that at the end we return HOME, after hazardous adventures. There's no place like the HOME-movie' (*Kicking the Pricks*, p. 108).

Jarman's quip gives an important clue to how he relates to his own past through these home movies. On the one hand, the films from the 1940s are a repository of childhood memories, in particular showing his mother as she would have looked in his earliest memories of her. But on the other hand, Jarman here signals the remove these films have from his life: they show a place that never quite existed, in that they produce a version of moments from a family history from a very partial perspective. Roland Barthes writes in *Camera Lucida* about his response to photographs of his recently deceased mother: 'I had no hope of "finding" her, I expected nothing from these "photographs of a being before which one recalls less of that being than by merely thinking of him or her" (Proust)'.[19] Although Barthes considers a series of still images of his mother rather than a moving sequence, his thoughts can be usefully considered in relation to Jarman's engagement with his family's home movies. In particular, Barthes looks at photographs of his mother before the time of his birth. He asks, 'Is History not simply that time when we were not born? I could read my nonexistence in the clothes my mother had worn before I can remember her'. Barthes continues, 'Here, around 1913, is my mother dressed up. [...] This is the only time I have seen her like this, caught in a History (of tastes, fashions, fabrics): my attention is distracted from her by accessories which have perished; for clothing is perishable, it makes a second grave for the loved being'.[20] The wide gap between one's own sense of autobiographical or personal history and one's family history is something that also interests Jarman. He inserts two sequences filmed by his grandfather showing his mother as a child (including the sequence of Grandma Mimosa at Sunday lunch from 1929, mentioned above), and it is difficult, as a viewer, not to read more affect into their inclusion – as Martin Frey does – than might have been intended. We do not have the same level of detail regarding Jarman's own responses to the 'no place' (*Kicking the Pricks*, p. 108) of his family's home movies as Barthes provides. Barthes' ruminations open up a space to think through the peculiar and dislocating sense of a history separate from one's own that belongs only to one's mother before the point that one existed.

Viewing the home movies as a 'safe haven' among childhood memories that include the 'distressing muscular Christianity' of boarding school, Frey reads their role in *The Last of England* as follows:[21]

> Here, in a manner related to the home-movie evenings of his childhood, the images of the home-movie fragments of his parents and grandparents symbolically become an opportunity for withdrawing, for an inner emigration, offering a view of a bygone, seemingly peaceful period in which there was still hope.[22]

Yet this reading layers the home movies with a sentimentality that seems foreign to Jarman. Jarman's friend and collaborator Simon Watney critiques the 'narrowness of [...] conventional pictures of family life' in 'Ordinary Boys', his essay on the particular poignancy of family portraits that feature oneself as a queer child, pointing to the way these images can provoke 'memories that signal some kind of dysfunction between one's sense of self and one's parents' expectations'.[23] Marianne Hirsch writes movingly on the deception and power of family images in *Family Frames: Photography, Narrative and Postmemory*, indicating the contradictions alive between visual representations of the family unit and the lives hidden behind the metaphorical masks they portray. One can see this theme explored in Alison Bechdel's *Fun Home: A Family Tragicomic* (2006), a memoir told in the form of a graphic novel, which rereads (and re-draws) family photographs and reinterprets events from Bechdel's adult perspective. Although Hirsch and Watney write about photographs rather than home movies, their readings apply across media. Ellis also argues that Jarman's engagement with his family's home movies is not purely sentimental:

> the home-movie shots do not function as a kind of generalized nostalgia for the middle-class nuclear family of the 1940s and 1950s; certainly, Jarman was scathing enough elsewhere about elements of his own childhood, and later

segments of the family footage implicate that particular family with the work of empire.[24]

Instead of offering an opportunity for 'withdrawing' into a 'bygone' age, Jarman's insertion of these home movies into his films is ideological, as well as personal.[25] Thinking not of the visions of Grandma Mimosa serving lunch in her 1920s dining room – 'no less than a miracle' (*Dancing Ledge*, p. 114) – but of the footage shot by Lance Elworthy Jarman, we receive images with no accompanying sound in 'the most brilliant colour' (*Dancing Ledge*, p. 114) that depict events that would have been unlikely to be remembered by its young subjects, Derek and Gaye. When he is asked in *Kicking the Pricks*, 'Do you remember being filmed?' Jarman replies, 'No' (p. 178).

The home movies show a halcyon past of eternal summer that simply didn't exist as it is seen on the screen. On a practical level, the peaceful scenes of the young children running across a meadow, watched over by their mother, have an important omission: by operating the camera, Lance Elworthy Jarman has effectively eliminated himself from the visual record of the family. The figure of the father watches over the scene or even, perhaps, directs it to some extent. Lance Elworthy Jarman died in November 1986, which enabled Derek Jarman to write about his father's rages with increased candour in *Kicking the Pricks*, which was published the following year. With characteristic humour, Jarman calls him 'the classic fag's father' (*Kicking the Pricks*, p. 122): Jarman's beloved Grandma Mimosa 'protected' the young Derek from his 'father's outbursts, which grew more severe as the war continued' (*Kicking the Pricks*, p. 121).

Yet even without this kind of biographical information to inflect our reading, we might understand the uncomplicated vision of the mother and children as an astute 'ideological target'.[26] Jarman commented, 'With *The Last of England* I've made a journey back of a different sort. *The Tempest* and *Caravaggio* allowed me to form a perspective, to stand back. Now I'm going back to my roots, to lay bare the contradictions' (*Kicking the Pricks*, p. 181). Jarman uses the home movies to signal the ambivalence of the post-war family structure as he had experienced it: uncovering the poisoned nature underneath a beautiful veneer of domesticity. I extend Wyatt's reading of the home movies as an 'ideological target' and suggest that the way he has made use of recordings of his own family's home movies as material, including the scenes of him as a young boy, informs his critique of the ideological structures that make up the nation: in this case, the family.[27]

It is important to consider what initial audiences would have understood from the home movies: here the materials around the release of the film are vital to its reception. There is little reason for the majority of the audience to immediately recognise that these films from the 1920s and 1940s relate to the specific family history of *The Last of England*'s director. However, interested members of the audience might guess or at least wonder. The short scenes might prompt interested viewers to explore more about its director and the source of these fragments. Prior to the release of the film, Jarman's audiences would have had access to very few materials relating to his early life: Jarman's first autobiographical text, *Dancing Ledge*, contains a picture of him as a baby sitting propped up on the fender of a car at his first birthday party (p. 16). Two black-and-white photographs are also included: a portrait of his grandmother Mimosa (*Dancing Ledge*, p. 42) in early middle age, and an intriguing, stylised photograph of a three-year-old Jarman in an all-in-one hooded romper suit, arms outstretched, with his young and stylish mother behind him (*Dancing Ledge*, p. 42). *Kicking the Pricks*, his next book of life-writing, does introduce the key to recognising that these sections of the film draw from his own childhood: a photo of Jarman with his mother and sister in a meadow that looks very similar to the scene shown in some of the Super 8s appears early in the book (p. 20) and he discusses the inclusion of the home movies at several points.

Despite these intertextual links that are available for those viewers who are sufficiently interested to discover them, the film enables the home movies to be viewed as simply another mode within the film, rather than necessarily a visual recollection of moments from Jarman's childhood. The ambiguity allows the home movies to play multiple roles. The home movies are noticeably thematically and stylistically different from the rest of the film, presenting generic characters and amateur stylistic techniques that indicate that they should be immediately read as home movies. As Jarman gives no context that might immediately and definitively situate the participants in the film within an understanding of his life on first watching, Jarman creates what Justin Wyatt terms a '"generic" home movie'.[28] And indeed this is what we read from the family sequences at first glance: a photogenic young family in suburban post-war Britain, a beautiful mother with two children in tow, the family home, a family dinner. The scenes add to the documentary feel of the film as a whole in an interesting way: their amateur and bland filmic characteristics anchor the surreal dystopia of much of the film to the real world. The home movies thus seem to evoke what Annette Kuhn describes as 'the *memory* of England which lies in a future'.[29]

Annette Kuhn asserts that *The Last of England* is a 'less personal film [...] than it may seem'. She considers that the home movies fulfil a more outward-looking function: 'A repertory of images of and from particular moments of the nation's past, with all the (sometimes contradictory or contested) meanings attaching to them in the present, emerges in this film as one [...] of its source materials'.[30] Building on this idea of the home movies, Sarah Street points out that moments of personal history are placed into conjunction with public history, noting the sequences of the plane Jarman's father flew in World War II as well as military parades in India. She suggests that, by bringing the personal and private into dialogue through these films, the film 'invites the viewer to contemplate a "queer" perspective on the iconography of nationalism'.[31] The idea of the family is tied firmly to the history of the nation, in particular the idea of the family the nation attempts to protect. Tilda Swinton observed of her experience during the making of the film that, in contrast to the 'intensely personal' film *The Garden*, 'the preoccupations of *The Last of England* were shared' (*Modern Nature*, p. 297).

The dream poet in *The Last of England*

Jarman uses a means of self-representation with a long history to explore the shared 'preoccupations' (*Modern Nature*, p. 297) of *The Last of England*: the framing device of the dream poet. This is a literary device used in *Pearl*, William Langland's *Piers Plowman* and in several of Geoffrey Chaucer's works, including *The House of Fame*, *The Book of the Duchess* and *The Parliament of Fowls*. Jarman explains that the film 'is held together by the presence of the author' (*Kicking the Pricks*, p. 188). Although the film repeatedly displays his body in several different guises, he remains oddly difficult to pin down. Dillon suggests: 'Although by now as political and outrageous as any Beat poet ever was, his poetic "I" is still remarkably self-effacing and difficult to locate'.[32] As mentioned earlier in the chapter, we respond to the director's use of himself in character as a dream poet who frames the scenes that comprise the film. The audience of *The Last of England* is intended to identify the figure seated at the desk, the origin of the visions in the film. At a remove geographically from the action of the film, he sits in a room and seems to create its activity through the movement of his fountain pen and his paintbrush on the page.

In *Kicking the Pricks*, Jarman describes the connection between his dream vision and its literary precedents:

> In dream allegory the poet wakes in a visionary landscape where he encounters personifications of psychic states. Through these encounters he is healed. *Jubilee* was such a healing fiction, it harked back to *Pearl* and *Piers Plowman*. Which was also a socio-political tract. In *Jubilee* the past dreamed the future present. *The Last of England* is the same form, though this time I have put myself into the centre of the narrative.
>
> Here the present dreams the past future. I wrote no script, it is held together by the presence of the author. This man is destitute, this is a marriage. Its

structure suggests a journey: pages turn in a book bringing with them new turnings in direction, building up an atmosphere without entering into traditional narrative. (*Kicking the Pricks*, p. 188)

I take the artist at his word: considering *The Last of England* and *Jubilee* as dream vision or dream allegory helps us to understand the set pieces within the films in the manner that was intended. The sequences within *Jubilee* are framed in a similar way to *The Last of England*: instead of an author–dreamer as the source of the dystopian visions, the occultist John Dee asks the angel Ariel to show Elizabeth I her kingdom, revealing modern Britain as a dystopian wasteland. Critics have pointed to the characters in the film as being reimagined 'Langlandian personifications': whereas *Piers Plowman* includes personifications of abstract qualities such as Conscience and Wit, *Jubilee* is similarly structured to include characters such as Crabs ('a lovelorn nymphomaniac') and Mad ('a revolutionary pyromaniac').[33]

Looking ahead to *The Last of England*, the allegorical approach to providing a bleak vision seen in *Jubilee* returns. The comparison to *Pearl* raises interesting questions for how we might want to read the structuring 'presence of the author' (*Kicking the Pricks*, p. 188). Concepts of selfhood in the Middle Ages of the *Pearl* poet were different. First, the term 'autobiography' did not exist. Second, understandings of life-writing were also different: the narrative of a life was intended to be exemplary and didactic, rather than displaying all the elements of a person's life and character. *Pearl* provides a partial account of a person's life in order to demonstrate how an individual overcame great adversity. In part, this demonstrates the development of a soul with the purpose of moving towards eternity: the narrative exists to teach by example (see also Abelard's *Historia calamitatum*, or Augustine's *Confessions*).

We are to read the film's fast-paced images of industrial decline as visual representations of his 'psychic states' (*Kicking the Pricks*, p. 188) in response to the decline of the nation. Robert Mills comments that:

> the film's kinship with dream allegory provides Jarman with a means of critiquing aspects of the world around him. Rather than issuing clear political statements, *The Last of England* dramatizes feelings, presenting them in a version of dreamtime; individual viewers respond by drawing their own conclusions.[34]

The 'Prospero' character, magus or dream poet who frames the narrative enables his audience to collaborate in the sharp socio-political critique portrayed by the moments within the film, and in doing so, perhaps access their therapeutic qualities: 'Through these encounters he is healed' (*Kicking the Pricks*, p. 188).[35] One example of this is the iconic scene where Tilda Swinton tears off her wedding dress under the red skies of abandoned docks.

Her gesture is a vision of freedom: it is a gesture that constitutes the character's escape from domestic servitude.

Yet if Jarman is placing himself in the position of dream poet, this has interesting consequences. *Pearl* is subtle and operates at many levels of meaning, yet its primary subject regards the difficulty the dreamer has in accepting the loss of his precious daughter, who died in infancy. When he sees a young woman, the 'perle' of the poem, in his dreams, the dreamer struggles to accept that he cannot reach her or have her.[36] His actions, trying to cross a stream to reach her, cause him to wake from the dream and thus to lose her once again. The narrator learns through his dream, yet J. J. Anderson suggests that this learning does not come easily: 'his acceptance is born out of resignation'.[37] This is a different reading from Jarman's. A medieval Christian's reluctant acceptance of loss and devastation seems to have little to do with the experience of being healed that Jarman describes. We watch a journey that, though bleak, holds some bright promise through a radical reappraisal of societal structures and a commitment to counterculture.

Jarman's self-representations are various. Jarman undoes the image of himself as steeped in the history of dream allegory: as he sets up the frame for the film, he is wearing a sailor's hat, which simultaneously places him in a very different tradition of queer representations of sailors. To return to Kenneth Anger's underground film *Fireworks* (1947), the dreamlike sequences loosely depict a young man picking up a sailor, then being queer-bashed by a group of sailors, before returning to a scene of desire involving the first sailor. There are multiple representations in camp culture that Jarman might be referencing: the sailors in Tom of Finland's kitsch erotic drawings, those in Paul Cadmus's drawings or the characters in Jean Genet's *Querelle de Brest* (1947), revisited in Rainer Werner Fassbinder's adaptation, *Querelle* (1982). To pursue the meaning on a literal level, sailors navigate the oceans, which might be understood as a continuation of the dream voyaging theme. In his role as director, Jarman is, so to speak, sailing the ship.

The dream poet in *The Garden*

The figure of the director – presented at times as a 'Prospero-like' character,[38] poet-dreamer or direct participant in the action of the film – emerges once again in *The Garden*, a film that has much in common stylistically with *The Last of England*. *The Garden* is similarly structured to avoid traditional narrative in favour of montage, repeated images and symbols. However, *The Garden* introduces curious tableaux of silent figures, an approach reprised in the later film, *Wittgenstein* (1993). It is a film that is broadly based on

118   *Luminous presence*

Figure 17 Jarman sleeps on his desk at Prospect Cottage as water drips down from the ceiling in *The Garden*.

Figure 18 Jarman sleeps on his desk at Prospect Cottage in *The Garden*.

Christ's passion, transposed to a queer context where Christ is divided into two young lovers (played by Johnny Mills and Keith Collins). It contains lyrical sequences, shot on the shingle and marshes of Dungeness. Its first moments set up the terms for much of what happens in the rest of the film. The film opens with a voiceover (read by Michael Gough), which offers up the contents of the film to its viewers:

> I want to share this emptiness with you; not fill the silence with false notes, or put tracks through the void. I want to share this wilderness of failure. The others have built you a highway, fast lanes in both directions. I offer you a journey without direction, uncertainty and no sweet conclusion. When the light faded, I went in search of myself. There were many paths and many destinations. (*The Garden*, 01:23–02:00)

When the voiceover ends, we hear Jarman's voice on the set, congratulating people on a good rehearsal and announcing that there will be a thirty-minute break. Someone yells, 'Quiet!' and a cello starts to play. Immediately after, the scene cuts to Jarman, the first figure to be seen, pacing in his garden at Prospect Cottage. This is followed by a slow-panning shot showing the interior of the study, filled with strange sculptures. Water drips from the ceiling onto the artefacts within, including – notably – onto a crucified Christ. The shot pans to Jarman, showing him asleep at his desk, hands outstretched (see Figure 17). Water falls from the ceiling onto his table and onto his right hand (*The Garden*, 02:30). He wakes and briefly looks around him. Five minutes in, and he is depicted as asleep again, resting on one of his large black square journals (see Figure 18). Water continues to pour onto the desk. He wakes and starts to look at the journal, before stretching out his hand to the dripping water.

In this sequence, we are invited to understand elements of the film as a kind of autobiographical project: it might be 'a journey without direction' (*The Garden*, 01:45), but it is also one 'in search of […] self' (*The Garden*, 01:54). It would be reasonable to read the 'I' figure in the voiceover as relating to Jarman himself and the film as introducing an intensely personal subject. However, the autobiographical project is by no means straightforward. As in *The Last of England*, Jarman complicates the meaning of his authorial presence from the outset. Again, as in *The Last of England*, the poem read at the beginning of the film seems to belong to the author and director, yet it is read out by someone different. The voiceover by Michael Gough enables us to interpret the speaker as not truly just one single person: the autobiographical project becomes a collaborative affair, mirroring the filmmaking process. It is a collaboration that extends out from the screen: we are invited to join in this quest for self. The speaker states, 'I offer you a journey without direction, uncertainty and no sweet conclusion' and tells us, 'when the light faded I went in search of myself. There were many paths and many destinations' (*The Garden*, 01:58). Jarman invites us to understand 'notions of selfhood as an open-ended journey'.[39] By placing his distinctive voice commenting on the quality of the rehearsal in his role as director next, Jarman breaks through the illusion of the film as being outside of time – a coherent imaginary world, and reminds us of its place as a performance, rehearsed and then filmed, directed by him.

Compellingly, the film invites us to dwell on the role of the sleeping body of the director, stretched across his desk, at night. Although complicated by the factors explored in the previous paragraph, we are invited to understand the authorial 'I' as stemming from Jarman himself. He thereby recalls the figure of the dream poet that frames *The Last of England*: this grounds the film in Jarmanian dream-time, giving its contents a visionary texture. Yet this time, the figure is less authoritative: Jarman's character, which Petrie had described as 'Prospero-like' in the earlier film, is now sleeping and less alert.[40] The water falling indoors belongs within his dreamscape, pointing to the disintegration of the illusion of domestic safety: the elements have entered the (unusual) domestic space. Dillon considers that these opening segments 'all work together to name Jarman as the creator-poet-magus', seeing him as in charge of the film regardless of the more tentative portrayal.[41] He likens the dripping water to the way the poetic school of Sergei Parajanov and Andrei Tarkovsky uses water to 'signal the poetic accident'.[42] These opening sequences bear further analysis and intertextual reading.

The opening voiceover invites us to share Jarman's quest for self, through a 'wilderness of failure' (*The Garden*, 01:35). If *Jubilee* and *The Last of England* recall in their documentary-cum-visionary style the medieval dream allegories *Pearl* and *Piers Plowman*, where the episodes encountered act as 'personifications of psychic states' (*Kicking the Pricks*, p. 188), then *The Garden* recalls the Old English preoccupation with the outsider figure: the solitary exiled speaker in *The Wanderer*, perhaps represented by the Christ-like figure walking in the film, and with the deeply Christian, mournful text, *The Dream of the Rood*. Jarman's biographer Tony Peake points out that the film was at times 'referred to by Jarman in his notes as *The Wanderer* or *The Dream of the Rood*, briefly became *The Garden of England*, then simply *The Garden*'.[43]

In particular, the footage at the beginning of *The Garden* references the beginning of *The Dream of the Rood* where the dreamer informs his readership that he will relate 'the best of dreams' (*swefna cyst*): a vision of 'a most splendid tree' (*syllicre treow*) that, though it is 'encrusted with gold' (*begoten mid golde*), is bleeding – or 'sweat[ing] from the right hand side' (*swætan on þa swiðran healfe*). In the second section, the tree – or rood – speaks, exclaiming that the soldiers left him 'standing drenched with moisture' (*standan steame bedrifenne*).⁴⁴ I quote the words of the poem in Old English alongside the Modern English translations, as these quotations highlight the multiple meanings of the words *swætan* and *steame*. As Éamonn Ó Carragáin and Richard North point out, blood in Old English poetry was sometimes called 'battle-sweat' (*hilde-swat*), 'as if fighting was a grim athletics, as if blood was produced naturally by strenuous activity'.⁴⁵ Looking to the second passage, according to Peter S. Baker, 'steame' can be translated as 'steam, moisture, or blood'.⁴⁶ The tree is the 'rood' or 'cross' of the poem, recalling the cross on which Christ died. Yet it also indicates Christ's body: the blood from the injury on the right-hand side is a reference to the dead body of Christ: 'But one of the soldiers with a spear pierced his side, and forthwith came there out blood and water'.⁴⁷ In the film, this image is depicted directly as the Christ figure shows the camera his wound (*The Garden*, 19:45). Robert Mills reads the opening to *The Garden* as an unequivocal reference to the poem: 'Jarman's vision of Christ's passion is similarly provoked by an experience of being drenched. The image of water flowing down like blood, from a visual image of the crucifixion, places Jarman himself in the position of the rood within the poem'.⁴⁸ This reading works within the wider narrative of *The Garden*: Jarman, like the two lovers, is imbricated in the representations of Christ's passion. They are situated within a lengthy history of suffering within a homophobic society.

I extend Mills's reading: on the one hand, Jarman situates himself as the rood itself, as Mills suggests. On the other hand, he is still placed within the centre of the screen as the origin of the visions that emerge from him. This second placement is also important: Ó Carragáin and North point out that 'the dreamer in the poem [...] is imagined as being far less educated than the people who heard or read this poem', thinking of him as 'an untutored Everyman'.⁴⁹ This reading might return us to the idea of the poet as introducing us into a shared 'wilderness of failure' (*The Garden*, 01:40): Jarman foregrounds his audience's interpretations of the events of the film, just as the dreamer in *The Dream of the Rood* foregrounds the religious interpretations of its own audience.

The cameraman on screen: interrogating the *auteur*

In both *The Last of England* and *The Garden*, Jarman complicates the symbolic function of the director as auteur in film by appearing on screen, camera in hand. Jarman has gained a reputation as an *auteur* and *enfant terrible*, in part down to the idiosyncratic nature of his films, which are easily recognisable as 'a film by Derek Jarman' (as he is listed at the beginning of *Edward II*). His expansive and wilfully unusual personality, made known through his wide circle of friends and acquaintances, and his fairly public private life, leaves a visible stamp on his cinema. Critics align him with other film authors who produce experimental art cinema: Andrei Tarkovsky and Sergei Parajanov, Jean Cocteau and Kenneth Anger, or Pier Paolo Pasolini and Rainer Werner Fassbinder. The concept of the *auteur*, which originated in French film criticism (see André Bazin's essay 'On the *politiques des auteurs*', 1957) revives, in Linda Haverty Rugg's words, 'a Romantic [...] notion of authorship as creative genius', often inviting critical analysis that draws heavily on biographical details.[50] This trajectory should be taken into account in our analysis of his self-representations, because the idea of the man as *auteur* – or, the 'Derek Jarman' brand – intersects in interesting ways with the self-representations we encounter in The Last of England and The Garden and this is certainly something Jarman capitalises on to great effect. The area that I will focus on is how Jarman plays with the idea of his role as film director in both films by appearing on screen with a Super 8 camera in hand.

Early in The Last of England, we see footage of Jarman, standing in a housing estate, his white sailor's hat shimmering out from the shaded scene (07:24). He stands, holding a Super 8 camera by his side, as the camera spins around him, presenting his stasis in a dizzying blur. It's just a brief shot within the fast-paced sequences that comprise the film, and it might be easy to miss. What commentary might Jarman have been making? The estate he stands in looks similar to the efficient post-war low-rise brick-built blocks found around Bermondsey, not far from his former Bankside studio. These are new homes built following the destruction that took place during the Second World War. Perhaps this footage marks a deliberate self-representative act that centres on his presence on the screen and the fact he is holding his camera, yet not using it. This shows a specific response to his function as 'Director' of the film, conceived of as a dream vision: the breakdown of his ability to bear witness by recording and thereby interpreting what he sees or dreams. We receive a self-reflexive scene where Jarman could be conceived of as both the imagined cameraman behind the shot we see and its subject. It is an autobiographical act, but not one that is attached to a sequential narrative. We might interpret it as a self-portrait in motion. We do not directly access any sense of interiority in this shot (there is no confessional voiceover; there is no direct speech), yet we are nonetheless given access to affect. We might read the emotion in the scene as paralysis, dizzying confusion, the pause of anxiety.

Moving on to The Garden, the role of the film director is interrogated in two key moments. He becomes, in Dillon's words, 'a creator figure who is simultaneously implicated in what he attacks'.[51] Acts of representation are not straightforward projects. Dillon usefully compares Jarman's presentation of himself as director to Pasolini's *La Ricotta* (1963), in which he casts Orson Welles as the director of a religious film, giving him sections of Pasolini's writing to read and thus setting him up as a complex, autobiographical figure who references Pasolini himself. The representation satirises the idea of the auteur by subverting Orson Welles's image as the epitome of directorial power and genius since *Citizen Kane* (1941), in which he famously acts as producer, co-screenwriter, director and star.

Early in *The Garden*, a Madonna (played by Tilda Swinton) and child are photographed by three paparazzi photographers dressed in black balaclavas and leather jackets (12:20–15:31). As the scene progresses, they become more and more intrusive and mob-like, harassing the Madonna until she breaks her pose and runs from the set. They pursue her across the marshes as she becomes increasingly desperate, eventually pushing her to the ground and wrestling with her. Jarman refers to them as 'terrorist photographers' in *Modern Nature* (p. 141), and they provide an intertextual link to *The Last of England*, using imagery established in the earlier film that locates the cameramen as terrorists. The most direct meaning of this scene is a commentary on British society and celebrity culture: calling the paparazzi 'terrorist photographers' pushes a trope we are familiar with to its extremes: tabloid newspapers are the unhappy result of popular demand for access to the lives of people within the public sphere. The scene recalls the paparazzi hounding of Diana, Princess of Wales, throughout the 1980s, and her increasingly panicked response to scrutiny. Ellis views this scene as a 'mirror' of Jarman's experiences with the tabloid press, especially after he made his HIV status public. This is also true.[52]

However, what is most interesting here is that Jarman also implicates himself. Dillon summarises: 'Having associated his directorial eye with figures of aggression and distaste, Jarman unleashes satirical effects that are never entirely self-righteous or simple in their targeting'.[53] Indeed, this is most clear in a set piece in which two bathing scenes seem to be taking place simultaneously: the two lovers (Johnny Mills and Keith Collins) bathe each other, cut with a scene in which one of the lovers seems to be caring for a younger boy (played by Jody Graber). These scenes of intimacy and domesticity are intercut by the unpleasant awareness that they are being watched. The young boy points directly at the camera, demonstrating it has become an unwelcome intrusion, and Johnny Mills physically pushes the camera away in a bid to protect the privacy of the scene (*The Garden*, 24:30, 24:47, 25:03). The tension escalates and we see disturbing footage of Jarman, in his trademark blue boilersuit, pursuing one of the lovers (Johnny Mills) across the sand as he films him (*The Garden*, 25:28, 25:32, 25:49). His satire is aimed at himself in his role as cameraman and director: making the private public is a pursuit tempered with ambivalence. In a different

Figure 19 Jarman sleeps on an iron bed in the sea at Dungeness, watched over by five figures. Still from Dungeness shoot of *The Garden*.

vein, one of the photographs from the Dungeness shoot of *The Garden* captures Jarman, looking through his Nizo Super 8, smiling behind the camera as he points it at the photographer, Liam Daniel (see Plate 5).

The dreamer and the sea

Jarman extends the Anglo-Saxon imagery of the dreamer to comment obliquely on HIV/AIDS with a striking self-representational act in *The Garden*.[54] In the film's most famous image, Jarman sleeps on an iron bed that has been placed in shallow waters at the edge of the sea. Five figures in flowing white skirts circle him as he sleeps, holding torches aloft (see Figure 19 and Plate 4). During the first sequence, he shifts slowly in his sleep, gripping the white sheet around him. The scene takes place to the sound of seagulls and what we see is intercut with close-ups of the sea, reflections of branches in still water and the shingle (*The Garden*, 08:07–09:30). At the midway point of the film, Jarman is now naked, curled into a foetal position. The sheet that previously covered him has fallen into the sea, and he rocks back and forth. Other images are intercut: many of the other characters within the film emerge briefly; this sleep is unsettled (*The Garden*, 40:11–40:45). A piercing, discordant sound punctures the soundtrack of strings: the score at this point conveys a strong sense of anxiety. On either side of the second sequence, we see him asleep at his desk in Prospect Cottage with water still dripping onto him. In both images, the domestic has been invaded by the elements: his house no longer provides shelter, his bed no longer affords him rest.

Given the context within the film, the image seems to be the most direct comment on the virus. The image brings to mind the protagonist of Thom Gunn's 'The Man With Night Sweats', transplanted into an allusive context at the edge of the sea:

> I wake up cold, I who
> Prospered through dreams of heat
> Wake to their residue,
> Sweat, and a clinging sheet.[55]

We see a different facet of the dreamer, as he switches roles between the visionary dream poet and a person undergoing physical suffering as a result of the virus. It is a self-representational act that adds to the film's stark commentary on the homophobic treatment of gay men. After all, the film appropriates the iconography of the story of Christ to concentrate on the persecution of gay men. He extends this persecution to martyrdom in the literal end to the lovers, yet mirrors this in his own self-representation, which acts as a counterpoise to the more overt violence in other parts of the film. Elsewhere, queer-bashing is rife: a gaggle of women pursue a person in drag and rip off her wig against the Denge Sound Mirrors at Dungeness, and the two lovers are tarred and feathered by a police officer. The image of Jarman in the bed, although less overtly violent, acts as a politically inflected reminder of the shockingly inadequate governmental responses to HIV/AIDS in the UK (and also in the US, where many of his friends had already fallen sick and died).

This is a moment when the biographical details behind the making of the film are most illuminating. In his journals published in *Modern Nature*, Jarman's commentary about the filming of the main sections of the film is quite sparse. He describes the filming on 1 September 1989:

> God what am I up to? No script!
> Is this OK, Derek?
> Yes!
> Is that OK, Del?
> Yes!
> I feel so old today, everyone is so young on this set. My hair is silver grey. I'm not filming – nor looking through any camera. My hand shakes too much.
> (*Modern Nature*, pp. 140–1)

Jarman does not go into much detail in his diaries about the difficulties he found participating in the hectic life on set. He had recently been very ill and would become more so during postproduction. Peake writes about his absences from postproduction as he found himself in hospital:

> Only with *The Garden* was he perhaps less than diligent, possibly because the film had already somewhat slipped from his grasp. As they persevered with the edit, Cartwright and Collins had always tried to bring what they could to the ward to show their director, only to find him too ill to react with any clarity.[56]

Cinema is a necessarily collaborative medium and Jarman had always worked more collaboratively than most. In the making of *The Garden*, this approach became essential. Peake suggests 'It was just as well Jarman believed as fiercely as he did in the "sublime anonymity" of the Middle Ages'.[57] In this film, the influence of Anglo-Saxon approaches to subjectivity and collaboration on Jarman's self-representational practices create useful ways to think through how one might use one's own body and subject position to provide social critique during a time of crisis. Rather than distancing the creative process from individual subjectivity, the collaborative approach might, in Petrie's words, be thought to 'bring it closer to the process of the making and remaking of subjectivity in that human beings are the product of an equally complex process of collaboration or interactivity'.[58] The complex ways in which Jarman uses self-representation to critique the social and governmental responses to HIV/AIDS are considered in much more detail in the following chapters, in particular in chapters 9 and 11.

Notes

1. *Kicking the Pricks*, p. 188.
2. Jean Genet, *Querelle de Brest* (Paris: Gallimard, 2002), p. 9. Translated as: 'The man who wears the uniform of the sailor is in no way pledged or bound to obey the rules of prudence.' Jean Genet, *Querelle of Brest*, trans. Gregory Streatham (London: Faber & Faber, 2015), p. 1.
3. Elizabeth W. Bruss, 'Eye for I: Making and Unmaking Autobiography in Film', in *Autobiography: Essays Theoretical and Critical*, ed. James Olney (Princeton, NJ: Princeton University Press, 1980), pp. 296–320 (p. 297); Tony Rayns, 'The "I-Movie"', in *The Garden: Salesbook* (London: The Sales Company, 1990), n.p.
4. Petrie, 'Autobiography and British Art Cinema', p. 64.
5. Annette Kuhn, *Family Secrets: Acts of Memory and Imagination*, 2nd edn (London: Verso Books, 2002), p. 121.
6. Jarman first used the technique of building a relentless sequence of fast-paced shots in the short film and music video *The Queen is Dead*, made for The Smiths

shortly before filming commenced on *The Last of England*. It contained three songs: 'The Queen is Dead', 'Panic' and 'There is a Light That Never Goes Out' (1986). The shots in the short film contain depressing, disaffected scenes of run-down buildings on fire intercut with shots of state pomp (footage of the Albert Memorial featured in the videos, a subject that recurs in *The Last of England*). *The Queen Is Dead*, dirs. Derek Jarman, Richard Heslop and John Maybury (1986).

7   Mark Turner, 'Gay London', in *London From Punk to Blair*, eds. Joe Kerr and Andrew Gibson, 2nd edn (London: Reaktion Books, 2012), pp. 50–61 (p. 51).
8   Dillon, *Derek Jarman and Lyric Film*, p. 163.
9   'Εξελόυμε' (Deliver Me). Two songs by Diamanda Galás are used in the soundtrack to the film, both taken from *Saint of the Pit* (1986), the second installment in her 'Masque of the Red Death' trilogy written in response to the HIV/AIDS crisis.
10 Petrie, 'Autobiography and British Art Cinema', p. 64.
11 Bruss, 'Eye for I', p. 297.
12 Ibid.
13 Ibid.
14 Rayns, 'The "I-Movie"', n.p.
15 Bruss, 'Eye for I', p. 312.
16 Justin Wyatt, 'Autobiography, Home Movies, and Derek Jarman's History Lesson', in *Between the Sheets, in the Streets: Queer, Lesbian, and Gay Documentary*, eds. Chris Holmlund and Cynthia Fuchs (Minneapolis: University of Minnesota Press, 1997), pp. 158–72 (pp. 158–9).
17 For a definition of the term 'personal cinema' in underground film, especially in a gay context, see Richard Dyer, *Now You See It: Studies on Lesbian and Gay Film* (London: Routledge, 1990), p. 172.
18 Martin Frey, *Derek Jarman – Moving Pictures of a Painter: Home Movies, Super 8 Films and Other Small Gestures*, trans. Michael Wetzel (La Vergne, TN: Ingram Content Group, 2016), p. 25.
19 Barthes, *Camera Lucida*, p. 63.
20 Ibid., p. 64.
21 Frey, *Derek Jarman*, p. 25; *Dancing Ledge*, p. 51.
22 Frey, *Derek Jarman*, p. 29.
23 Watney, *Imagine Hope*, pp. 30–1.
24 Ellis, *Angelic Conversations*, p. 145.
25 Frey, *Derek Jarman*, p. 29.
26 'Jarman's choice of the home movie as an ideological target is astute.' Wyatt, 'Autobiography', p. 161.
27 Wyatt, 'Autobiography', p. 161.
28 Wyatt, 'Autobiography', p. 160.
29 Kuhn, *Family Secrets*, p. 109.
30 Ibid., pp. 109, 110.
31 Sarah Street, *British National Cinema* (London: Routledge, 2009), p. 175.
32 Dillon, *Derek Jarman and Lyric Film*, p. 164.
33 Mills, *Derek Jarman's Medieval Modern*, p. 165.

34 Mills, *Derek Jarman's Medieval Modern*, p. 167.
35 Petrie, 'Autobiography and British Art Cinema', p. 64.
36 *Pearl*, in *Sir Gawain And The Green Knight/Pearl/Cleanness/Patience*, ed. J. J. Anderson, new edn (London: W&N, 1996), pp. 1–46 (p. 1).
37 J. J. Anderson, 'Introduction', in *Sir Gawain And The Green Knight/Pearl/Cleanness/Patience*, ed. J. J. Anderson, new edn (London: W&N, 1996), pp. ix–xxi (p. x).
38 Petrie, 'Autobiography and British Art Cinema', p. 64.
39 Mills, *Derek Jarman's Medieval Modern*, p. 117.
40 Petrie, 'Autobiography and British Art Cinema', p. 64.
41 Dillon, *Derek Jarman and Lyric Film*, p. 184.
42 Ibid.
43 Peake, *Derek Jarman*, p. 443.
44 All Old English quotes from *The Dream of the Rood*. Lines 1, 4, 7, 20, 62. The original Old English is taken from Peter S. Baker, *An Introduction to Old English* (Malden, MA: Wiley-Blackwell, 2003), based on the tenth-century Vercelli Book, pp. 201–2. The translations in quotation marks are taken from Éamonn Ó Carragáin and Richard North, 'How Christian is OE Literature? *The Dream of the Rood* and Anglo-Saxon Northumbria', in *Beowulf and Other Stories: A New Introduction to Old English, Old Icelandic and Anglo-Norman Literatures*, eds. Joe Allard and Richard North, 2nd edn (Harlow: Routledge, 2011), pp. 160–88 (pp. 161, 166). The final translation is taken from Mills, *Derek Jarman's Medieval Modern*, p. 163.
45 Ó Carragáin and North, 'How Christian is OE Literature?', p. 167.
46 Baker, *Introduction to Old English*, p. 296.
47 *The Bible*, John 19.17.
48 Mills, *Derek Jarman's Medieval Modern*, p. 163.
49 Ó Carragáin and North, 'How Christian is OE Literature?', p. 167.
50 André Bazin, 'On the *politiques des auteurs* (April 1957)', trans. Peter Graham, in *Cahiers du Cinéma: The 1950s: Neo-Realism, Hollywood, New Wave*, ed. Jim Hillier (Cambridge, MA: Harvard University Press, 1985), pp. 248–59. See also 'The Auteur Theory' in Peter Wollen, *Signs and Meanings in the Cinema*, 5th edn (London: Palgrave Macmillan on behalf of the British Film Institute, 2013), p. 58–96. Quotation: Linda Haverty Rugg, *Self-Projection: The Director's Image in Art Cinema* (Minneapolis: University of Minnesota Press, 2014), p. 4.
51 Dillon, *Derek Jarman and Lyric Film*, p. 185.
52 Ellis, *Angelic Conversations*, p. 186.
53 Dillon, *Derek Jarman and Lyric Film*, p. 185.
54 I discuss the famous image of Jarman lying in sea kale, another distinctive self-representation in *The Garden*, in the conclusion to this book (see Plate 6).
55 Thom Gunn, *The Man With Night Sweats* (London: Faber & Faber, 2002), p. 57.
56 Peake, *Derek Jarman*, p. 456.
57 Ibid.
58 Petrie, 'Autobiography and British Art Cinema', p. 65.

Plate 1 Jarman in front of a rainbow, 1993.

Plate 2 Jarman in a cameo role as a cardinal in *Caravaggio*.

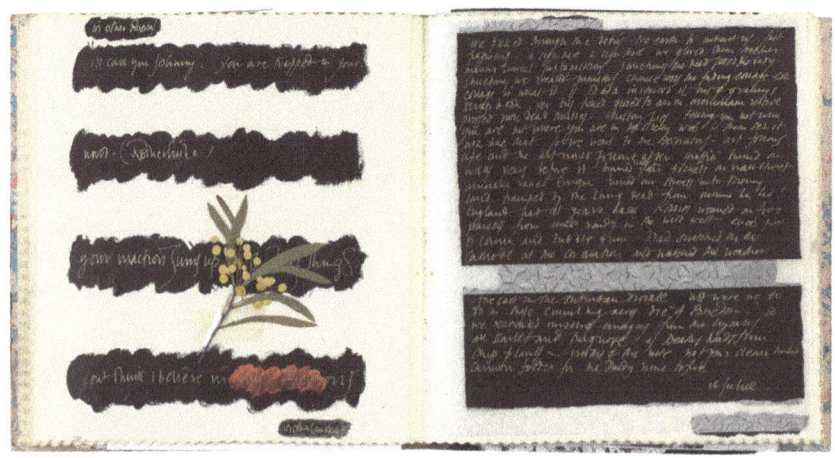

Plate 3 Spread from Jarman's sketchbook 'The Last of England'.

Plate 4 Jarman sleeps on an iron bed in the sea, watched over by figures with flaming torches. Still from Dungeness shoot of *The Garden*.

Plate 5 Jarman. Still from Dungeness shoot of *The Garden*.

Plate 6 Jarman lying in *Crambe maritima*. Still from Dungeness shoot of *The Garden*.

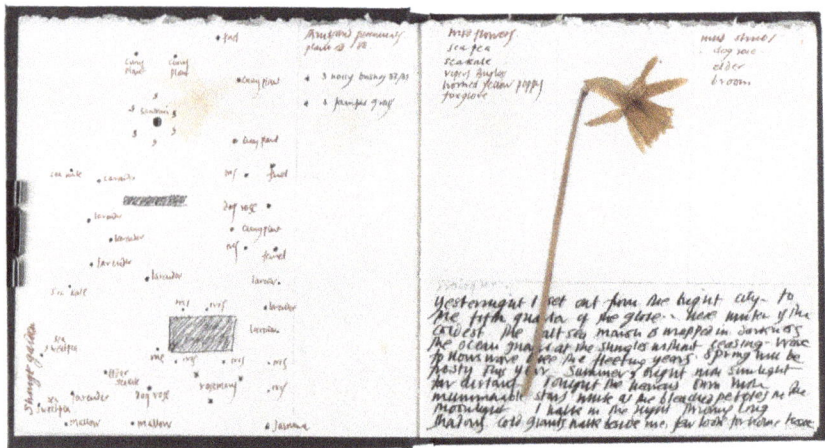

Plate 7 Pages from Jarman's journal 'The Garden', showing a planting plan, a prose journal entry and a pressed daffodil from his garden.

Plate 8 Set of contacts from Priory Road, summer 1965.

Plates 9 and 10 Jarman at work on *Blood* in Richard Salmon's studio, 1992.

Plate 11 Jarman in front of *Dead Sexy*, May 1993.

Plate 12 Jarman, *One Day's Medication*, 1993.

Plate 13 Jarman in the garden at Prospect Cottage in the snow.

Plate 14 The Prospect Cottage garden in full bloom, June 2014.

Plate 15 The sunroom in Prospect Cottage, looking out onto part of the garden, June 2018.

Plate 16 Jarman's profile in front of a screening of *Blue*.

Plates 17 and 18 Jarman in Monet's garden at Giverny, 1993.

7

Modern Nature: Haunting, flowers and personal mythologies

Derek Jarman's haunting diary *Modern Nature* (1991) is his best-known book of life-writing. It is a departure from his previous life-writing: rather than presenting varied recollections in 'non-narrative blocks' (such as in *Dancing Ledge* and *Kicking the Pricks*), or written to accompany the release of a film (such as *Derek Jarman's Caravaggio* and *War Requiem*), it is structured chronologically, under dated entries spanning from 1989 through to the end of 1990.[1] Its entries span many themes. The activities of each day spark memories and reflections that range across Jarman's childhood to his present. The book is set in a starkly different landscape from his previous published life-writing. It describes Jarman's new life in the small fisherman's hut Prospect Cottage in Dungeness – Britain's only desert – on the southernmost tip of the Kentish coast, where he had been living part-time since he bought it in 1987 (see Figure 20). The activity of constructing the unusual shingle garden and improving the cottage provides a positive focus for his days, and he includes many observations about the changing garden in his diary. But the landscape is also battered by the sea and by harsh coastal winds (see Figure 21). The desolate setting inflects the text – Jarman shares a more melancholy and sustained depressive state than in his previous works. Although Jarman reflects upon his film career and writes about the making of *The Garden*, which took place during the period covered by the diaries, the text feels at a remove from the bustling world of film. Instead, its main topic is the effects of AIDS on him, his friends and many of those around him. During the course of the diary, Jarman writes about his transition from being HIV-positive to the symptomatic stage of AIDS. In careful detail, he presents the effects of illness on his body and his responses to its changes. It also makes much mention of the ghosts of past friends and lovers, acting as elegy and testimony.

Interwoven with his memories of his community and his past are his observations about the plants and flowers of Prospect Cottage's garden. Added to these, he places quotations from medieval and Renaissance herbals to develop recurring symbols that offer an unusual queer history and

130   *Luminous presence*

Figure 20 Jarman standing in the doorway of Prospect Cottage, 1990.

Figure 21 Spread from Jarman's earlier sketchbook 'Borrowed Time', 1987. It shows an example of his journal entries written up carefully in his distinctive handwriting and juxtaposed with photographs of the changeable landscape of the sea at Dungeness.

commentary. His preoccupation with excavating the uses of plants found in these herbals intertwines with his experience of AIDS-related illness. Olivia Laing considers *Modern Nature* 'a memoir-cum-plantsman's diary, written as a kind of spell against the devastations of AIDS'.[2] On one level, this is so – yet Jarman's message is far from consolatory. He constantly questions the idea of the garden as a source of refuge and of hope for a spiritual if not a physical cure. He writes: 'I plant my herbal garden as a panacea, read up on all the aches and pains that plants will cure – and know they are not going to help. The garden as pharmacopoeia has failed' (*Modern Nature*, p. 179). Rather, by citing the potentially curative powers of some of these herbs, he sought to draw attention to the 'hegemony of the medical establishment on knowledge concerning health and life'.[3]

The text was written with the intention of bearing witness to the effects of HIV/AIDS on Jarman and those around him. Indeed, Peake suggests that Jarman saw himself as 'writing specifically for the young men of the nineties', corroborating Jarman's intention but drawing attention to the way the text is angled towards the generation of queer young men who would be coming of age and seeking precedents in the years following its publication.[4] One might also consider that AIDS journals act as a political provocation that, by bearing witness to the effects of HIV/AIDS, provide, as Ross Chambers comments, 'a reproach, to those who, at the best of times, would like to see gay people [...] just give up and disappear'.[5] Yet this has not been the sum of his readership. *Modern Nature* prompted affective investment from a wide-ranging readership. Indeed, following *Modern Nature*'s publication, he received a mass of 'unbidden letters', demonstrating that he was becoming not only well-known, but much loved.[6] Naturally, many letters came from young gay men, but they also came from gardeners, students wanting to write on his cinema, young people seeking to enter the film world and those who simply wanted to thank him for touching their lives.[7] More recently, the writer Olivia Laing calls *Modern Nature* 'sublime' and lists it as one of the books that most inspires her work, and in June 2019 BBC Radio 4 picked *Modern Nature* for 'Book of the Week', with readings by actor Rupert Everett.[8]

Of Jarman's life-writing, *Modern Nature* is the text that has attracted the most critical attention. Daniel O'Quinn draws out the ways in which 'gardening is an emergency praxis' that opens up a consideration of 'the relationship between time and community'.[9] Derek Duncan points to the ways in which *Modern Nature* and Paul Monette's *Borrowed Time* enact their politics: 'to secure for their authors a public space in which to act out their bodily and psychic disarray'.[10] Brophy dedicates a chapter to the book in *Witnessing AIDS*, wherein she considers how Jarman's investment in queer pedagogy is enacted in it. Ellis devotes only limited space to a consideration of the diary in *Derek Jarman's Angelic Conversations*, but returns to it in two articles – one that seeks to identify Jarman's continued interest in early modern objects in the diary and one that looks to the relationship he had with the land as a queer materiality of dirt.[11] Tom Ratekin also dwells on the text in a chapter on postmodern memoir, framing devices and ways of gaining control of one's image in *Final Acts*.[12] Deborah Esch comments on representations of Jarman in the media and on his response to these representations in *Modern Nature*.[13]

Modern Nature presents a wonderfully complex account of Jarman's investment in excavating queer and alternative histories, advancing a pedagogical ideal for the future and gardening as a means to explore alternative models for living. Considering the artists Gilbert & George, Jarman admits that 'like them, I can find strength in flowers, boys, and childhood memories' (*Modern Nature*, p. 91). He here identifies three recurring motifs in the diary.

Can diary provide testimony?

Modern Nature's form can be best described as a revised diary, written with an eye to its publication. 'I'm writing a diary, which I'm publishing', Jarman reports telling a journalist from *The Sun* (*Modern Nature*, p. 94). Peake notes that the diary 'had been accepted for publication by Mark Booth at Century' in early 1990, and that 'Jarman shaped the raw material into the book it would become' between September and the end of that year, with the help of Shaun Allen, who had helped edit *Dancing Ledge*, and Keith Collins.[14] Michael O'Pray points out that although 'As a journal, *Modern Nature* reveals a different side of him [from the polemical protagonist of *Dancing Ledge* or *At Your Own Risk*]; nevertheless, it was commissioned, and must have been written with that in mind'.[15] Jarman too observes that he had always been 'conscious [...] of the limitations and loyalties' of the diary 'as I have always been aware that it would be published' (*Modern Nature*, p. 298). Though Jarman mentions the diary's 'limitations and loyalties', he does not directly name what these are for him. A diary openly pursued with a view to publication greatly changes its orientation by questioning the public–private dichotomy by which a purely private diary is defined. Although this does not exclude the possibility of the 'intimate self-analysis associated with the *journal intime*', it is a major shift in the terms under which one decides what to record.[16]

His diary is inseparable from identity politics: as a famous gay man who, during the period in which the diary's commission was confirmed, knew he was now at the symptomatic stage of AIDS, his diary becomes more than a personal document. He writes: 'My sense of confusion has come to a head, catalysed by my public announcement of the HIV infection. Now I no longer know where the focus is, for myself, or in the minds of my audience' (*Modern Nature*, p. 25). Recording the events of his everyday life would necessarily include a volume of writing on the effects of AIDS-related illnesses. The diary becomes a witnessing document, charting the progress of its author's health. By transforming his thoughts and body into what Derek Duncan terms 'the focus of public surveillance', Jarman might significantly add to work that sought to change the terms of HIV/AIDS representation.[17] By adding his own changing perspective in the first person – unlike the greater volume of AIDS memoirs written by relatives discussed in the introduction to this book – Jarman seeks to provide representation unmediated by damaging tropes circulating about 'person[s] with AIDS'.[18] Ross Chambers writes that AIDS journals 'look forward as enunciations to a future in which they will be read, and the open-endedness of their chronicle structure implies this prospectivity as much as the thematics of survival does'.[19] This is crucial: its politics work by enabling a future audience to bear witness to the diary's events.

Even so, Jarman writes of his caution about exposing his feelings of loss – 'Our happy years were punched off course by the gods' (*Modern Nature*, p. 98). He writes an entry that details some telephone contact with his friend, the film director Howard Brookner, who 'can only groan now, his bright mind slowly invaded by a terrible infection that is depriving him gradually of his faculties' (*Modern Nature*, p. 54). The one-sided conversation causes him to reflect on his friend's visit to Dungeness the previous March, during which they 'walked in a storm along the Ness'. Brookner 'had a sudden nose bleed' – a visible sign of the illnesses he was constantly fending off – but 'wouldn't admit it', and 'kept on smiling' 'all through last summer' (*Modern Nature*, p. 54). Although Jarman shares in his diary that the call left him 'confused, fearful, and terribly sad', he then writes: 'Emotions frozen for fear of filling the world with tears'. This marks a conflict between his desire to record events and emotions in his diary, and his fear that if he shares them it will be too much – the world will be overwhelmed by this record of sadness. Brophy considers his hesitation a sign that he fears not only 'the exposure' but also 'the sentimentalization of his concerns'.[20]

In a long diary entry that recalls some holidays spent with an aunt in Kilve, Somerset, as a child, while his parents were living in Pakistan, Jarman mentions Dorothy Wordsworth's journal written in nearby Alfoxden almost 200 years before he was there, aged 11, ranging over Danesborough, exploring the beach and making drawings of what he found. He quotes from her journal, drawing parallels between her explorations and his own as a boy, where he '*sat a considerable time upon the heath, its surface restless and glittering with motion of the withered grasses, and the waving of the spider's threads*' (italics in original).[21] He then mentions that he returned to Kilve three years ago, attempting to find Aunt Isobel – but had found 'the house was deserted' and 'no record' of a number for her in any nearby towns (*Modern Nature*, p. 69). Recalling us to his present setting by the sea at Dungeness, Jarman writes, 'The cold wind has fallen, the sea has turned an opaque jade', as he 'rummage[s]' through his books for 'Dorothy's journal' (*Modern Nature*, p. 69), which he uses to illustrate the passage he is writing. An elegy follows, part of which is reproduced below:

> I have no words
> My shaking hand
> Cannot express my fury
> Sadness is all I have,
> Cold, cold, cold they died so silently
>
> (*Modern Nature*, p. 69)

Jarman relates his excavations of his childhood, his reading history and the poignancy of being unable to find a trace of his aunt, who might by then have passed away, to a present of grief. The poem is a bleak elegy for dead friends, used in the voiceover to *The Garden*. Dorothy Wordsworth's journal helps him make sense of his boyish world – the clarity with which she conveys what he could see then in Somerset (quoted above), and now in Dungeness ('*I never saw such a union of earth, sky and sea: the clouds beneath our feet spread themselves to the water, and the clouds of the sky almost joined them*' (*Modern Nature*, p. 69, italics in original)). Jarman's return to her words to describe his boyish experience and contemporary setting seems to echo his own desire to provide a journal that might be used by others in future years. However, he undoes his reliance on books, words or writing – his belief that it is possible to communicate effectively in diary form – 'I have no words', he writes in the poem, just 'sadness' and 'fury'. Jim Ellis observes that 'Jarman's text is [...] haunted, by old friends and lovers and by obsolete but still useful ways of knowing and being'.[22] In Jarman's entry above, the haunting is prompted by memories of place and of Dorothy Wordsworth's writing about the environment. Elsewhere, he writes that 'a sprig of lavender held in the hand or placed under the pillow enables you to see ghosts, travel to the land of the dead' (*Modern Nature*, p. 55). Carla Freccero suggests that the 'willingness to be haunted is an ethical relation to the world, motivated by a concern not only for the past but also for the future'.[23] His shared ruminations on his personal, cultural and social history form an ethics of engagement. But writing a personal account that acts as testimony or elegy is a fraught activity because of the awareness of the gap between one's experience, under pressurised circumstances, and how these experiences might be received by those outside the crisis. I return to the impact of HIV/AIDS in each chapter for the remainder of this book. Finally, although Collins has said that Jarman 'seemed ambivalent about publication, once instructing me that on his death he would like them to be burnt', this mood can't have been constant: after all, he chose to fulfil the commission for *Modern Nature*, and discussed plans for a further collection – that would posthumously become *Smiling in Slow Motion* – with the same publishing house.[24]

On the diary form

Jarman's choice of the diary form allows him the freedom to share his shifting subjectivity in a way that feels as unmediated as possible and seems to offer the potential for greater immediacy. A diary 'fixes the portrait of the writer's daily reality without any concern for continuity', proposes Georges Gusdorf, the French philosopher and epistemologist.[25] The freedom to choose how to represent oneself is radically different from an autobiography. Literary autobiographies, rather than simply recording the events of a life, construct it in formal and social terms. Gusdorf views a properly autobiographical text as one that brings the ideal man, in his 'special unity and identity across time', into being.[26] John Sturrock continues this argument, stating that 'autobiography wills the unity of its subject', following Nietzsche.[27] But Jarman, by using this diary or journal format, is not limited by trying to present a fixed, perhaps ossified identity or subjectivity: his understanding of himself, his personal history and histories of other kinds is able to shift as the diary proceeds.

In her study of postmodern life-writing, Gunnthorunn Gudmundsdottir points out that the diary form is 'usually free of any hierarchical interpretation of events; the mundane and the eventful are all allocated the same space and form'.[28] The quotidian and the significant are structured under the same organising principles. The diary's structure is bound by the metronomic progression of time: each entry, theoretically, was written on the date printed above it, and no entry is privileged above another in terms of sequence – although it may be, in terms of length or depth of content. There is a contract in this type of writing that implies that the date above each piece marks the actual date on which it was written. But although the days pass page by page, the content described within each entry is not bound by the same logic: although the entry might concern itself with the quotidian, it might, conversely, refer to any event either in Jarman's history or other world events, a certain memory, film, author, historical event or theme. Jarman refers to this process as 'diary after the event'.[29]

The entries that make up *Modern Nature* are often allusive and always fragmentary. Thoughts and ideas are often brief, made distinct from one another by the use of a simple paragraph separator symbol. Even so, Jarman worries that by editing and shaping the diary entries prior to publication, he has created a text that is more cohesive than his life really was. *Modern Nature* is preoccupied with 'the potentially deforming pressures of writing for public consumption'.[30] For example, writing from the hospital where he was being treated for tuberculosis, Jarman claims: 'This diary gives the wrong impression, it's much too focused. I'm emerging from a strange dream' (*Modern Nature*, p. 275). In drawing our attention to the seeming focus that emerges from his account of illness, he highlights the gaps that are elided by the diary form. The silence between entries or paragraphs might contain so much that he was unable to record. By summarising them, even in brief diary form, he believes he has smoothed over too many of the fissures. Even in doing something that could potentially give the closest account of the events of his life, he is painfully aware of its limitations.

At the end of *Unbecoming*, Eric Michaels's account of the last year of his life (1987–88), sits a brief text on gay politics from 1982. In it, Michaels argues that older gay men

> need to take some responsibility for our own history, for conveying it to our young. It is not nostalgia. If one is going to go to all the trouble to be gay, one ought to do a more interesting and useful job of it. Models exist in our very recent past. They should be recalled.[31]

Simon Watney considers 'this was in large part the underlying motive behind his AIDS diary', which ranges over its fiercely intelligent author's opinions, experiences of AIDS-related illnesses, theorising about death and about the process of recording it in his diaries, and tirades against Brisbane.[32] It could well have been Jarman writing. Yet far from offering a sanitised model, Michaels, like Jarman, offers an alternative to the good 'AIDS patient': in Penny Taylor's photograph, printed on the cover of Michaels's book, he strikes a defiant pose that highlights the extensive lesions from Kaposi's sarcoma. Ross Chambers focuses on the importance of form for Michaels, who 'implies that the looseness and disunity of the diary form – its lack of formal cohesion – is part and parcel of an overall tactics of untidiness as a mode of resistance […]', part 'of a project of survival', that stands in contrast to the tidy, well-behaved and sanitised world of hospital treatments.[33] He rails against what Eve Kosofsky Sedgwick has termed 'the hygienic imperative' in contemporary cultures, i.e. 'the overarching, hygienic Western fantasy of a world without any more homosexuals in it'.[34] Instead, a diary that ranges from a patient's accounts of his maladies to a searing political critique, fails to be easy to listen to or to account for. Jarman similarly demonstrates resistance to the dominant cultural script of the 'person with AIDS' (as described in G. Thomas Couser's breakdown of different kinds of AIDS narrative available, or as seen in films such as *Philadelphia*, 1993), by providing a record of his subjectivity through this terrible time.[35] His record, though it appears to be ordered through the chronological progression of dated entries, 'lacks formal cohesion' as an intended political effect – to undermine a sense of progression, or thematic unity.[36]

Personal mythologies

Though the journals contain great thematic breadth, there are particular devices that recur. One of these is that Jarman uses observations about his physical environment in order to introduce 'spots of time' from his past. He intertwines his experiences of HIV/AIDS with moments from his childhood, recollections from his career and interesting counter-histories, including constructing one around the symbolism and medical uses of different plants. Quotations from medieval and Renaissance herbals help to develop recurring symbols that offer an unusual queer history and commentary, in which the uses of flowers and plants found in these herbals intertwines with his experience of AIDS-related illness. The plants he discovers or grows in his garden provide what Jim Ellis calls 'time-travelling worm holes'.[37]

He uses material from both obscure and pedestrian sources, allowing his dialectic to emerge through a careful reading of the choices he made in juxtaposing one text with another. He occasionally presents the information with an accompanying explanation:

> A personal mythology recurs in my writing, much the same way poppy wreaths have crept into my films. For me this archaeology has become obsessive, for the 'experts' my sexuality is a confusion. All received information should make us inverts sad. But before I finish I intend to celebrate our corner of Paradise, the part of the garden the Lord forgot to mention. (*Modern Nature*, p. 23)

In this passage, Jarman clearly describes his political and artistic project. He links his present to the history of 'experts' on sexuality, such as Havelock Ellis's theory of sexual inversion.[38] He also claims space for queer desire despite its absence from normative – Christian – culture. In most of the other comparable arrangements, however, he allows these snippets to speak for themselves. For example, Jarman tells an anecdote about his night-time fear of a Swiss clock – 'a gruff little owl whose eyes moved in time to the tick' – that his parents had put up in his room while he was sleeping. On leaping out of his own room in fear to his parents' bed, his father 'laughed: "Don't be such a pansy, Derek"' (*Modern Nature*, p. 29). This tableau clearly remained with him not just because of the hurt caused or the sense of injustice Jarman felt at the time, but also because of the carelessly inflected homophobia of which a later Derek would become aware. Jarman uses this memory to launch into a list of associations about the flower:

The Pansy

Viola tricolor, heartease, tickle-my-fancy, love-in-idleness, or herb trinity. The juice of it on sleeping eyelids will make a man or woman dote upon the next live creature they see, if you would have midsummer's dreams. A strong tea made of the leaves will cure a broken heart; for our pansy is strongly aphrodisiac, its name, pensée, *I think of you*. If it leads you astray, don't worry: the herbal says it cures the clap; for 'it is a Saturnine plant of a cold slimy viscous nature … an excellent cure for venereal disorder'. (*Modern Nature*, p. 29)

The passage continues along the same lines as is shown above, demonstrating Jarman putting into practice the ideas he set out in the previous extract. Each snippet combines to produce a startling effect in order not only to delight and entertain, but to re-inscribe a collection of meanings culled from cultural memory onto a symbol that has become solely one of disparagement in the twentieth century: something entirely different and wonderfully multivalent to the point of contradiction. The associations are allowed to speak for themselves.

In the first five months depicted in *Modern Nature*, we find Jarman looking inward. It is a melancholy text: a sustained attempt to re-evaluate and try to knit together a history relevant to him. Jarman is constantly attempting to find a path between how to represent his own history, and how to find precursors in the histories he has read. As a prominent figure in gay culture, he felt a responsibility to try to make sense of the histories that affected his generation and his community (as echoed in his contemporary Eric Michaels's journals, quoted earlier in this chapter). In this mode, he explores negative tropes – like the term 'pansy' explored above, that have continued to crop up as schoolyard slurs. In *Smiling in Slow Motion*, he describes his friend's reaction to reading *Modern Nature* shortly after its publication: 'Ken […] found my depressed self quite different from the self on the set of *Edward* that he knew. "Liverish," I said, "those TB bugs jaundice the view, like cracked and yellowing varnish"' (p. 31). Indeed, he considers his 'garden is a memorial, each circular bed and dial a true lover's knot – planted with lavender, helichryssum and santolina' (*Modern Nature*, p. 55).

In this 'jaundice[d]' mode, his journal entries are often at their most haunting: 'Flowers spring up and entwine themselves like bindweed along the footpaths of my childhood', Jarman states (*Modern Nature*,

p. 7). Flowers in their wonderful specificity – snowdrops, fritillaria, wild columbine – recall his past, but the manner in which they do so is not uninflected. The Royal Horticultural Society informs us that 'Hedge bindweed or bellbind (*Calystegia sepium*) with its pure white trumpet flowers is a familiar sight, choking plants in borders and twining around any plant shoot or cane'.[39] The flowers Jarman here refers to behave like weeds that grasp and bind other plant life. But in *Modern Nature*, the flowers entwine themselves – the gaze is inward. One imagines a young Derek walking in a country garden, his ankles caught by vines. His older self stands in a garden and finds himself propelled backwards by these pointers to an earlier time: all childhood memories are situated in garden spaces within his mind.

Jarman has internalised the external world of his childhood, thus its prompts make memories bloom. 'These spring flowers are my first memory, startling discoveries; they shimmered briefly before dying, dividing the enchantment into days and months, like the gong that summoned us to lunch' (*Modern Nature*, p. 7). The garden space is not figured as neutral in either example I discuss: his descriptions of nature are rarely purely lyrical, and often feature a sense of enclosure, claustrophobia or even death. Jarman makes it clear very early on that, for him, flowers mark time's passage via their swift 'startling' life and death. Flowers, common on the one hand, yet monumental on the other in their invocations of the human history of symbols – like gongs that conjure ritual alongside the regular beat of everyday life – mark out Jarman's thematic link between quiet, rural everyday encounters and his personal history.

On narcissi

The garden and its contents act as emblems that recall not only Jarman's personal history, but also a more collective history of queer desire. Each type of flower calls attention to itself: to the physical attributes of the object as it exists in time, plant lore, recalling the history of England, and the history of its symbols over time. He dwells in particular on the associations of daffodils, an interest replicated in his journals (see Plate 7). On Tuesday, 7 February, Jarman has 'counted well over 50 buds on the daffodils I planted last year' (*Modern Nature*, p. 12). The physical plants, along with some other details to do with some other bulbs he has planted, are recorded. He then presents us with a wealth of history about 'Daffodowndillies', from their beauty (Hill finds them 'good for shew'), their sweet smell (Gerard's *Herbal* mentions Theocretius's line 'Narcisse good in scent'), to other details, including the unexpected information that the 'bulbs were used by Galen, surgeon of the school of gladiators, to glue together great wounds and gashes' (*Modern Nature*, p. 12). One gets the impression he is gathering up all this knowledge in order to save it from loss – because it is valuable to those who can see the relevance of this kind of project as producing and sustaining shared cultural histories.

The results are not simply a collection of trivia though they are that as well: the collection could be presented as a book of historical curiosity. But Jarman has evoked a flower of myth, whose beauty and scent are constant across centuries – carried by the Romans across Europe in the 'back-packs of Roman soldiers' (*Modern Nature*, p. 12). They are not only attractive, but have healing properties, binding the wounds of men thus soothing the after-effects of battle. Around the time that Jarman was in his late teens, there was a vogue for homoerotic historical films, such as *Ben-Hur* (1959) and *Spartacus* (1960), which may well have been influential. The lesbian writer Mary Renault's historical novels, such as *The Mask of Apollo* (1966), use classical Greek settings, and were very popular in the 1950s and 1960s. Her contemporary novel *The Charioteer* (1953) tells the story of two gay servicemen who model their relationship upon ideals expressed in Plato's *Symposium*. Similarly, lesbian writer Marguerite Yourcenar's *Memoirs of Hadrian* (1951), expressed as a letter to Marcus Aurelius, dwells on the Roman's love for the youth Antinous. The muscle magazine *Physique Pictorial* was launched in 1951, often including Greek- and Roman-themed softcore porn photos. Jarman's *Sebastiane* is certainly influenced by the classical revival that took place during his early twenties. In late 1991, Jarman comments 'In ancient Rome, I could have married a boy; but in the way that ideals seem to become their shadows, love came only to be accepted within marriage' (*At Your Own Risk*, p. 4). Ancient Greece and Rome are suggestive sites to dwell on because they fuse homoeroticism with the birth of Western art and culture.[40]

'Daffodils "come before the swallows dare and take the winds of March with beauty." When I read these words they are tinged with sadness, for the seasonal nature of daffodils has been destroyed by horticulturists who nowadays force them well before Christmas' (*Modern Nature*, p. 12). Modern time is no longer equivalent to time in the annals he is picking through to find these resonant examples, or even to the time of his childhood. Contemporary horticulturists can adapt their practices to outsmart the seasons. Jarman then reflects, 'perhaps my nostalgia is out of place – now daffodils are plentiful; and mushrooms, once a luxury, are ladled out by the pound' (*Modern Nature*, p. 12).

On Monday, 13 February, 'the first of the daffodils opens, bowed almost to the ground by the inclement weather' (*Modern Nature*, p. 13). By Thursday, 23 February, 'the hail came with the dark [...]. My poor daffodils, which greeted me on my return [from Berlin], are now beaten to the ground' (*Modern Nature*, p. 17). The growth and destruction that the weather enacts upon the garden attain a metaphorical importance: the drama that is played out on the landscape evokes related symbolic dramas for Jarman. After informing us that these flowers have been broken by the harsh weather, he steps straight into myth:

> Narcissus is derived not from the name of the young man who met his death vainly trying to embrace his reflection in crystal water, but from the Greek narkao (to benumb); though of course Narcissus, benumbed by his own beauty, fell to his death embracing his shadow. Pliny says '*Narce Narcissum dictum non a fabuloso puero*,' named Narcissus from *narkê*, not from the fabled boy. Socrates called the plant 'crown of the infernal gods' because the bulbs, if eaten, numbed the nervous system. Perhaps Roman soldiers carried it for this reason (rather than for its healing properties) as the American soldiers smoked marijuana in Vietnam.
>
> This prompted me to ring Matthew Lewis, the portrait photographer, and ask him if he would take a photo of a young man holding a daffodil. Last year he took a beautiful portrait of a handsome Italian, stripped to the waist, holding a lemon, the juice of which he used to dissolve heroin to fill his syringe. Narcissus, narcotics, self-absorption: benumbed retreat into self. (*Modern Nature*, pp. 17–18)

The journey of associations shown in this passage demonstrates the range and confidence Jarman displays when sorting through history to attempt to make sense of it – to draw parallels and draw out new meanings. Daffodils are an obvious choice for focus. There is much to be unpacked in relation to their symbolic value. The flower's foremost association is with the Narcissus myth. According to Ovid, the first daffodil grew from the spot on which Narcissus died: 'The body, however, was not to be found – / only a flower with a trumpet of gold and pale while petals'.[41] In David Raeburn's translation of the *Metamorphoses*, the most poignant moment, as Narcissus falls in love not with the 'Legions of lusty men and bevies of girls [who] desired him' but with himself, is described as follows: 'He fell in love with an empty hope, / a shadow mistaken for substance'.[42] In his 1914 essay *On Narcissism*, Sigmund Freud claimed:

> We have discovered, especially clearly in people whose libidinal development has suffered some disturbance, such as perverts and homosexuals, that in their later choice of love-objects they have taken as a model not their mother but their own selves. They are plainly seeking *themselves* as a love-object, and exhibiting a type of object-choice which must be termed 'narcissistic'.[43]

This work has left a negative legacy that has remained influential in popular culture, retaining an unwarranted level of currency over almost a century.

Jarman offers a critical investigation of the history of the flower, perhaps in order to provide an alternative history system. He insists upon the primacy of the lesser-known meaning of the flower's name: ναρκάω, to numb, recorded in Pliny the Elder's *Natural History*. The emphasis on another version of history, where things don't mean quite what they did before – or at least, what you thought they meant – and where there is more than one truth, is typical of Jarman's revisionary project. By privileging Pliny the Elder's interpretation over more common, simplified versions, he presents an alternative view. I think it is important that Jarman creates an alternative history but then, by suggesting the idea for the Lewis portrait, encourages the two histories to exist side by side, and thus makes them new. And, it should be noted, that Pliny's translation of ναρκάω as solely 'to numb' is reductive: it can also be translated as 'to grow stiff', a translation that, had Jarman been aware of it, may well have pleased him and found its way into this passage.

The daffodil, according to Vickery's *A Dictionary of Plant Lore* (1995), is 'considered by many to be unlucky, and they will not have the flowers in their house because they hang their heads, bringing tears and unhappiness. The sweet-scented old fashioned white narcissus, also called scented lily or white lily, is also known as grave flooers [sic] and unlucky to take indoors'.[44] But named 'Daffodowndilly', the flowers become provincial, affectionate and playful. A slippage from Asphodel, they become knowable – William Wordsworth's daffodils 'tossing their head in sprightly dance'.[45]

To focus so heavily on this particular flower's associations is appropriate. As O'Quinn points out, the 'allegory is palpable':

> just as violets and daffodils and poppies make a living among the stones in the shadow of the nuclear plant which overlooks his cottage, so also Jarman and the communities invoked – PWAs, queers, communists, inverts, and saints – demonstrate their strength and their resilience in the face of the personal, cultural, and social crisis of Thatcherite Britain.[46]

However, Jarman concludes: 'Narcissus, narcotics, self-absorption: benumbed retreat into self' (*Modern Nature*, p. 18). By externalising this train of thought, and involving Matthew Lewis in his idea for a further portrait, Jarman has made the daffodil issue directly about queer art, while simultaneously turning back in on himself. There's something seductive here that mirrors the quite narcissistic pleasure of writing one's life: deciding that what one experiences, in its singularity, should become representative to others. Peake informs us that 'With a young photographer called Matthew Lewis, he [Jarman] discussed producing a book of photographs (half his, half Lewis's) called *Narkao*'.[47]

'Red Pentel Duels' and reinvention

Keith Collins, in his preface to *Kicking the Pricks*, tells us that 'Derek extensively re-edited and re-ordered the text, scrubbing out the past, inverting meanings, ruthlessly cutting so that pages were returned bleeding from their red Pentel duels – a process of revision and re-invention that was characteristic in his painting, writing, film editing, and personal history' (*Kicking the Pricks*, preface). This process of revision has been demonstrated earlier in this chapter in relation to the recurrent floral emblems, but Jarman's technique is the same when using the events of his own life. For example, Jarman returns several times in his life-writing to the house on the lakeside of the Lake Maggiore and the boy, Davide, whom he meets there. Below are three versions of the memory. The first is found in the handwritten journal 'Dancing Ledge' (parts of which would become his first published diary, *Dancing Ledge* in 1984):

> May 1946 Largo Maggiore
>
> I'm four years old. The sound of swallows itys itys itys I lie awake in a grand old mahogany bed staring at the high ceiling of my bedroom, which glows pearly white in the early morning sunlight. Itys itys itys in the yard Davido the handsome one, who rows across the lake throws me high in the air and takes me hunting on the handlebars of his bike is whistling Dolce Fa Niente.[48]

The second is from *Modern Nature*, written in early 1989 from the silence of Dungeness:

> *Villa Zuassa 1946*
>
> In 1946 we flew to Italy, where my father after some months became Commandant of the airfield in Rome, and a witness in the Venice war trials. Villa Zuassa was requisitioned for us – a large house on Lake Maggiore, with extensive gardens on the lakeside.
>
> *Beautiful Flowers And How To Grow Them* – a few months after my fourth birthday my parents gave me this large Edwardian garden book full of delightful watercolour illustrations and neat little line drawings [...]

This is followed by eleven lyrical paragraphs about the setting, the garden, the contents of *Beautiful Flowers* and related associations, following which Jarman returns to the story:

> After breakfast Davide, her [the housekeeper's] handsome eighteen year old nephew, would place me on the handlebars of his bike and we'd be off down country lanes – or out on to the lake in an old rowing boat, where I would watch him strip in the heat as he rowed round the headland to a secret cove, laughing all the way. He was my first love. (*Modern Nature*, p. 10)

Composing *At Your Own Risk* late in 1991, Jarman describes the same sequence once again:

HOW DAVIDE TURNED MY HEAD

In 1946, my father was posted to Italy. Overnight home was transformed from the bleak wartime married quarters with their coke stoves and mildew to a villa on Lake Maggiore.

Villa Zuassa had beautiful gardens. There I chased lizards among the enormous golden pumpkins that grew along the gravel paths, played hide-and-seek in alleys banked with camellias, or crept off to the gatehouse where a little old lady in the blackest mourning fed armies of silk-worms on trays in the gloom of her front room. She would give me caterpillars and cocoons to take home, and I would be driven back through the woods by her grandson Davide on the handlebars of his bike. He would stop and hoist me on his shoulders to pick a particular flower.

Davide was my first love and the love was returned. He stripped off and rowed me on the lake as summer storms blew in from the mountains. This love was my great secret. If only this innocent idyll could have continued. But after a brief summer we left for Rome. (*At Your Own Risk*, pp. 14–15)

In *Modern Nature*, the entwined memories of the house, the garden and the boy are contextualised: they take place 'a few months after [his] fourth birthday'. He provides a stream of lyrical impressions of childhood: the rain, the profusion of green, and much-loved books acquire a totemic quality; the rush of a precocious infatuation that he remembers in motion, from the heady vantage point of 'the handlebars of his bike'. In its position, this tone makes sense: Jarman places this in the month that begins with his statement that flowers act as bindweed in his memory.

During this February, the changes he sees in his Dungeness garden spark recollections of gardens that strongly recall his past. These start with those of the private house Villa Zuassa, but progress to the public Borghese Gardens, National Trust property Sissinghurst, and his family garden in Cambridge. The earlier passage, from 1982, makes no explicit mention of Jarman's feelings for the older boy, content with describing him as 'the handsome one', and spells 'Davide' 'Davido'. *At Your Own Risk* has a different purpose. Although a touch of the lyricism remains, it is truncated from two pages to a paragraph. The title of the extract, 'HOW DAVIDE TURNED MY HEAD', explicitly suggests its conclusion – his youthful love. However, in this passage, Jarman does not point out that at the time he was only four. The way that he inflects the passage ('Davide was my first love and the love was returned'; 'he stripped off and rowed me on the lake'; 'This love was my great secret') makes it sound almost like a teenage love affair, drawing attention to the romantic passion that a small child is quite capable of feeling. The result is markedly different from the earlier passage. On the one hand, this process of rewriting creates a productive tension between what John Sturrock describes as 'the writer's will to singularity and the autobiographical act itself, which restores by conventional and rhetorical means the harmony between the writer and a community of readers'.[49] From Dungeness, Jarman writes that 'I sit here in the dark holding a candle that throws my divided shadow across the room, and gathers my thoughts to the flame like moths' (*Modern Nature*, p. 20). A 'divided shadow' might be read as twinned versions of the same events – the difference between two shadows cast from the same object, but onto different walls, from different angles.

In seeking this 'singularity', even between his own texts, Jarman enacts the perspective that one cannot maintain anything other than a fractured identity.[50] He is unable and unwilling to make a fixed shape from the fragments that make up a life: all structures and stories are temporarily imposed upon his material. This creates a further interesting tension between Jarman and his readers. Sturrock describes the 'will to association [that] lies in the existence of autobiography itself, as the most sociable of literary acts'.[51] How should one reconcile the social nature of the autobiographical act with the instability of this genre – and in particular, the instability of Jarman's inconsistent autobiographical representations? Jarman was dismissive of the postmodernism that characterised the late 1980s and early 1990s ('Everywhere there is the failure of nerve, failure of intellect: look at the ghastly Legoland of post-modernism thrown up without a care for social value', *Smiling in Slow Motion*, pp. 233–4). Nonetheless, he produced work that was a product of its time in terms of its preoccupation with fragmented, time-based subjectivities. In the light of his illnesses, Jarman may also have wanted to create hybrid, reconsidered versions of events described several years earlier: the knowledge of one's mortality does much to sharpen observations over time.

As a famous man, Jarman had the opportunity to use his public status to challenge versions of the truth and to drive political meanings in a more artistic way. In the spin on events Jarman puts on the Davide story in *At Your Own Risk*, he is pushing this youthful encounter: emphasising it as a political act. Jarman writes about the process of life-writing in *Modern Nature*: 'One part of me hates the idea of the author, I recognise the importance of individual experience but it is also important to understand that we are related to one another as we are individualised' (*Modern Nature*, p. 212). It makes sense to use your own experience in different ways for wider effect.

Yet Jarman also problematises his own memories and disquieting cultural tropes in order for him to grasp the patterns he is trying to fashion, albeit fleetingly, from his life and history. But, in the end, issues tend to be dropped unresolved: a point of departure, or a topic for debate. There is no final answer. This seems to be a result of his desire to create an allusive form that interprets his past while simultaneously proving that the same form is a conceit thus can never be definitive. Speaking of himself, Roland Barthes wrote in *Roland Barthes by Roland Barthes*: 'Liking to find, to write *beginnings*, he tends to multiply this pleasure: that is why he writes fragments: so many fragments, so many beginnings, so many pleasures (but he doesn't like the ends: the risk of the rhetorical clausule is too great'.[52]

Notes

1. Dillon, *Derek Jarman and Lyric Film*, p. 228.
2. Alain de Botton et al., 'Essential Reading: Nine Experts on the Books That Inspired Them', *Observer*, 8 January 2017, www.theguardian.com/books/2017/jan/08/essential-reading-experts-inspiration-film-law-philosophy-economics-history-psychology-music-nature (accessed 26 November 2017). Olivia Laing wrote the foreword to a new edition of *Modern Nature*, published by Vintage in May 2018.
3. Jim Ellis, 'Renaissance Things: Objects, Ethics, and Temporalities in Derek Jarman's *Caravaggio* (1986) and *Modern Nature* (1991)', *Shakespeare Bulletin*, 32.3 (2014), 375–92 (p. 389).
4. Peake, *Derek Jarman*, p. 488. Peake was writing about Jarman's sense of an audience for *At Your Own Risk*, published in 1992, the year after *Modern Nature*.
5. Chambers, *Facing It*, p. 7.
6. Peake, *Derek Jarman*, p. 480.
7. For a detailed list of anecdotes about the different letters Jarman received, see Peake, *Derek Jarman*, pp. 480–1.
8. De Botton et al., 'Essential Reading'.
9. Daniel O'Quinn, 'Gardening, History and the Escape from Time: Derek Jarman's *Modern Nature*', *October*, 89 (Summer 1999), 113–26 (p. 116).
10. Derek Duncan, 'Solemn Geographies: AIDS and the Contours of Autobiography', *a/b: Auto/Biography Studies*, 15.1 (Summer 2000), 22–36 (p. 33).
11. See Jim Ellis, 'The Temporality of Dirt: Queer Materiality in Jarman's *Modern Nature*', *ESC: English Studies in Canada*, 40.2 (2014), 9–13, and Ellis, 'Renaissance Things'.
12. See Tom Ratekin, *Final Acts: Traversing the Fantasy in the Modern Memoir* (Albany: State University of New York Press, 2010), pp. 107–38.
13. Deborah Esch, *In the Event: Reading Journalism, Reading Theory* (Stanford, CA: Stanford University Press, 2000), pp. 116–34.
14. Peake, *Derek Jarman*, p. 462.

15 Michael O'Pray, *Derek Jarman: Dreams of England* (London: British Film Institute, 1996), p. 14.
16 Chambers, *Facing It*, p. 5.
17 Duncan, 'Solemn Geographies', p. 25.
18 Douglas Crimp, 'Introduction', *October*, 43 (Winter 1987), 3–16 (p. 4).
19 Chambers, *Facing It*, p. 7.
20 Brophy, *Witnessing AIDS*, p. 30.
21 Dorothy Wordsworth, quoted in *Modern Nature*, p. 68.
22 Ellis, 'The Temporality of Dirt', p. 11.
23 Carla Freccero, *Queer/Early/Modern* (Durham, NC: Duke University Press, 2006), p. 75.
24 Keith Collins, 'Editor's Preface', in *Smiling in Slow Motion*, n.p.
25 Georges Gusdorf, 'Conditions and Limits of Autobiography', in *Autobiography: Essays Theoretical and Critical*, ed. and trans. James Olney (Princeton, N.J.: Princeton University Press, 1980), p. 35.
26 Ibid.
27 John Sturrock, *The Language of Autobiography: Studies in the First Person Singular* (Cambridge: Cambridge University Press, 1993), p. 18.
28 Gunnthorunn Gudmundsdottir, *Borderlines: Autobiography and Fiction in Postmodern Life Writing* (Amsterdam: Editions Rodopi, 2003), p. 26.
29 Cited in Peake, *Derek Jarman*, p. 321.
30 Brophy, *Witnessing AIDS*, p. 30.
31 Eric Michaels, *Unbecoming* (Durham, NC: Duke University Press, 1997), p. 129.
32 Simon Watney, 'Introduction', in Eric Michaels, *Unbecoming* (Durham, NC: Duke University Press, 1997), pp. xxi–xxv (p. xxiv).
33 Chambers, *Facing It*, p. 10.
34 Sedgwick, *Epistemology of the Closet*, p. 41.
35 Tim Lawrence, 'AIDS, the Problem of Representation, and Plurality in Derek Jarman's *Blue*', *Social Text: Queer Transexions of Race, Nation and Gender*, 52–53 (Autumn–Winter 1997), 241–64 (p. 243).
36 Chambers, *Facing It*, p. 10.
37 Ellis, 'The Temporality of Dirt', p. 11.
38 See Havelock Ellis and John Addington Symonds, *Sexual Inversion: A Critical Edition*, ed. Ivan Crozier (Basingstoke: Palgrave Macmillan, 2008), p. 96.
39 Royal Horticultural Society, 'Bindweed', n.d., http://apps.rhs.org.uk/advicesearch/Profile.aspx?pid=241 (accessed 16 March 2012).
40 Jarman's passage on the importance of rosemary for remembrance also draws from classical culture. 'In ancient Greece young men wore garlands of rosemary in their hair to stimulate the mind; perhaps the gathering of the Symposium was scented with it' (*Modern Nature*, p. 9).
41 Ovid, *Metamorphoses*, trans. David Raeburn (London: Penguin, 2004) p. 116.
42 Ibid., pp. 109, 112.
43 Sigmund Freud, 'On Narcissism: An Introduction', in *The Freud Reader*, ed. Peter Gay (London: Vintage, 1995), pp. 545–61 (p. 554).

44 Roy Vickery, *A Dictionary of Plant Lore* (Oxford University Press, Oxford: 1995), p. 35.
45 William Wordsworth, 'I Wandered Lonely As a Cloud', *The Norton Anthology of Poetry*, 4th edn, eds. Margaret Ferguson, Mary Jo Salter, Jon Stallworthy (New York: W. W. Norton, 1996), pp. 732–3.
46 O'Quinn, 'Gardening, History and the Escape from Time', pp. 115–16.
47 Peake, *Derek Jarman*, p. 427.
48 Derek Jarman, 'Dancing Ledge' journal (1982), Box 17, *Derek Jarman's Papers*, BFI Archive (London).
49 Sturrock, *The Language of Autobiography*, p. 12.
50 Ibid.
51 Ibid., p. 18.
52 Roland Barthes, *Roland Barthes by Roland Barthes*, trans. Richard Howard (New York: Hill and Wang, 1977), p. 94.

8

Queer Edward II: 'Are *you* a closet bigot?'

Derek Jarman's political anger underlies his oeuvre.[1] In the hostile climate of Britain under Margaret Thatcher (1979–90) and her successor John Major (1990–97), he re-evaluates history, rehabilitating queer cultural figures from the past and using their lives as material to inform how to live in a time of crisis. The resurgence of state-sanctioned homophobia in the 1980s following the beginning of the AIDS crisis prompted a considered reaction from many within LGBTQ+ communities. This cultural climate of activism was brought into sharp focus following the reintroduction of legislative initiative 'Clause 28' in December 1987 (passed into law as Section 28 in May 1988), which prohibited local authorities from 'promoting homosexuality by teaching or by publishing material', or to 'promote the teaching in any maintained school of the acceptability of homosexuality as a pretended family relationship'.[2]

Organisations including direct action groups ACT UP London, OutRage! and the Sisters of Perpetual Indulgence, as well as the lobbying group Stonewall, campaigned against the introduction of the clause as a discriminatory, intolerant and unjust law. Whether through protests, direct action, theatrical zaps or directly approaching MPs and Peers, these direct action groups advocated for political and social change. After publicly declaring his HIV-positive status in 1987, Jarman became an active political campaigner for the first time. As well as being a protestor himself, Jarman used his writing, life and films to manifest his commitment to speaking out, activism and political action to redress inequalities.[3]

This chapter discusses the role of the text *Queer Edward II*, which was published alongside the release of Jarman's film adaptation of Christopher Marlowe's *Edward II* in the early summer of 1991. The inscription states that the book is '*dedicated to: the repeal of all anti-gay laws, particularly Section 28*', and the book is far more than a published script to complement the film. I consider its role as an artefact, distinct from the film that prompted its production, and examine how it operates as a queer activist text that both acts as a marker of solidarity for its queer readers and an unexpected means of protest. The book provides a focused reaction against Section 28 to a much greater extent than the film in part by foregrounding the figure of the queer child alongside the slogans that punctuate the text. By rehabilitating the context and history of the book, which has to date not received significant scholarly attention, this essay demonstrates its relevance to understandings of Jarman's varied body of work.

In his journal *Smiling in Slow Motion*, Jarman reports, 'At six the screening of Edward for the investors – a great success. Colin MacCabe said Kit Marlowe would have smiled, it was a great improvement on the original' (p. 18). Jarman places MacCabe's comment prominently throughout *Queer Edward II*: it has a running title of *'improved by* DEREK JARMAN' on the recto pages. A collaboration and a bricolage, the book combines photographs, provocative slogans, an 'improved' version of Marlowe's play, and diaristic comments from Jarman, Tilda Swinton (the film's Isabella and a recurrent presence in Jarman's films) and associate director Ken Butler. Jarman collects fragments from other texts – whether early modern, medieval or even from the writings of church fathers – and combines these with the detritus of his everyday life: gifts from friends, memories or notes made in the margins of a working script. Presenting and using diverse aspects of queer lives, the resulting script is a highly unusual activist statement that remains effective more than twenty years on. The way Jarman melds personal commentaries on a theatrical event with the remnants of Marlowe's text produces new connections that explore Jarman's ideas of the interconnectedness of queer experience.

The book's presentation encapsulates the approach of its contents. The regal cover design – gold lettering on thick, burgundy cartridge – is at first glance traditional. However, Jarman's use of large gold letters to spell out 'Queer', with its camp excess, points to the way the book's contents ransack the past to comment on the present. On the title page of *Queer Edward II*, Jarman comments 'How to make a film of a gay love affair and get it commissioned. Find a dusty old play and violate it'. The film was produced by Working Title producers Antony Root and Steve Clark-Hall, and funded by the BBC and British Screen. Naturally, commissions come with constraints. Michael O'Pray comments that 'In conversation with myself and Colin MacCabe on the day he handed in the script to the BBC, Jarman with some glee promised an *Edward II* which would be a "blue movie" filled with explicit fucking – an orgy of sex'.[4] This plan changed, however, throughout the working process. Following the film's production, Jarman comments, 'George is to recut the boys fucking from the first sequence of Edward for the BBC's screening next week. We are hoping they will have a change of heart but we are trapped. The commissioning editors are allies, but above them are Mrs Thatcher's accountants' (*Smiling in Slow Motion*, p. 18).[5]

In contrast, *Queer Edward II* was not subject to the considerations of the BBC, but instead offered Jarman freer rein to pursue his agenda. In his biography of Jarman, Peake describes the inception of the book:

> Initial attempts to interest a publisher in a combination of the original play script and the film script, plus a commentary and a plethora of illustrations in the form of design sketches and stills, had failed. Meanwhile, Jarman had been speaking to a new collaborator, a young man called Malcolm Sutherland who was well versed in desktop publishing. Sutherland and Jarman decided to produce the book themselves, whereupon the BFI came to their rescue. Colin MacCabe put an office in Soho at their disposal and, on the understanding that the two authors would take responsibility for the design and compilation of the book, agreed to pay their basic costs, then print and distribute the finished article.[6]

Unmediated by investors seeking to shape the content, this varied text, as Ellis points out, works 'not to take us behind the scenes, but rather to show us the continuity between what is happening in front of the camera and what is happening all around it'.[7] This chapter examines how Jarman juxtaposes different eras, voices and genres to produce his activist text. To contextualise how unusual this film script is, I will briefly touch on the publication of film scripts, which often form quite an unpromising genre. *Queer Edward II* is startling because of what it's not. For example, Faber published a series of film scripts in the 1990s, including Jarman's *War Requiem*. All the scripts in this series are very similar to a play script, with a few grainy stills from the film. *War Requiem* does not contain any of the elucidatory introductory material that scripts from plays often include. Any audience would be intensely specialised, for keen fans of a particular film. *Queer Edward II* is very different – an example of what Jarman does when given a free hand to make the kind of text he wanted to make.

Jarman has produced what is at times a highly personal book, but one that always seeks to use what Joan Scott describes as this 'authority of experience' to enact Jarman's commitment to what he calls 'politics in the first person' (*At Your Own Risk*, p. 121).[8] When *Edward II* was released, Jarman had been famous for some time, predominantly for his work as an art-house filmmaker. His first feature film, *Sebastiane*, drew attention for its entirely Latin script and explicit depictions of homosexual desire. His biopic, *Caravaggio*, was reviewed extensively in the national press. As such, he was in a position to use his influence in order to publicise and combat the repressive turn that Britain had taken in the wake of the AIDS crisis under Thatcher's third-term government, which was complicit with – nay, encouraged – the resurgence in homophobia across the country.

This context was recently discussed by performer and director Neil Bartlett and AIDS activist Simon Watney in a conversation titled 'Remembering

Derek', on what would have been Jarman's 72nd birthday on 31 January 2014: in the intense homophobia in the decade following the arrival of the HIV/AIDS epidemic in Britain, just walking past newsagents became a trial due to the virulent homophobic sentiments in newspaper headlines by much of the press.[9] Jackie Stacey notes that the virus prompted 'an increased pathologization of homosexuality, associating it with promiscuity, disease and a risk to both public health and morality'.[10] A social environment that refused to differentiate between queer relationships and the spread of HIV enabled the conception of Section 28. The association between sexual object choice and disease, including in the wording of Section 28, enabled queer relationships to become a fraught public issue: by being seen to curtail access to information, particularly in schools, the government sought to intervene in the formation of sexual behaviour and thus ensure the safety of the wider population. However, by excluding LGBT support groups and appearing to prevent teachers from speaking out against victims of homophobic bullying, the clause was endangering vulnerable children. In addition, the idea that homosexuality could be 'promoted' indicated the government believed that queer desire was a negative choice that children could be persuaded to make, and the clause gave the impression that the state-sanctioned homophobia, whether inside or outside the classroom.

In *Queer Edward II*, Jarman creates a politically engaged text that often uses an interesting combination of autobiographical subject matter alongside the figure of the young Jody Graber, the actor who played Prince Edward in the film, to draw attention to the faulty reasoning of advocates of the clause. By drawing on the viewpoints of a variety of contributors, Jarman demonstrates the relevance of the project to a wider community, explored later in this chapter.

Who wrote *Queer Edward II*? On multiple authorship

Queer Edward II contains a range of voices: there is considerable complexity behind the construction of the text. The screenplay was adapted from Marlowe's play by two people: Jarman and Stephen McBride (who also appeared in *The Garden*), and thus contains the authorial decisions of three distinct individuals. Another collaborator, Greg Taylor, provided the slogans that dominate each page. The commentary running down the right of the page is predominantly shaped by Jarman's recollections and notes, but also contains asides by close friends and collaborators Tilda Swinton and Ken Butler. Pascale Aebischer notes that 'Significantly, Jarman co-authored the book with Tilda Swinton and Ken Butler, that is, with two collaborators who were immersed in feminist performance practice and queer theory'.[11] The pair contributed to many of the decisions on set. Their theoretical engagement complicates any sense in this text that the commentary is simply a collection of notes in the margin of a script. Ken Butler's voice is denoted by '(G)', short for Ghost Director, and Swinton's by '(IR)', for Isabella Regina. These voices rarely enter into the commentary, however, although Butler's voice became more frequent as filming progressed and Jarman sometimes found himself too unwell to direct. In a book with approximately eighty pages containing these diaristic notes, Butler has thirteen brief statements, Swinton only six. Nearly all the commentary is written by Jarman, with the three occasionally in conversation with one another about events on set. Although the text contains multiple voices, Jarman worked closely with just one other collaborator when compiling the book, as described by Peake earlier in this chapter. This was a practice that Jarman returned to when compiling *At Your Own Risk* later that year. Peake explains that 'because his health made collaboration with others more pressing than ever, he worked on the book with a handful of young men who could help with the research'.[12] Jarman enlisted Sutherland's help once again, along with Collins and others. It was expedient for Jarman to work with others partly because of his increasingly fragile health, but partly because this working style allowed for a multiplicity of voices to influence the finished project.

Does the variety of voices in *Queer Edward II* affect how we should read the creative or political purpose of the text, and can it be read as authored by Jarman? Due to the way Jarman uses material from his own life, there is a temptation to read his work as a specifically autobiographical project. The commentary in *Queer Edward II* contains highly personal details regarding his failing health. If a reader is never quite sure who authored the text, the specific, personal elements become less individual and instead more easily interpretable as material to underline a furious, activist attack on state responses to the AIDS crisis and homosexuality more generally. He is uninterested in displaying a unity of vision, concentrating instead on the richness of the ideas that come out of this collaborative working process. As the director of a film, he relies on the talents of co-workers, who all produce work under the director's 'brand'. Don Boyd, the producer for several of Jarman's films, commented in his introduction to *War Requiem* that Jarman's 'collaborative intense working process, which is unique in the cinema of today, has its precedents in the studios of the Italian Renaissance, where painters employed other highly creative craftsmen and artists to help them execute their work'.[13] Having found this working style fruitful, Jarman transfers it from one medium into another: here, it facilitates the production of this book. The fluidity of authorship in *Queer Edward II*, however, is ultimately controlled by Jarman. The running title

Figure 22 Prince Edward (Jody Graber) in *Queer Edward II*, p. 33.

of the script, '*improved by* DEREK JARMAN', humorously demonstrates this control.

'Save queer children from straight parents': Representing the queer child

Queer Edward II has spare, elegantly arranged pages. Each recto is dominated by a photograph by Liam Daniel, taken during the filming of *Edward II*.[14] The verso is divided into several sections. A confrontational slogan is provided by Greg Taylor, one of the text's contributors. A short sequence taken from Stephen McBride and Jarman's adaptation of Marlowe's text runs down the left-hand side and down the central margin, there is a commentary in italics mainly from Jarman, but occasionally with sentences from Swinton and Butler.

The pages devoted to the section in the film labelled 'Sequence 16' in *Queer Edward II* bear further analysis (pp. 32–3). This single spread from the book demonstrates the book's potential as an activist text. The scene heading describes 'Mortimer and chorus, who resemble the benches of the House of Commons, in the shadows discover the weeping queen with Prince Edward' (*Queer Edward II*, p. 32). A brief dialogue between Mortimer

(Nigel Terry) and the chorus describes the queen's abject state. In the film, the scene is short: the chorus, unlit, loom behind the seated queen (Tilda Swinton), as the young prince (Jody Graber) plays at her feet. They discuss her pain but, significantly, do not engage with her. The scene in the film is a departure from Marlowe's text, where Mortimer Junior (as he is known in the play) converses with the queen.[15] Significantly for my argument, Marlowe makes no indication that Prince Edward is present.

In contrast, the focus of this sequence in *Queer Edward II* is the onlooker, the young Edward. The photographic frame is filled with the prince (see Figure 22). The shot is striking for its near-symmetry: the disk of his mother's wide-brimmed hat forms a halo that continues out of the shot, as he faces the camera. His features are large and feminine; his lips are glossed. The heavy tweed jacket that he is wearing looks too big for him and recalls the weekend tweed of the upper classes. It's overly grown-up for the little boy, who seems dwarfed by its sloping shoulders. Standing between traditional gender stereotypes, the boy is intended to form a disruptive image to *Edward II*'s adult audience in 1991: the figure of the queer child. Kathryn Bond Stockton explores the idea of the queer child as a retrospectively constituted phenomenon. 'The child is precisely who we are not and, in fact, never were. It is the act of adults looking back', she argues.[16] What is illuminating here is that Stockton demonstrates how we overlay our nostalgia on our understanding of the child, meaning we only see our own desire to recognise a queer childhood rather than the child itself. By 'child' I mean not someone of any particular age, but rather the idea of the child – the fiction of the child that is reproduced by adults looking back upon their own pasts, but fundamentally altering it by bringing to bear many of the attitudes and experiences of the intervening years on their interpretation of this history. Jarman, here, plays with this notion: in the context of Section 28's aim to restrict access to education regarding queer experience, Jarman recognised the political importance of highlighting adults' wilfully blinkered understanding of childhood experience. Further, Jarman's focus on the queer child offers a challenge to what Lee Edelman argues is the dominant conception of 'the child' as the keystone of a politics of compulsory heterosexual reproductive futurism. To unpack this, the child is a symbol of the product of, and future for, reproduction and traditional family structures. Jarman disrupts this notion, this 'sentimentalized cultural identification' overlaid upon the child, by presenting a symbolic child who does not conform to type.[17]

Jarman extends this presentation further in the book than in the film through his use of accompanying commentary and through the use of the large slogan 'PENETRATE *the Rambo Bimbo DIVIDE*'. The commentary that runs down the right margin of the verso begins by describing this scene in *Edward II*. Jarman comments, 'Chorus materialises like shadows. Jody switches on a flashing robot. This is the third film we've made together. He was happy not to be in pyjamas again. Did you wear your mother's clothes?' (*Queer Edward II*, p. 32). The actor who plays the prince is referred to by his real name, which indicates that we can read the image as depicting the young actor himself (see Figure 23). By both highlighting the identity of the young actor and by confronting his readership with a direct question, Jarman demonstrates the relevance of the choices within the film to the world outside it. In this instance, he invites his readers to recall their childhood transgressions in order to demonstrate the artificial nature of the social constructions that are subsequently forced upon us. Martin Quinn-Meyler suggests that Edward/Jody demonstrates that 'existing efforts at compulsory heterosexist education are not only unacceptable, but also ultimately futile'.[18] Jarman argues that for many, childhood sexuality emerges well before most adults are willing to admit. As he points out in his polemic book of life-writing, *At Your Own Risk*, 'I was aware of my sexuality at nine, which makes a nonsense of an age of consent of twenty-one and of the ideas of CONVERSION, PERVERSION and COR-RUPTION of youth' (p. 20). In addition, as Pascale Aebischer notes, 'The boy's transgressive cross-dressing is clearly inspired not by his homosexual father and his partner, whose gender performances are masculine even as their desires are same-sex, but by the exaggerated femininity of his heterosexual mother'.[19] The film goes further than this: the boy does not self-present entirely as female. In this photograph, a promotional still from the film, he blends a variety of traditionally gendered clothes, as he does in the final sequences where he wears a smart, black suit but with Isabella's earrings and high heels (see Figure 24). It is this selective transformation that is particularly queer, because it demonstrates a refusal to be bound by any gender category.

'I wish *my* aunt were a lesbian': The importance of queer history

Jarman uses the figure of the prince to represent a collective queer childhood.[20] In *Queer Edward II*, he doesn't significantly differentiate between fragments from his own, and from others' lives, instead insisting on the equal power of these plural personal histories. One example of how he encourages this reading is his use of Prince Edward/Jody. O'Pray cites an interview in which Jarman mentions that 'there is an element of young Edward being me but everyone identifies with the child and he is the same child in all my films'.[21] This is important: Jarman allows that the child represents himself as a child, but he is also very open to others seeing the

Queer Edward II: *'Are you a closet bigot?'*   157

Figure 23 Prince Edward (Jody Graber) in *Edward II*.

Figure 24 Prince Edward (Jody Graber) dancing on the caged Queen Isabella (Tilda Swinton) and Mortimer (Nigel Terry) in *Edward II*.

boy as representative of their own childhood selves – whether his friends and colleagues or the audience of the film. He promotes the hermeneutic possibilities of his work, which enables others to participate in it through self-identification.

Jarman explains the importance of representing his own life near the beginning of *At Your Own Risk*. As this book mentions previously, a significant motivation for introducing autobiographical elements into his work and for searching out histories that would undo the 'absence of the past' (*At Your Own Risk*, p. 30) was that he felt a pressing responsibility to provide this social act. As with Prince Edward/Jody, the child not only has a representative function for Jarman himself, but also shares his meaning, standing for any child – and any of our childhoods. As a result, Jarman seeks to depict a queer lineage across time.

By adapting *Edward II* – a story of queer desire composed in the late sixteenth century but referring to events from the early fourteenth – Jarman demonstrates the continuity of queer desire across time, including the late twentieth century of the film's production. By searching for this lineage, Jarman provides an important social record that seeks to inscribe queer experience into history by rehabilitating the queer context of the lives of important cultural figures from the past. Jarman began to pursue these connections while he was taking his first degree in the early sixties at King's College London. He comments: 'I began to read between the lines of history. The hunt was on for forebears who validated my existence' (*At Your Own Risk*, p. 46). He found what he was looking for, taking pleasure in investigating, for example, the Queer Renaissance of 'Lorenzo di Medici, Michelangelo, Leonardo [...] Caravaggio, Shakespeare, Marlowe, [and] Bacon' (*At Your Own Risk*, p. 46).

Jarman further deepens his response to Edward II's history in *Queer Edward II* by culling quotes from other sources. Reprising his scholarly background, Jarman created what Ellis terms a 'Queer Period', where Jarman demonstrates a complex engagement with these historical paradigms. He uses them not to 'revisit an imagined past of grace, simplicity and noble suffering', but instead to create activist work that speaks to the present.[22] He starts to explore the notion that the power of the English state has relied on the repression of homosexuality since the time of Edward II. Following Jarman's diagnosis as HIV positive in late 1986, his work could no longer simply search for forebears, but began to represent homophobic panic throughout the ages in order to comment on the urgent crises in the present.

The notes to the right of the play text that form a running commentary throughout *Queer Edward II* continue with a succession of snippets taken from Jarman's reading about the Plantagenets. This begins '*Medieval fag-lore. Queer hares. "The hare grows a new anus each year"*' Jarman pauses to interrupt '*(lucky for some)*' before continuing – '"*hyenas alternate between male and female each year." A confusion of lusty imaginings in the mind of Clement of Alexandria*' (*Queer Edward II*, p. 32). Dating from the first century AD, the Epistle of Barnabas contains the above lore, which was picked up on and developed by Clement of Alexandria during the following century. These gems were incorporated into the *Physiologus*, which Barbara Creed describes as 'One of the most widely read books of the medieval period, said to be as popular as the Bible', and which John Boswell calls 'a manual of piety, a primer of zoology, and a form of entertainment'.[23]

Jarman follows this excerpt with a statement from '*Ugly Archbishop Carey*', declaring that '"*Gay men are unfit to be ordained as priests*"' (*Queer Edward II*, p. 32). George Carey had been enthroned as Archbishop of Canterbury less than a month after *Edward II* finished filming, at the time that Jarman was preparing the text for *Queer Edward II*. Jarman then returns to religious forefathers, citing fourth-century Archbishop of Constantinople, Saint John Chrysostum: '"*And this is not even the worst, which is that this outrage is perpetrated with the utmost openness*"' (*Queer Edward II*, p. 32). In parentheses, Jarman quips '*(Where was he?)*'. Subsequently, Jarman quotes the medieval chronicler and Benedictine monk Ralph Higden, author of the *Polychronicon*: '*Edward in fact delighted inordinately in the vice of sodomy*'. Jarman juxtaposes the logical '*confusion*' and prurient '*outrage*' (*Queer Edward II*, p. 32) about queer encounters from up to 2,000 years ago with contemporary opinions. This demonstrates the utter backwardness of Britain in 1991 by highlighting the lack of progress in the thinking of those in positions of authority, in this case within the church.

'Out, proud and livid': Activism in *Queer Edward II*

Jarman demonstrated his belief in the force of queer activism not only through his involvement with protests or by bringing those involved in activist groups into his films, but in his writing.[24] Just as Jarman used his celebrity status to draw attention to political agendas such as the 'Equality Now' campaign by the direct action group OutRage!, he hoped to raise political consciousness amongst his readers. One of the most visible ways that Jarman attempts this in *Queer Edward II* is by using the queer trope of subverting dominant discourses in order to demonstrate how easy it is to deconstruct them. By demonstrating how prone to disassembly these 'residual biases' are, Jarman thereby hopes to cause those who propound them to reconsider these formerly stable categories.[25]

The choice of words displayed as the large slogan that dominates the verso of 'Sequence 16' states: '*PENETRATE the Rambo Bimbo DIVIDE*' (*Queer Edward II*, p. 32). This imperative invites reading directly in relation to the photograph of young actor Jody Graber to the right, sitting outside of Marlowe's text or Jarman's adaptation of it. In this context, the '*Rambo Bimbo DIVIDE*' describes how most of Western society brings its children up to enact their gender roles unambiguously. This choice of vocabulary points to the caricatured fairy tale in which the attractive but mentally inferior bimbo defers to the aggressive attentions of Sylvester Stallone's Rambo, willingly complicit in her subordination. Imperatives we have been given from a young age – for example, either to 'be a man' or be scolded 'that's not very ladylike' – serve to inculcate this fixed sense of gender.[26] To use the verb 'penetrate' rather than, for example, smash or collapse, is confrontational, especially when coupled with this image of a child: it draws our attention to fraught understandings of childhood and sexual activity. Jarman thereby highlights how we tend retrospectively to project adult interpretations of childhood sexuality onto children. Following Stockton's hypothesis in *The Queer Child*, this projection is often problematically entwined with inflections of morality, innocence and guilt.

The queer child is just one example of the borders between the work of art and the world breaking down. The OutRage! demonstration scene in the film clearly shows us the continuity between what is happening in front of the camera and what is happening all around it. In this scene, Isabella coldly denounces her husband from an empty room as opposing forces approach one another on the ground. Her army is comprised of riot police, ominously striking their batons against their shields and advancing in formation. Edward (Stephen Waddington), on the other hand, is shown rallying his supporters: a group of OutRage! activists chant slogans and wave banners as the demonstration descends into violence against the ill-armed protestors. As Peter Tatchell comments, 'We were in a section of the film which spliced the real story of *Edward II*'s homophobic murder with real life queer activism against anti-gay violence'.[27] By making this link explicit, *Edward II* denies that there are borders between the film and the world. This is even more prominent in *Queer Edward II*, where activist slogans are present on every page. Dillon notes that 'The slogans shout down the poetry, [and] are happily reductive [...]. But why choose Marlowe at all if one is just going to run down the past?'[28] In *Queer Edward II*, Jarman explains: 'In our film all the OutRage boys and girls are inheritors of Edward's story' (p. 146). The 'happily reductive' nature of the OutRage! slogans, rather than 'shout[ing] down the poetry', productively clash with Jarman's choice of material from the past.[29] In his next book of life-writing, *At Your Own Risk*, Jarman uses hostile quotes culled from the media in order to demonstrate the pressing need for activism and the legitimacy of such a move when traditional tactics have gone unnoticed. *Queer Edward II* uses a different tactic – slogans from collaborator Greg Taylor, some of which are from OutRage!, which invert well-known examples of prejudice and censure against gay men and lesbians, including:

'Open your mind *not* your big mouth' (p. 34)
'*our* orientation is not *your* decision' (p. 38)

'**anus** – the last place the government […/ …] should be poking its nose' (pp. 80, 82)
'if you must be heterosexual, please *try* to be discreet' (p. 104)
'Get cured – HOMOPHOBIA is a social disease' (p. 106)
'you're ignorant, arrogant & boring – we're just a little queer' (p. 108)
'So, what do you think caused your heterosexuality?' (p. 112)

Initiated in 1990, OutRage!, the group that claims to 'puts the camp into campaigning', drew 'largely on camp and parody, with bold slogans and a series of photographic stunts which accompanied researched press releases and handouts'.[30] Jarman's adoption of their approach disarms through its camp, almost absurd, humour.

'Intercourse has never occurred in private'

Jarman finishes the commentary on the page of *Queer Edward II* that I have been discussing (pp. 32–3) with the following: '*I first fucked with a young man in the basement of 64, Priory Road. I was 23, it was 1965*' (p. 32).[31] It is direct and possibly confrontational to some readers, but it is also collaborative in the way it talks about sex: instead of 'I fucked' or 'he fucked me,' suggesting either passivity or its converse, it's 'I fucked with'. Here, Jarman refuses the power dynamic inherent in the more common structure of this phrase. Following on from Higden's declaration that Edward '*delighted inordinately in the vice of sodomy*' (*Queer Edward II*, p. 32), Jarman's spare autobiographical statement seems both poignant and mundane. Why does Jarman mention this formative sexual experience here? One of Jarman's workbooks for the *Edward II* film contains a photograph of the young Jarman, reading in a garden, pasted into its inside front cover (see Figure 25). In the notes to the published *Derek Jarman's Sketchbooks*, Collins has commented: 'An ancient photograph of Derek [. . .] whilst a student at the Slade. The photograph is weirdly inserted into this sketchbook'.[32] Jarman's handwritten note to the side of the photograph reads 'Lawrence found this in clearout'.[33] Jarman's early book of life-writing, *Dancing Ledge*, holds a very similar photograph taken on the same occasion, with the caption 'In the garden at Priory Road, 1965' (*Dancing Ledge*, p. 68). One could suggest that Jarman's discovery of the photograph prompted this memory of a formative sexual experience in *Queer Edward II*. The chance reminder of a certain time, the basement flat in a middle-class Victorian house in West Hampstead, is used to wed the work to the reality from which it has been constructed. Jarman uses material from his private self to show the pressing need to revisit and reinterpret the historical status quo. As the only fragment

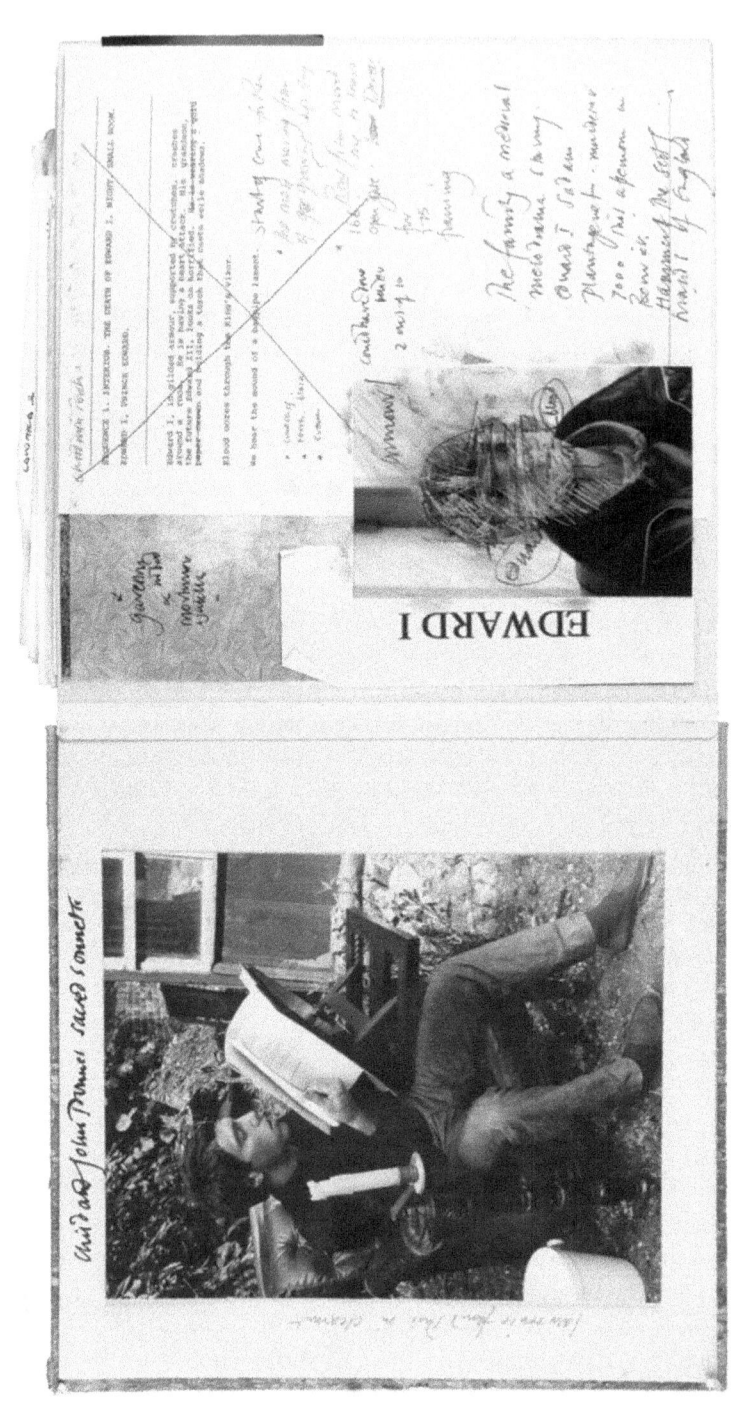

Figure 25 Spread from one of Jarman's 'Edward II' journals, showing a collage of personal and work material.

to be dated in this series, it leaves an impression that the other quotations are as likely to have been penned in the present day as in the past, and thus require active intervention to disrupt their continuation.

Alongside one of the Lightborn/Edward dungeon sequences in *Queer Edward II*, Jarman comments: '*The past is the past, as you try to make material out of it, things slip even further away*' (*Queer Edward II*, p. 86).[34] Using this inevitable loss to his advantage, Jarman's practical use of the past thoughtfully addresses the homophobia of the oppressive political climate of the then present. He juxtaposes these different historical registers on the page, then underscores this approach by drawing from much more recent history, in the form of the personal testimonies of ordinary gay men whose life stories were not yet finished, including his own. These histories become a wealth of evidence of experience, inciting political anger. Jarman shows how this anger can be transformed into activist interventions, such as this text, to promote social change. It's Jarman's use of childhood, however, that becomes especially divisive. In both *Queer Edward II* and *At Your Own Risk*, Jarman confrontationally foregrounds arguments concerning queer childhood and sexual activity at a young age in order to provoke his audience. By doing so, he hoped to rouse even more of his audience and readers into action, in a time of crisis under a government that continued to legislate against its own citizens.

Notes

1 The quote in the chapter title is from Derek Jarman, *Queer Edward II* (London: British Film Institute, 1991), p. 6. Further references are given within the text.
2 'Section 28: Prohibition on Promoting Homosexuality'.
3 See, for example, Jarman's account of his part in the OutRage! protest march that ended at Bow Street Police Station, famous as the station Oscar Wilde was taken to following his arrest (*Smiling in Slow Motion*, p. 77).
4 O'Pray, *Derek Jarman*, p. 184.
5 Here, 'the boys' denotes the two hustlers depicted naked on p. 7 of *Queer Edward II*, performed by Mark Davis and Andy Jeffrey. Margaret Thatcher had been out of office for more than six months at this point, but Jarman did not differentiate between her tenure and the government under John Major.
6 Peake, *Derek Jarman*, p. 471.
7 Ellis, *Angelic Conversations*, p. 206.
8 Scott, 'The Evidence of Experience', p. 780.
9 Neil Bartlett and Simon Watney, 'Remembering Derek', talk at King's College London Chapel, 31 January 2014, www.kcl.ac.uk/cultural/culturalinstitute/whatson/talksevents/Jarman-events-programme.aspx#RememberingDerek. Examples of homophobic newspaper headlines from the front pages of papers

including the *Sun, News of the World, Daily Mail*, and *Daily Mirror* are given in Jarman's *At Your Own Risk* (pp. 105–11). See also Terry Sanderson's "Mediawatch" column in *Gay Times*, which records the extent of press homophobia in the 1980s.

10 Jackie Stacey, 'Promoting Normality: Section 28 and the Regulation of Sexuality', in *Off-Centre: Feminism and Cultural Studies*, eds. Sarah Franklin, Celia Lury and Jackie Stacey (London: Harper Collins Academic, 1991), pp. 284–304 (p. 284).
11 Aebischer, *Screening Early Modern Drama*, p. 49. Aebischer notes that Butler had studied English at Sussex under Jonathan Dollimore and Alan Sinfield, and had written to Jarman about hearing Michel Foucault speak in America (p. 30).
12 Peake, *Derek Jarman*, p. 489.
13 Don Boyd, 'Introduction by Don Boyd', in *War Requiem*, by Derek Jarman (London: Faber, 1989), pp. vii–x (p. vii).
14 Credited as Liam Longman in the 1991 edition of *Queer Edward II*. The quote in the subheading is from *Queer Edward II*, p. 24.
15 See Christopher Marlowe, *Edward II*, 2nd edn (London: William Jones, 1594; London: Bloomsbury, 1997), pp. 28–9: scene 4, lines 193–229. This edition divides the play into scenes, rather than acts and scenes.
16 Kathryn Bond Stockton, *The Queer Child: Or Growing Sideways in the Twentieth Century* (Durham, NC: Duke University Press, 2009), p. 5.
17 Lee Edelman, *No Future: Queer Theory and the Death Drive* (Durham, NC: Duke University Press, 2004), p. 11.
18 Martin Quinn-Meyler, 'Opposing "Heterosoc": Derek Jarman's Counter-Hegemonic Activism', in *By Angels Driven: The Films of Derek Jarman*, ed. Chris Lippard (Trowbridge: Flicks Books, 1996), pp. 117–34 (p. 126).
19 Aebischer, *Screening Early Modern Drama*, p. 54.
20 The quote in the subheading is from *Queer Edward II*, p. 40.
21 Michael O'Pray, 'Edward II: Damning Desire', *Sight and Sound*, 1.6 (1991), 8–11 (p. 11).
22 Jim Ellis, 'Queer Period: Derek Jarman's Renaissance', in *OutTakes: Essays on Queer Theory and Film*, ed. Ellis Hanson (London and Durham, NC: Duke University Press, 1993), pp. 288–315 (p. 288).
23 Barbara Creed, 'Lesbian Bodies: Tribades, Tomboys and Tarts', in *Sexy Bodies: The Strange Carnalities of Feminism*, eds. Elizabeth Grosz and Elspeth Probyn (London: Routledge, 2013), pp. 86–103 (p. 96); John Boswell, *Christianity, Social Tolerance, and Homosexuality: Gay People in Western Europe from the Beginning of the Christian Era to the Fourteenth Century* (Chicago: University of Chicago Press, 1981), p. 141.
24 The quote in the subheading is from *Queer Edward II*, p. 96.
25 Thomas Cartelli, '*Queer Edward II*: Postmodern Sexualities and the Early Modern Subject', in *Marlowe, History, and Sexuality: New Critical Essays on Christopher Marlowe*, ed. Paul Whitfield White (New York: AMS Press, 1998), pp. 213–24 (p. 213).

26 See Judith Butler, *Gender Trouble: Feminism and the Subversion of Identity*, new edn (London: Routledge, 1999), pp. 3–44.
27 Quoted in Lucas, *OutRage!*, p. 58.
28 Dillon, *Derek Jarman and Lyric Film*, p. 204.
29 Ibid.
30 Ian Lucas, *Impertinent Decorum: Gay Theatrical Manoeuvres* (London: Cassell, 1994), pp. 111, 160.
31 The quote in the subheading is from *Queer Edward II*, p. 90.
32 Quoted in Farthing and Webb-Ingall, 'An Introduction to the Sketchbooks', p. 208.
33 Ibid. Both photographs are by Raymond Dean. See Plate 8 for a contact sheet of portraits of Jarman from the garden of Priory Road, on the same day in summer 1965.
34 See Lee Benjamin Huttner, 'Body Positive: The Vibrant Present of Derek Jarman's *Edward II* (1991)', *Shakespeare Bulletin*, 32.3 (2014), 393–412.

9

At Your Own Risk: A Saint's Testament

'We have moved into a little office above Ann Summers' sex shop with a view down Old Compton Street, enough room to swivel a chair, "AYOR" written on the doorbell', Derek Jarman writes in *Smiling in Slow Motion* on 21 October 1991 (p. 59). Jarman composed the slim, polemic text *At Your Own Risk: A Saint's Testament* (1992) between late 1991 and early 1992. He enlisted the help of several young friends, who interviewed him extensively about his past, assisted him with the research, then helped to shape the collected material. Colin MacCabe, Jarman's producer, lent them the tiny office described above for the process. The following day, Jarman began: 'I picked up my silver pen fizzing with fury and took the first stab at *AYOR*. The new office is a fine place to write' (*Smiling in Slow Motion*, p. 60). As the project continued, the walls of the office became a collage of newspaper clippings: the tabloid assault in the wake of the AIDS crisis was kept in full view.

This chapter examines the personal and political significance of Jarman's self-representations in *At Your Own Risk*. I illustrate how Jarman constructs the text in the context of the AIDS epidemic and his own positive status, using his own history alongside the personal histories of others to mark out a newly visible space for himself and other gay men in what he found to be an often homophobic culture. Using hostile quotes culled from the media, Jarman demonstrates the pressing need for activism and the legitimacy of such a move when traditional tactics have gone unnoticed. The book's title raises some of these concerns. In gay listings magazines, the more dangerous places to cruise are labelled 'At Your Own Risk'. The text is subtitled '*A Saint's Testament*', a reference to his recent canonisation by the Sisters of Perpetual Indulgence. A *testament* is a final statement. In legal terms, it is the last indication of one's will predetermining how one's property will be divided following one's death. But it also derives from the Latin *testor*: to bear witness. The book attempts to do both, providing what he knew may well have ended up being his final statement, in which he bears witness to hostility in institutions such as the media, government, police and school system. Ellis comments: 'As with all saints, private passions become [...] the catalyst for public dramas'.[1] The book uses collage to juxtapose 'private passions' with the 'public dramas' that seek to expose and thereby contain sexualities. As Michael Warner and Lauren Berlant point out, despite the insistence of normative heterosexual culture that sex belongs in the private realm, 'intimacy itself is publicly mediated' *already*.[2] In *At Your Own Risk*, Jarman shows many examples of overt public mediation and regulation.

At Your Own Risk is Jarman's most focused and chronologically driven book of life-writing. Unlike the earlier *Kicking the Pricks*, which is arranged in a loosely thematic way, *At Your Own Risk* is structured chronologically. It is divided into sections, one for every decade of Jarman's life. He re-examines his memories of important episodes from each decade, presenting a carefully arranged portrait of parts of his life, in the knowledge that he is almost at the end of it. The past, however, is not unassailable: Jarman always sees the past in terms of the present, hence the chronology of the book is interrupted by relevant comments and events from the time that Jarman was preparing the text. In addition, Jarman inserts contemporaneous (though undated) diary entries about his night-time visits to the cruising ground of Hampstead Heath.

At Your Own Risk does 'politics in the first person' (p. 121). By the time of its composition, Jarman was a famous man. As such, he was in a position where he was able to use his own life in order to publicise the histories of the decades he describes and thereby educate his readers about their recent heritage. Jarman was part of a gay cultural efflorescence that drew on personal stories, alongside the testimonies of friends and predecessors, to create a politically engaged body of work that would serve to disrupt the historical status quo and draw attention to the severe issues that gay men faced in the present. For many, it became essential to combat the sinister turn that Britain had taken in the wake of the AIDS crisis, under Thatcher's third term in power, which was complicit with the resurgence in homophobia across the country (see the discussions of Section 28 in the Introduction and in Chapter 9). Jarman's response was to create a moving, tender and radicalising testimony of his life and his community, thereby raising the possibility of politicising his audience. Relying on radical tactics drawn from the then-nascent fields of queer politics and theory, he demonstrates the instability and thus foolishness of some mainstream categorisations of queer experience by inverting these dominant discourses and turning the ire of 'heterosoc' back upon itself.[3] As a result of the underlying political aims of the *At Your Own Risk* project, the slant given to Jarman's personal experiences is more polarised than elsewhere in his oeuvre because they are present specifically to demonstrate homophobia in practice.

Smiling in Slow Motion describes Jarman's part in the launch of the 'Equality Now' campaign by OutRage!, demanding the repeal of anti-gay laws. The campaign began on Thursday, 6 February 1992 with a large protest organised by Peter Tatchell. Campaigners met at Bow Street Police Station, where Oscar Wilde was first taken after his arrest, before they attempted to march on Parliament. Jarman was prevailed upon to make a short speech to the crowd, his public profile being an excellent way to attract media attention for the campaign. Jarman writes in his diary, 'I said goodbye to HB who we decided should not be arrested this time as there is a deadline to finish AYOR' (*Smiling in Slow Motion*, p. 77). When they reached Charing Cross Road, which marks the one-mile line from Parliament that demonstrations cannot cross without special permission, the group sat in the middle of the road, wrapped in their banners, and waited their turn to be arrested. The following day, Jarman 'Finished AYOR once and for all. Celebratory scrambled egg on toast at the café with HB. A sombre photo in the *Guardian* [of Jarman after his arrest] peering out of the police van. The intervention made all the major news bulletins and most of the papers' (*Smiling in Slow Motion*, p. 77). Tatchell describes *At Your Own Risk* as 'in many ways Derek's political testament', and its composition was also a complement to the activism he was involved in at the time.[4]

A portrait of homophobia in Britain, 1940s–1990s

In *At Your Own Risk*, Jarman draws a portrait of a homophobic Britain from the 1940s to the 1990s, focusing on his perspective as a gay man. Near the book's opening, he starkly lists his relation to the law:

> For the first twenty-five years of my life I lived as a criminal, and the next twenty-five were spent as a second-class citizen, deprived of equality and human rights. No right to adopt children – and if I had children, I could be declared an unfit parent; illegal in the military; an age of consent of twenty-one; no right of inheritance; no right of access to a loved one; no right to public affection; no right to an unbiased education; no legal sanction of my relationships and no right to marry. These restrictions subtly deprived me of my freedom. (*At Your Own Risk*, p. 4)

Taking stock from the perspective of 1992, aged 50, he writes 'angrily' (*Smiling in Slow Motion*, p. 3), 'fizzing with fury' (p. 60) – the accumulated difficulties of existing as a gay man in society thrown into sharp relief in the years following the start of the AIDS crisis, when, for example, 'no right of access to a loved one' or 'no right of inheritance' took on a particularly painful meaning for many.

In the early sections of the book, he describes incidents where public figures were involved in public shamings, especially when their sexual encounters had taken place in public spaces. His account of the 1940s includes a long extract from Tom Driberg's diary *Ruling Passions*. Driberg, who was then Labour Member of Parliament for Maldon, writes about an incident in which he is discovered by the police in a compromising position with a 'flaxen-haired and smilingly attractive' Scandinavian sailor in a Central London air-raid shelter in 1943. 'Och, ye bastards – ye dirty pie o' whoors…', Driberg reports one policeman as exclaiming 'in a tone of angry disgust' (quoted in *At Your Own Risk*, p. 11): the reach of the law is enacted under putatively moral grounds.[5]

Jarman juxtaposes public hysteria in the newspapers with accounts of his contemporary experiences on Hampstead Heath, the characters he met there and the stories they shared with him. For example, he quotes from an article in the *Sunday Chronicle*, 1955, in which Barbara Cartland denounces 'the hydra-headed monster of masculine perversion' and incites her readers to 'DESTROY THIS EVIL!' (quoted in *At Your Own Risk*, p. 21). In contrast, 'We wandered from the path and got lost in the woods' (*At Your Own Risk*, p. 8), he writes of one episode, presenting a vision of the Heath as a place of kindness, intimacy and community – far from the perspective of Barbara Cartland or Mary Whitehouse. In the 1950s, he uses his own negative experiences of public school life to demonstrate the foolish and damaging strictures of such a system of authority. He presents this against a backdrop of the Montagu and Wildeblood trial in 1953, inserting parts of its transcript verbatim (see *At Your Own Risk*, pp. 24–5). He comments: 'I was dimly aware that this national scandal related to me, though I had no words to describe it' (*At Your Own Risk*, p. 25).

The 1960s and 1970s are presented as a relatively happy time. He spent the latter part of the decade exploring the pubs and clubs of London, and learning codes such as Polari. Jarman writes that 'the whole decade [1960s] passed quite innocently' – as 'there was still a large amount of restraint on my part' (*At Your Own Risk*, p. 54). But by the end of the decade, 'everyone I knew, knew everyone else, and everyone I knew had slept with everyone else. We all lived together as a generation, not as a family' (*At Your Own Risk*, p. 64). He was living in warehouses as an artist: 'My life had fluidity and possibility' (*At Your Own Risk*, p. 64). He also describes the queer spaces of New York's derelict warehouses and bathhouses, where 'The lid was off; the dance was on' (*At Your Own Risk*, p. 81). Out at Fire Island during the summer of 1974, 'This world had a simplicity that I never encountered in "civilised" surroundings. [...] Out alone at night, I was a traveller. Power, privilege, even good looks, and certainly money, disappeared in that dark' (*At Your Own Risk*, p. 80). Jarman compellingly and sentimentally presents memories of the sexual utopia of his youth, especially in the 1970s. Shadows are always present, however, in particular in the form of Harvey Milk's murder in 1978, the resultant trial and the San Francisco riots of the following year.

The 1980s form the focus of the book, describing the shock of HIV alongside its history and its representations in the UK media. 'I wouldn't wish the eighties on anyone, it was the time when all that was rotten bubbled to the surface', he comments (*At Your Own Risk*, p. 95). He reviews his response to his HIV-positive diagnosis (as initially reported in *Kicking the Pricks*. See the section 'Nothing to be afraid of?' in Chapter 5). Now, with five years' hindsight, he writes, 'I became frightened of myself' and commented, 'All life became a problem, and I solved this by shutting my physical self like a clam. For a while, I could have been a model for the Conservative Family Association' (*At Your Own Risk*, p. 95). The text is interspersed with headlines from the front pages of the tabloid press: 'AIDS BLOOD IN M&S PIES PLOT', 'THE NIGHT I MET MP IN GAY CLUB', 'GAY SANTA GETS SACK', 'SEX BOYS FOR SALE AT QUEEN'S GROCERS', 'VILE BOOK IN SCHOOL – PUPILS SEE PICTURES OF GAY LOVERS' (*At Your Own Risk*, p. 105).

Some of these provocative headlines from the tabloid press would be revisited in Jarman's *Queer* series of paintings. These were large in scale and collaborative: Jarman used the help of artist Piers Clemett to help him produce seventeen large paintings in just fourteen days. Each canvas was pasted with photocopies of the bigoted newspaper front pages before being smeared with paint.[6] Some, like *Blood* (1992), had words scratched into the paint as it dried, overlaying the tabloid prints with Jarman's own inscriptions (see plates 9 and 10).

As Jarman wrote *At Your Own Risk* in 1991–92 the section on the 1990s is its slimmest. Not only had the decade only just begun, but Jarman was also aware it would likely mark the end of his story. He caps off the text by including a press release that describes his canonisation by the San Francisco LGBT activist group the Sisters of Perpetual Indulgence:

> *Film director Derek Jarman will be canonised as a saint by the gay order of nuns, the Sisters of Perpetual Indulgence, at his famous garden in Dungeness, Kent. This is in recognition of his films and books, for all he does for the lesbian and gay community, and because 'he has a very sexy nose'.* (*At Your Own Risk*, p. 131)

He thereby places himself within his own history and passes on the baton to a younger generation of gay men. *At Your Own Risk* creates an important historical document, describing the years Jarman lived through from the war almost to the end of the twentieth century.

Hidden from history

At Your Own Risk provides an important social record that forms part of a wider body of work that seeks to inscribe gay experience into history. In films such as *Caravaggio* and *Edward II*, and his earlier diary *Modern Nature*, Jarman rehabilitates the queer context of the lives of important cultural figures from the past (as I discuss in the section 'Jarman's use of the past' in Chapter 3 and the section 'The importance of queer history' in Chapter 8 on the texts that were published alongside these films). As I have previously discussed, Jarman began to pursue queer connections with the past through which to reassess the present while he was taking his first degree in the early 1960s at King's College London. He comments, 'It may seem ludicrous now that stumbling on Marlowe's outing speech from *Edward II* could be an eye-opener' (*At Your Own Risk*, p. 46). Jarman refers to the speech in which Mortimer Senior calls for his nephew to ignore the relationship between Edward and Gaveston. After all, Marlowe's Mortimer Senior comments:

> Great Alexander loved Hephaestion;
> The conquering Hercules for Hylas wept;
> And for Patroclus stern Achilles drooped.
> And not kings only, but the wisest men:
> The Roman Tully loved Octavius,
> Grave Socrates, wild Alcibiades.[7]

Recalling the passage, Jarman comments, 'The Greeks knew how to live', and writes that he found reading predecessors such as Sappho and Plato 'a revelation' (*At Your Own Risk*, p. 46). Marlowe sought to trace a queer genealogy from ancient Greece and Rome to medieval England. The approach has been taken up by others. Oscar Wilde, for example, famously calls on the 'great affection [...] between David and Jonathan, such as Plato made the very basis of his philosophy, and such as you find in the sonnets of Shakespeare and Michelangelo' in his courtroom defence of 'the Love that dare not speak its name' on 30 April 1895.[8] Edward Carpenter also provides an extended list of queer lovers throughout history in *Homogenic Love, and its Place in a Free Society* (1894). One can find similar, more recent genealogies within the work of other gay writers, historians and artists from the 1970s to the 1990s. For example, John Rechy's *The Sexual Outlaw: A Documentary* (1977) lists Michelangelo, Da Vinci, Socrates, Proust, Shakespeare and Tchaikovsky. The edited collection of scholarship, *Hidden From History: Reclaiming the Gay and Lesbian Past* (1989) and Gregory Woods's *A History of Gay Literature: The Male Tradition* (1998) explore the impulse to excavate these histories and create genealogies through repeated lists of queer figures from history. Woods comments on the rationale for the list: 'The eclecticism and unpredictability of the list, emphasised by its not being presented in any logical order, is part of the point: not only are we everywhere, but we always were'.[9] It is a political tactic to insist on recognising a tradition – that, though it has always existed, will only be rehabilitated through '*recitation*' that might result in a newly acknowledged queer canon in which the queer content is not excised.[10]

Though the repetition of lists of queer figures from history and culture is nothing new, it is a tactic that Jarman, Neil Bartlett and others returned to as one way to respond to the urgent demands of the present. With the advent of HIV/AIDS, Jarman's and others' relationship to history became more complex and urgent. History became more than a way to understand oneself by forging an identity whose origins can be traced back to past lives and in which the pressing issues of the day could be combated by using the past. It also became a matter of using much more recent history, in the form of the personal testimonials of ordinary gay men whose life stories were not yet finished, as well as the record left by the media and by government action, to address the most important issues and rouse people into visible action. For example, Neil Bartlett's performance 'A Vision of Love Revealed in Sleep' (1987) works to 'celebrate the beauty and daring' of its subject, the Victorian painter Simeon Solomon, while giving a personal account of homophobic persecution in 1980s London.[11] Similarly, Bartlett's *Who Was That Man? A Present for Mr Oscar Wilde* (1988) is a self-reflexive, autobiographical text that identifies the contemporary significance of Wilde and other precursors for a gay identity during a time of crisis. *At Your Own Risk* reports a history of struggle – 'I had to write of a sad time as a witness', Jarman comments (*At Your Own Risk*, p. 134). However, it does so as a way to dream of 'a better future' (p. 134): Jarman writes movingly, 'As the shadows closed in, the stars came out' (p. 134).

Family photographs

The collection of personal photographs printed in *At Your Own Risk* heightens the sense of it being foremost an autobiographical text that ties Jarman's personal and family details to broader historical currents in the media, in politics and in the courts. The book contains personal photographs depicting the stages of his life. In the first block of photographs (between p. 42 and p. 43), Jarman presents what Linda Haverty Rugg terms the 'naïve' use of photographs 'where simulacra of family albums [...] appear as a "natural" and expected supplement to the autobiographical text'.[12] The first in the series is a conservatively posed image of Jarman's mother, Betty, as a young woman, which is followed by a similar portrait of his father, Lance. They do not make eye contact with the camera (differently from the photographs in *Kicking the Pricks* discussed in the sections 'On the family' and 'The Terror in a Photo' in Chapter 4). A photograph of the couple leaving church on their wedding day follows, incidentally located underneath an arrangement of the narcissi that would play a significant role in Jarman's later work. We then see a photograph of Betty with infants Derek and his sister Gaye, alongside other photographs of Jarman as a young boy. Jarman also appears as a teenage schoolboy in uniform, then dressed for a night out. Seven years elapse before the next photograph, showing a more relaxed Jarman at a gallery opening in 1967. Jarman's first love, Ron, is the subject of the next image, in which he is depicted with only his head visible above the surface of a swimming pool. This sequence represents the first half of Jarman's life and can be termed his upbringing up until the point he came out and began his mature life as an adult and as an artist.

Simon Watney, whose archive of homophobia in the media provided the content for much of *At Your Own Risk*, wrote an essay looking at images of his past, 'Ordinary boys', that reflects upon the significance of domestic photography. Like Jarman, Watney divides his representations of himself into two distinct categories: for Watney, the watershed was before and after he went to college. Describing the function of domestic photography as 'to impart the semblance of retrospective coherence to family life', Watney describes the vulnerability that he felt – and that he suspects other gay children of his generation felt – to 'parents' fantasies about who they are'.[13] Watney describes the dislocation between his memory of being an awkward, anxious little boy and the way he appears in a photograph depicting him learning to read: 'I am shocked to discover that the picture reveals nothing of the terrible secret' of Watney's sexuality.[14] The photograph of the teenage Jarman described as 'A night out, 1960', shows him in slightly oversized dinner jacket next to a smiling, coiffed woman in a white stole and circle skirted dress. Jarman is looking down, his arms stiffly pressed to his sides; the woman is looking past Jarman, over to the right of the picture frame (*At Your Own Risk*, p. 153). What does the image show other than a snap taken at just the wrong moment? Is there a 'terrible secret' to be read in it? By placing the photograph in this defiant text, Jarman encourages his readers to carefully examine the image and search for traces of the man he would become.

The second block of photographs in *At Your Own Risk* falls late in the text and shows a different kind of content (between p. 107 and p. 108). The first image in this sequence shows Jarman in his late twenties, crouching, nude, a dishevelled artist with curling, longish hair. This is followed by a glamorous photograph of Jarman in semi-drag: dressed up in tights, heels, a bathing cap and sunglasses, interviewing a friend. We then see a happy nude in Roman sandals, on location during the filming of *Sebastiane*.[15] There then follows a snapshot of Jarman on a demonstration in 1991, the young lovers from *The Garden* embracing, then three images of Jarman by Howard Sooley, all from 1991. In the first, he poses as Nosferatu, at first glance a silly posture but one that is reminiscent of the press portrayal of men with HIV/AIDS as predatory and sinister vampires in the plot of a gothic horror story.[16] The second photograph shows Jarman being canonised in a glittering silver gown by the Sisters of Perpetual Indulgence. The third shows him standing pensive and dour outside Prospect Cottage. Taken not long before the time of writing, these final Sooley portraits resonate with the text. They show Jarman in the incarnation in which he composed the text we're reading.

The images are there to provide evidence about the referentiality of the text to a real life lived, and to sate the reader's curiosity. We have become accustomed to looking at photographs within autobiographies that are placed among the text without special comment on what is shown. In the case of *At Your Own Risk*, the list describing the contents of each photograph is presented as the very last page of the appendix. There is no other mention of the images or what they signified to Jarman. Their presence alone is sufficient. Looking particularly at the second set of personal photographs, one might conclude that the need to record and to prepare an archive is of intense importance, especially in the early AIDS years. In Watney's essay on personal photography, he comments 'My Extended Family album is now something more than a partial record of my life: it has become an archive, one fragment of the much greater enterprise that is modern gay history'.[17] Neil Bartlett also describes the important archival quality of photographs depicting the intimacies of gay life and friendships in *Who Was That Man?*. He explains:

> Somewhere in the house, flat or room of each of my lovers and friends there is a draft of a book like this one. [...] I know that he has a record collection, a drawer of photographs, a wall of pictures [...]. If you or he can 'read' this collection of words and images, with all its attendant justifications, juxtapositions and cross-references, you will have a gay story, a history.[18]

Jarman allows the images to form an unspoken addition to the book, adding to its archival quality and to its status as a historical document produced in a threatened present. Although the insertion of photographs – of a particular life, with its accordant ties of family, friends and work – places the text firmly within a tradition of autobiography, whether in a straightforward definition of the category or not, Jarman's text is complicated by their presence.[19] They indicate how merged his personal life and the political project he seeks to further by using his life as material have become.

'SEX AT NINE': Polarising childhood

One of the ways in which Jarman creates a shared history project is by examining the most radicalising events from his own life alongside the lives of his contemporaries.[20] His focus on what has been hidden from history is his attempt to write these experiences – often of injustice, often of sex, love or community – into a longer-lasting story. For example, Jarman's depiction of his school years, described in the 1950s section of *At Your Own Risk*, is superimposed upon those of others. Jarman begins the 1950s with a quote designed to both shock and amuse: 'I am a schoolboy with nine inches – meet me here tomorrow at 4.00 (Serious)' (*At Your Own Risk*, p. 19). There is no further explanation or indication of its origins, but it would be reasonable to assume it to be copied from anonymous graffiti on a toilet wall. The combination of the explicit alongside the youthful exaggeration and immature register of the finishing note '(Serious)' marks it out as *genuine evidence*. The following page also contains another disruptive heading: 'SEX AT NINE' (*At Your Own Risk*, p. 20). He thereby introduces a far more polarised vision of Jarman's encounter with another boy at Hordle than that presented in earlier autobiographical texts.

To illustrate the importance of the version of the tale used in *At Your Own Risk*, I will catalogue its earlier forms. Jarman first wrote about this in *Dancing Ledge*, where he relates:

> At nine I discovered that sleeping with someone was more fun than sleeping alone and climbed into my mate Gavin's bed. Cuddling each other alleviated some of the isolation of boarding school. This wholly innocent affair was destroyed by a jealous dormitory captain. (*Dancing Ledge*, p. 18)

Here loneliness requires the salve of bodily warmth and comfort: Jarman picks the words 'wholly innocent' to emphasise a lack of sexual implications in their actions. The episode in Jarman's next book of life-writing, *Kicking the Pricks*, is presented similarly:

> My first confrontation with oppression was in the cold dormitory of a British preparatory school [...]. My crime [...] [was that] I had crossed over the dormitory and climbed into the bed of another nine year old; the action was quite innocent, neither of us could have foreseen the consequences. (*Kicking the Pricks*, p. 19)

The passage above shows Jarman beginning to revise the representation he chooses in *Dancing Ledge*, where the matter is 'wholly innocent'. Here, the event is again described as 'innocent', but the following clause demonstrates the innocence as being directly related to the boys being unaware that a 'crime' was being committed: without knowing the consequences, innocence is preserved. He here elides the crux of the story as it would be presented in the two versions that follow. This shows Jarman starting to revise his earliest representation in *Dancing Ledge*, as he defines his understanding that there is no reason why specifically sexual intentions in boys of nine should be perceived as anything other than 'wholly innocent'. In a journal entry from 1989 that would be published in *Modern Nature*, Jarman has greatly changed his approach to this memory:

> In the early hours Johnny and I shared our secrets, clambering onto each other's beds like the heroes of Edwardian picture books. Skinny nine year olds, we explored the contours of forgotten landscapes. The imaginary worlds of Prester John – and of Big Foot, Tight Arse, Stiff Cock. (*Modern Nature*, p. 50)

The passage is presented lyrically. The boys are represented nostalgically, as 'heroes' from the (recently) bygone age of Edwardian childhood – and a childhood fictionalised within 'picture books'. Here, however, he relates their nocturnal explorations as a quest. Instead of privileging their loneliness and innocence as he does in *Dancing Ledge* and *Kicking the Pricks*, he presents them both as wonderstruck children embarking on their first adventures – innocent, but of a sexually explorative nature.

The final telling of the episode is found in *At Your Own Risk*. After the heading 'SEX AT NINE', introduced above, Jarman writes bluntly and furiously: 'I was unsuccessfully trying to fuck the boy in the bed next to mine – quite unaware that I was doing anything out of the ordinary – when the sky fell in as we were ripped apart like two dogs' (*At Your Own Risk*, p. 20). He returns to the episode later in the chapter, under the heading: 'ARE THERE ANY PARENTS WITH THEIR EYES OPEN?': 'At nine, I was caught in bed with Gavin – thrown onto the floor by the headmaster's wife, lectured publicly and whipped' (*At Your Own Risk*, p. 36). The tone is markedly different. The shared exploration of *Modern Nature* has transformed into an event where the sole agency belongs to Jarman. Curt, purged of any trace of lyricism and sentimentality, the passages transform an adventure into its barest reality. It's bitter: that the boy Jarman's attempts were 'unsuccessful' lends further pathos to the punishments he received. He describes the treatment of their discovery in a bestial way to highlight his anger and his pain following the response from the figures of authority. The capitalised section headings read as newspaper headings – unmeasured, but also lending a tone of authority, like that of the media, to the 'articles'. The change in name from the 'Gavin' from three of the four reports to the 'Johnny' found in *Modern Nature* is explained by Jarman's use of the name Johnny as a generic term for queer boys, which he used at least from the late 1980s onwards. Changing the name to Johnny underlines Jarman's point that his experiences could be anybody's story. A final note about this episode: Peake notes that 'the headmasters of Hordle deny any knowledge of it, as does the boy into whose bed Jarman crept'.[21]

Returning to the structure of the stories of childhood sexuality related at the beginning of the 1950s section of *At Your Own Risk*, the deeply personal passage ends with the gossip that his friend 'Jimmy told Michael that at twelve he was hanging around Glasgow bus station hoping some man would "shove it up him" – a youth intent on corrupting the middle-aged' (*At Your Own Risk*, p. 20). The point of this barrage of episodes: the anonymous (the graffiti), the personal ('SEX AT NINE'), and the stories of childhood shared among friends ('Jimmy told Michael…') is twofold. Firstly, in political terms, it unavoidably demonstrates that children, even (or especially) those 'smarting under the tortured system' of a public school environment, will never act as the adults governing them might choose to believe. Jarman uses a significant memory from his past in a context that reduces its individuality by its placement. This raises the question of how far the autobiographical content in *At Your Own Risk* is subsumed by Jarman's broader conception of gay lives and the significant markers that they are likely to include. He deliberately produces a story that could be anyone's story.

Secondly, it is significant that his varied sexual 'evidence of experience' is presented in a deliberately antagonistic way.[22] Lindsay Anderson, another child of empire, though two decades older than Jarman, depicts a similar setting to that which Jarman underwent at Hordle, followed by Canford, in his 1968 film *If…*. Though based on a school in the 1960s rather than Jarman's 1950s, Anderson depicts the same stuffiness, claustrophobia and exploitative power relationships depicted against a background of what Jarman terms 'muscular Christianity' (*Dancing Ledge*, p. 51). The three rebels in *If…* responded to their incarceration by launching a violent attack on the pupils, teachers and parents on Founder's Day, shooting whoever they could. Jarman sums up the feeling of disenfranchisement: 'No man is an island, but each man created his own island to cope with the prejudice and censure. The time for politeness had to end' (*At Your Own Risk*, p. 23). Shock tactics became a crucial strategy, as it was possible to ignore the AIDS crisis in the UK. Jarman comments that 'If you were not at the receiving end of this mayhem, you could be unaware of it' (*At Your Own Risk*, p. 95). Shockingly, as Watney points out, 'Mrs Thatcher did not even mention AIDS in her memoirs'.[23] Watney neatly summarises:

> Activism is a politics of emergencies, and becomes necessary when powerful institutions stubbornly refuse to listen to reasonable, well informed, democratic arguments. It is a politics of last resort, necessary when all other attempts at dialogue and negotiation have failed.[24]

In the schoolboy examples in *At Your Own Risk*, Jarman uses shock tactics to make visible his activist campaign for sufficient AIDS education.

Jarman's examples prove the idiocy of the idea that children need to remain uneducated in order to be protected. Jarman uses evidence from a letter he had received from a sixteen-year-old boy. The boy had written, '*The whole concept of childhood is suspect. I was having sex at twelve*' (*At Your Own Risk*, p. 28, italics in original). Jarman responds, 'A scenario for disaster! As a twelve year old you become HIV+, and then you fuck the whole school! The epidemic is potentially uncontrollable. The only solution is discussion rather than censure' (*At Your Own Risk*, p. 28). His own unhappy experiences as a schoolboy – the lack of an unbiased and informative sexual education, for one – prompted him to evaluate how to respond in the present: 'I've remained angry about it ever since and, because it made me desperately unhappy as an adolescent, it's one of the motivating forces in what I've done with my life' (*At Your Own Risk*, p. 35). It is this 'motivating force' that underpins *At Your Own Risk*. Its aim was to provide a document that would not only educate its audience and provide examples of living history, but also serve to change the minds of those who would rather not educate young people, as a result of Section 28, despite the urgency of the AIDS crisis.

Against 'heterosoc'

When Jarman discusses gay autobiography early in *At Your Own Risk*, he writes, 'There's a huge self-censorship because we're terrified of betraying ourselves. We don't want people to know' (p. 30). What is crucial here is that he is writing in the present tense. This is an interesting move: coupled with his use of the nominative plural, he includes himself within a current problem. This book would seek to do away with this sense of secrecy, but this comment raises the question of how we as readers can trust or use such evidence of experience provided in the text. To explore this, one might consider who the text's audience is, and examine how this might affect the potential effectiveness of the text as a means to incite social change.

As explored earlier in this chapter, Jarman demonstrates his commitment to queer activism not only through his involvement with protests but in his writing, and *At Your Own Risk* is a political manifesto as well as an autobiographical text. Just as Jarman uses his own status as a famous man to draw attention to political agendas, campaigns and direct action from OutRage!, he hopes to use this same status to raise political consciousness among his readers. One of the main ways that Jarman attempts this is by using the queer trope of subverting dominant discourses in order to demonstrate how easy it is to deconstruct them, as discussed in the previous chapter in relation to *Queer Edward II*.

For example, Jarman inverts examples of 'prejudice and censure' (*At Your Own Risk*, p. 23) against gay men and turns them inside out. Direct statements are inserted into the autobiographical collage:

> *Heterosexuality isn't normal, it's just common.* (*At Your Own Risk*, p. 19)[25]
>
> Heterosexuality: what is it? how is it caused? (*At Your Own Risk*, p. 45)
>
> It eventually dawned on me that heterosexuality is an abnormal psychopathic state composed of unhappy men and women whose arrested emotions, finding no natural outlet, condemned them to each other and lives lacking warmth and human compassion. (*At Your Own Risk*, p. 60)

His approach is not always so direct: Jarman also makes light of the things that 'heterosoc' picks on, while simultaneously indicating a different history:

> Hampstead Heath is in the news, the *Standard* has discovered an 'orgy bush'. You can buy these in the garden centre at Camden and plant them in your front garden. The orgy bush has beautiful red berries and is traditionally used to decorate your homes at Christmas to celebrate the birth of Jesus who loved John. (*At Your Own Risk*, p. 23)

It is hard not to be disarmed by Jarman's style, swept along in the fun of seeing him striking back in a playful way that proves the idiocy of statements that are all too commonplace. It is clear that this anger is a productive reaction against the perverse behaviour of individuals such as Barbara Cartland and Mary Whitehouse and certain voices in the media.[26] However, Jarman's approach was not happily received by everyone, including the liberal press. Catherine Bennett, whose article I discuss in connection to the reception of *Smiling in Slow Motion*, responds as follows:

> Jarman has always adopted a haughty tone about heterosexuals, but what's new, in this book, is the political hectoring; from patently just demands for homosexual civil rights, to aggressive claims for indulgence, and assertions of gay superiority over brutish 'heterosoc'.[27]

Bennett's negative response to what she sees as simply a 'haughty' and 'hectoring' attitude raises a rather pertinent question. Can this particular strain of queer activism work when its audience doesn't know anything about the concept in advance? In the same interview, Jarman explains his approach:

> 'I've been living with newspapers saying these things about me for the last 50 years,' Jarman says, to explain his sub-Wildean paradoxes, 'so one voice turns round, and it absolutely is agent provocateur stuff. It is a perverse thing, to say everything that's been levelled at gay people, back!'
>
> It's a taste of 'our' own medicine. But isn't it equally silly?
>
> 'No, it isn't, because it provokes people – it has provoked you very deeply,' Jarman retorts, triumphantly. 'The liberal consensus is quite happy, as long as it doesn't cross their paths'.[28]

Jarman indicates that this provocation is a useful critical response. However, in order for a mainstream audience to be provoked, it would have to read – and be encouraged to read – the book.

At the beginning of the book, Jarman writes that 'To those who have not lived it, it might appear opaque; those of us who are living it will recognise the map' (*At Your Own Risk*, p. 5). At the end of the book, Jarman's closing 'benediction' begins: 'but as I leave you Queer lads'.[29] He here implies that the audience of the book is definitely and specifically these 'Queer lads', namely a younger generation of gay men. His intended audience places the jibes at 'heterosoc' into interesting relief. From some angles, the book appears to be a brave, hostile, political affront seeking to force its likewise hostile readers to reassess their narrow opinions and begin to understand the perspective of those living under the shadow of the AIDS crisis. However, as Jarman deliberately frames the text in order that it should not fully make sense to anyone without a gay, male, London-centred background (or at least the tools required to read this background), it is not truly aimed at the 'heterosoc' Jarman would seek to alter. Instead, its truer aim is to politicise a young, queer readership via education presented in polemical style. Jarman was more than aware of the need for a contemporary historical gay education, writing: 'I had to write of a sad time as a witness', then asking these 'lads' to: 'please read the cares of the world that I have locked in these pages' (*At Your Own Risk*, p. 134). I wonder whether this question of audience relates back to Jarman's feeling that there is still self-censorship: there is no point being brave if your target can't hear you. It's quite interesting that the book is written within a framework that seeks to reassess and do away with fixed boundaries of identity, while simultaneously re-restricting the audience. Alan Sinfield comments that dissident discourses, such as the queer approach Jarman takes in *At Your Own Risk*, 'can always, ipso facto, be discovered reinscribing that which it proposes to critique. [...] All stories comprise within themselves the ghosts of the alternative stories they are trying to exclude'.[30]

Notes

1 Ellis, *Angelic Conversations*, p. 222.
2 Lauren Berlant and Michael Warner, 'Sex in Public', *Critical Inquiry*, 24.2 (Winter 1998), 547–66 (p. 553).
3 Term used throughout *At Your Own Risk*, pp. 4, 19, 23, 34, 35, etc.
4 Peter Tatchell, 'Peter Tatchell on Derek Jarman', interviewed by Andy Kimpton-Nye, 2003, www.400blows.co.uk/inter_tatchell.shtml (accessed 4 February 2013).
5 Tom Driberg, *Ruling Passions: The Autobiography of Tom Driberg*, 1st edn (London: Jonathan Cape, 1977), pp. 144–6. Rather than resulting in Driberg's arrest, the story has a happy ending: Driberg presented his calling card, which had the pseudonym he used for his popular column in the *Express* and the words 'Member of Parliament'. The young police officer responded, 'Good God, man, *I've read ye all of my life!*' (Driberg, *Ruling Passions*, p. 145) and let him off. Driberg later posted him a respectable bribe of some book tokens, then met him for some drinks in a pub. Some years later, he received news of the man's death in a personal letter from his wife, with the information that he had always held Driberg in high regard. The anecdote is a tale of the hypocrisy of the law, and the ability of status to raise one above it.
6 For both an account of the production of the *Queer* paintings and an overview of Jarman's series of paintings, see Joanna Shepard, 'Painting on Borrowed Time: Jarman's Media and Techniques', in *Derek Jarman: PROTEST!*, eds. Seán Kissane and Karim Rehmani-White (London: Thames and Hudson, 2020), pp. 92–9.
7 Marlowe, *Edward II*, pp. 36–7, 4:392–8.
8 Oscar Wilde quoted in Merlin Holland, *The Real Trial of Oscar Wilde* (London: Fourth Estate, 2003), p. 213.
9 Woods, *A History of Gay Literature*, p. 4.
10 De Certeau, *Everyday Life*, p. 186.
11 Neil Bartlett, 'A Vision of Love Revealed in Sleep (Part One)', in *Solo Voices: Monologues 1987–2004* (London: Oberon, 2005), pp. 15–46, p. 15.
12 Rugg, *Picturing Ourselves*, p. 2.
13 Watney, *Imagine Hope*, p. 30.
14 Ibid., p. 29.
15 Jarman's friend Ken Hicks, the photographer, whose death Jarman would eulogise in *Smiling in Slow Motion*, p. 241. See discussion in the section 'Testimony and elegy' in Chapter 10.
16 For a discussion of monstrosity and vampiricism in filmic representations of AIDS, see the chapter 'AIDS and its Metaphors: (Re)imaging the Syndrome' in

Niall Richardson, *The Queer Cinema of Derek Jarman: Critical and Cultural Readings* (London: I. B. Tauris, 2009), pp. 173–200.
17 Watney, *Imagine Hope*, p. 34.
18 Neil Bartlett, *Who Was That Man? A Present for Mr Oscar Wilde* (London: Serpent's Tail, 1988), p. 24.
19 See Adams, *Light Writing*, pp. 1–25.
20 The quote in the subheading is from *At Your Own Risk*, p. 20.
21 Peake, *Derek Jarman*, p. 31.
22 Jarman's experiences are worlds apart from the underage sexuality depicted in Felice Picano, *Like People in History* (London: Abacus, 1996) when the wealthy, flamboyant – and underage – Alastair Dodge is discovered with a Sicilian gardener in California in 1961. A court case is brought against the gardener, but the adults view the teenaged Alastair as beyond reproach.
23 Watney, *Imagine Hope*, p. 3.
24 Ibid., p. 11.
25 Taken from Dorothy Parker.
26 Jarman quotes Barbara Cartland's article about 'the monster of masculine perversion', which I raise earlier in this chapter. For Mary Whitehouse's attack on Jarman, see Peake, *Derek Jarman*, p. 357.
27 Catherine Bennett, 'Lesson of the Gay Guru: "I've known all my life that there was this immense anger, a sort of fury, and that it could be used fruitfully." Catherine Bennett on Derek Jarman, auteur, artist, activist – and very, very angry', *Guardian*, 9 April 1992.
28 Bennett, 'Lesson of the Gay Guru'.
29 Ellis, *Angelic Conversations*, p. 222; *At Your Own Risk*, p. 134.
30 Alan Sinfield, *Faultlines: Cultural Materialism and the Politics of Dissident Reading* (Oxford: Clarendon Press, 1992), p. 47.

10

Smiling in Slow Motion: Testimony and elegy

In a letter published on the front page of the *Independent* in May 1993 as part of a campaign to halt the closure of St Bartholemew's Hospital, Derek Jarman wrote that 'Without our past our future cannot be reflected, the past is the mirror'.[1] At the time, he was still regularly keeping a journal that examined his past and commented on his present (see Figure 26). Published for the first time in 2000, *Smiling in Slow Motion* contains diary entries spanning almost three years, dated between May 1991 (eight months after *Modern Nature* closes) and early 1994. Collins collated and edited the entries after Jarman's death, following the techniques he used when he worked on Jarman's previous diaries. He consulted many of Jarman's closest friends and colleagues in the process. *Smiling in Slow Motion* spans almost 400 pages of small type and includes two sections of photographs. The entries range over work and social commitments, commentaries about the expansion of Prospect Cottage and the development of its garden, and the increasingly frequent challenges of illness and hospital stays.[2]

Whereas the text for *Modern Nature* had been specifically conceived of as a book prior to its composition, the final results of *Smiling in Slow Motion* were not designed in the same structured way, though Jarman had intended publication of some kind. It spans a long period, and many different registers and modes of living. Jarman worked on several significant projects during the course of the journal: he wrote *At Your Own Risk* and *Chroma*, made the films *Wittgenstein* and *Blue*, worked on scripts for film projects that remained unmade including *The Raft of the Medusa* and an adaptation of James Purdy's *Narrow Rooms*, helped prepare a Japanese book of his film stills, *Freeze Frame*,[3] and created two major series of large paintings, *Queer* (Manchester Art Gallery, 1992) and *Evil Queen* (1993).[4] He travelled to film festivals and kept a hectic social schedule. He also had periods of intense illness and began to suffer from increasingly harrowing periods of ill health (one diary detailing some of the hospital stays during this time was lost in a taxi in May 1993).[5] In the midst of such freneticism, the diary took a sideline at times. He continued to be photographed by Howard

Figure 26 Jarman writing at Barts Hospital, early 1993.

Sooley, whose portrait of him in front of *Dead Sexy* (part of the *Evil Queen* series) is shown in Plate 11.

Of all Jarman's life-writing, *Smiling in Slow Motion* is the collection of published diary entries that can be best understood as an AIDS journal. Jarman is at the symptomatic stage of AIDS for its duration, and it ends with the death of its author. The *Observer* summarised the book in six stark words: 'The director's record of his decline'.⁶ Ross Chambers reminds us of 'the rhetorical stakes of writing an AIDS diary': 'Why would a person at the symptomatic stage of AIDS wish to write a diary? What are the responsibilities of those who survive the diary's author as its readers? What kind of "facing up" is entailed in these practices of writing and of reading?'⁷ As in Jarman's earlier *Modern Nature* and *At Your Own Risk*, life-writing is a critical political practice of bearing witness to the dual impact of HIV/AIDS and censure from institutions: 'I had to write of these sad times as a witness', Jarman explains at the end of *At Your Own Risk* (p. 134). Similarly, some of Jarman's art at the time provides a witnessing function: *One Day's Medication* (1993) glues seventeen different bottles, vials and packets of his medication onto a canvas (see Plate 12). Yet according to Chambers 'an act of witnessing [...] implies a certain belief in there being a future', and Jarman's decision to sustain his writing through the early 1990s is a testament to that future.⁸

Reception of *Smiling in Slow Motion*

None of Jarman's journals has received much sustained critical attention, but *Smiling in Slow Motion* in particular has as yet received little of note, except Neil Bartlett's new introduction to the 2018 Vintage Classics reissue.⁹ During the time that elapsed between Jarman's last diary entry (early 1994) and its publication in 2000, the social landscape had changed. At the time of the publication of *Modern Nature* and *At Your Own Risk*, AIDS-related illnesses and death was a daily reality for many. Following the announcement in 1996 of new combination therapies involving protease inhibitors, the medical picture changed. As a result, by the time the diaries were published in mid-2000, the experience of a now-deceased figure from the generation who suffered in a way that for the most part, most newly diagnosed HIV-positive people in the Western world no longer have to, had over the course of just half a decade become more of a history than a living event. Without the urgency, perhaps the diary entries seemed to have lost their immediacy. Alternatively, people have perhaps found themselves more drawn to the earlier journal *Modern Nature*, which features a more sustained development of major themes and an enhanced coherence as a collection of journal entries.

Whatever the reason, of the collections of critical prose based solely on Jarman's work and published after 2000, the year *Smiling in Slow Motion* came out, none index the book, though most extensively refer to *Modern Nature*.¹⁰ Brophy devotes the first chapter of her 2004 study of AIDS writing to *Modern Nature*, but does not mention the later diaries. Michael Charlesworth covers the text in just two pages in his 2011 monograph.[11] There are only a handful of journal articles or book chapters that include similarly brief comments.[12] Indeed, Ashlee Polatinsky mentions *Smiling in Slow Motion* in a paper about South African AIDS diaries predominantly to wonder why it hasn't been written about more. At present, the reviews in newspapers form the most complete response to the book's contents.

Smiling in Slow Motion was reviewed quite prominently in the national press, coming out as it did only a few months after Tony Peake's well-received biography, which would have helped return Jarman's work to the public eye following the flurry of obituaries and essays that emerged after his death six years earlier. It was reviewed extensively in *The Times* (which published full-length reviews on both 5 and 8 July 2000) and the *Guardian*, and gained a short review in the *Independent*'s review section. *The Times* published a glowing full-length review of *Smiling in Slow Motion*, in which journalist Michael Arditti commented that he found 'diarist' 'the profession' Jarman 'most consistently' practised, and a 'perfect forum for […] his talent', finding that 'the journals provide an authoritative literary portrait of gay life in the second half of the 20th century'.[13] He draws apt but obvious comparisons between Jarman's status in the UK and Edmund White's in the US, born as they were into the same generation and writing autobiographical texts that focus on the development of their sexuality. Yet the praise was measured. Arditti contends that Collins's editing 'has served Jarman's interests less well, not only by retaining too many mawkish references to himself but by failing to supply a single footnote'.[14] Indeed, the diaries are a sprawling and tender record of Jarman's love for him, which Collins acknowledges in an interview with *The Times*: 'The hardest thing was editing a 300-page love letter to yourself. […] I wanted it to be his voice that people hear so I was restrained'.[15]

The focus on editing style – or supposed lack thereof – is mirrored in Julie Burchill's damning review in the *Guardian*, where she calls Jarman 'a man with a cauliflower where his ear for language should have been'.[16] The article is written to be confrontational, unmeasured and provoke laughs, and has little to do with the book itself. One gets the impression she has not read much of the text (she does not mention that the text charts his illnesses and eventual death, and has been published as a posthumous labour of love). Simon Watney provides an interesting point of view to explain her callousness: 'Hired by the national press, the anti-gays could hardly wait to dissociate themselves from the communities from which they had come, which had made their early careers possible, and where their genius had perhaps been under-appreciated. Julie Burchill, Andrew Sullivan, [etc.] pointed the way'.[17] Regardless of reviews such as Burchill's, the public bought the book: it came third in The *Observer*'s bestseller list of the top five film books sold in the week ending 29 July 2000, when it sold 176 copies.[18]

Jarman on the reception of his life-writing

In the journals collected in *Smiling in Slow Motion*, Jarman comments on the reception of two of his earlier books of life-writing. On *Modern Nature*, he reports receiving 'a letter from Peter Burton at *Gay Times* saying they would not feature *Modern Nature* as it conflicted with other material they are publishing, I'm not very lucky in that magazine – I'm either the butt of their scorn, or second-hand' (*Smiling in Slow Motion*, p. 22). Jarman believed that he had been ostracised by the gay press, and returns to the topic of the *Gay Times* several times in his life-writing. The following year, Jarman writes of 'a long conversation with a charming young man on the Heath' (*Smiling in Slow Motion*, p. 168) about a critical review of *At Your Own Risk* that did find its way into *Gay Times*. Jarman contends that 'the great queer artists dealt with the negatives, this is why Pasolini and Genet will last long after *Gay Times* is forgotten in a world of false hope and illusion fed by adverts' (*Smiling in Slow Motion*, p. 168). He summarises his disdain for what he considers the mainstreaming and whitewashing of queer experience that the publication represents:

> The concept of positive images was born out of gay liberation in the 1970s; *Gay Times* is of that time and Brighton-based. I don't know how one should describe Brighton, perhaps Façade Amnesia, the town for gay people. There are no queers there, it is often violent, has a huge sex-for-money scene – as there is no other employment. (*Smiling in Slow Motion*, p. 168)

This rant is a reminder that Jarman could be said to have stood outside the gay mainstream (as the 1980s wore on). In *Modern Nature*, *At Your Own Risk* and *Smiling in Slow Motion*, he is keen to set himself within a tradition of encounters unbound by scenes, class or connection. Of the nocturnal world of cruising on Fire Island, which I discuss in Chapter 9, he comments: 'Out alone at night, I was a traveller. Power, privilege, even good looks, and certainly money, disappeared in that dark' (*At Your Own Risk*, p. 80). Here and elsewhere he advocates for the reclamation of the cruising ground as a heterotopia unbound by the hierarchies of 'power, privilege, even good looks'. The queer utopia is one that can encompass ambivalence. During the night at the Heath in which he converses about the *Gay Times* review, he comments: 'Conversation rambled through the night. I wish it were raining, rain concentrates the mind, the blue sky is an illusion, behind lies an infinite black' (*Smiling in Slow Motion*, p. 169).

Earlier that year, he describes being visited for an interview with Catherine Bennett from the *Guardian*. 'I could feel there were going to be no smiles or jokes. The interviewer was so obviously disturbed by *AYOR*', he comments, 'I sensed that behind all this questioning she wanted me to say "Yes I do have unsafe sex" so they could put a tombstone over me' (*Smiling in Slow Motion*, pp. 110–11). When the interview was published less than a week later, Jarman responded: 'Why are people so negative? The phobias leapt out of the journalist's averted eyes – the interview was so seedy' (*Smiling in Slow Motion*, p. 113). The journalist describes *At Your Own Risk* as 'his most disjointed autobiographical hodge-podge to date', feeling that 'After all, Jarman had already shared the rest of his life (quite enough of it for anyone) in *Dancing Ledge*, his first "autobiographical collage"'.[19] Bennett calls on the terms 'hodge-podge' and 'autobiographical collage' to suggest disapproval. The former especially suggests a confused, heterogeneous mixture. On Jarman's discovery that he was HIV positive, Bennett writes, 'Courageously, if unnecessarily, he announced it to the world'.[20] For her to describe the act of the first famous British person to publicly announce his positive status as unnecessary displays her lack of understanding regarding anything of the political situation over the previous decade. After speaking to Bennett, Jarman writes that 'By the end of the interview I saw not a chink of understanding and felt either I was mad, or so old I could no longer communicate with those who had grown to adulthood in the 1980s' (*Smiling in Slow Motion*, p. 111).

The encounter is not atypical, and after all, Bennett is looking to entertain the *Guardian*'s readership. Yet the thoughtless and at times homophobic response is a reaction against Jarman's experiences in the 'Edenic pleasure ground' of Hampstead Heath at night, and his mobilisation of children's sexual encounters (see the discussion in the section 'Polarising childhood' in Chapter 8 on *At Your Own Risk* and similar arguments in the section 'Representing the queer child' in Chapter 9 on *Queer Edward II*).[21] By raising controversial topics and using his own life as material, he courts disapproval, as he has been doing throughout his career. Yet he anticipates finding a sympathetic readership, and his aim is to expose hypocrisy and expand the limits of what is acceptable through honest communication. Jarman states: 'I didn't discover my sexuality to sell *in* – I want change' (*Smiling in Slow Motion*, p. 168).

Testimony and elegy

What is important about *Smiling in Slow Motion* is not its evenness or the way that it was edited, but its status as a social document. Brophy points to 'the overlapping representational contracts of testimony, obituary, and elegy' in her discussion of *Modern Nature*.[22] As the 1990s commenced, as recorded in *Smiling in Slow Motion*, his work had become even more urgent as the people around him died in ever greater numbers, and his own AIDS-related illnesses grew worse. At a time of great suffering and sadness, the way that Jarman has collected, stored and kept alive many individuals' stories has an important archival quality, not only for himself, but also for others.

Jarman transcribed his later diary entries into large, square journals from Venice in his gorgeous artists' hand using an antique fountain pen and black ink. Often the journals contain photographs or other mementos, along with letters and cuttings from the press. This therefore makes this act of diary-writing a specific kind of collecting and preserving. Jarman preserves not only his own everyday accounts but the more exciting parts of other people's, and most extensively as elegy after they have died. When he discovers that Ken Hicks (a photographer, who played the character Adrian in *Sebastiane*) has died, he eulogises him via lively recollections about the young Ken posing naked for a Super 8 and making love to Jarman in Anthony Harwood's mirrored flat in Sloane Square. Another memory surfaces: 'I'm glad that his youthful vigour is preserved on film', Jarman comments. He recalls: 'There's a moment in *Sebastiane* when he surfaces from the water, smiling in slow motion' (*Smiling in Slow Motion*, p. 241). When Jarman receives news of former boyfriend Patrik Steede's death, he devotes four pages to amusing anecdotes that present Steede indulgently. He distils the unusual, striking or comic: 'He had a mind as sharp as a razor and would tell you the worst about himself', 'He laughed quickly and often, and was able to move in [to Jarman's Bankside warehouse]' (*Smiling in Slow Motion*, p. 94), 'Pat was a gigolo, rich ladies, rich men. He brought the perception of an acid drop into their bland and repetitive lives. He was the perfect company at dinner and was always paid for' (*Smiling in Slow Motion*, p. 95). Jarman summarises his friends' personalities and tries to bring their behaviour to life in his diaries' pages: 'Patrik was always planning to do this and that, but to have completed any of these dreams would have grounded him like a paragraph in this diary' (*Smiling in Slow Motion*, p. 96). These vignettes are precious among the scattered record of Jarman's everyday life.

Late in *Smiling in Slow Motion*, Jarman includes an entry that lists the friends he had lost to AIDS-related illnesses to date. 'This is a terrible destruction of my friends', he writes, before listing sixteen men alongside their occupation, including David Dipnall, art student; Rudolf Nureyev, dancer; Patrik Steede, writer; Howard Bruckner, film-maker; and Robert Mapplethorpe, photographer. 'There are six or more others dying, including myself', he finishes (*Smiling in Slow Motion*, p. 326). There is a sense that the elegies that he writes about others, along with the record of his own life, are offered as part of a larger gay archive. In *Imagine Hope*, Simon Watney quotes James Baldwin, who once observed in an interview with Ida Lewis that 'I'm a witness. That's my responsibility. I write it all down'.[23] The idea that the self-positioned 'witness' has a clear 'responsibility' is central to the life-writing that emerged in the wake of the AIDS crisis and is a key factor in Jarman's diaristic project.

Ross Chambers's second book on AIDS writing, *Untimely Interventions*, contextualises this mode of writing within the twentieth-century genre of autobiographical trauma narratives. He points out that 'it remains relatively easy for "unaffected" majorities [...] to sleep on, more or less blissfully oblivious or indifferent to, and undisturbed by, what is nevertheless *happening*', and in this context draws parallels between soldiers' descriptions of their experiences during World War I, Holocaust testimonies and narratives from people with AIDS-related illnesses.[24] Specific literary interventions by authors writing from their own experience have a special kind of power. The authority generated by the immediacy of the experience is what holds our attention. As a result, Chambers argues:

> What witnessing texts [...] therefore work to require us to acknowledge is that the 'alien' scene, the 'other' context, is *also* a part of culture [...]. Witnessing is, in that sense, an ethical practice [...] that seeks to inculcate a sense of shared (because cultural) responsibility that it is only too easy – for other cultural reasons – to deny.[25]

To write one's witness statement is to take the ethical step – to enable others to understand one's reality and thus effect change.

Jarman's swift production and publication of *At Your Own Risk*, which he describes in *Smiling in Slow Motion* (see my account at the beginning of Chapter 8), demonstrates this practice of bearing witness. *Smiling in Slow Motion*, in its contemplation of the everyday as experienced by someone declining throughout several serious illnesses, ending with premature death, demonstrates an equally valuable way to undertake this 'ethical practice'. As 'politics in the first person' (*At Your Own Risk*, p. 121), the act of writing a diary bears witness to a reality that cannot be as fully realised when it is less personal and therefore less immediate. As I mentioned earlier in this chapter, Jarman's act of diary-writing looks forward to a time when the journals will be compiled, published and then read by a wider readership: his act 'implies a certain belief in there being a future', even if not for him.[26]

Trusting that these entries will reach a future readership, like much of his preceding work, Jarman bears witness to a history of crisis by recording the physical effects of AIDS-related illnesses, but not displaying them visually. The film *Blue* in particular relies upon his ability to avoid 'the overdetermined body images of the person with AIDS' (I examine how in Chapter 11, which deals with the representation of Jarman's illnesses in *Blue* and *Chroma*).[27] From the mid-1980s onwards, mainstream art dealing with the virus predominantly featured visual representations of people suffering from illnesses commonly associated with AIDS – the disfiguring lesions caused by Kaposi's sarcoma, the yellowing skin caused by consumption of the drug AZT, the brittleness of someone who has been suffering over a long period. Paul Julian Smith points to AIDS activist Douglas Crimp's response to much portrait photography of people with AIDS, noting that 'they strip their subjects of dignity and take pleasure in bringing to light visible evidence of the invisible virus in, say the lesions of Kaposi's sarcoma'. The result is that subjects seem imprisoned in a Foucauldian 'trap of visibility'.[28] Demonstrating against an exhibition of Nicholas Nixon's photography at the New York Museum of Modern Art in 1988, the refrain of direct action advocacy group ACT UP was 'Stop looking at us. Start listening to us'.[29] In this context, Jarman's decision not to visually document and display his body can be considered 'an urgent, politicized response to other unsatisfactory representations of the AIDS crisis'.[30]

In the record of his illnesses in *Smiling in Slow Motion*, Jarman attempted to communicate the awful effects of illness without depicting them. He is frank about his own illness: 'My stomach collapsed this morning for a second time. The whole of my dinner with Richard shat out as I opened the door – indescribable mess. I cried, more in fury than anything else, as HB cleaned it up' (*Smiling in Slow Motion*, p. 294). This is one incident among many and needs little commentary. He demonstrates continual honesty and commitment to the continual act of bearing witness to the degradation of the virus. The purpose in describing but not showing the effects of the virus is very different: the speaking or writing subject retains a powerful agency, not the onlooker. Jarman insists on the necessity for language rather than self-image to bear ethical witness – with what Alan Sinfield termed 'civil intimacy' – to the individually embodied effects of the HIV/AIDS crisis, even though sometimes language might fail.[31]

Narcissi

Smiling in Slow Motion demonstrates a clear break from the prose style of *Modern Nature*. Once the diary entries that comprised *Modern Nature* had ceased in September 1990, there was a gap in his published writing for approximately eight months. During this time, he edited the diary entries for *Modern Nature*. Once he took up his diary again in May 1991, his concerns had changed, and the energies he could devote to writing had reduced. He continued to write about the landscape in Dungeness, as well as the effects of the seasons on his garden, yet his writing had become more spare. The way Jarman's use of the daffodils motif changes over time in *Smiling in Slow Motion* shows how far his writing has altered since the highly allusive prose of much of *Modern Nature*. As I discuss in section 'On narcissi' in Chapter 7 on *Modern Nature*, Jarman had returned to the daffodil as a symbol through which to collect and understand conceptions of sexuality throughout time. The daffodils in his Dungeness shingle garden prompted a chain of associations in the early spring of 1989. In the journal entries collected in *Smiling in Slow Motion*, daffodils are no longer presented in the same way, retreating to a more simple horticultural presence in the later journals. The first mention of them is during the first spring recounted in the book, 1992:

> Busy as a lark, industrious as a bumble bee – I saw a large one in my daffodils. HB hates daffodils, says they look vulgar. Here they stand surreal in the shingle, quite out of place. Mrs Jekyll would laugh at them but they bring in the spring and once, when they were rare in the shops, were such a treat. (*Smiling in Slow Motion*, p. 103)

The seasons, the weather, and the progress of the garden are documented, but not in the same way that is found in *Modern Nature*. The delight, and the research into the significance of each plant, is missing. Instead, Jarman produces a simpler record. Several years earlier, Jarman included streams of consciousness about Roman soldiers' use of the plant as a numbing agent. Now, the only mention of their heritage is an aside that Gertrude Jekyll, the gardener famous for working with Lutyens throughout the late Victorian and Edwardian periods, would find their presence a curious lapse in taste. Strikingly, Collins's feelings and his tastes are here given prominence, and Jarman's response ('once, when they were rare in the shops, were such a treat') sounds like the utterance of an old man.

By the following spring, the first daffodils are mentioned in spare prose. The seasons' passing is described as follows: 'This morning grey and cold, the dead light of February. My daffodils flare into life to illuminate the spring' (*Smiling in Slow Motion*, p. 308). Shortly afterwards, Jarman mentions 'glimpses of daffodils in parks and squares' (*Smiling in Slow Motion*, p. 314) but does not elaborate further. He then uses them to describe the weather: 'It is so cold outside, the daffodils have all wilted, even the tough artichoke is lying flat' (*Smiling in Slow Motion*, p. 318). In these three examples, it is clear that while the presence of daffodils is still of interest to Jarman, he lacks the energy or desire to flesh out his thoughts more fully. As a result, the diary entries prove more of an archive than an analysis: they exist as a record of time passing. There is just one last return to the excitement contained in his earlier prose style. In April 1993, during one of Jarman's later hospital stays, he describes a scene: 'HB shocked us by picking up a daffodil and plunging it into the liquid nitrogen for burning my molluscum. It came out smoking. He flicked it with his finger and it shattered into a thousand pieces' (*Smiling in Slow Motion*, p. 330). The event marks the end of an era.

Writing towards death

The entries in *Smiling in Slow Motion* no longer comprise folklore or modern myth-making: Jarman had become less concerned with presenting material from his personal research in order to draw parallels and useful contrasts across texts and across history. References to culture via books, music or films are more of a simple record of his reading and the music that he listened to. He listened to 'Janáček's violin concert' and 'Delius's *Sea Drift*', 'read Richardson's book on Picasso and *The Beggar's Opera*', 'Read Horace's *Odes*' and 'sat and listened to Whitman's poems set by George Crumb'.[32] There is little discussion, which is especially noteworthy when contrasted with his earlier easy style of slipping cultural references into everyday descriptions, as discussed in Chapter 7. The *Smiling in Slow Motion* record produces a useful archive to draw from when investigating what Jarman was most influenced by during these years. They are notes towards a record of everyday existence. It would be easy to draw conclusions about the weakening Jarman's lessening involvement with the material around him, but I wonder whether instead it marks a change in register towards the everyday, away from the historically oriented. Five months before his death, and very late in the diaries (he would write just a further ten pages of entries), Jarman writes:

> I just downed a sizzlingly peppery tomato juice. I often wonder as I write this diary whether I should put down 'deep' insights, but perhaps the surface is more interesting and alive like the skin and really those other revelations are better left in the past as teenage memories. (*Smiling in Slow Motion*, p. 377)

The inevitable and necessary focus on his physical present, and the resultant effects on his energy levels and capacity to work, has prompted a release from the project he has been working on for much of his adult life: to 'see everything through the past' (*Smiling in Slow Motion*, p. 46) in order to compose, or give light to, the queer canon he found missing throughout his adolescence. Jarman's prose has simplified: he is preoccupied with colour, effect, physical changes and weaknesses, and is now able to listen to a symphony as any listener – not to inform future work, but just as part of his everyday life. This is no longer 'diary after the event' but a contemporaneous record of loss and of illness.[33] These diaries exist as a record of illness, and of friends' lives, among the fragments of the final years of his life.

Notes

1 Derek Jarman, 'Why shutting Barts would be a crime', *Independent*, 4 May 1993. The high-profile campaign was successful.
2 Plate 13 captures Jarman in the garden at Prospect Cottage in the snow. Plate 15 shows the finished sunroom, part of the extension to Prospect Cottage.
3 Derek Jarman, *Freeze Frame*, ed. Takashi Asai (Tokyo: Uplink, 1993). A thick quarto volume containing more than 300 still images from films by Derek Jarman, including *Sebastiane*, *Jubilee*, *The Tempest*, *Imagining October*, *The Last of England*, *Edward II* and *Blue*. Most of the pages are full page colour plates. The book is not analysed here as a separate instance of Jarman's life-writing as it is primarily a visual record of his feature films, with very occasional brief fragments of text.
4 The paintings that comprise both *Queer* and *Evil Queen* were created collaboratively, as has been mentioned elsewhere in this book. Karl Lydon joined Piers Clemett to help Jarman create the paintings that would form the *Evil Queen* series.
5 Reported in *Smiling in Slow Motion*, p. 341.
6 'Books: The Observer Bestseller Lists: Top 5 Film Books', *Observer*, 6 August 2000.
7 Chambers, *Facing It*, p. vii.
8 Ibid., p. viii.
9 Neil Bartlett, 'Introduction', in *Smiling in Slow Motion: The Journals of Derek Jarman, 1991–1994*, by Derek Jarman, ed. Keith Collins (London: Vintage Classics, 2018), pp. vii–xix.
10 See Pencak, *The Films of Derek Jarman*; Rowland Wymer, *Derek Jarman* (Manchester: Manchester University Press, 2005); Richardson, *The Queer Cinema of Derek Jarman*; Ellis, *Angelic Conversations*; and Charlesworth, *Derek Jarman*.
11 Charlesworth, *Derek Jarman*, pp. 173–4.
12 See Ashlee Polatinsky, 'Living Between Deaths: Temporality and the South African AIDS Autopathography', *English Studies in Africa*, 52.1 (2009), 38–49; Chris Steyaert, 'Queering Space: Heterotopic Life in Derek Jarman's Garden', *Gender, Work and Organization*, 17.1 (2010), 45–68; Kevin Barry, 'How Things Can Be Beautiful: Signs, Patches, and Assignats', in *L'Empreinte des choses*, ed. André Topia (Paris: Presses Sorbonne Nouvelle, 2007), pp. 131–46 (p. 132).
13 Michael Arditti, 'Fighting the Dying of the Light', *The Times*, 8 July 2000.
14 Ibid.
15 Penny Wark, 'A Labour of Love', *The Times*, 19 June 2000.
16 Julie Burchill, 'Books: Diary of a Nobody, Part Two; Julie Burchill Charts The Moans And Minutiae Of Derek Jarman's Journal', *Guardian*, 15 July 2000.

17 Watney, *Imagine Hope*, p. 18. Watney's term 'anti-gays' refers to those who had deliberately set themselves apart from their recent GLF-era predecessors and queer contemporaries. For a useful critique of these perspectives, as found in Mark Simpson, ed., *Anti-Gay* (London: Freedom Editions, 1996), see José Esteban Muñoz, *Disidentifications: Queers of Color and the Performance of Politics* (Minneapolis: University of Minnesota Press, 1999), pp. 111–12.
18 'Books: The Observer Bestseller Lists: Top 5 Film Books'.
19 Bennett, 'Lesson of the Gay Guru'.
20 Ibid.
21 Ibid.
22 Brophy, *Witnessing AIDS*, p. 34.
23 Watney, *Imagine Hope*, p. 22. The quote comes from Ida Lewis, 'Conversation: Ida Lewis and James Baldwin', in Fred L. Stanley and Louis H. Pratt, eds, *Conversations with James Baldwin* (Jackson: University Press of Mississippi, 1989), pp. 83–92 (p. 92).
24 Ross Chambers, *Untimely Interventions: AIDS Writing, Testimonial, and the Rhetoric of Haunting* (Ann Arbor: University of Michigan Press, 2004), p. xviii.
25 Ibid., p. xix.
26 Ibid., p. viii.
27 Lawrence, 'Derek Jarman's *Blue*', p. 243.
28 Paul Julian Smith, 'Blue and the Outer Limits', *Sight and Sound*, 3.10 (1993), 18–19 (p. 18).
29 Watney, *Imagine Hope*, p. 101.
30 Moor, 'Spirit and Matter', p. 50.
31 Alan Sinfield, 'Thom Gunn and the Largest Gathering of the Decade', *London Review of Books*, 14.3 (1992), 16–17 (p. 17).
32 *Smiling in Slow Motion*, p. 22 (Tuesday, 18 June 1991); p. 29 (Wednesday, 3 July 1991); p. 62 (Tuesday, 24 December 1991); p. 122 (Sunday, 3 May 1992); p. 173 (Saturday, 18 July 1992).
33 Jarman quoted in Peake, *Derek Jarman*, p. 321.

11

'A kind of bliss': *Blue* and *Chroma*

Colour seems to have a Queer bent!
(Derek Jarman, *Chroma*, p. 58)

Colour is 'a kind of bliss [...] like a closing eyelid, a tiny fainting spell', Roland Barthes wrote in response to the work of artist Cy Twombly.[1] Barthes diagnoses the 'blissful' presence of colour in Twombly's fragmentary, highly personal oeuvre: colour can elicit a curious physical response in those who view his work. Colour precipitates a moment held between embodiment and sublimity: the 'pleasure of a gesture' that the crayon's scratches record invites moments of transcendence in the pieces' viewers.[2] Looking outwards prompts its inverse – a looking inwards – the 'closing eyelid' a physical signal that one is entering into an interior kind of consciousness. Colour becomes a way to bypass image, or language, to prompt direct communion between artist and audience. This chapter explores how Derek Jarman has written searchingly about colour in relation to his own life, in particular the colour blue. Jarman's *Chroma* (1994), which contains the script of his film *Blue* (1993), uses colour as a mode of life-writing, engaging with Ludwig Wittgenstein's work on colour to explore the logic that informs his perceptions. He strives to articulate and thus expand the limits of what language can do and thereby extend what he can communicate about himself. This chapter examines Jarman's engagement with the social and intellectual history of the colour blue, and explores how he engages with colour as a means of splitting meaning into innumerable parts. Barthes' emotive reading of colour in Twombly's canvases sheds light on Jarman's dispersed and fragmentary autobiographical projects, showing us how he uses colour to traverse culturally constituted boundaries within ourselves – the division between the corporeal, emotional and intellectual – and between ourselves and others.

Jarman sought to understand his experiences of colour in relation to a range of intellectual precedents. He places autobiographical fragments alongside quotations about colour from artists and thinkers throughout history who had queer encounters. He combines them to construct a lineage of colour knowledge: a queer history of colour. Measuring his relationship to the spectrum in this way allows him to talk about his experiences as a queer man. By denaturalising and complicating our understandings of colour, Jarman creates unusual activist work that unmasks the structure of socially constituted knowledge, which has the potential to gather a community of queer readers around it. As Jarman quips, 'Colour seems to have a Queer bent!' (*Chroma*, p. 58).

Concentrating on colour is an unexpected and powerful method to communicate about extremes of experience. As this book records, Jarman was bearing witness during a time of crisis: he battled the homophobic governmental and media responses to the HIV/AIDS crisis in Britain, including the reintroduction of Section 28 in 1988. As a prominent HIV-positive man, he consistently created art from material drawn from his own life, blending visionary queer politics with experimental modes of self-representation. By presenting an unwavering blue screen in his last film, *Blue*, created from the majority of the 'Into the Blue' chapter of *Chroma*, he refuses his readership and audience what Tim Lawrence summarises as 'the overdetermined body images of the person with AIDS' (see Plate 16).[3]

He uses colour instead of image to communicate the details of his suffering from late-stage AIDS-related illnesses – the pains of the body with shingles, the loss of sight due to cytomegalovirus, recurrent pneumonia, the indignity and discomfort of chronic diarrhoea – and associated invasive medical treatments. By doing this, Jarman provides an imaginative means of enacting the ACT UP refrain: 'Stop looking at us. Start listening to us'.[4] Jarman employs the colour blue to access complex emotions towards the end of his life, as he is going blind and dying from AIDS-related illnesses: he questions whether colour can allow him to access the limitless, or the transcendent, yet always returns to the body. Doing away entirely for the need for a problematically inflected image of the 'person with AIDS', colour promotes ethical spectatorship: it is a means to bear witness to the terrible effects of the virus as he was drawing to the end of his life.

Jarman writes searchingly about colour to illuminate issues relating to how we deal with some of the most significant human experiences and how we communicate these in language. This chapter seeks to distil the perceptions, relations and genealogies generated by his queer meditations on colour, and considers what they suggest about queer aesthetic modes of navigating personal and political crises of embodiment.

On the colour blue

The colour blue has a long social and intellectual history. The pigment was associated with wealth, from the point that the semi-precious stone lapis lazuli began to be mined in Afghanistan over 3,000 years ago and exported across the ancient world at great expense. In Ancient Egypt, blue was believed to protect the dead against evil in the afterlife. Dark blue was widely used in the Byzantine Empire to decorate churches: it symbolised the infinite expanse of the sky. However, a cheaper version of blue dye, woad, could be created from plants. For the Romans, blue dye was used to colour the clothes of working people. It was also associated with barbarians and with mourning. In the art and life of the early Middle Ages across Europe, blue was used to colour the garments of poor working people. It was not until the status of the Virgin Mary increased and her habit changed to the expensive hue ultramarine, created from lapis lazuli, that blue became associated with holiness.

The colour blue has been used by various prominent artists, filmmakers and musicians. Notably, Pablo Picasso's blue period (1901–04), during which he painted using predominantly blue and green tones, commenced following the suicide of his friend Carlos Casagemas and provides a record of his subsequent depression. The blues is a genre of music that often incorporates narratives of personal misfortune and structural racism. Miles Davis's album *Kind of Blue* (1959) is the most famous example of modal jazz. Maggie Nelson's lyrical text *Bluets* (2009) is a meditation on the colour blue, which is used as a tool to help her untangle the intensity of her feelings resulting from loss. Carol Mavor's evocative essay collection *Blue Mythologies: Reflections on a Colour* (2013) draws from the history of art, photography, literature and her own memories. The French film *La vie d'Adèle* (dir. Abdellatif Kechiche, 2013) is translated for its North American release as *Blue is the Warmest Color*. Blue in this case refers to Adèle's lover Emma's blue hair, which symbolises desire, first love and loss. Anne Carson wrote on the colour blue in *The Blue of Distance*, published to accompany a group exhibition at the Aspen Art Museum, Colorado. Featuring drawing, photography, sculpture and sound art by the artists Felix Gonzalez-Torres, Roni Horn, Catherine Opie, Cy Twombly, Cerith Wyn Evans and others, it is a reflection on the colour blue's relationship to absence, desire and distance.

We are accustomed to understanding the colour blue as pointing towards the precious, the infinite and the holy: a tangle of cultural associations from different sources that Jarman references copiously in his texts. But, as Wittgenstein points out, 'Someone who speaks of the character of a colour is always thinking of just *one* particular way it is used'.[5]

For Jarman, 'Blue is the universal love in which man bathes – it is the terrestrial paradise' (*Chroma*, p. 108), among other attributes. His affinity with this particular pigment stems from his interest in the avant-garde artist Yves Klein, who sought to attain 'the expression of an inner spiritual meaning' in his extensive series of blue paintings (1957–62), made from International Klein Blue (IKB).[6] Klein attached particular significance and meanings to certain pigments. He derived some of this symbolism from Max Heindl, the seventeenth-century Rosicrucian philosopher, who believed that blue was the highest of all colours and represented the spirit freed from matter. Jarman references this Rosicrucian thinking when he comments, 'Blue transcends the solemn geographies of human limits' (*Chroma*, p. 109). Furthermore, early versions of Jarman's idea for a film about the painter Klein were titled 'Bliss,' recalling Barthes' response to Twombly's deployment of colour: 'Color … [is] a kind of bliss'.[7]

'The problem with books of colour is that they turn out like shopping lists', observes Jarman in a journal entry written while he was preparing the content for *Chroma* (*Smiling in Slow Motion*, p. 199). The French social historian Michel Pastoreau charts the popularity of the colour blue in *Blue: The History of a Color* (2001) through a string of examples; William Gass, the American writer and former philosophy professor, indulges an obsession with lists in *On Being Blue: A Philosophical Enquiry* (1975). Jarman's *Chroma* sometimes tends towards the same. Yet this is purposeful. In her essay 'Giotto's Joy', Julia Kristeva 'unpicks the mystical blue' of the Scrovegni Chapel, Padua.[8] She uses the example of the chapel to make a wider observation about colour: 'Color achieves […] the laying down of One Meaning so that it might at once be pulverized, multiplied into plural meanings. Color is the shattering of unity'.[9] Colour is a site to explore what Karen Barad describes as the 'ongoing, open-ended, entangled material practices' through which 'the social and the scientific are co-constituted'.[10] The propulsive forces of 'shattering' and 'entangle[ment]' that Kristeva and Barad highlight are critical to an understanding of queer aesthetic modes of crisis. Although a colour's symbolic resonances might be contradictory – splintered, variant – the colour itself contains these meanings in complex, palimpsestic form.

On an abiding interest in Wittgenstein

Colour's ability to pulverise, multiply and shatter meaning is one of its most important qualities for Jarman.[11] Colour provides him with a medium through which to explore the complications and contradictions inherent in how he can express his embodiment. But there is a related attribute that demands attention: the discussion of colour places the juncture of human perception with language in sharp focus. Jarman is preoccupied with this difficulty: we must face the discursive limits of language to usefully define and thereby share our internal and physical worlds. He engages with the Austrian-British philosopher Ludwig Wittgenstein, who repeatedly uses colour to demonstrate his theories about the limits of language and its logical structures. Throughout his writing, from the early *Tractatus Logico-Philosophicus* (1921) to *Philosophical Investigations* (published posthumously in 1953) and *Remarks on Colour* (published posthumously in 1977) that rebutted much of his earlier work, Wittgenstein offers examples of colour in order to demonstrate his larger theories about language and logic. He contended that like language, our understanding of colour is part of a shared system of usage within culture, and therefore scientific investigations into the nature of colour (by, for example, Isaac Newton) can only be secondary to an understanding of how words denoting colour are used in a particular culture. This is because colour perception is contextual and deeply personal: Wittgenstein points to 'the indeterminateness in the concept of colour or again in that sameness of colour'.[12] Although Jarman calls the hue 'the universal love in which man bathes' (*Chroma*, p. 108), he immediately undoes a sense of the universal by adding alternate, often contradictory meanings. Colour provides a distilled demonstration of our inability to share an exact understanding of the world with one another. This method is a means of attempting to get closer to a fuller understanding of the world, simultaneously accepting the futility of any such task.

It is not coincidental that Jarman produced a startling, pared-down biopic of the philosopher, which in turn directly informed his research and writing in *Chroma*, as well as his final film, *Blue*. Described by Jarman as 'my harlequin book' (*Smiling in Slow Motion*, p. 143), *Chroma* was predominantly written during the summer of 1992 alongside the production of *Wittgenstein* (1993) and comprises one of his most unusual books of life-writing. The idea for the book was sparked in part by Jarman's lifelong preoccupation with aesthetic concerns but also, more directly, by his biographical research on the philosopher that took place over the same period. On 31 May 1992, Jarman wrote: 'I dreamt all night of writing a book on colour, not scientific or in any way academic, free floating through the spectrum. Maybe the *Tractatus* unlocked it' (*Smiling in Slow Motion*, p. 134).

At the beginning of *Philosophical Investigations*, Wittgenstein comments, 'I should not like my writing to spare other people the trouble of thinking. But, if possible, to stimulate someone to thoughts of his own'.[13] Jarman absorbs his idea, producing vivid writing that shares Wittgenstein's fragmentary approach, prompting his readers to consider the reasons for particular elisions, juxtapositions and contradictions. Reading Jarman and Wittgenstein together, one notices how Jarman transposes Wittgenstein's form and ideas into political ends. Unsettling our understanding of how we experience the world is a way of creating space for alternative ways of living.

Jarman's collage technique in *Blue* and *Chroma*

Blue, the last film that Jarman would release, is a moving and radical exploration of the bodily disintegration he endured as a result of a number of AIDS-related illnesses, including the loss of his sight. Justin Remes describes it as 'one of the most profound meditations on death in the history of cinema'.[14] 'Conceptually challenging and formally severe', the film comprises an unchanging field of deep ultramarine – the pigment used by Yves Klein in his series of blue paintings (1957–62) and named International Klein Blue – for 79 minutes.[15] Its soundtrack incorporates four voices (Nigel Terry, John Quentin, Tilda Swinton and, on occasion, Jarman) reading a script that intertwines three recognisable strands: reflections on the colour blue, a dreamlike account of a boy called Blue and autobiographical fragments, the most sustained of which deal with his treatment for blindness. The spoken elements make up just 22 minutes of material. Sound effects such as noise from traffic, the buzz of a café and birdsong accompany the voices, along with a minimalist score by long-time collaborator Simon Fisher Turner, who brings in musicians to create fragments of sound.[16]

The text that provides the script for the film is published inside *Chroma: A Book of Colour*. In *Chroma*, Jarman's writing is not organised chronologically, but is divided into chapters, each of which focuses on a different colour of the spectrum: 'Into the White', 'On Seeing Red', 'Green Fingers'. Yet even here, Jarman considers not only the colours of the rainbow (or the rainbow flag), but includes the monochromatic white, black and grey, and the shimmering gold and silver, as well as modalities such as translucence and iridescence. More unusual yet are the chapters on figures from history, including Marsilio Ficino, the Renaissance philosopher renowned for re-popularising the works of Plato, and Isaac Newton, who discovered that light, refracted through a prism, decomposes into the colours of the visible spectrum. The result, *Chroma*, is described by Ellis as 'an autobiographical experiment for a subject-in-process', formed from, as Dillon notes, 'a kind of critical collage that is more familiar from American experimental writing'.[17] Its methods also have precedents in Jarman's own work: those seen in the journals published as *Modern Nature* and the scrapbook-polemic *At Your Own Risk*, which use collage as a means not only to construct life narrative, but also to speak back to the cultural forms within which the narrative exists. Reading queer filmmaker Jonathan Caouette's autobiographical documentary *Tarnation*, Anna Poletti argues that its collage aesthetics can be read as a 'practice' that can provide a 'periperformative' revision of the documentary memoir form.[18] I further develop Poletti's argument, viewing the way Jarman uses collage as a queer practice of survival in his writing that also seeks to change the terms of his representation by 'cobbling together ways to attach to the world that cannot be subsumed into an identity or bionarrative'.[19]

Each chapter of *Chroma* and the colour it concerns is formed by a collage comprised of three main areas. He collects theories of colour from philosophers, scientists and writers to include, among others, Pliny, Leonardo da Vinci, Isaac Newton, Johann Wolfgang von Goethe and Ludwig Wittgenstein. He intersperses these with fragments of poetry concerning colour from Sappho, Ovid, Dante, Wilfred Owen, T. S. Eliot and himself. Working in relationship with these quotations, Jarman uses the colour under consideration as a prompt for his own memory, adding memoir-like vignettes. Inspired by Kasimir Malevich's statement 'In art there is need for truth, not sincerity' (quoted in *Chroma*, p. 3), Jarman incants: 'May my black Waterman ink spill out the truth' (*Chroma*, p. 3) – linking his thoughts with the material traces left by his fountain pen. Peake describes the process: 'Writing in longhand on whatever sheets of paper he had to hand, he jotted down ideas, anecdotes and autobiography in the order they came to him. His only focus was the colour under consideration'.[20] Often wearing an article of clothing to match the colour chapter he was working on, he connected his body to his work on the project: the chapter 'On Seeing Red' sees him 'sitting here writing this in a bright red T-shirt from Marks and Spencer. I shut my eyes. In the dark, I can remember the red, but I cannot see it' (*Chroma*, p. 33). Here he demonstrates how everyday humdrum experience sits in tandem with the more theoretical. He links his body to some of the associations of the colour red, such as blood, anger and passion, yet undercuts them with the banality of the t-shirt's quotidian origins. A defiant celebration of the richness of visual culture, the book was written at a hectic pace before he became too weak and unwell to continue.

On colour and queerness

Not only does Jarman celebrate the diversity of different perceptions of colour in *Chroma*, he also deploys this exploration of visuality to create queer countercultural discourse, through two different means. In the first, he makes use of Wittgenstein's technique of collating different ways to conceptualise colour. Wittgenstein juxtaposes different understandings of colour in order to point out the gulf between individual subjectivities, as well as to politicise colour. Wittgenstein wonders: 'couldn't there be [...] people whose colour concepts deviate from ours?' He challenges his readership to understand that 'not every deviation from the norm must be a blindness, a defect'.[21] Jarman's project works to break down the concept of an essential meaning, to demonstrate how contextual and mutable meaning is. Following Wittgenstein, Jarman comments: 'I know that my colours are not yours' (*Chroma*, p. 42) and, in his introduction to the published scripts for *Wittgenstein*, Jarman asks 'What is a picture of Queer? There is no one picture' (*Wittgenstein*, p. 64). The concern with colour in both *Chroma* and the film *Blue* comprises a commentary on perception: marking the diverse experiences in the world and thereby making a lyrical yet urgent case for the acceptance of queer lives, in the midst of the HIV/AIDS crisis and Jarman's own suffering. He thereby draws attention to the multiplicity of ways in which sexuality manifests. Ellis summarises the link between the two: 'Queerness, like color, is a matter of definition and usage; queer doesn't designate a stable thing or identity but rather a way of being in the world, an ethics of existence'.[22] In *Chroma*, Jarman points out the multiple meanings and uses of colour as a resistant act.

Others have used colour as a means by which to reclaim queer histories. Building on Jarman's project, the artist David Batchelor accuses Western culture of being inherently anti-colour in *Chromophobia* (2000), a slim text that argues that the chromophobic impulse is apparent in 'the many and varied attempts to purge colour from culture, to devalue colour, to diminish its significance, to deny its complexity'.[23] He points to the othering of colour: 'colour is made out to be the property of some 'foreign' body – usually the feminine, the oriental, the primitive, the infantile, the vulgar, the queer or the pathological'.[24] Batchelor points to these negative representations in order to undo them in an act of reclamation.

In contrast, Jarman collates histories of colour that persistently link to the history of sexuality. 'The forward exploration of Colour is Queer,' Jarman announces in his introduction to the *Wittgenstein* script, 'Leonardo in his notebook, Newton's *Optics* and Ludwig's *Remarks on Colour*' (p. 64). Here, he draws out a lineage between his work on colour and that of precursors who also worked on colour and desired men. He extends this lineage in *Chroma*, assembling evidence to support this assertion in the chapter on the humanist philosopher Marsilio Ficino:

> In the 1430s a fourteen year old boy could be burnt at the stake for an act of sodomy – this would not happen in Florence again. Platonism confirmed that it was right and proper to love someone of your own sex – a more practical way of viewing sexuality than the church's blueprint of DON'Ts. The modern world received the message with open arms and Botticelli, Pontormo, Rosso, Michelangelo and Leonardo stepped from the shadows. (*Chroma*, p. 58)

Ficino's work translating Plato into Latin and attempting a revival of his Academy served to bring the *Symposium* into public view and had some influence on the Italian Renaissance and the development of European philosophy. Jarman here draws a lineage from Plato through to the sexually ambiguous artists of the Italian Renaissance, to Newton's work on the division of light into the colours of the spectrum in the seventeenth and eighteenth centuries, through to the tortured Wittgenstein in the twentieth century. As well as drawing attention to the changing perceptions of sexuality over time, by drawing from what we know of the lives of philosophers, artists and scientists who demonstrated attraction to men, Jarman seeks to forge a queer lineage to inform his understanding of himself as a queer subject with a history. As Ellis notes when summarising *Chroma* 'historicizing inevitably means politicizing, or, at the very least, making visible connections that generally go unnoticed'.[25] Making history visible is a political act.

Extending queer genealogies into the contemporary

In *Bluets*, a slender, fragmentary meditation on loss, Maggie Nelson makes visible a link between three of her primary influences: Goethe, Wittgenstein and Jarman. Unlike Jarman, she aligns the colour blue to the body not primarily in terms of sexuality, but in terms of trauma. Concentrating on colour becomes an acute way of describing and sharing painful personal experience. She points to something curious that links the three writers: each of them wrote his book on colour during a period marked by mental or physical darkness, or both. She presents the following in sequence, wondering about but not stating the connection between the three:

> 23. Goethe wrote *Theory of Colours* in a period of his life described by one critic as 'a long interval, marked by nothing of distinguished note.' Goethe himself describes the period as one in which 'a quiet, collected state of mind was out of the question.' Goethe is not alone in turning to color at a particularly fraught moment. Think of filmmaker Derek Jarman, who wrote his book *Chroma* as he was going blind and dying of AIDS, a death he also forecast on film as disappearing into a 'blue screen'. Or of Wittgenstein, who wrote his *Remarks on Colour* during the last eighteen months of his life, while dying of stomach cancer. He knew he was dying; he could have chosen to write on any philosophical problem under the sun. He chose to write about color. About color and pain.[26]

The unwritten final link is that she, too, wrote her book on colour during a particularly fraught period, emotionally speaking. She is gesturing towards, but not articulating directly, a holistic link between how we experience pain and a desire to analyse colour. As contemporary critical theory increasingly conceptualises emotion as 'materially embodied, discursively constituted', it doesn't seem dissonant for Nelson to group Goethe's uncollected state of mind with the late illnesses of Wittgenstein and Jarman.[27] What connects the three men with her text in this excerpt is the way each looks to colour to test the limits of how far one can communicate about pain.

Bluets generates meaning through juxtaposition. By abutting autobiographical vignettes with quotations from poets such as Frank O'Hara, Gertrude Stein and Mallarmé, songwriters Joni Mitchell and Leonard Cohen, and her main referents Goethe and Wittgenstein, she places her memories in dialogue with them. Differently from Jarman's queer collage technique, one of the effects of her writing is that 'other people's sentences blend into Nelson's; they seem to belong there, as residents of her mind she must contend with'.[28] Jarman allows the genealogies of colour he collates to accrue meaning through accumulation. Nelson, however, further develops Jarman's approach. She uses these referents to test her ideas against – she holds up to the light fragments of others' thought that help us get closer to, if not inside, her relentless self-questioning.

In *Giving an Account of Oneself*, Judith Butler comments that 'the "I" has no story of its own that is not also the story of a relation – or set of relations – to a set of norms', and both Jarman and Nelson test their understanding of themselves by placing their contentions in relation to a series of ideas from intellectual and cultural precedents.[29] Part of the purpose of this activity is to examine how their choice of precedents might be productively different from the culturally accepted norms that surround them, broadly unquestioned by wider society. Nelson's method is complicated and further politicised in *The Argonauts*, which explores the nuances of her particular experiences of queer kinship – the changes to her body during her pregnancy and childbirth that take place in tandem with the changes in her partner Harry Dodge's body as he commences hormone therapy and top (gender-confirmation) surgery. In *The Argonauts*, she pays homage to 'the many-gendered mothers of my heart', a phrase she borrows from the poet Dana Ward, for the powerful revolutionary work of many feminist, queer, anti-racist thinkers, writers, activists and artists of different genders who have nurtured her thinking or provided her with intellectual precedents. 'I was cruising for intellectual mothers', she says of her college-age self.[30] Butler considers this desire for origins in terms that speak both to Nelson's process and relate back to Jarman's: 'If the "I" is not at one with moral norms, this means only that the subject must deliberate upon these norms, and that part of deliberation will entail a critical understanding of their social genesis and meaning'.[31] Questioning social structures unearths a desire to find a different kind of origin.

On colour and the ethics of bearing witness

Jarman's *Chroma* has in common with Nelson's *Bluets* and *The Argonauts* the way they create fragmentary texts that seek to create new genealogies of meaning and ways of being. Nelson writes about some queer issues that affect our contemporary moment – transitioning and queer kinship – whereas *Chroma* bears witness to the preceding history of crisis. Jarman here records the physical effects of the AIDS-related illnesses that affected him. This project relies upon his ability to provide an account of himself to his readership. Jarman made the decision to create this work with no accompanying series of images. In doing so, he avoids what Tim Lawrence refers to as the 'Overdetermined body images of the person with AIDS'.[32] As I raise in my discussion of *Smiling in Slow Motion*, from the mid-1980s onwards, mainstream art dealing with the virus predominantly featured visual representations of people suffering from illnesses commonly associated with AIDS, in ways that strip their subjects of agency and dignity. In this context, Jarman's decision not to visually document and display his body in *Blue* or *Chroma* can be considered 'an urgent, politicized response to other unsatisfactory representations of the AIDS crisis'.[33]

Jarman's project in *Blue*, as in *Chroma*, enacts the message from the ACT UP demonstrators. Written and audible expressions of the corporeal are here intentionally mediated to avoid an audience that gives precedence to the biological over the political, discursive aspects of his self-representations. It is important that in the 'Into the Blue' chapter of *Chroma*, as in the film, we read about the ravages the virus has inflicted on Jarman's body, but we do not see its effects. However, as Patrizia Lombardo comments, speaking about the film version, *Blue*, 'With a violent leap, the most bodyless film ever produced projects the human body in its most cruel and unspeakable presence'.[34] Yet the purpose in describing but not showing the effects of the virus is very different: the speaking or writing subject retains a powerful agency, not the onlooker. Jarman insists on the necessity for language rather than self-image to bear ethical witness – with what Alan Sinfield termed 'civil intimacy' – to the individually embodied effects of the HIV/AIDS crisis, even though sometimes language might fail.[35]

Equally important, Jarman uses the colour blue to access complex emotions as he is going blind and dying. At times, the colour is used by Jarman, along with its evocative history and symbolic resonances, to gesture towards the limitless or transcendental. As he was losing his sight and therefore to the ability to access the colour blue outside his imagination, its spiritual aspects come to the fore. Much has been written about the more transcendental passages in Jarman's *Blue*, which also feature in *Chroma*: 'Blue an open door to soul' (p. 112), 'Blue of my dreams' (p. 108), 'Blue transcends the solemn geographies of human limits' (p. 109). In her essay on the film, Kate Higginson raises some of the meanings that *Blue* creates: 'contemplation, joy, spaciousness, immateriality, and the sea'.[36] The colour blue represents a release from 'the pandemonium of image' (*Chroma*, p. 112), perhaps in a gesture towards something more spiritual.[37] She explores Jarman's role as a 'seer,' one whose literal blindness is compensated for with divine insight, building on Andrew Moor's comments on *Blue* as a political intervention in and against the regime of visuality. She theorises the final scene of *Blue* – a vision of 'an eternal queer sanctuary on the seabed' – as Jarman's prophecy of a 'queer h(e)aven' that attempts to mitigate the losses from AIDS.[38]

However, Justin Remes rebuts Higginson's reading that Jarman might be providing a 'consolatory vision'.[39] He considers Higginson's perspective 'too intent on salvaging some kind of religious impulse from the film,' explaining that 'there is no reason to suppose that IKB has the same spiritual import in *Blue* that it had in the hands of Klein'.[40] He comments that 'Blue no longer connotes heaven but an empty sky', and raises Dillon's similar reading of Jarman's use of the colour: 'a visual absence, a nothingness before the abyss of death'.[41] As Tracy Biga points out, blue is used by Jarman as 'variously a color, a person or agent, a mood, a concept and a thing'.[42] Although Higginson's focus on a sense of 'an eternal queer sanctuary' may be an overemphasis, her essay usefully summarises a critical tension in Jarman's work: '*Blue* negotiates, and essentially stages a dialogue between, the material realities of AIDS and a desire to escape the same'.[43]

'Into the Blue'

Although much has been written about the potentially transcendental aspects of the film *Blue*, the ways Jarman portrays the 'material realities of AIDS' in *Blue* and *Chroma* have been afforded less attention.[44] Writing about colour offers him an unusual and effective way to communicate about the litany of AIDS-related illnesses that he suffered from, the physical pain and the resulting series of medical treatments. Jarman teases out connections between colour and his treatments at St Bartholomew's Hospital for blindness, particularly in the chapter of *Chroma* that would become the text for the film *Blue*, 'Into the Blue'. The chapter contains deadpan reports of the indignities caused by Jarman's loss of sight that bear closer examination. Tania, one of the owners of Maison Bertaux, a pâtisserie Jarman frequented regularly in Soho's Greek Street, tells him: '"Your clothes are on back to front and inside out"' (*Chroma*, p. 107). Jarman confronts the change his loss of sight forces on his capacity to perform the basic function of getting dressed. Any pathos is tempered by his matter-of-fact approach: 'Since there were only two of us here I took them off and put them right then and there' (*Chroma*, p. 107). Later, 'I step off the kerb and a cyclist nearly knocks me down' is directly followed by 'I step into a blue funk' (*Chroma*, p. 107). As Jarman steps into the road, he feels his new vulnerability sharply: the metaphorical movement into a state of depression, confusion and fearfulness echoes his physical movement. In this example, Jarman weaves his fragmentary narratives together by careful deployment of different cultural uses of the word blue.

A related device is deployed in the fragment that follows his movement into a 'blue funk' (*Chroma*, p. 107), which describes a medical procedure familiar to many readers from routine eye tests:

> The doctor in St Bartholemew's Hospital thought he could detect lesions in my retina – the pupils dilated with belladonna – the torch shone into them with a terrible blinding light.
> Look left
> Look down
> Look up
> Look right.
>
> Blue flashes in my eyes. (*Chroma*, p. 107)

The doctor's instructions to look in each direction are to some degree comforting in their predictability and their thoroughness. Yet Jarman's reference to the substance used to dilate his pupils defamiliarises the experience by causing his readers to pause and consider the multiple meanings here at work. The drug belladonna, meaning 'beautiful woman' in Italian, was so named for its historical use by women for cosmetic purposes. Women used eye drops prepared from the poisonous plant to dilate their pupils, an effect thought to be alluring. Also commonly known as deadly nightshade, it is one of the most toxic plants in the West. Its full name is *Atropa belladonna*, thought to have been named after the Greek goddess Atropos, the oldest of the three fates and the one who ended the life of mortals by cutting the thread of their lives with scissors. Atropine sulphate, derived from the plant, is still used in ophthalmology as a mydriatic.

The mention of the substance 'belladonna' (*Chroma*, p. 107) would not have been accidental. Jarman makes frequent reference to herbal lore throughout his journals, especially in those published within *Modern Nature* (see the section 'Personal mythologies' in Chapter 7) where, for example, he uncovers the historical uses and folkloric associations of plants such as pansies, rosemary and daffodils. He then repurposes them to create a queer history that works by complicating our understanding of the diversity of symbolic resonances alive in common plants and by extension our everyday experience. In the passage cited above, Jarman uses the term 'belladonna' (*Chroma*, p. 107) so as to draw on the plant's historical resonances and thereby draw ironic attention to the material effects of HIV/AIDS. The first irony at play is that the substance is being used for a purpose very far from making Jarman attractive in the manner of a historical Italian *bella donna*: the substance is used to allow the doctor to see the extent of the retinal damage wrought by cytomegalovirus, a virus often seen in patients with compromised immune systems, that caused his loss of vision. The second, and related, irony is that the full name of the plant, Atropa belladonna, merges two meanings: the Greek fate of death with the cosmetically enhanced, seductive woman. The stock character of the femme fatale emerges at the conjunction of these two meanings, acting here as a metonym for the HIV/AIDS virus.

The last line in the passage, 'Blue flashes in my eyes' (*Chroma*, p. 107), refers to the sharp light of the doctor's torch on Jarman's damaged retinae, connecting the diary report of Jarman's experience of the medical procedure to the other strands of the chapter 'Into the Blue' through colour. Here, the colour blue is used as a tool to help communicate the sometimes alienating embodied experiences of treatment for AIDS-related illnesses. This is a method that recurs throughout *Chroma*. He links intense physical experiences with the colour blue, thereby placing them on a continuum of colour that, through association and connection, helps him communicate what he himself, at times, finds hard to relate to. Colour becomes a means to bear witness and allow his readership to engage in ethical spectatorship.

Jarman's journey through light and pigment produces searching and moving personal testimony, creating 'luminous presence' (*Chroma*, p. 151) that advances our understanding of how we might construct genealogies of meaning outside of mainstream discourse. Colour is a special, productive site in his life-writing because of its 'ontological indeterminacy', which enables those who interrogate it to demonstrate the instability of meaning and, in doing so, the multiplicity of possible meanings.[45] By exploring what Karen Barad describes as 'the inescapable entanglement of matters of being, knowing, and doing', Jarman seeks to advance a sense of the connectedness of the discursive and the material, in which no priority is given to either side.[46] He juxtaposes material from his own life with material collated from others, in often fragmentary or unresolved ways: as Jarman writes in *Chroma*, 'For Blue there are no boundaries or solutions' (p. 115).

Jarman uses Wittgenstein's work to demonstrate the range of perspectives that are possible in the world. He explores two personal perspectives regarding colour in particular: the at once transcendent and deeply embodied sense of colour as a route into communicating about great pain. Jarman uses colour as a way to bear witness during the HIV/AIDS crisis to the terrible effects of the virus, as he was drawing to the end of his life. He uses colour to mobilise affect and a sense of community in his readership for urgent political purposes. As Roger Hallas points out, 'Bearing witness involves an address to an other; it occurs only in a framework of relationality, in which the testimonial act is itself witnessed by another'.[47] Jarman is self-reflexively reliant on his reader's capacity to partake in ethical spectatorship.

Notes

1. Roland Barthes, *The Responsibility of Forms: Critical Essays on Music, Art, and Representation*, trans. Richard Howard (Berkeley: University of California Press, 1985), p. 166.
2. Ibid.
3. Lawrence, 'Derek Jarman's *Blue*', p. 243.
4. Watney, *Imagine Hope*, p. 101.
5. Ludwig Wittgenstein, *Remarks on Colour: Parallel Text*, ed. G. E. M. Anscombe, trans. Linda L. McAlister, new edn (Oxford: John Wiley & Sons, 1979), p. 12e.
6. Wymer, *Derek Jarman*, p. 170.
7. Barthes, *The Responsibility of Forms*, p. 166. For information about the development of 'Bliss', including an early related live performance with Derek Jarman and Tilda Swinton at the Lumière, St Martins Lane, see Peake, *Derek Jarman*, pp. 475–8.
8. Tessa Laird, 'Getting the Blues – Sex, Words and the Hues', *The Weeklings*, 2014, www.theweeklings.com/tlaird/2014/10/15/getting-the-blues-sex-words-and-the-hues (accessed 16 July 2018). The Scrovegni chapel's fresco cycle, recounting the Christian salvation story, covers the walls and ceiling. It is remarkable in part for its use of colour: Giotto used a deep ultramarine to cover the ceiling and as the background for the frescoes on each of the walls, which saturates the onlooker's field of vision.
9. Julia Kristeva, 'Giotto's Joy', in *Desire in Language: A Semiotic Approach to Literature and Art*, ed. Leon S. Roudiez, trans. Thomas Gora, Alice Jardine and Leon S. Roudiez, revised edn (New York: Columbia University Press, 1980), pp. 210–36 (p. 221).
10. Karen Barad, *Meeting the Universe Halfway: Quantum Physics and the Entanglement of Matter and Meaning* (Durham, NC: Duke University Press, 2007), p. 168.
11. 'Color achieves the momentary dialectic of law – the laying down of One Meaning so that it might at once be pulverized, multiplied into plural meanings. Color is the shattering of unity', Kristeva, 'Giotto's Joy', p. 221.
12. Wittgenstein, *Remarks on Colour*, p. 4e.
13. Ludwig Wittgenstein, *Philosophical Investigations*, trans. G. E. M. Anscombe, new edn (Oxford: Wiley-Blackwell, 1973), p. viii.
14. Justin Remes, *Motion(Less) Pictures: The Cinema of Stasis* (New York: Columbia University Press, 2015), p. 112.

15 Ellis, *Angelic Conversations*, p. 235.
16 Contributors include John Balance and Peter Christopherson from cult queer experimental band Coil, a capella gothic rock band Miranda Sex Garden and sound architect Brian Eno. For an analysis of the particular resonances of sound in Jarman's audio-visual project, see Jacques Khalip, '"The Archaeology of Sound": Derek Jarman's *Blue* and Queer Audiovisuality in the Time of Aids', *differences*, 21.2 (2010), 73–108.
17 Ellis, *Angelic Conversations*, p. 234; Dillon, *Derek Jarman and Lyric Film*, p. 229.
18 Poletti, 'Periperformative Life Narrative: Queer Collages', p. 362.
19 Ibid., p. 376.
20 Peake, *Derek Jarman*, p. 501.
21 Wittgenstein, *Remarks on Colour*, p. 3e.
22 Ellis, *Angelic Conversations*, p. 235.
23 David Batchelor, *Chromophobia* (London: Reaktion Books, 2000), p. 22.
24 Ibid., pp. 22–3.
25 Ellis, *Angelic Conversations*, p. 235.
26 Maggie Nelson, *Bluets* (Seattle, WA: Wave Books, 2009), p. 10.
27 Brophy and Hladki, 'Visual Autobiography', p. 6; Nelson, *Bluets*, p. 10.
28 Moira Donegan, 'Gay as in Happy', *N+1*, 23 (Fall 2015), https://nplusonemag.com/issue-23/reviews/gay-as-in-happy (accessed 5 December 2016).
29 Judith Butler, *Giving An Account of Oneself*, p. 8.
30 Maggie Nelson, *The Argonauts* (Minneapolis, MN: Graywolf Press, 2016), pp. 57–8.
31 Judith Butler, *Giving an Account of Oneself*, p. 8.
32 Lawrence, 'Derek Jarman's *Blue*', p. 243.
33 Moor, 'Spirit and Matter', p. 50.
34 Patrizia Lombardo, 'Cruellement Bleu', *Critical Quarterly*, 36.1 (1994), 131–3 (p. 133).
35 Sinfield, 'Thom Gunn', p. 17.
36 Kate Higginson, 'Derek Jarman's "Ghostly Eye": Prophetic Bliss and Sacrificial Blindness in *Blue*', *Mosaic*, 41.1 (2008), 77–94 (p. 78).
37 The artist Georgia O'Keeffe also turned to the colour blue in her late works. In 1972, she lost much of her eyesight due to macular degeneration. After this point, she produced a series of abstract watercolours in a deep blue. Following her encroaching blindness, she shares with Jarman an instinctual engagement with pure colour: 'The fathomless blue of Bliss' (*Chroma*, p. 115).
38 Higginson, 'Derek Jarman's "Ghostly Eye"', pp. 78–9.
39 Ibid., p. 78.
40 Remes, *Motion(Less) Pictures*, p. 118.
41 Ibid., p. 119; Dillon, *Derek Jarman and Lyric Film*, p. 237.
42 Tracy Biga, 'The Principle of Non-Narration in the Films of Derek Jarman', in *By Angels Driven: The Films of Derek Jarman*, ed. Chris Lippard (Wiltshire: Flicks Books, 1996), pp. 12–30 (p. 26).
43 Higginson, 'Derek Jarman's "Ghostly Eye"', pp. 79–80.

44 Ibid., p. 80. The quote in the subheading is from *Chroma*, p. 103.
45 Nelson, *The Argonauts*, p. 15.
46 Barad, *Meeting the Universe Halfway*, p. 27.
47 Roger Hallas, *Reframing Bodies: AIDS, Bearing Witness, and the Queer Moving Image* (Durham, NC: Duke University Press, 2010), p. 10.

12

Derek Jarman's Garden: A therapy and a pharmacopoeia

Like all true gardeners I'm an optimist
(Jarman, *Kicking the Pricks*, p. 151)

Small pleasures must correct great tragedies, therefore of gardens in the midst of war I boldly tell
(Vita Sackville-West)[1]

When keen gardener Howard Sooley began to visit Prospect Cottage regularly in 1991, Keith Collins commented: 'With his collaboration the garden entered its second phase', and 'slowly the garden acquired a new meaning'.[2] Sooley's help was instrumental in helping Derek Jarman to develop the garden space. He had excellent horticultural knowledge and a keenness to provide practical assistance by working in the garden and driving Jarman to nurseries. For Collins, the landscape surrounding Prospect Cottage acted as a pathetic fallacy for the first few years at Prospect Cottage: 'the plants struggling against biting winds and Death Valley sun merged with Derek's struggle with illness' (*Derek Jarman's Garden*, Preface). The landscape transformed into a vibrant memento mori: 'the flowers blossomed while Derek faded' (*Derek Jarman's Garden*, Preface). Sooley began to photograph the garden from his first visit onwards and continued to document both the plant life and Jarman from then until his death. The results of these three final years of photography are collated in *Derek Jarman's Garden* (1995), alongside some accompanying writing by Jarman from the final year of his life. The writing in the book mirrors some of the content of journal entries in *Smiling in Slow Motion* from 1993 – descriptions of the garden's form and contents, the progress of particular plants, elegies for dead friends and mention of hospital stays. The book, as Melissa Zeiger puts it, 'is both a how-to gardening book and a meditation on crisis'.[3]

Derek Jarman's Garden was a project that Jarman intended to be published, but it was prepared posthumously by Sooley and Collins. It holds more illustrations than there are pages (150 illustrations, ninety in colour, across

142 pages), making its final form a departure from the books of life-writing Jarman had been preparing during the early 1990s. The numerous large images depict a place flooded with sunlight. The images provide a highly coloured record of the garden at the most mature stage that Jarman would see it. It also contains a number of Sooley's portraits of Jarman during these final years – in the garden at Dungeness, on the shingle beach and during a final holiday to Monet's garden in Giverny (see plates 17 and 18). It raises some of the same topics as the diaries previously published as *Modern Nature*. For example, towards the beginning of the book, Jarman comments: 'flowers sparkled in my childhood as they do in a medieval manuscript' (*Derek Jarman's Garden*, p. 11). Flowers act as illumination in his memory – marking particular moments of being as significant. Jarman also explains once again: 'I saw [the garden] as a therapy and a pharmacopoeia' (*Derek Jarman's Garden*, p. 12), an idea he raises and responds to in *Modern Nature* (see the beginning of Chapter 7). Jarman emphasises the space as most important for the plainest purposes it serves: to provide enjoyment and healing to those who tend it, even as it also 'registers his pain and rage'.[4]

The garden book records the garden's rhythms. For those who take the time to notice, the aesthetic effect of time passing on the land becomes an end in itself. On sea kale: 'They look their best in sunlight after rain as the leaves are designed to catch the rain and feed it to the centre of the plant: the beads of water glittering on the plant are an ecstasy' (*Derek Jarman's Garden*, p. 18). The kale ages as the season progresses, 'The flowers then turn into seeds – which look like a thousand peas. They lose their green and become the colour of bone. At this stage they are at their most beautiful' (*Derek Jarman's Garden*, p. 16). The *Crambe maritima* is shown in photographs at all stages of its life, including the dried-out plant Jarman mentions. At its most obvious symbolic level, the garden, represented in *Derek Jarman's Garden*, was an enactment of the struggle between an oppressive society and dissidents who disprove the logic of governing structures. Indeed, as Melissa Zeiger argues, the garden 'forms part of a conversation about the rarely simple relation of the aesthetic to political work, to ideals of social justice, and to the anti-inertial and oppositional'.[5] Plants that weren't meant to survive in the harsh landscape prove tenacious and soon thrive. Chris Steyaert describes the garden as a Foucauldian 'heterotopic space', which the practice of gardening transforms from 'a spatial politics of (sexual) difference into one of queering spaces'.[6] A garden would normally be contained by boundary walls, yet the housing in Dungeness has none. In this odd, shingle landscape, Jarman participated in a mode of life that exists in opposition to the segmentation and regimentation of the suburban English dream.

Writing *Derek Jarman's Garden*

The writing that fills Jarman's garden book is a departure from his recent books of life-writing. Its focus is the garden, and it was written with its final purpose in mind. It provides a narrative to guide readers through the background to the garden – the physical place, its importance for Jarman and the plants that fill it. Its writing explains the context for the garden – a notable departure from earlier life-writing that often provided context allusively, partially, or through juxtaposition. It begins with the search for some antique secateurs for Sooley, showing a simplified reproduction of Jarman's handwritten piece on the verso and neat printed text on the recto. Gardening implements are pictured along the right-hand margin, carefully arranged on the page. From the outset, the book provides a sense that it is preserving the trace of Jarman's handwriting like a flower pressed in a daybook (see Figure 27).

Sections begin with an introduction to their contents: 'I was always a passionate gardener –' (*Derek Jarman's Garden*, p. 11), 'When I came to Dungeness in the mid-eighties, I had no thought of building a garden' (p. 12), 'At first, people thought I was building a garden for magical purposes – a white witch out to get the nuclear power station' (p. 47). The text provides information about certain plants – the native 'Sea kale', or '*Crambe maritima*', which is edible, 'but a radiologist told me that they accumulate radioactivity from the nuclear power station more than any other plant' (*Derek Jarman's Garden*, p. 15); 'The gorse is wonderful in the winter' (p. 21); 'viper's bugloss' (p. 52); 'valerian', linked to his childhood, where 'it clung to the old stone walls of the manor at Curry Mallet, and grew in the garden of the bomb-damaged house at the end of the road which the airman Johnny, my first love, took me to on his motorbike' (p. 53). He describes his bees, which produce 'Dungeness gold' (*Derek Jarman's Garden*, p. 55) and describes the restoration of the inside of Prospect Cottage. The descriptions are practical, for the most part, and less personal than the registers found in the diaries collected as *Modern Nature* and *Smiling in Slow Motion*. It strikes a similar tone to that which his friend Beth Chatto would use in her garden book, *Beth Chatto's Gravel Garden* (2000), half a decade later.

Halfway through the book, several poems are reproduced. The melancholy poems are set in the landscape of the Ness and dwell on mortality, AIDS, loss and self-doubt. The first asks '*Is there nothing but mortality?*' (*Derek Jarman's Garden*, p. 73). The second is written on the occasion of Jarman's friend Howard Brookner's death in New York: '*How can anything endure / the terrible rising of the sun, / the death of a thousand summers?*', Jarman asks. '*All our memories are wasted*', he laments, '*the wild night fucking*

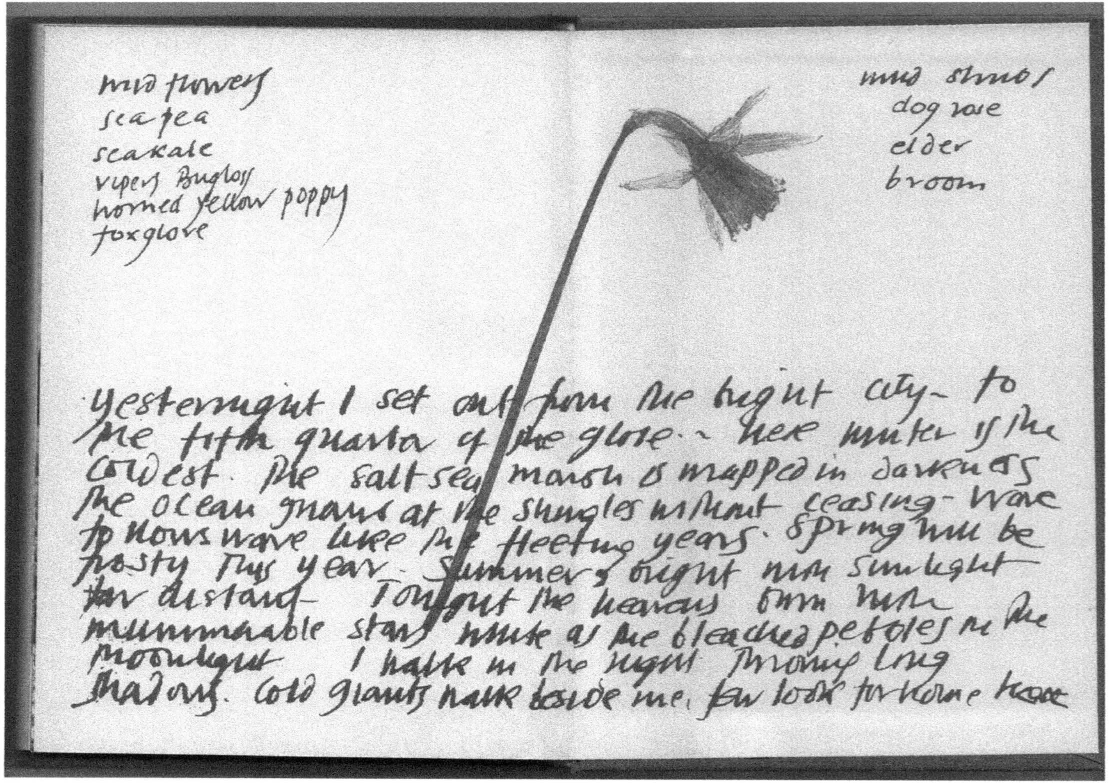

Figure 27 Simplified version of a page from Jarman's journal 'The Garden', printed on the inside front cover of *Derek Jarman's Garden*.

you / on the floor of Heaven –' (*Derek Jarman's Garden*, p. 74). The elegy is placed opposite a black and white image of Jarman's rust sculptures in the shingle in the foreground, with the looming power station Dungeness B on the horizon. The next poem asks: '*Did you imagine* [...] / *that I would be left / to bear witness to our friendship?*' (*Derek Jarman's Garden*, p. 77). The memorable voiceover to *The Garden*, also printed in *Modern Nature*, recurs here: '*I walk in this garden / holding the hands of dead friends*' (*Derek Jarman's Garden*, p. 81), a poem with a clear predecessor in William Blake's 'The Garden of Love'. Blake's poem contains the lines: 'And I saw it was filled with graves, / And tomb-stones where flowers should be'. In Blake's garden, sexuality is also circumscribed: 'Priests [...] bind [...] with briars my joys & desires'.[7] The moment in *The Garden* is often quoted in critical writing about Jarman. Chris Lippard and Guy Johnson find the poem notable as the sole 'direct expression of both anger and grief' within the film, providing an interpretation of the events showed on screen rather than solely allowing the action to remain a parable.[8] Its repetition in the garden book is a stark reminder to the book's readers about Jarman's circumstances. George McKay marks the difference between this poem – 'not light of touch and witty' – and the content of the rest of the gardening book. He quotes part of the poem, which 'tells of disease and death, which were his companions in the years he was building the garden, and of the desire for the plant to return next season, *alive*'.[9]

In April 1989, Jarman described his garden as 'a memorial, each circular bed and dial a true lover's knot – planted with lavender, helichryssum and santolina' (*Modern Nature*, p. 55). He explains that 'a sprig of lavender held in the hand or placed under the pillow enables you to see ghosts, travel to the land of the dead' (*Modern Nature*, p. 55). Seven months later, he reiterates the commemorative nature of the space: 'The garden is built for dear friends / Howard, Paul, Terence, David, Robert, and Ken, / And many others, each stone has a life to tell' (*Modern Nature*, p. 178). The garden is a text that can be read as a place of remembrance. The garden becomes an oblique form of life-writing, in which 'each stone has a life to tell'. The garden acts as a place to celebrate dead friends as well as being a site of historical re-evaluation using the plants that feature there. As O'Quinn explains, Jarman's gardening is 'an emergency praxis whose imperative opens onto a motivated consideration of the relationship between time and community'.[10] The inclusion of these moving poems shows the garden not only as a memorial, but also as memento mori, showing Jarman reflecting on the transience and fragility of his own life, and the lives of those close to him: '*Our life will pass away like traces of a cloud / and be scattered like mist / that is chased by the rays of the sun*' (*Derek Jarman's Garden*, p. 77). It deals with grief and uncertainty: '*A fathomless lethargy has swallowed me, / great waves of doubt broken me, / all my thoughts washed away'* (*Derek Jarman's Garden*, p. 82).

During this section of reflection in poetry, the brilliant sun-filled landscape is replaced. Jarman comments on the poems: 'A cold, grey day. I write these poems, and while the poems form the rain blows in' (*Derek Jarman's Garden*, p. 89). Images show the bleakness of the grey landscape, and the drama of the sea. Nevertheless 'as the day draws to a close, sunlight floods the Ness and the wet shingle glistens like pearls of Vermeer light' (*Derek Jarman's Garden*, p. 89). The shifting moods of the landscape track the shifting emotions that follow from grief, as well as providing some relief. Towards the end of the book, two more diary-like entries indicate Jarman's world away from the garden. One starts: 'Wednesday evening' at 'St. Bartholemew's hospital', and explains 'I've found that hospital is perfect for writing, at four or five in the morning (*Derek Jarman's Garden*, p. 121). Another, dated 'May 2', begins: 'Bart's let me off the drip and Howard and I took off to Dungeness' (*Derek Jarman's Garden*, p. 130). It then describes the garden as being 'filled with the flowers of spring' such as 'the first white campion, blue-eyed forget-me-nots and banks of marigolds' (*Derek Jarman's Garden*, p. 30). The entries serve to ground the book in Jarman's context, but say very little about his own illnesses. The circumstances are implied, but this book is about his relationship to the garden, above all else. The book, like the garden, is 'therapeutic in its peacefulness' (*Derek Jarman's Garden*, p. 132), as well as being a memorial site.

The book finishes *in media res*:

> The foxgloves that march like soldiers in platoons along the lake have a scent that is hardly present at all.
>
> The seaweed's back. (*Derek Jarman's Garden*, p. 140)

It is apt that the book finishes in mid-stride – the book considers the turning of the earth and the cycles of the garden. Yet in this case, there is no end – *'the terrible rising of the sun'* (*Derek Jarman's Garden*, p. 74) will continue, as will the AIDS deaths Jarman laments.

Monet's garden at Giverny

Derek Jarman's Garden contains three portraits of Jarman taken during his final holiday: a trip to France with Sooley to visit Monet's garden (see plates 17 and 18). The holiday itself is described at length in *Smiling in Slow Motion* (pp. 351–7), and more briefly in *Derek Jarman's Garden*:

> Monet's garden at Giverny is an Edwardian garden of borders and gravel paths. Huge rose pergolas run riot. It is the shaggiest garden in the world,

only possible to describe in the flecks and dabs of colour in his paintings. Although the white wisteria on the bridge was nearly over and the lilies not yet out, the main garden was a mass of irises, peonies and dew-laden roses.

It is such a contrast to the desert of Dungeness – rich, watery and sheltered behind its poplars. I doubt there is a plant that wouldn't thrive there. (p. 134)

The above passage, printed in the garden book, is derived from Jarman's journal entry for Thursday 27 May 1993 in *Smiling in Slow Motion* (pp. 352–3), shortened through multiple ellipses. Giverny maintained its place in Jarman's imagination and the description of his trip to the garden quoted above gives the impression of a garden overladen with richness, colour and sensuality. Sooley's images from the day show the 'shaggiest garden in the world' (*Derek Jarman's Garden*, p. 134), and its famous bridge over the lily ponds. Portraits of Jarman in loose mid-blue cotton dungarees, a thick woollen tweed jacket, a draped snood scarf and a startling scarlet flat cap. He is wearing perfectly circular old-fashioned glasses. He holds a cane and his face is drawn, but its deep tan colour (the result of the medication AZT) makes him look like a distinguished Frenchman. He cuts a dashing though fragile figure. Jarman comments on his appearance and his hat in *Smiling in Slow Motion*: 'Everyone said: "*Bonjour M. l'ambassadeur*" – who waddled along the path with his stick, bright-red hat and owlish glasses' (*Smiling in Slow Motion*, p. 353).

Jarman does not mention a previous attempt to visit the gardens around seven years earlier. In *Kicking the Pricks*, Jarman describes an excursion with a friend, Rick, to visit Monet's gardens: 'It's late May so the garden should be a paradise' (p. 148). When they arrive, the pair 'glimpse the garden from the road'. Jarman narrates the scene: 'At the door we are stopped by an American lady in a neat blue uniform. "I'm sorry," she says, "but the gardens are closed till four for a private function." [...] We didn't bother to argue, just turned home sadly, shut out of the garden' (*Kicking the Pricks*, pp. 148–9). He uses the events described as an allegory of his wider political battle, understood within the context of paradise. Monet's garden was the garden that he had dreamt of since childhood, representing a bright, verdant perfection. Jarman concludes: 'As we left we glimpsed the garden bathed in a golden glow. The magic garden, fatal to enter, don't go there 'cos it's fallen into the hands of demons' (pp. 149–51). Monet's garden has been transformed from a private, artistic space of inspiration and refuge now that it has entered the public domain (similar to his disdain for Vita Sackville-West's gardens at Sissinghurst losing touch with their origins by falling into 'the institutional hands of the National Trust', *Modern Nature*, p. 15). Jarman specifically wrought the anecdote to demonstrate oppression – implying one's sexuality means that one will be shut out from certain places, or modes of experience. It is notable, however, that the woman who bars their entrance is not saying that the gates would be closed forever. It is Jarman and his friend who provide the constraints at the time that this happened: they simply didn't have the time to wait – 'My friends, the bluebells are flowering in the woods of Kent – now do you wait for someone to tell you you can film them? They'll have died before you get an answer' (*Kicking the Pricks*, p. 169).

The garden as paradise

In *Kicking the Pricks*, Jarman asks: 'Why shouldn't I invite people into another garden, rather than walk in theirs?' (p. 108). Jarman was preoccupied with the idea of paradise. In *Smiling in Slow Motion*, he mentions his affinity with the mood of the *Pearl* poet. The fourteenth-century poem *Pearl* describes a dreamer who, having fallen asleep in an 'erber grene' (green garden), dreams of a paradisiacal garden on the other side of the riverbank to where he is situated.[11] The garden here represents an earthly reminder of the Garden of Eden from which man has been expelled. The recurrent visibility of the Eden myth demonstrates the battleground of the mythical site of the original heterosexuality and its alternatives. Peake explains what underlies Jarman's concept of the garden as an Eden-like space: as a site for the family, for childhood and for innocent pursuits, the garden holds a special significance. Focusing on the representations of the family in the garden taken by Jarman's grandparents that Jarman reappropriated in his early Super 8s, Peake comments that:

> The flickering images record a way of life that has vanished forever; a lost Eden, but an Eden, too, that is haunted by the spectre of what lay behind it. Little wonder that when Jarman came to pick up a camera of his own, his work should be steeped in a sense of paradise lost, a paradise which, even as he yearned for it, he mistrusted, because he knew that somewhere, somehow, it was poisoned.[12]

The notion of a 'poisoned' garden – an apparent perfection which is rotten despite its image – is echoed throughout Jarman's conceptions of the garden space in his memoirs. However, Dungeness is his individual, intentionally peculiar, artistic vision. He uses the garden space as a way of writing about his own life: the changes he enacts upon the land itself are as much a part of his autobiographical project as the representations of them in text or film. He states: 'Paradise haunts gardens, and some gardens are paradises. Mine is one of them' (*Derek Jarman's Garden*, p. 40).

The book preserves the garden as a 'paradise' (*Derek Jarman's Garden*, p. 40), in the most mature form that Jarman would see it, and sold well following its publication. By carefully describing the garden with text and image, Jarman and Sooley can protect its symbolism from loss if, following his death, it ceases to exist. Represented in full bloom and in sunshine, the garden will live on in a manner of speaking even if the physical garden dies away. Until 2018, Collins maintained and even added to the garden to the extent that he was warned not to continue to expand: he has said that 'English Nature have written to me to say: "Do not gardenise any more"' (see Plate 14 for a photograph of the garden in full bloom in 2014).[13]

Following Collins' death, ArtFund launched a highly successful campaign in 2020 to fundraise to buy Prospect Cottage, conserve its contents and restore and maintain the garden. Promoted by Tilda Swinton and in the national press, the campaign drew much attention and raised more than the £3.5 million needed to succeed. Creative Folkestone will now oversee a programme of artist residencies and public visits, as well as events that will bring Jarman's work into view in Kent. Jarman's garden has also been the subject of an exhibition at Lambeth's Garden Museum in 2020, 'Derek Jarman: My Garden's Boundaries are the Horizon'. The exhibition tells the story of the garden at Prospect Cottage and shares some of Jarman's work across media including film stills, artworks and garden journals. A beautifully illustrated book with photographs of the garden by Howard Sooley as well as several essays reflecting on the garden, *Derek Jarman: My Garden's Boundaries are the Horizon*, accompanies the exhibition. Although beyond the scope of this book, it will be important to attend to the ways that these acts of preservation and engagement with Jarman's home and garden shift his legacy over time.

Notes

1 Vita Sackville-West, *The Garden* (London: Michael Joseph, 1946; London: Frances Lincoln, 1989), p. 13.
2 Keith Collins, 'Preface', in Derek Jarman, *Derek Jarman's Garden, with Photographs by Howard Sooley* (London: Thames and Hudson, 1995), p. 5. Further references are given within the text.
3 Melissa Zeiger, '"Modern Nature": Derek Jarman's Garden', *Humanities*, 6.22 (2017), 1–12 (p. 2).
4 Zeiger, '"Modern Nature"', p. 2.
5 Ibid.
6 Steyaert, 'Queering Space', p. 45.
7 William Blake, 'The GARDEN of LOVE', *Songs of Innocence and of Experience* (1794), Copy B, Object 43 (British Museum, London), reproduced on *The William Blake Archive*, www.blakearchive.org/copy/songsie.b?descId=songsie.b.illbk.43 (accessed 11 June 2021).

8 Chris Lippard and Guy Johnson, 'Private Practice, Public Health: The Politics of Sickness and the Films of Derek Jarman', in *Fires Were Started: British Cinema and Thatcherism*, ed. Lester Friedman (Minneapolis: University of Minnesota Press, 1993), pp. 301–14 (p. 311). It is also quoted in part by Brophy, *Witnessing AIDS*, p. 32; Ellis, *Angelic Conversations*, p. 193; Peake, *Derek Jarman*, p. 442; Richardson, *The Queer Cinema of Derek Jarman*, pp. 192–3.
9 George McKay, *Radical Gardening: Politics, Idealism and Rebellion in the Garden* (London: Frances Lincoln, 2011), p. 145.
10 O'Quinn, 'Gardening, History and the Escape from Time', p. 116.
11 *Pearl*, p. 2, line 38.
12 Peake, *Derek Jarman*, p. 11.
13 Keith Collins, quoted in Michael Leapman, 'A Profusion of Plants in a Driftwood Oasis', *Independent*, 10 June 1995, www.independent.co.uk/arts-entertainment/a-profusion-of-plants-in-a-driftwood-oasis-1586025.html (accessed 28 October 2012).

Conclusion: 'The past is the mirror'

The purpose of this book has been to examine how Derek Jarman enacted 'politics in the first person' (*At Your Own Risk*, p. 121) throughout his life-writing.[1] He used repeated acts of experimental self-representation and a commitment to rehabilitating queer pasts to inform his powerful, imaginative activist response to the HIV/AIDS crisis. His life-writing forms a moving and highly original account of his experiences with the virus, bearing witness to its effects on his body as well as to the casualties among his friends. It also acts as a furious backlash against the resurgence of hostility towards queer people in the 1980s in the wake of HIV/AIDS, especially following the revival in the UK of what would be passed into law as Section 28 in 1988. This book also uncovers the range and power of his earlier life-writing, in which he began using material from his own life to inform his film and writing work. He called on transhistorical, allegorical forms of self-representation that take inspiration from diverse periods including the classical period of Ancient Greek history, the medieval period and the Renaissance. Jarman used interdisciplinary methods across media – film, writing and art – to create urgent work that communicated his visionary queer politics with 'testamentary force'.[2] This is the first book-length study of his published books, almost all of which are autobiographical.

Jarman used collage technique and collaborative methods to create life-writing that acts as a queer practice of survival during a period where queer identities were often erased, diminished or dismissed. In *Borrowed Time*, Paul Monette notes that 'a gay man seeks his history in mythic fragments [...] Fragments are all you get. You jigsaw the rest with your heart'.[3] Jarman took the same approach. By collating and juxtaposing quotations from diverse periods and artistic registers, he sought to create new, queer genealogies of meaning, knowing and understanding that are nevertheless in touch with their pasts. For example, *Queer Edward II* examines medieval homophobia in the ruling classes and Church fathers, while also invoking the figure of the queer child to examine a history of harm and to look forward to reparations that may be possible in an imagined future. In a different register,

Chroma collates different impressions of colour from artists and philosophers in order to create a queer history of colour as a means to expand the limits of what is communicable through language. In the earlier text *Derek Jarman's Caravaggio* and the short film *Ostia*, he plays with identity, taking on aspects of the identities of queer icons whom he identifies with. As a scrapbooker, Jarman is 'an active participant in reshaping and re-presenting content', engaging with the past yet 'reshaping' it in order to try to represent new ways of living.[4]

Jarman almost always worked collaboratively to create work that, while using his own life as material, sought to use said material to work towards a politics much larger than himself. As I have argued in the chapter on *Queer Edward II*, though we are sometimes unsure which of the text's authors has contributed which bit to the final text, the collaboration allows multiple voices to enrich the final product. Jarman is not interested in displaying a unity of vision, but instead concentrates on the richness of ideas that stem from a collective working process. As the director of a film, he relies on the talents of co-workers, all of whom produce work under the director's 'brand'. As he found this working style so fruitful, he transferred it to other media, facilitating the swift production of multiple books. As his health began to fail, working collaboratively became essential, enabling him to contribute urgent work including *Blue*, dealing with his failing sight; another biopic, *Wittgenstein*; the polemic texts *At Your Own Risk* and *Chroma*; the AIDS diary *Modern Nature*; the large canvases reproduced in *Queer* and *Evil Queen*; the texts that would become *Smiling in Slow Motion* and *Derek Jarman's Garden*; and many more unrealised projects besides.

Jarman's life-writing was created during a period of crisis, and performs a special kind of activism, which is, as Simon Watney summarises, 'a politics of emergencies', a tactic necessary when institutions 'stubbornly refuse to listen to reasonable, well informed, democratic arguments'.[5] By working with others and using juxtaposition as a generative strategy, Jarman was able to create activist work that uses his shifting experiences to add to debates on queer rights, education and politics. His self-representations have often overlapped with his presentation of queer figures from history. Examples include his engagement with the life of Caravaggio in *Derek Jarman's Caravaggio*, his performance in the role of Pier Paolo Pasolini in his friend Julian Cole's student film *Ostia*, and the ways he layers temporalities in *Queer Edward II*. In each, he refracts different self-representations that use, critique or create a queer past.

In his autobiographical meditation on Oscar Wilde and queer spaces in London, Neil Bartlett reflects: 'I subject the story of my own life as a gay man to constant scrutiny; we all do. We have to, because we're making it up as we go along'.[6] Jarman took the same approach, yet extended this 'constant scrutiny' to include repeated communication in the form of new pieces of life-writing – diaries, collaged lyric essays, and autobiographical film and painting. As a result, his life-writing and shifting self-representations should be interpreted as a critical, mature career-long project. This book understands Jarman's life-writing as a project that extended across his career, but in its most focused form between the composition of *Dancing Ledge*, starting in 1982 and his death in February 1994.

Jarman practised serial life-writing because doing so enabled him to share his changing subjectivity as he underwent acute shifts: as the HIV/AIDS crisis worsened, he discovered he was HIV-positive, became a public figurehead and started to suffer from a series of AIDS-related illnesses. His responses in his life-writing are swift, as he did not know how long he would be able to continue to work, and provisional, as he tracked his changing experiences and perspectives. As well as being serial, Jarman's life-writing is also dispersed. He describes his life-writing in *At Your Own Risk* as 'a series of introductions to matters and agendas unfinished. Like memory, it has gaps, amnesias, fragments of past, fractured present' (p. 5). It is incomplete, rather than a relation of completed statements. In this book, I have commented on a number of events that recur across his life-writing to indicate how his approach to his past changes over time, at times becoming more polarised and at times appearing to change with the retelling. For example, his recollections of the magical time he spent as a young child in the Villa Zuassa by Lago Maggiore where he experiences his first attraction is presented lyrically in *Dancing Ledge*, but becomes more adversarial in later volumes. Similarly, the 'destruction wrought at Hordle [...] [that] grew like a poison vine' that Jarman describes in *Dancing Ledge* (p. 50) is mobilised in a more confrontational style in later text *At Your Own Risk*. Moments from his past remain 'matters and agendas unfinished' (*At Your Own Risk*, p. 5), picked over and examined from new angles. Under the fraught conditions Jarman was working in, memories took on new inflections and required retelling.

Generosity and visions for the future

One of Jarman's most apparent traits is the generosity with which he shared his own life. His life-writing demonstrates this openness, cataloguing his sustained belief in the critical importance of talking candidly about experiences of childhood, sex, love, cruising, community, friendship, homophobia and HIV/AIDS. Jarman did this not because he believed his experiences to be of singular importance, but because to do so was an essential political response to a life lived in a country that had remained homophobic and inhospitable through every period of his life. As a famous film director, he had a platform and an audience. By naming the realities of one queer life in many ways, from different angles, he added his voice to those which had previously been silenced. The ways he shares his life are often confrontational, engaging with contentious and perhaps challenging areas of queer experience. Brophy comments on the 'shifting dynamics of mourning and memory, blend[ed] [...] with a good deal of polemic' in the AIDS memoirs she analyses, including Jarman's.[7]

His life-writing offers an alternative from mainstream forms of representation of queer lives and HIV-positive subjects, retaining agency while communicating complex, often melancholic moods. He challenges the idea of the 'person with AIDS' as a victim or as abject.[8] One of the most familiar photographs of him is from the Dungeness shoot of *The Garden*, showing him lying blissful, eyes closed, in a clump of sea kale (see Plate 6). He is wearing a crown of golden twigs punctuated with red, contrasting with a shiny black PVC coat. Here, he engages religious iconography in playful juxtaposition with fetish and with the fleshly leaves of the *Crambe maritima*. Yet he does not shy away from confronting prejudice about practices deemed unacceptable by much of the mainstream: he offers detailed accounts of his night-time encounters on Hampstead Heath, proffering a lyrical vision of the site as a queer utopia where differences go unremarked. He adds a significant voice to those combating harmful representations in the media. Across his published life-writing and in his appearances in his films post-HIV diagnosis, he enacts the ACT UP demand to 'Stop looking at us. Start listening to us'.[9]

The last words that Jarman would write are printed in *Smiling in Slow Motion*. A final entry reads: 'Birthday fireworks', and then, 'HB true love' (*Smiling in Slow Motion*, p. 388). The book includes scans of the handwritten journal entry: his beautiful handwriting has become shaky and uncertain. Neil Bartlett writes movingly about these final, devastating words in his introduction to the reissued journals. He comments, 'In this particular journal, nothing is too private to be recorded, and nothing is so public as to prevent it from being taken personally' (*Smiling in Slow Motion*, p. xviii). Even at the last, Jarman's life is art. Of the fireworks display Jarman records in his journal, Bartlett writes, 'in retrospect a firework is surely what Derek was. He was noisy, glittering and public; he was exact in his trajectory, and expansive when he exploded'... the comparison goes on. A person of great illumination, Jarman 'spread [...] life and colour across even (and especially) the darkest of nights' (*Smiling in Slow Motion*, p. xviii). What a way to think about Jarman – through his own words at the end – a crystallisation of his impact:

> Luminous presence
> Here and gone.[10]

Notes

1 The quote in the chapter title is from Derek Jarman's letter to the *Independent* campaigning against the proposed closure of Barts Hospital: 'Why shutting Barts would be a crime', *Independent*, 4 May 1993.
2 Hollinghurst, '*A Boy's Own Story*'.
3 Paul Monette, *Borrowed Time: An AIDS Memoir* (London: Collins Harvill, 1988), p. 22.
4 Brinkman, 'Scrapping Modernism', p. 47.
5 Watney, *Imagine Hope*, p. 3.
6 Bartlett, *Who Was That Man?*, p. 30.
7 Brophy, *Witnessing AIDS*, p. 12.
8 Lawrence, 'Derek Jarman's *Blue*', p. 243.
9 Quoted in Watney, *Imagine Hope*, p. 101.
10 *Chroma*, p. 151.

Bibliography

Aaron, Michele, ed., *New Queer Cinema: A Critical Reader* (Edinburgh: Edinburgh University Press, 2004)
Acker, Kathy, *My Death My Life by Pier Paolo Pasolini* (London: Pan, 1984; repr. in *Literal Madness*, New York: Grove, 1988), pp. 171–393
Ackerley, J. R., *My Father And Myself* (London: Bodley Head, 1968; repr. New York: NYRB Classics, 2006)
Adams, Timothy Dow, *Light Writing & Life Writing: Photography in Autobiography* (Chapel Hill: University of North Carolina Press, 2000)
Aebischer, Pascale, 'Renaissance Tragedy on Film: Defying Mainstream Shakespeare', in *The Cambridge Companion to English Renaissance Tragedy*, ed. Emma Smith and Sullivan Jr, Garrett A. (Cambridge: Cambridge University Press, 2010), pp. 116–31
—, *Screening Early Modern Drama: Beyond Shakespeare* (Cambridge and New York: Cambridge University Press, 2013)
—, 'Shakespearean Heritage and the Preposterous "Contemporary Jacobean" Film: Mike Figgis's *Hotel*', *Shakespeare Quarterly*, 60.3 (2009), 279–303
—, '"To the Future": Derek Jarman's *Edward II* in the Archive', *Shakespeare Bulletin*, 32.3 (2014), 429–50
Agoston, Laura Camille, 'Sonnet, Sculpture, Death: The Mediums of Michelangelo's Self-Imaging', *Art History*, 20.4 (1997), 534–55
Aldrich, Robert, *Gay Life Stories* (London: Thames and Hudson, 2012)
Ali, Tariq, 'Arts: "No Bums or Willies Please, Derek": With Derek Jarman's Long-Awaited Diaries Set to Be Published next Month, Tariq Ali Recalls the Time They First Met – Looking out on a Radioactive Sea, Discussing Ludwig Wittgenstein', *Observer*, 18 June 2000
Almodóvar, Pedro, *Almodóvar on Almodóvar* [1996], ed. Frederic Strauss, trans. Yves Baignères, rev. edn (London: Faber & Faber, 2006)
Anderson, J. J., 'Introduction', in *Sir Gawain And The Green Knight/Pearl/Cleanness/Patience*, ed. J. J. Anderson, new edn (London: W&N, 1996), pp. ix–xxi
Anderson, Linda, 'Autobiographical Travesties: The Nostalgic Self in Queer Writing', in *Territories of Desire in Queer Culture: Refiguring Contemporary Boundaries*, eds. David Alderson and Linda Anderson (Manchester: Manchester University Press, 2000), pp. 68–81
—, *Autobiography* (London: Routledge, 2000)
Arditti, Michael, 'Fighting the Dying of the Light', *The Times*, 8 July 2000
Armstrong, Raymond, 'More Jiggery Than Pokery: Derek Jarman's *Edward II*', in *British Queer Cinema*, ed. Robin Griffiths (London: Routledge, 2006), pp. 145–56

Arterburn, Jerry, and Stephen F. Arterburn, *How Will I Tell My Mother? A True Story of One Man's Battle With Homosexuality and AIDS* (Nashville: Thomas Nelson, 1990)
'Art of the Garden', 2004, www.tate.org.uk/whats-on/tate-britain/exhibition/art-garden (accessed 30 November 2012)
Ashley, Kathleen, Leigh Gilmore and Gerald Peters, eds., *Autobiography and Postmodernism* (Amherst: University of Massachusetts Press, 1994)
Baker, Peter S., *An Introduction to Old English* (Malden, MA: Wiley-Blackwell, 2003)
Baker, Rob, *The Art of AIDS: From Stigma to Conscience* (New York: Continuum, 1994)
Banash, David, *Collage Culture: Readymades, Meaning, and the Age of Consumption* (Amsterdam: Editions Rodopi, 2013)
Barad, Karen, *Meeting the Universe Halfway: Quantum Physics and the Entanglement of Matter and Meaning* (Durham, NC: Duke University Press, 2007)
Barry, Kevin, 'How Things Can Be Beautiful: Signs, Patches, and Assignats', in *L'Empreinte Des Choses*, ed. André Topia (Paris: Presses Sorbonne Nouvelle, 2007), pp. 131–46
Barthes, Roland, *Camera Lucida: Reflections on Photography*, trans. Richard Howard (London: Vintage, 2000)
—, *Mythologies*, trans. Annette Lavers (London: Vintage, 1993)
—, *The Responsibility of Forms: Critical Essays on Music, Art, and Representation*, trans. Richard Howard (Berkeley: University of California Press, 1985)
—, *Roland Barthes by Roland Barthes*, trans. Richard Howard (New York: Hill and Wang, 1977)
Bartlett, Neil, 'Introduction', in *Smiling in Slow Motion: The Journals of Derek Jarman, 1991–1994*, by Derek Jarman, ed. Keith Collins (London: Vintage Classics, 2018), pp. vii–xix
—, *Skin Lane* (London: Serpent's Tail, 2007)
—, 'A Vision of Love Revealed in Sleep (Part One)', in *Solo Voices: Monologues 1987–2004* (London: Oberon, 2005), pp. 15–46
—, *Who Was That Man? A Present for Mr Oscar Wilde* (London: Serpent's Tail, 1988)
—, and Simon Watney, 'Remembering Derek', talk at King's College London Chapel, 31 January 2014.
Batchelor, David, *Chromophobia* (London: Reaktion Books, 2000)
Bax, Dominique, and Cyril Béghin, *Derek Jarman – Jean Cocteau: Alchimie* (Bobigny: Magic Cinema, 2008)
Bazin, André, 'On the *politiques des auteurs* (April 1957)', trans. Peter Graham, in *Cahiers du Cinéma: The 1950s: Neo-Realism, Hollywood, New Wave*, ed. Jim Hillier (Cambridge, MA: Harvard University Press, 1985), pp. 248–59
Bechdel, Alison, *Fun Home: A Family Tragicomic* (London: Jonathan Cape, 2006)
Benini, Stefania, *Pasolini: The Sacred Flesh* (Toronto: University of Toronto Press, 2015)
Benjamin, Walter, *The Arcades Project*, trans. Howard Eiland and Kevin McLaughlin (Cambridge, MA: Harvard University Press, 2002)
Bennett, Catherine, 'Lesson of the Gay Guru', *Guardian*, 9 April 1992
Bennett, Jill, *Empathic Vision: Affect, Trauma, and Contemporary Art* (Stanford, CA: Stanford University Press, 2005)
Bennett, Susan, *Performing Nostalgia: Shifting Shakespeare and the Contemporary Past* (London: Routledge, 1996)

Bergman, David, *Gay American Autobiography: Writings from Whitman to Sedaris* (Madison: University of Wisconsin Press, 2009)
Bergman, Susan, *Anonymity: The Secret Life of an American Family* (New York: Farrar, Straus and Giroux, 1994)
Berlant, Lauren, and Michael Warner, 'Sex in Public', *Critical Inquiry*, 24.2 (Winter 1998), 547–66.
Bersani, Leo, *Is the Rectum a Grave?: And Other Essays* (Chicago: University of Chicago Press, 2009)
—, and Ulysse Dutoit, *Caravaggio* (London: British Film Institute, 1999)
—, and Ulysse Dutoit, *Caravaggio's Secrets* (Cambridge, MA: MIT Press, 2001)
Bible, The, Authorized King James Version, eds. Robert Carroll and Stephen Prickett (Oxford: Oxford University Press, 1998)
Biga, Tracy, 'The Principle of Non-Narration in the Films of Derek Jarman', in *By Angels Driven: The Films of Derek Jarman*, ed. Chris Lippard (Wiltshire: Flicks Books, 1996), pp. 12–30
Blake, William, 'The GARDEN of LOVE', *Songs of Innocence and of Experience* (1794), Copy B, Object 43 (British Museum, London), reproduced on *The William Blake Archive*, www.blakearchive.org/copy/songsie.b?descId=songsie.b.illbk.43 (accessed 11 June 2021)
'Books: The Observer Bestseller Lists: Top 5 Film Books', *Observer*, 6 August 2000
Boswell, John, *Christianity, Social Tolerance, and Homosexuality: Gay People in Western Europe from the Beginning of the Christian Era to the Fourteenth Century* (Chicago: University of Chicago Press, 1980)
de Botton, Alain, Helena Kennedy, Mark Kermode et al., 'Essential Reading: Nine Experts on the Books That Inspired Them', *Observer*, 8 January 2017, www.theguardian.com/books/2017/jan/08/essential-reading-experts-inspiration-film-law-philosophy-economics-history-psychology-music-nature (accessed 26 November 2017)
Boule, Jean-Pierre, *Herve Guibert: Voices of the Self* (Liverpool: Liverpool University Press, 1999)
—, *HIV Stories: The Archaeology of AIDS Writing in France, 1985–1988* (Liverpool: Liverpool University Press, 2002)
Boyd, Don, 'Introduction by Don Boyd', in *War Requiem*, by Derek Jarman (London: Faber, 1989), pp. vii–x
Brabazon, Tara, 'At Your Own Risk: Derek Jarman and the (Semiotic) Death of a Film Maker', *Social Semiotics*, 3.2 (1993), 183–200
—, 'Reading Tilda: A Swinton Guide through Bodily Textualisation', *Semiotics*, 4.1–2 (1994), 9–30
Bradford, Richard, ed., *Life Writing: Essays on Autobiography, Biography and Literature* (Basingstoke: Palgrave Macmillan, 2010)
Bravmann, Scott, *Queer Fictions of the Past: History, Culture, and Difference* (Cambridge: Cambridge University Press, 1997)
Bray, Alan, *Homosexuality in Renaissance England* (London: Gay Men's Press, 1982)
Brinkman, Bartholomew, 'Scrapping Modernism: Marianne Moore and the Making of the Modern Collage Poem', *Modernism/Modernity*, 18.1 (2011), 43–66
Brisolin, Viola, *Power and Subjectivity in the Late Work of Roland Barthes and Pier Paolo Pasolini* (Oxford: Peter Lang, 2011)
Bristow, Joseph, 'Being Gay: Politics, Identity, Pleasure', *New Formations*, 9 (Winter 1989), 61–81
—, *Effeminate England: Homoerotic Writing after 1885* (New York: Columbia University Press)

Brockelman, Thomas P., *The Frame and the Mirror: On Collage and the Postmodern* (Evanston, IL: Northwestern University Press, 2001)
Brophy, Sarah, *Witnessing AIDS: Writing, Testimony, and the Work of Mourning* (Toronto: University of Toronto Press, 2004)
—, and Janice Hladki, 'Visual Autobiography in the Frame: Critical Embodiment and Cultural Pedagogy', in *Embodied Politics in Visual Autobiography*, eds. Sarah Brophy and Janice Hladki (Toronto: University of Toronto Press, 2014), pp. 3–30
Brouillette, Sarah, *Literature and the Creative Economy* (Stanford: Stanford University Press, 2017)
Bruhm, Steven, *Reflecting Narcissus: A Queer Aesthetic* (Minneapolis: University of Minnesota Press, 2001)
Bruss, Elizabeth W., *Autobiographical Acts: The Changing Situation of a Literary Genre* (Baltimore, MD: Johns Hopkins University Press, 1976)
—, 'Eye for I: Making and Unmaking Autobiography in Film', in *Autobiography: Essays Theoretical and Critical*, ed. James Olney (Princeton, NJ: Princeton University Press, 1980), pp. 296–320
Burchill, Julie, 'Books: Diary of a Nobody, Part Two; Julie Burchill Charts The Moans And Minutiae Of Derek Jarman's Journal', *Guardian*, 15 July 2000
Burger, Glenn, and Steven F. Kruger, *Queering the Middle Ages* (Minneapolis: University of Minnesota Press, 2001)
Burger, Peter, *Theory of the Avant-Garde* (Manchester: Manchester University Press, 1984)
Burston, Paul, *What Are You Looking at?: Queer Sex, Style and Cinema* (London: Cassell, 1995)
Butler, Judith, 'Critically Queer', *GLQ: A Journal of Lesbian and Gay Studies*, 1.1 (1993), 17–32
—, *Gender Trouble: Feminism and the Subversion of Identity*, new edn (London: Routledge, 1999)
—, *Giving an Account of Oneself* (New York: Fordham University Press, 2005)
Calhoun, Dave, 'The Genius of Derek Jarman', *Time Out London*, 2 June 2008, p. 14
Campbell, Jan, and Janet Harbord, eds., *Temporalities, Autobiography and Everyday Life* (Manchester: Manchester University Press, 2002)
Canning, Richard, 'The Literature of AIDS', in *The Cambridge Companion to Gay and Lesbian Writing*, ed. Hugh Stevens (Cambridge: Cambridge University Press, 2010), 132–47
Cardullo, Bert, '"Outing" Edward, Outfitting Marlow: Derek Jarman's Film of *Edward II*', *Literature/Film Quarterly*, 37.2 (2009), 86–96
Carlin, John, 'David Wojnarowicz: As the World Turns', in *Tongues of Flame*, eds. David Wojnarowicz and Barry Blinderman (Normal: Illinois State University, 1990), pp. 21–33
Carpenter, Edward, *Homogenic Love, and its Place in a Free Society* (Manchester: Labour Press Society, 1894)
Cartelli, Thomas, '*Queer Edward II*: Postmodern Sexualities and the Early Modern Subject', in *Marlowe, History, and Sexuality: New Critical Essays on Christopher Marlowe*, ed. Paul Whitfield White (New York: AMS Press, 1998), pp. 213–24
Carter, Erica, and Simon Watney, eds., *Taking Liberties: AIDS and Cultural Politics* (London: Serpent's Tail, 1989)
Certeau, Michel de, *The Practice of Everyday Life*, trans. Steven Rendall (Berkeley: University of California Press, 1988)
Chambers, Ross, *Facing It: AIDS Diaries and the Death of the Author* (Ann Arbor: University of Michigan Press, 1998)

—, *Untimely Interventions: AIDS Writing, Testimonial, and the Rhetoric of Haunting* (Ann Arbor: University of Michigan Press, 2004)
Charlesworth, Michael, *Derek Jarman*, Critical Lives (London: Reaktion Books, 2011)
Chatto, Beth, *Beth Chatto's Gravel Garden* (London: Frances Lincoln, 2000)
Chedgzoy, Kate, *Shakespeare's Queer Children: Appropriation in Contemporary Culture* (Manchester: Manchester University Press, 1995)
Cheney, Patrick, '*Edward II*: Marlowe, Tragedy, and the Sublime', in *The Cambridge Companion to English Renaissance Tragedy*, eds. Emma Smith and Garrett A. Sullivan, Jr (Cambridge: Cambridge University Press, 2010), pp. 174–87
Chisholm, Dianne, *Queer Constellations: Subcultural Space in the Wake of the City* (Minneapolis: University of Minnesota Press, 2005)
Christiansen, Keith, 'Low Life, High Art', *New Republic*, 8 December 2010, https://newrepublic.com/article/79749/life-art-paintings-carvaggio (accessed 10 May 2021)
Christopher, James, 'How to Repeat the Unique?', *The Times*, 20 February 2008
Cixous, Hélène, *Hélène Cixous: Rootprints: Memory and Life Writing*, ed. Mireille Calle-Gruber, trans. Eric Prenowitz, first English edn (London: Routledge, 1997)
Coe, Jonathan, 'Books: Honest Views from Prospect Cottage', *Guardian*, 8 August 1991
Cohen, Ed, *Talk on the Wilde Side: Towards a Genealogy of a Discourse on Male Sexualities* (London: Routledge, 1992)
Cohler, Bertram J., *Writing Desire: Sixty Years of Gay Autobiography* (Madison: University of Wisconsin Press, 2007)
Coil, 'Ostia (the Death of Pasolini)', *Horse Rotorvator* [music track, cass] Perf. Stephen Thrower, Peter Christopherson and John Balance with Billy McGee, Some Bizzare Records, UK, 1986. 6mins 20secs.
Collard, Cyril, *Savage Nights* [1989], trans. William Rodarmor (London: Quartet Books, 1993)
Collins, Keith, 'Preface', in *Derek Jarman's Garden, with Photographs by Howard Sooley*, by Derek Jarman (London: Thames and Hudson, 1995), n.p.
Connolly, Mary Kate, ed., *Throwing the Body into the Fight: A Portrait of Raimund Hoghe* (Bristol: Intellect, 2013)
Connor, Steven, *Postmodernist Culture: An Introduction to Theories of the Contemporary* (Oxford: Blackwell, 1997)
Conway, Jill Kerr, *When Memory Speaks: Reflections on Autobiography* (New York: Alfred Knopf, 1998)
Cook, Matt, *Queer Domesticities: Homosexuality and Home Life in Twentieth-Century London* (Basingstoke: Palgrave Macmillan, 2014)
—, 'Sex Lives and Diary Writing: The Journals of George Ives', in *Life Writing and Victorian Culture*, ed. David Amigoni (Aldershot: Ashgate, 2006), pp. 195–215
—, 'Taking Sexual Politics Home: Derek Jarman and Queering Domesticity', paper presented at the Sexuality at Home conference, University College London, 2012, www.ucl.ac.uk/urbanlab/news/SexualityatHome (accessed 4 February 2013)
—, 'Wilde Lives: Derek Jarman and the Queer Eighties', in *Oscar Wilde and Modern Culture: The Making of a Legend*, ed. Joseph Bristow (Athens: Ohio University Press, 2008), pp. 285–304
Cook, Matt, ed., with Robert Mills, Randolph Trumbach and H. G. Cocks, *A Gay History of Britain: Love and Sex between Men since the Middle Ages* (Oxford: Greenwood World, 2007)
Couser, G. Thomas, *Memoir: An Introduction* (Oxford: Oxford University Press, 2011)

—, *Recovering Bodies: Illness, Disability and Life-Writing* (Madison: University of Wisconsin Press, 1997)

—, and Joseph Fichtelberg, eds., *True Relations: Essays on Autobiography and the Postmodern* (Westport, CT: Greenwood Press, 1998)

Cox, Elizabeth, *Thanksgiving: An AIDS Journal* (New York: Harper & Row, 1990)

Creed, Barbara, 'Lesbian Bodies: Tribades, Tomboys and Tarts', in *Sexy Bodies: The Strange Carnalities of Feminism*, eds. Elizabeth Grosz and Elspeth Probyn (London: Routledge, 2013), pp. 86–103

Crimp, Douglas, *AIDS Demo Graphics* (Seattle, WA: Bay, 1990)

—, 'Introduction', *October*, 43 (Winter 1987), 3–16

—, *Melancholia and Moralism: Essays on AIDS and Queer Politics* (Cambridge, MA: MIT Press, 2002)

Crisp, Quentin, *The Naked Civil Servant* (London: Jonathan Cape, 1968; London: Harper Perennial, 2007)

—, *Resident Alien: The New York Diaries*, ed. Donald Carroll (London: HarperCollins, 1996)

Dave, Paul, *Visions of England: Class and Culture in Contemporary Cinema* (Oxford: Berg, 2006)

David, Hugh, *On Queer Street: A Social History of British Homosexuality, 1895–1995* (London: HarperCollins, 1997)

Davies, Terence, *Hallelujah Now* (London: Penguin, 1993)

Del Re, Gianmarco, *Derek Jarman* (Milan: Il Castoro, 2005)

Delany, Samuel R., *The Motion of Light in Water: Sex and Science Fiction Writing in the East Village, 1957–1965* (New York: Arbor House, 1988)

Delvaux, Martine, 'The Garden as Memento Mori: Derek Jarman and Jamaica Kincaid', *Canadian Woman Studies/Les Cahiers de La Femme*, 21.2 (2001), 135–8

'Derek Jarman's Angelic Conversations', *The Criterion Collection*, 6 December 2009, www.criterion.com/current/posts/1324-derek-jarman-s-angelic-conversations (accessed 17 December 2012)

Derrida, Jacques, *The Ear of the Other: Otobiography, Transference, Translation: Texts and Discussions with Jacques Derrida*, ed. Christie McDonald, trans. Peggy Kamuf and Avital Ronell (Lincoln: University of Nebraska Press, 1988)

—, *The Post Card: From Socrates to Freud and Beyond*, trans. Alan Bass (Chicago: University of Chicago Press, 1987)

Dickinson, Goldsworthy Lowes, and Noel Annan, *The Autobiography of G. Lowes Dickinson and Other Unpublished Writings*, ed. Dennis Proctor (London: Gerald Duckworth, 1973)

Dillon, Steven, *Derek Jarman and Lyric Film: The Mirror and the Sea* (Austin: University of Texas Press, 2004)

Dinshaw, Carolyn et al., 'Theorizing Queer Temporalities Roundtable', *GLQ: Journal of Lesbian and Gay Studies*, 13.2–3 (2007), 177–95

Dixon, Wheeler Winston, 'Derek Jarman and Lyric Film: The Mirror and the Sea', *Film Quarterly*, 59.3 (2006), 70–1

Dollimore, Jonathan, *Sexual Dissidence: Augustine to Wilde, Freud to Foucault* (Oxford: Clarendon Press, 1991)

Donegan, Moira, 'Gay as in Happy', *N+1*, 23 (Fall 2015), https://nplusonemag.com/issue-23/reviews/gay-as-in-happy (accessed 5 December 2016)

Donnelly, Sue, 'Coming Out in the Archives: The Hall-Carpenter Archives at the London School of Economics', *History Workshop Journal*, 66.1 (2008), 180–4

Doty, Alexander, *Making Things Perfectly Queer: Interpreting Mass Culture* (Minneapolis: University of Minnesota Press, 1993)
Doty, Mark, *Heaven's Coast: A Memoir* (New York: HarperCollins, 1996)
Dreuilhe, Emmanuel, *Mortal Embrace: Living with AIDS*, trans. Linda Coverdale (New York: Hill and Wang, 1988)
Driberg, Tom, *Ruling Passions: The Autobiography of Tom Driberg*, 1st edn (London: Jonathan Cape, 1977)
Duberman, Martin, *Midlife Queer: Autobiography of a Decade, 1971–1981* (Madison: University of Wisconsin Press, 1998)
—, Martha Vicinus and George Chauncey, Jr., eds., *Hidden from History: Reclaiming the Gay and Lesbian Past* (New York: New American Library, 1989)
Duncan, Derek, 'Solemn Geographies: AIDS and the Contours of Autobiography', *a/b: Auto/Biography Studies*, 15.1 (2000), 22–36
Duve, Pascal de, *Cargo Vie* (Paris: Jean-Claude Lattès, 1992)
Dyer, Richard, *The Culture of Queers* (London and New York: Routledge, 2002)
—, 'Getting Over the Rainbow: Identity and Pleasure in Gay Cultural Politics', in *Silver Linings: Some Strategies for the Eighties*, eds. George Bridges and Rosalind Brunt (London: Lawrence & Wishart, 1981), pp. 53–67
—, *Heavenly Bodies: Film Stars and Society*, 2nd edn (London: Routledge, 2003)
—, *The Matter of Images: Essays on Representation*, 2nd edn (London: Routledge, 1993; 2002)
—, *Now You See It: Studies on Lesbian and Gay Film* (London: Routledge, 1990)
Eagleton, Terry, *The Illusions of Postmodernism* (Oxford: Blackwell, 1996)
Eakin, Paul John, *Fictions in Autobiography: Studies in the Art of Self Invention* (Princeton, NJ: Princeton University Press, 1985)
—, *Living Autobiographically: How We Create Identity in Narrative*, trans. Christine M. Rose (Ithaca, NY: Cornell University Press, 2008)
—, 'Relational Selves, Relational Lives: The Story of the Story', in *True Relations: Essays on Autobiography and the Postmodern*, eds. G. Thomas Couser and Joseph Fichtelberg (Westport, CT: Hofstra University and Greenwood Press, 1998), pp. 63–81
—, *Touching the World: Reference in Autobiography* (Princeton, NJ: Princeton University Press, 1992)
Edelman, Lee, *Homographesis: Essays in Gay Literary and Cultural Theory* (New York: Routledge, 1994)
—, *No Future: Queer Theory and the Death Drive* (Durham, NC: Duke University Press, 2004)
Edmundson, Mark, 'Taking Leave', *London Review of Books*, 11.5 (1989), 22–3
Egan, Susanna, 'Encounters in Camera: Autobiography as Interaction', *MFS – Modern Fiction Studies*, 40.3 (1994), 593–618
—, *Mirror Talk: Genres of Crisis in Contemporary Autobiography* (Chapel Hill and London: University of North Carolina Press, 1999)
Ehrenstein, David, 'Review: *Dancing Ledge* by Derek Jarman', *Film Quarterly*, 39.1 (1985), 57–8
Ellis, Havelock, and John Addington Symonds, *Sexual Inversion: A Critical Edition* [1896], ed. Ivan Crozier (Basingstoke: Palgrave Macmillan, 2008)
Ellis, Jim, *Derek Jarman's Angelic Conversations* (Minneapolis: University of Minnesota Press, 2009)
—, 'Queer Period: Derek Jarman's Renaissance', in *OutTakes: Essays on Queer Theory and Film*, ed. Ellis Hanson (London and Durham, NC: Duke University Press, 1993), pp. 288–315

—, 'Renaissance Things: Objects, Ethics, and Temporalities in Derek Jarman's *Caravaggio* (1986) and *Modern Nature* (1991)', *Shakespeare Bulletin*, 32.3 (2014), 375–92

—, 'Strange Meeting: Wilfred Owen, Benjamin Britten, Derek Jarman and the War Requiem', in *The Work of Opera: Genre, Nationhood, and Sexual Difference*, eds. Richard Dellamora and Daniel Fischlin (New York: Columbia University Press, 1997), pp. 277–96

—, 'The Temporality of Dirt: Queer Materiality in Jarman's *Modern Nature*', *ESC: English Studies in Canada*, 40.2 (2014), 9–13

Esch, Deborah, *In the Event: Reading Journalism, Reading Theory* (Stanford, CA: Stanford University Press, 2000)

Farthing, Stephen and Ed Webb-Ingall, 'An Introduction to the Sketchbooks', in *Derek Jarman's Sketchbooks*, eds. Stephen Farthing and Ed Webb-Ingall (London: Thames and Hudson, 2013), pp. 24–7

Fisher, Celia, *Flowers in Medieval Manuscripts*, 1st edn (Toronto: University of Toronto Press, 2004)

—, *The Medieval Flower Book*, 1st edn (London: British Library, 2008)

Fletcher, Martin, 'Bombs of Bitterness – At Your Own Risk: A Saint's Testament by Derek Jarman', *New Statesman & Society*, 5.202 (1992), 38

Fone, Byrne R. S., *Hidden Heritage: History and the Gay Imagination* (New York: Irvington Publishers, 1981)

Foucault, Michel, *The History of Sexuality*, vol. 1, *The Will To Knowledge* (1976), trans. Robert Hurley (London: Penguin, 1998)

—, 'Of Other Spaces: Utopias and Heterotopias (1967)', trans. Jay Miskowiec, *Architecture/Mouvement/Continuité*, 5 (1984), 46–9

Freccero, Carla, *Queer/Early/Modern* (Durham, NC: Duke University Press, 2006)

Freeman, Elizabeth, *Time Binds: Queer Temporalities, Queer Histories* (Durham, NC: Duke University Press, 2010)

Freeman, Mark, *Rewriting the Self: History, Memory, Narrative* (London: Routledge, 1993)

Freud, Sigmund, 'On Narcissism: An Introduction', in *The Freud Reader*, ed. Peter Gay (London: Vintage, 1995), pp. 545–61

Frey, Martin, *Derek Jarman – Moving Pictures of a Painter: Home Movies, Super 8 Films and Other Small Gestures*, trans. Michael Wetzel (La Vergne, TN: Ingram Content Group, 2016)

Friedman, Lester, ed., *Fires Were Started: British Cinema and Thatcherism* (Minneapolis: University of Minnesota Press, 1993)

Frith, Simon, '*Queer Edward II* (Book Review)', *Sight and Sound*, 1 (1991), p. 32

Gage, John, *Colour and Culture: Practice and Meaning from Antiquity to Abstraction*, new edn (London: Thames and Hudson, 1995)

—, *Colour and Meaning: Art, Science and Symbolism*, new edn (London: Thames and Hudson, 2000)

Gamble, Andrew, *The Free Economy and the Strong State* (Basingstoke: Macmillan Education, 1988)

Garden Museum, *Derek Jarman: My Garden's Boundaries are the Horizon* (London: Garden Museum, 2020)

Gardner, David, 'Perverse Law: Jarman as Gay Criminal Hero', in *By Angels Driven: The Films of Derek Jarman*, ed. Chris Lippard (Wiltshire: Flicks Books, 1996), pp. 31–64

Garfield, Simon, *The End of Innocence: Britain in the Time of AIDS* (London: Faber, 1995)

Gass, William H., *On Being Blue: A Philosophical Inquiry* [1975], reissue edn (Boston: David R. Godine, 2007)
Gay Men's Oral History Group, *Walking After Midnight: Gay Men's Life Stories* (London: Routledge, 1989)
Genet, Jean, *Journal Du Voleur* (Paris: Folio, 1949)
—, *Querelle de Brest* (Paris: Gallimard, 2002)
—, *Querelle of Brest*, trans. Gregory Streatham (London: Faber and Faber, 2015)
Gide, Andre, *If It Die* [1935], trans. D. Bussy, new edn (Middlesex: Penguin Books, 1977)
—, *Journals: 1889–1949*, ed. Justin O'Brien, trans. J. O'Brien, new edn (Penguin Books, 1991)
Gilmore, Leigh, *The Limits of Autobiography: Trauma and Testimony* (Ithaca, NY: Cornell University Press, 2001)
—, 'The Mark of Autobiography: Postmodernism, Autobiography, and Genre', eds. Kathleen Ashley, Leigh Gilmore and Gerald Peters (Amherst: University of Massachusetts Press, 1994), pp. 3–21
Ginsberg, Allen, 'Gay Sunshine Interview', *College English: The Homosexual Imagination*, 36.3 (1974), 392–400
Goethe, Johann Wolfgang von, *Theory of Colours*, trans. Charles Lock Eastlake (London: John Murray, 1840; Cambridge, MA: MIT Press, 1989)
Goldberg, Jonathan, ed., *Queering the Renaissance* (Durham, NC: Duke University Press, 1993)
—, *Sodometries: Renaissance Texts, Modern Sexualities* (Stanford, CA: Stanford University Press, 1992)
Graham-Dixon, Andrew, *Caravaggio: A Life Sacred and Profane* (London: Penguin, 2011)
Green, Charles, *The Third Hand: Collaboration in Art from Conceptualism to Postmodernism* (Minneapolis: University of Minnesota Press, 2001)
Greenberg, David F., *The Construction of Homosexuality* (Chicago: University of Chicago Press, 1988)
Grieve, Mrs Maud, *A Modern Herbal* (London: Cape, 1931)
Griffin, Gabriele, *Representations of HIV and AIDS: Visibility Blue/s* (Manchester: Manchester University Press, 2001)
Griffiths, Robin, ed., *British Queer Cinema*, new edn (New York: Routledge, 2006)
—, *Queer Cinema in Europe* (Chicago: University of Chicago Press, 2009)
Gudmundsdottir, Gunnthorunn, *Borderlines: Autobiography and Fiction in Postmodern Life Writing* (Amsterdam: Editions Rodopi, 2003)
Guibert, Hervé, *Cylomegalovirus: A Hospitalization Diary*, trans. Clara Orban (Lanham, MD: University Press of America, 1996)
—, *To The Friend Who Did Not Save My Life*, trans. Linda Coverdale (New York: Atheneum, 1991)
Gunn, Thom, *The Man With Night Sweats* [1992] (London: Faber & Faber, 2002)
—, and Ander Gunn, *Positives* (London: Faber and Faber, 1966)
Gusdorf, Georges, 'Conditions and Limits of Autobiography', in *Autobiography: Essays Theoretical and Critical*, ed. and trans. James Olney (Princeton, NJ: Princeton University Press, 1980), pp. 28–48
Hacker, Jonathan, and David Price, *Take Ten: Contemporary British Film Directors* (Oxford: Oxford University Press, 1991)
Hall, Peter, *Peter Hall's Diaries: The Story of a Dramatic Battle*, ed. John Goodwin (London: Hamilton, 1983)

Hall, Stuart, *The Hard Road to Renewal: Thatcherism and the Crisis of the Left* (London: Verso, 1988)
—, ed., 'The Work of Representation', in *Representation: Cultural Representations and Signifying Practices*, ed. Stuart Hall (London: Sage, 1997), pp. 1–47
Hallas, Roger, *Reframing Bodies: AIDS, Bearing Witness, and the Queer Moving Image* (Durham, NC: Duke University Press, 2010)
Halperin, David M., *How to Do the History of Homosexuality* (Chicago: University of Chicago Press, 2002)
—, *One Hundred Years of Homosexuality: And Other Essays on Greek Love* (New York: Routledge, 1990)
Hanson, Ellis, ed., *OutTakes: Essays on Queer Theory and Film* (Durham, NC: Duke University Press, 1993)
Hartley, L. P., *The Go-Between* (London: Penguin Books, 1958)
Harvey, David, *The Condition of Postmodernity: An Enquiry into the Origins of Cultural Change* (Oxford: Basil Blackwell, 1989)
Hassan, Ihab, *The Dismemberment of Orpheus: Toward a Postmodern Literature*, 2nd edn (Madison: University of Wisconsin Press, 1982)
Hebdige, Dick, *Hiding in the Light: On Images and Things* (London: Comedia, 1987)
—, *Subculture: The Meaning of Style* (London: Routledge, 1988)
Hegarty, Paul, *Noise/Music: A History* (New York, London: Continuum, 2009)
Helms, Alan, *Young Man from the Provinces: A Gay Life before Stonewall* (Minneapolis: University of Minnesota Press, 2003)
Hesford, Wendy S., *Framing Identities: Autobiography and the Politics of Pedagogy* (Minneapolis: University of Minnesota Press, 1999)
Hewer, Paul, 'Consuming Gardens: Representations of Paradise, Nostalgia and Postmodernism', *European Advances in Consumer Research*, 6 (2006), 327–31
Hewison, Robert, *Future Tense: A New Art for the Nineties* (London: Methuen, 1990)
Hibbard, Howard, *Caravaggio* (New York: Harper and Row, 1983)
Hidalgo Ciudad, Juan Carlos, 'Marlowe, Jarman, and *Edward II*: Use or Abuse', *Sederi*, 8 (1997), 291–5
Higginson, Kate, 'Derek Jarman's "Ghostly Eye": Prophetic Bliss and Sacrificial Blindness in *Blue*', *Mosaic*, 41.1 (2008), 77–94
Higgs, David, ed., *Queer Sites: Gay Urban Histories since 1600* (London and New York: Routledge, 1999)
Hill, John, *British Cinema in the 1980s: Issues and Themes* (Oxford: Clarendon Press, 1999)
—, 'The Rise and Fall of British Art Cinema', *Aura*, 6.3 (2000), 18–32
Hind, John, 'Derek Jarman: "So Mum Covered Me in Cooking Oil. Then Dad Came Home"', *Guardian*, 15 February 2014, www.theguardian.com/film/2014/feb/15/derek-jarman-covered-in-cooking-oil (accessed 16 February 2014)
Hirsch, Marianne, *Family Frames: Photography, Narrative and Postmemory* (Cambridge, MA: Harvard University Press, 1997)
Hobbs, Christopher, 'Derek Jarman', *Sight and Sound*, 4 (1994), 7
Hogan, Rebecca, 'Engendered Autobiographies: The Diary as a Feminine Form', in *Autobiography and the Question of Gender*, ed. Shirley Neuman (London: Frank Cass, 1991), pp. 95–107
Holland, Merlin, *The Real Trial of Oscar Wilde* (London: Fourth Estate, 2003)
Holleran, Andrew, *Dancer from the Dance* (New York: William Morrow, 1978; repr. New York: Perennial, 2001)

Hollinghurst, Alan, 'Alan Hollinghurst on Edmund White's Gay Classic A Boy's Own Story', *Guardian*, 10 June 2016, www.theguardian.com/books/2016/jun/10/edmund-white-a-boys-own-story-rereading-gay-literature (accessed 12 November 2017)

Holman, C. Hugh, *A Handbook to Literature*, based on the original edn by William Flint Thrall and Addison Hibbard, 4th edn (Indianapolis, IN: Bobbs-Merrill, 1980)

Houlbrook, Matt, *Queer London: Perils and Pleasures in the Sexual Metropolis, 1918–1957* (Chicago: University of Chicago Press, 2005)

Howard, Ed, 'Derek Jarman's *At Your Own Risk: A Saint's Testament*', *Slant*, 28 April 2010, www.slantmagazine.com/house/2010/04/derek-jarmans-at-your-own-risk-a-saints-testament (accessed 2 February 2013)

Hudson, Rock, and Sara Davidson, *Rock Hudson: His Story* (London: Weidenfeld & Nicolson, 1986)

Hughes, Ted, and Fay Godwin, *Remains of Elmet* (London: Faber and Faber, 1979)

Humphrey, Daniel, 'Authorship, History and the Dialectic of Trauma: Derek Jarman's *The Last of England*', *Screen*, 44.2 (Summer 2003), 208–15

Hutcheon, Linda, *A Poetics of Postmodernism: History, Theory, Fiction* (New York: Routledge, 1988)

—, *The Politics of Postmodernism*, 2nd edn (London: Routledge, 2002)

Huttner, Lee Benjamin, 'Body Positive: The Vibrant Present of Derek Jarman's *Edward II* (1991)', *Shakespeare Bulletin*, 32.3 (2014), 393–412

Ingram, Gordon Brent, Anne-Marie Bouthillette and Yolanda Retter, eds., *Queers in Space: Communities, Public Places, Sites of Resistance* (Seattle, WA: Bay Press, 1997)

Isherwood, Christopher, *Christopher and His Kind* [1976] (London: Vintage Books, 2012)

—, *Lions and Shadows* (New York: Vintage Classics, 2013)

Ivory, James, 'Pier Paolo Pasolini: A Life in Poetry', in *The Selected Poetry of Pier Paolo Pasolini: A Bilingual Edition*, by Pier Paolo Pasolini, ed. and trans. Stephen Sartarelli (Chicago: University of Chicago Press, 2014), pp. 1–58

Jacobus, Mary, *Reading Cy Twombly: Poetry in Paint* (Princeton, NJ: Princeton University Press, 2016)

Jameson, Fredric, 'Postmodernism: Or, the Cultural Logic of Late Capitalism', *New Left Review*, 1.146 (1984), 53–92

Janes, Dominic, *Visions of Queer Martyrdom from John Henry Newman to Derek Jarman* (Chicago: University of Chicago Press, 2015)

Jarman, Derek, *At Your Own Risk: A Saint's Testament* [1992] (London: Vintage, 1993)

—, *Blue* (London: Koenig Books, 2008)

—, *Chroma: A Book of Colour – June '93* [1994] (London: Vintage, 1995)

—, 'Damning Desire (Interview with Derek Jarman)', ed. Michael O'Pray, *Sight and Sound*, 1 (1991), 8–12

—, *Dancing Ledge*, ed. Shaun Allen (1984, repr. London: Quartet Books, 1991)

—, *Derek Jarman's 'Caravaggio': The Complete Film Script and Commentaries* (London: Thames and Hudson, 1986)

—, *Derek Jarman's Garden, with Photographs by Howard Sooley* (London: Thames and Hudson, 1995)

—, *Evil Queen: The Last Paintings* (Manchester: University of Manchester Press and Whitworth Art Gallery, 1994)

—, *A finger in the fishes mouth* (Bettiscombe, Dorset: Bettiscombe Press, 1972; repr. London: Test Centre, 2014)
—, *Freeze Frame*, ed. Takashi Asai (Tokyo: Uplink, 1993)
—, *Kicking the Pricks* (first published as *The Last of England*, London: Constable, 1987; new edn London: Vintage, 1996)
—, *Luminous Darkness: The Exhibition of Derek Jarman* (UPLINK, 1990)
—, *Modern Nature: The Journals of Derek Jarman* (London: Century, 1991; repr. London: Vintage, 1992)
—, 'P. P. P. in the Garden of Earthly Delights', *Afterimage*, 12 (Autumn 1985), 22–5
—, *Queer* (Manchester: Manchester City Art Galleries, 1993)
—, *Queer Edward II* (London: British Film Institute, 1991)
—, *Smiling in Slow Motion*, ed. Keith Collins (London: Century, 2000)
—, *Today and Tomorrow* (London: Richard Salmon, 1991)
—, *Up in the Air: Collected Film Scripts* (London: Vintage, 1996)
—, *War Requiem* (London: Faber, 1989)
—, and Ken Campbell, 'Derek Jarman and Ken Campbell, in Conversation', Institute of Contemporary Arts, London, 1984, http://sounds.bl.uk/View.aspx?item=024M-C0095X0085XX-0100V0.xml (Accessed 10 May 2021)
—, Terry Eagleton and Ken Butler, *Wittgenstein: The Terry Eagleton Script, The Derek Jarman Film* (London: British Film Institute, 1993)
'Jarman2014', www.jarman2014.org (accessed 9 August 2017)
Jay, Paul, 'Posing: Autobiography and the Subject of Photography', in *Autobiography and Postmodernism*, eds. Kathleen M. Ashley, Leigh Gilmore, and Gerald Peters (Amherst: University of Massachusetts Press, 1994), pp. 191–211
Johnson, Barbara, 'Whose Life Is It, Anyway?', in *The Seductions of Biography*, eds. Mary Rhiel and David Suchoff (New York: Routledge, 1996), pp. 119–21
Johnson, Fenton, *Geography of the Heart: A Memoir* (New York: Scribner, 1996)
Jones, Amelia, *Body Art/Performing the Subject* (Minneapolis: University of Minnesota Press, 1998)
—, Julia Peyton-Jones and Tilda Swinton, *Derek Jarman: Brutal Beauty* (Verlag der Buchhandlung Walther König, 2008)
Kantrowitz, Arnie, *Under the Rainbow – Growing Up Gay* (New York: William Morrow, 1977)
Kechiche, Abdellatif, dir., *Blue Is the Warmest Color* (Wild Bunch, 2013)
Keenan, David, *England's Hidden Reverse: A Secret History of the Esoteric Underground* (London: SAF, 2003)
Khalip, Jacques, '"The Archaeology of Sound": Derek Jarman's *Blue* and Queer Audiovisuality in the Time of AIDS', *Differences*, 21.2 (2010), 73–108
Kincaid, Jamaica, *My Brother* (New York: Farrar, Straus and Giroux, 1997)
King, Nicola, *Memory, Narrative, Identity: Remembering the Self* (Edinburgh: Edinburgh University Press, 2000)
Kissane, Seán, and Karim Rehmani-White, eds. *Derek Jarman: PROTEST!* (London: Thames and Hudson, 2020)
Kitson, Michael, *The Complete Paintings of Caravaggio* (New York: Henry N. Abrams, 1967)
Kramer, Larry, *Faggots* [1978] (New York: Avalon Travel Publishing, 2000)
—, *The Normal Heart*, new edn (London: Nick Hern Books, 2011)
Kristeva, Julia, *Black Sun: Melancholia and Depression*, trans. Leon S. Roudiez (New York: Columbia University Press, 1989)

—, 'Giotto's Joy', in *Desire in Language: A Semiotic Approach to Literature and Art*, ed. Leon S. Roudiez, trans. Thomas Gora, Alice Jardine and Leon S. Roudiez, rev edn (New York: Columbia University Press, 1980), pp. 210–36

Kruger, Steven F., *AIDS Narratives: Gender and Sexuality, Fiction and Science: Gender, Sexuality, Fiction and Science* (New York: Routledge, 1997)

Kuhn, Annette, *An Everyday Magic: Cinema and Cultural Memory* (London: I. B. Tauris, 2002)

—, *Family Secrets: Acts of Memory and Imagination*, 2nd edn (London: Verso Books, 2002)

—, *The Power of the Image: Essays on Representation and Sexuality* (London: Routledge, 1994)

Kuspit, Donald B., 'Collage: The Organizing Principle of Art in the Age of the Relativity of Art', in *Relativism in the Arts*, ed. Betty Jean Craige (Athens: University of Georgia Press, 1983), pp. 123–47

Laing, Olivia, 'Introduction', in *Modern Nature: The Journals of Derek Jarman*, by Derek Jarman (London: Vintage Classics, 2018), pp. vii–xiii

Laird, Tessa, 'Getting the Blues – Sex, Words and the Hues', *The Weeklings*, 15 October 2014, www.theweeklings.com/tlaird/2014/10/15/getting-the-blues-sex-words-and-the-hues (accessed 16 July 2015)

Laub, Dori, 'Bearing Witness or the Vicissitudes of Listening', in *Testimony: Crises of Witnessing in Literature, Psychoanalysis, and History*, eds. Shoshana Felman and Dori Laub (New York: Routledge, 1992), pp. 57–74

Lawrence, Tim, 'AIDS, the Problem of Representation, and Plurality in Derek Jarman's *Blue*', *Social Text: Queer Transexions of Race, Nation and Gender*, 52–53 (Autumn–Winter 1997), 241–64

Leader, Zachary, 'Introduction', in *On Life-Writing*, ed. Zachary Leader (Oxford: Oxford University Press, 2015), pp. 1–6.

Leap, William, *Public Sex, Gay Space* (New York: Columbia University Press, 1999)

Leapman, Michael, 'A Profusion of Plants in a Driftwood Oasis', *Independent*, 10 June 1995, www.independent.co.uk/arts-entertainment/a-profusion-of-plants-in-a-driftwood-oasis-1586025.html (accessed 28 October 2012).

Lejeune, Philippe, 'The Autobiographical Contract', trans. R. Carter, in *French Literary Theory Today*, ed. Tzvetan Todorov (Cambridge: Cambridge University Press, 1982), pp. 192–222

—, *On Autobiography*, ed. Paul John Eakin, trans. Katherine Leary (Minneapolis: University of Minnesota Press, 1989)

—, *On Diary*, eds. Jeremy D. Popkin and Julie Rak, trans. Katherine Durnin (Honolulu: University of Hawai'i Press, 2009)

Lévi-Strauss, Claude, *The Savage Mind*, trans. George Weidenfeld & Nicolson (London: Weidenfeld & Nicolson, 1966)

Lewis, Ida, 'Conversation: Ida Lewis and James Baldwin', in *Conversations with James Baldwin*, eds. Fred L. Stanley and Louis H. Pratt (Jackson: University Press of Mississippi, 1989), pp. 83–92

Lippard, Chris, ed., *By Angels Driven: The Films of Derek Jarman* (Wiltshire: Flicks Books, 1996)

—, and Guy Johnson, 'Private Practice, Public Health: The Politics of Sickness and the Films of Derek Jarman', in *Fires Were Started: British Cinema and Thatcherism*, ed. Lester Friedman (Minneapolis: University of Minnesota Press, 1993), pp. 301–14

Lombardo, Patrizia, 'Cruellement Bleu', *Critical Quarterly*, 36.1 (1994), 131–3

Love, Heather, *Feeling Backward: Loss and the Politics of Queer History* (Cambridge, MA: Harvard University Press, 2007)
Lucas, Ian, *Impertinent Decorum: Gay Theatrical Manoeuvres* (London: Cassell, 1994)
—, *OutRage!: An Oral History* (London: Cassell, 1998)
Lyotard, Jean-François, *The Postmodern Condition: A Report on Knowledge*, trans. Geoff Bennington and Brian Massumi (Minneapolis: University of Minnesota Press, 1984)
MacCabe, Colin, 'Derek Jarman: Obituary', *Critical Quarterly*, 36.1 (1994), v–ix
—, 'A Post-National European Cinema: A Consideration of Derek Jarman's *The Tempest* and *Edward II*', in *Screening Europe: Image and Identity in Contemporary European Cinema*, ed. Duncan Petrie (London: BFI Publishing, 1992), pp. 9–18
McKay, George, *Radical Gardening: Politics, Idealism and Rebellion in the Garden* (London: Frances Lincoln, 2011)
—, 'Radical Plots: The Politics of Gardening', *Independent*, 23 October 2011, www.independent.co.uk/property/gardening/radical-plots-the-politics-of-gardening-2277631.html (accessed 30 November 2012)
Mackay, James, *Derek Jarman: Super 8* (London: Thames and Hudson, 2014)
—, 'James Mackay's Papers: Proposal for a "Derek Jarman Interactive Monograph", British Film Institute Seminar and Miscellaneous Papers' (University of Exeter Special Collections, 1991)
—, 'Low-Budget British Production: A Producer's Account', in *New Questions of British Cinema*, ed. Duncan Petrie (London: BFI Publishing, 1992), pp. 52–64
McSmith, Andy, *No Such Thing As Society* (London: Constable, 2011)
Maguire, Richard, 'The Relics of St David Wojnarowicz: The Autobiography of a Mythmaker', in *Life Writing: Essays on Autobiography, Biography and Literature*, ed. Richard Bradford (Basingstoke: Palgrave Macmillan, 2010), pp. 247–68
de Man, Paul, 'Autobiography as De-Facement', *MLN*, 94.5 (1979), 919–30
Marcus, Laura, *Auto/Biographical Discourses: Criticism, Theory, Practice* (Manchester: Manchester University Press, 1994)
Marlowe, Christopher, *Edward II*, eds. Martin Wiggins and Robert Lindsey, 2nd edn (London: William Jones, 1594; London: Bloomsbury, 1997)
Martin, Robert K., *The Homosexual Tradition in American Poetry* (Austin: University of Texas Press, 1979)
Mattison, Robert Saltonstall, 'Robert Rauschenberg's Autobiography: Context and Meaning', *Wallraf-Richartz-Jahrbuch*, 59 (1998), 297–305
Maupin, Armistead, *Tales Of The City* [1978] (London: Black Swan, 1993)
Mavor, Carol, *Blue Mythologies: Reflections on a Colour* (London: Reaktion Books, 2013)
Melson, James, *The Golden Boy* (Binghampton, NY: The Haworth Press, 1992)
Michaels, Eric, *Unbecoming* (Durham, NC: Duke University Press, 1997)
Mieli, Mario, *Homosexuality and Liberation: Elements of a Gay Critique*, trans. D. Fernbach (London: Gay Men's Press, 1980)
Mighall, Robert, 'Review: Books: Paperbacks', *Observer*, 11 March 2001
Miller, Nancy K., *But Enough About Me: Why We Read Other People's Lives* (New York: Columbia University Press, 2002)
Miller, Tim, *Shirts and Skin* (Los Angeles: Alyson Publications, 1997)
Mills, Robert, *Derek Jarman's Medieval Modern* (Cambridge: D. S. Brewer, 2018)
Mitchell, W. J. Thomas, *Blake's Composite Art: A Study of the Illuminated Poetry*, reprint edn (Princeton, NJ: Princeton University Press, 1983)

Mohanty, Chandra Talpade, 'Feminist Encounters: Locating the Politics of Experience', in *Social Postmodernism: Beyond Identity Politics*, eds. Linda Nicholson and Steven Seidman (Cambridge: Cambridge University Press, 1995), pp. 68–86

Moir, Alfred, *Caravaggio* (New York: Harry N. Abrams, 1989)

Monette, Paul, *Becoming a Man: Half a Life Story* (New York: Harcourt Brace Jovanovich, 1992)

—, *Borrowed Time: An AIDS Memoir* (London: Collins Harvill, 1988)

Monk, Claire, '"The Shadow of This Time": Punk, Tradition, and History in Derek Jarman's Jubilee (1978)', *Shakespeare Bulletin*, 32.3 (2014), 359–73

Monk, Ray, '*Wittgenstein* (Film Review)', *Times Literary Supplement*, 19 March 1993, p. 16

Moor, Andrew, 'Spirit and Matter: Romantic Mythologies in the Films of Derek Jarman', in *Territories of Desire in Queer Culture: Refiguring Contemporary Boundaries*, eds. David Alderson and Linda Anderson (Manchester: Manchester University Press, 2000), pp. 49–67

Moore, Oscar, *PWA: Looking AIDS in the Face* (London: Picador, 1996)

Morris, Scott, 'A Finger in the Fishes Mouth: The Legacy of Derek Jarman', *The Literateur*, http://literateur.com/a-finger-in-the-fishes-mouth-the-legacy-of-derek-jarman (accessed 9 August 2017)

Morrison, Richard, 'Derek Jarman: The Final Interview, Thursday November 18, 1993', *Art & Understanding: The International Magazine of Literature and Art about AIDS*, April 1994, 17–22

Muñoz, José Esteban, *Cruising Utopia: The Then and There of Queer Futurity* (New York: New York University Press, 2009)

—, *Disidentifications: Queers of Color and the Performance of Politics* (Minneapolis: University of Minnesota Press, 1999)

Murphy, Timothy F., and Suzanne Poirier, eds., *Writing AIDS: Gay Literature, Language and Analysis* (New York: Columbia University Press, 1993)

Nawrocki, Jim, 'Motion Paintings', review of *Derek Jarman* by Michael Charlesworth, *The Gay & Lesbian Review*, July–August 2012.

Nelson, Emmanuel S., *Contemporary Gay American Novelists: A Bio-Bibliographical Critical Sourcebook* (Westport, CT: Greenwood Press, 1993)

Nelson, Maggie, *The Argonauts* (Minneapolis, MN: Graywolf Press, 2016)

—, *Bluets* (Seattle, WA: Wave Books, 2009)

Normand, Lawrence, '"Edward II", Derek Jarman, and the State of England', in *Constructing Christopher Marlowe*, eds. J. A. Downie and J. T. Parnell (Cambridge: Cambridge University Press, 2000), pp. 177–93

—, 'Jarman, Derek' in *The Gay and Lesbian Literary Heritage: A Reader's Companion to the Writers and Their Works, from Antiquity to the Present*, ed. Claude J. Summers (New York: Routledge, 2002), pp. 405–6

Ó Carragáin, Éamonn, and Richard North, 'How Christian is OE Literature? *The Dream of the Rood* and Anglo-Saxon Northumbria', in *Beowulf and Other Stories: A New Introduction to Old English, Old Icelandic and Anglo-Norman Literatures*, eds. Joe Allard and Richard North, 2nd edn (Harlow: Routledge, 2011), pp. 160–88

O'Donnell, Katherine, and Michael O'Rourke, eds., *Queer Masculinities, 1550–1800: Siting Same-Sex Desire in the Early Modern World* (Basingstoke: Palgrave Macmillan, 2006)

Olney, James, ed., *Autobiography: Essays Theoretical and Critical* (Princeton, NJ: Princeton University Press, 1980)

—, *Memory and Narrative: The Weave of Life-Writing* (Chicago: University of Chicago Press, 1998)
—, ed., *Metaphors of Self: The Meaning of Autobiography* (Princeton, NJ: Princeton University Press, 1972)
—, ed., *Studies in Autobiography* (Oxford: Oxford University Press, 1988)
O'Neill, John, *The Poverty of Postmodernism* (London: Routledge, 1995)
O'Pray, Michael, *Avant-Garde Film: Forms, Themes and Passions* (New York: Columbia University Press, 2003)
—, 'Britannia on Trial: An Interview with Derek Jarman', *Monthly Film Bulletin*, 53 (1986), 100–1
—, 'The British Avant-Garde and Art Cinema from the 1970s to the 1990s', in *Dissolving Views : Key Writings on British Cinema*, ed. Andrew Higson (London: Cassell, 1996), pp. 178–90
—, ed., *The British Avant-Garde Film, 1926–1995: An Anthology of Writings* (Luton: University of Luton Press, 1996)
—, *Derek Jarman: Dreams of England* (London: British Film Institute, 1996)
—, 'Derek Jarman's Cinema: Eros and Thanatos', *Afterimage*, 12 (Autumn 1985), 6–21
—, 'Edward II: Damning Desire', *Sight and Sound*, 1.6 (1991), 8–11
—, 'Philosophical Extras (Derek Jarman's Film 'Wittgenstein')', *Sight and Sound*, 3 (1993), 24–5
O'Quinn, Daniel, 'Gardening, History and the Escape from Time: Derek Jarman's Modern Nature', *October*, 89 (Summer 1999), 113–26
Orr, John, 'The Art of National Identity: Peter Greenaway and Derek Jarman', in *British Cinema: Past and Present*, eds. Justine Ashby and Andrew Higson (London: Routledge, 2000), pp. 327–38
Orton, Joe, *The Orton Diaries*, ed. John Lahr (London: Minerva, 1989)
Otto, Walter Friedrich, *Dionysus: Myth and Cult* (Bloomington: Indiana University Press, 1965)
Overbeek, Henk, *Global Capitalism and National Decline: The Thatcher Decade in Perspective* (London: Unwin Hyman, 1990)
Ovid, *Metamorphoses*, trans. David Raeburn (London: Penguin, 2004)
'Paradise On Sea', *Observer*, 4 June 1995, p. 74
Parsons, Alexandra, 'History, Activism, and the Queer Child in Derek Jarman's Queer Edward II (1991)', *Shakespeare Bulletin*, 32.3 (2014), 413–28
—, 'A Meditation on Color and the Body in Derek Jarman's *Chroma* and Maggie Nelson's *Bluets*', *a/b: Auto/Biography Studies*, 33.2 (2018), 375–93
Pascal, Roy, *Design and Truth in Autobiography* (Cambridge, MA: Harvard University Press, 1960)
Pasolini, Pier Paolo, *Bestemmia* in *Tutte le poesie*, ed. Walter Siti, vol. 2 (Milan: Mondadori, 2003), pp. 995–1115
Pastoureau, Michel, *Blue: The History of a Color* (Princeton, NJ: Princeton University Press, 2001)
Patton, Cindy, *Inventing AIDS* (London: Routledge, 1990)
Peabody, Barbara, *The Screaming Room: A Mother's Journal of Her Son's Struggle with AIDS* (San Diego, CA: Oak Tree Publications, 1986)
Peake, Tony, *Derek Jarman* (London: Little Brown, 1999)
Pearl, in *Sir Gawain And The Green Knight/Pearl/Cleanness/Patience*, ed. J. J. Anderson, new edn (London: W&N, 1996), pp. 1–46
Pearl, Monica B., *AIDS Literature and Gay Identity: The Literature of Loss* (New York: Routledge, 2013)

Pencak, William, *The Films of Derek Jarman* (Jefferson, NC: McFarland, 2002)
Pericolo, Lorenzo, and David M. Stone, *Caravaggio: Reflections and Refractions* (Farnham: Ashgate, 2014)
Perloff, Marjorie, *The Futurist Moment: Avant-Garde, Avant Guerre, and the Language of Rupture* (Chicago: University of Chicago Press, 1986)
—, *Wittgenstein's Ladder: Poetic Language and the Strangeness of the Ordinary* (Chicago: University of Chicago Press, 1996)
Petrie, Duncan, 'Autobiography and British Art Cinema: The Films of Bill Douglas, Terence Davies and Derek Jarman', in *Biographie als religiöser und kultureller Text [Biography as a Religious and Cultural Text]*, ed. Andreas Schule (Munster: Lit Verlag, 2002), pp. 55–66
Phelan, Shane, *Playing with Fire: Queer Politics, Queer Theories* (New York: Routledge, 1997)
Phillips, Tom, 'Down among the Rushes: *Dancing Ledge* by Derek Jarman', *Times Literary Supplement*, 4227 (6 April 1984), 367
Picano, Felice, *Like People in History* (London: Abacus, 1996)
Pinfold, Michael John, 'The Performance of Queer Masculimity in Derek Jarman's *Sebastiane*', *Film Criticism*, 23.1 (1998), p. 74
Plummer, Ken, *Telling Sexual Stories: Power, Change and Social Worlds* (London and New York: Routledge, 1994)
Polatinsky, Ashlee, 'Living Between Deaths: Temporality and the South African AIDS Autopathography', *English Studies in Africa*, 52.1 (2009), 38–49
Poletti, Anna, 'Periperformative Life Narrative: Queer Collages', *GLQ: A Journal of Lesbian and Gay Studies*, 22.3 (2016), 359–79
Porter, Kevin, and Jeffrey Weeks, *Between the Acts: Lives of Homosexual Men, 1885–1967* (London: Routledge, 1991)
Posner, Donald, 'Caravaggio's Homo-Erotic Early Works', *Art Quarterly*, 34 (1971), 301–24
Potter, Jennifer, 'Stranger than Paradise', *Guardian*, 15 June 1995
Proust, Marcel, *In Search Of Lost Time Vol 1: Swann's Way* [1913–1927], trans. C. K. Scott Moncrieff, D. J. Enright, and Terence Kilmartin, New Edition (London: Vintage Classics, 1996)
Puglisi, Catherine, *Caravaggio* (London: Phaidon Press, 2000)
Pullen, Christopher, *Gay Identity, New Storytelling and the Media* (Basingstoke: Palgrave Macmillan, 2009)
Purdy, James, *Narrow Rooms* (London: Gay Men's Press, 1985)
Quinn-Meyler, Martin, 'Opposing "Heterosoc": Derek Jarman's Counter-Hegemonic Activism', in *By Angels Driven: The Films of Derek Jarman*, ed. Chris Lippard (Trowbridge: Flicks Books, 1996), pp. 117–34
Ratekin, Tom, *Final Acts: Traversing the Fantasy in the Modern Memoir* (Albany: State University of New York Press, 2010)
Rayns, Tony, *The Garden: Salesbook* (London: The Sales Company, 1990)
Rechy, John, *City of Night* [1963] (London: Souvenir Press, 2009)
—, *The Sexual Outlaw: A Documentary* (New York: Random House, 1977)
Reed, Jeremy, 'Living up to the End', *The Times*, 5 July 2000
Rees, A. L., *A History of Experimental Film and Video*, 2nd edn (Basingstoke: Palgrave Macmillan, 2011)
Remes, Justin, *Motion(Less) Pictures: The Cinema of Stasis* (New York: Columbia University Press, 2015)
Renault, Mary, *The Charioteer* (London: Longmans, Green and Co, 1953)

—, *The Mask of Apollo* (London: Longmans, Green and Co, 1966)
Rich, Adrienne, 'Invisibility in Academe', in *Blood, Bread, and Poetry: Selected Prose 1979–1985* (New York: Norton, 1986), pp. 198–201
Richards, Jane, 'THE FLOWER AND THE GLORY; While Derek Jarman Was Grappling with Death, He Was Also Coaxing Alive a Garden from Hostile Ground. Howard Sooley Kept This Photographic Record, Now on Show in London', *Guardian*, 16 May 1995
Richardson, Niall, *The Queer Cinema of Derek Jarman: Critical and Cultural Readings* (London: I. B. Tauris, 2009)
—, 'The Queer Performance of Tilda Swinton in Derek Jarman's *Edward II*: Gay Male Misogyny Reconsidered', *Sexualities: Studies in Culture and Society*, 6.3–4 (2003), 427–2
Riley, Charles A., *Color Codes: Modern Theories of Color in Philosophy, Painting and Architecture, Literature, Music and Psychology*, new edn (Hanover, NH: University Press of New England, 1996)
Robinson, Paul A., *Gay Lives: Homosexual Autobiography from John Addington Symonds to Paul Monette* (Chicago: University of Chicago Press, 1999)
Royal Horticultural Society, 'Bindweed', n.d., http://apps.rhs.org.uk/advicesearch/Profile.aspx?pid=241 (accessed 16 March 2012)
Rugg, Linda Haverty, *Picturing Ourselves: Photography and Autobiography* (Chicago: University of Chicago Press, 1997)
—, *Self-Projection: The Director's Image in Art Cinema* (Minneapolis: University of Minnesota Press, 2014)
Rumble, Patrick A., and Bart Testa, eds., *Pier Paolo Pasolini: Contemporary Perspectives* (Toronto: University of Toronto Press, 1994)
Rusk, Lauren, *The Life Writing of Otherness: Woolf, Baldwin, Kingston, and Winterson* (London: Routledge, 2002)
Sackville-West, Vita, *The Garden* (London: Michael Joseph, 1946; London: Frances Lincoln, 1989)
Sarkonak, Ralph, *Angelic Echoes: Hervé Guibert and Company* (Toronto: University of Toronto, 2017)
Saunders, Max, *Self Impression: Life-Writing, Autobiografiction, and the Forms of Modern Literature* (Oxford: Oxford University Press, 2010)
Sborghi, Anna, 'Reconfiguring the Past into the Present: Derek Jarman's Elaboration of Heritage Culture', *Textus: English Studies in Italy*, 29 (2007), 481–95
Schehr, Lawrence R., 'Thanatopsis: Writing and Witnessing in the Age of AIDS', *Modern Fiction Studies*, 48.3 (2002), 746–50
Schneider, Laurie, 'Donatello and Caravaggio: The Iconography of Decapitation', *American Imago*, 33.1 (1976), 76–91
Schulman, Sarah, *The Gentrification of the Mind: Witness to a Lost Imagination* (Berkeley: University of California Press, 2012)
Schwenger, Peter, 'Derek Jarman and the Colour of the Mind's Eye', *University of Toronto Quarterly*, 65.2 (1996), 419–26
Scott, Joan W., 'The Evidence of Experience', *Critical Inquiry*, 17.4 (1991), 773–97
'Section 28: Prohibition on promoting homosexuality by teaching or by publishing material', Local Government Act 1988, www.legislation.gov.uk/ukpga/1988/9/section/28/enacted (accessed 4 December 2017)
Sedgwick, Eve Kosofsky, *Between Men: English Literature and Male Homosocial Desire* (New York: Columbia University Press, 1985)
—, *Epistemology of the Closet* (Berkeley: University of California Press, 1990)

—, *Tendencies* (London: Routledge, 1994)
—, *Touching Feeling* (Durham, NC: Duke University Press, 2003)
Sexual Offences Act 1967, 1967, www.legislation.gov.uk/ukpga/1967/60/pdfs/ukpga_19670060_en.pdf (accessed 16 February 2013)
Shepard, Joanna, 'Painting on Borrowed Time: Jarman's Media and Techniques', in *Derek Jarman: PROTEST!*, eds. Seán Kissane and Karim Rehmani-White (London: Thames and Hudson, 2020), pp. 92–9
Shepherd, Simon, and Mick Wallis, eds., *Coming on Strong: Gay Politics and Culture* (London: Routledge, 1989)
Sheringham, Michael, and Johnnie Gratton, 'Tracking the Art of the Project: History, Theory, Practice', in *The Art of the Project: Projects and Experiments in Modern French Culture*, eds. Michael Sheringham and Johnnie Gratton (New York: Berghahn Books, 2005), pp. 1–30
Shields, David, *Reality Hunger: A Manifesto* (London: Penguin, 2011)
Shilts, Randy, *And the Band Played on: Politics, People, and the AIDS Epidemic*, 20th Anniversary rev edn. (New York: Griffin, 2007)
Siciliano, Enzo, *Pasolini: A Biography*, trans. John Shepley (New York: Random House, 1982)
Silverstein, Charles, and Edmund White, *The Joy of Gay Sex: An Intimate Guide for Gay Men to the Pleasures of a Gay Lifestyle* (New York: Simon and Schuster, 1978)
Silverstone, Catherine, 'Editorial: Derek Jarman and "the Renaissance"', *Shakespeare Bulletin*, 32.3 (2014), 329–36
—, 'Remembering Derek Jarman: Death, Legacy, and Friendship', *Shakespeare Bulletin*, 32.3 (2014), 451–70
Simons, John, 'Elizabethan Texts in the Work of Derek Jarman', in *Elizabethan Literature and Transformation, Salzburg Conference on Elizabethan Literature and Transformation*, ed. Sabine Coelsch-Foisner (Tübingen: Stauffenburg-Verlag, 1999), pp. 263–72
Simpson, Mark, ed., *Anti-Gay* (London: Freedom Editions, 1996)
Sinfield, Alan, *Cultural Politics, Queer Reading* (London: Routledge, 1994)
—, *Faultlines: Cultural Materialism and the Politics of Dissident Reading* (Oxford: Clarendon Press, 1992)
—, *Gay and After* (London: Serpent's Tail, 1998)
—, *Literature, Politics, and Culture in Postwar Britain* (London: Athlone Press, 1997)
—, *On Sexuality and Power* (New York: Columbia University Press, 2004)
—, 'Thom Gunn and the Largest Gathering of the Decade', *London Review of Books*, 14.3 (1992), 16–17
—, *The Wilde Century: Effeminacy, Oscar Wilde and the Queer Movement* (London: Cassell, 1994)
Smith, Ali, 'Introduction', in *Chroma: A Book of Colour–June '93*, by Derek Jarman (London: Vintage Classics, 2019), pp. vii–xv
Smith, Anna Marie, *New Right Discourse on Race and Sexuality: Britain, 1968–1990* (Cambridge and New York: Cambridge University Press, 2008)
Smith, Paul Julian, 'Blue and the Outer Limits', *Sight and Sound*, 3.10 (1993), 18–19
Smith, Sidonie, 'Performativity, Autobiographical Practice, Resistance', *a/b: Auto/Biography Studies*, 10.1 (1995), 17–33
—, *Reading Autobiography: A Guide for Interpreting Life Narratives* (Minneapolis: University of Minnesota Press, 2010)
—, and Julia Watson, eds., 'Introduction', in *Getting a Life: The Everyday Uses of Autobiography* (Minneapolis: University of Minnesota Press, 1996), pp. 1–24

Sobchack, Vivian, *Carnal Thoughts: Embodiment and Moving Image Culture* (Berkeley: University of California Press, 2004)
—, 'Fleshing Out The Image: Phenomenology, Pedagogy, and Derek Jarman's Blue', in *New Takes in Film-Philosophy*, eds. Havi Carel and Greg Tuck (New York: Palgrave Macmillan, 2011), pp. 191–206
Sontag, Susan, *Illness as Metaphor and AIDS and Its Metaphors* [1978] (New York: Anchor Books, 1990)
—, *On Photography* [1977] (London: Penguin, 2008)
—, *Regarding the Pain of Others* (London: Penguin, 2004)
Sooley, Howard, 'Derek Jarman's Hideaway', *Guardian*, 17 February 2008, www.guardian.co.uk/lifeandstyle/2008/feb/17/gardens (accessed 30 November 2012)
Spear, Thomas C., 'Edmund White on Queer Autofiction, Biography, and Sidafiction', *a/b: Auto/Biography Studies*, 15.2 (2000), 261–76
Spender, Stephen, *World Within World: The Autobiography of Stephen Spender* [1951], new edn (London: Faber and Faber, 1991)
Stacey, Jackie, 'Promoting Normality: Section 28 and the Regulation of Sexuality', in *Off-Centre: Feminism and Cultural Studies*, eds. Sarah Franklin, Celia Lury and Jackie Stacey (London: Harper Collins Academic, 1991), pp. 284–304
Stanley, Liz, and Helen Dampier, 'Simulacrum Diaries: Time, the "Moment of Writing," and the Diaries of Johanna Brandt-Van Warmelo', *Life Writing*, 3.2 (2006), 25–52
Stein, Gertrude, *Q.E.D.* [Originally published in the collection *Things as They Are*, 1950] (Paris; Montréal: Remue Menage, 2005)
—, *The Autobiography of Alice B. Toklas* [1933], new edn (London: Penguin Classics, 2001)
Stewart, Alan, '*Edward II* and Male Same-Sex Desire', in *Early Modern English Drama: A Critical Companion*, eds. Garrett A. Sullivan, Jr., Patrick Cheney, and Andrew Hadfield (Oxford: Oxford University Press, 2006), pp. 82–95
Steyaert, Chris, 'Queering Space: Heterotopic Life in Derek Jarman's Garden', *Gender, Work and Organization*, 17.1 (2010), 45–68
Stillinger, Jack, *Multiple Authorship and the Myth of Solitary Genius* (Oxford: Oxford University Press, 1991)
Stockton, Kathryn Bond, *The Queer Child: Or Growing Sideways in the Twentieth Century* (Durham, NC: Duke University Press, 2009)
Stone, David, 'Self and Myth in Caravaggio's "David and Goliath"', in *Caravaggio: Realism, Rebellion, Reception*, ed. Genevieve Warwick (Newark: University of Delaware Press, 2006), pp. 36–46
Stoschek, Julia, Jon Savage and Simon Field, *Derek Jarman: Super8* (Dusseldorf: Buchhandlung Walther Konig, 2010)
Street, Sarah, *British National Cinema* (London: Routledge, 2009)
Stribling, Thomas B., with Verne Becker, *Love Broke Through: A Husband, Father, and Minister Tells His Own Story* (Grand Rapids, MI: Zondervan, 1990)
Sturrock, John, *The Language of Autobiography: Studies in the First Person Singular* (Cambridge: Cambridge University Press, 1993)
Summers, Claude J., ed., *The Gay and Lesbian Literary Heritage: A Reader's Companion to the Writers and Their Works, from Antiquity to the Present* (New York: Routledge, 2002)
Swindells, Julia, *The Uses of Autobiography* (London: Taylor & Francis, 1995)
Swinton, Tilda, 'In the Spirit of Derek Jarman', *Guardian*, 17 August 2002, www.theguardian.com/film/2002/aug/17/books.featuresreviews (accessed 28 May 2019)

—, 'Foreword', in *Derek Jarman's Sketchbooks*, eds. Farthing, Stephen, and Ed Webb-Ingall (London: Thames and Hudson, 2013) pp. 18–19

Symonds, John Addington, *The Memoirs*, ed. Phyllis Grosskurth, 1st edn (London: Hutchinson, 1984)

Szabados, Bela, and Christina Stojanova, eds., *Wittgenstein at the Movies: Cinematic Investigations* (Lanham, MD: Lexington Books, 2011)

Tagg, John, *The Burden of Representation: Essays on Photographs and Histories* (London: Macmillan, 1988)

Tambling, Jeremy, *Becoming Posthumous: Life and Death in Literary and Cultural Studies* (Edinburgh: Edinburgh University Press, 2001)

Tatchell, Peter, 'Peter Tatchell on Derek Jarman', interviewed by Andy Kimpton-Nye, 2003, www.400blows.co.uk/inter_tatchell.shtml (accessed 4 February 2013)

Teeman, Tim, 'Non-Fiction (Review of Smiling in Slow Motion)', *The Times*, 24 February 2001

Thirlwell, Adam, 'Reality Hunger: Pasolini's Seductive Utopian Vision', *Bookforum* (June/July/Aug 2014), www.bookforum.com/print/2102/pasolini-s-seductive-utopian-vision-13281 (accessed 12 June 2021)

Thomson, Heidi, 'Wordsworth's "Song for the Wandering Jew" as a Poem for Coleridge', *Romanticism*, 21.1 (2015), 37–47

Tobias, Andrew, writing as John Reid, *The Best Little Boy in the World* (New York: Ballantine Books, 1998)

Tóibín, Colm, *Love in a Dark Time: Gay Lives from Wilde to Almodovar* (New York: Scribner, 2002)

Todd, Matthew, 'Introduction', in *At Your Own Risk: A Saint's Testament*, by Derek Jarman, ed. Michael Christie (London: Vintage Classics, 2019), pp. vii–xii

Trimm, Ryan S., 'Nation, Heritage, and Hospitality in Britain after Thatcher', *CLCWeb: Comparative Literature and Culture*, 7.2 (2005), https://docs.lib.purdue.edu/clcweb/vol7/iss2/8/ (accessed 11 May 2021)

Turner, Mark, *Backwards Glances: Cruising the Queer Streets of New York and London* (London: Reaktion Books, 2003)

—, 'Derek Jarman in the Docklands: *The Last of England* and Thatcher's London', in *Taking Place: Location and the Moving Image*, eds. John David Rhodes and Elena Gorfinkel (Minneapolis: University of Minnesota Press, 2011), pp. 77–97

—, 'Gay London', in *London From Punk to Blair*, eds. Joe Kerr and Andrew Gibson, 2nd edn (London: Reaktion Books, 2012), pp. 50–61

Turner, Simon Fisher, 'Simon Fisher Turner On Derek Jarman's Blue', *The Quietus*, 18 February 2014, http://thequietus.com/articles/05380-world-aids-days-simon-fisher-turner-on-derek-jarman-s-blue (accessed 5 December 2016)

Tweedie, James, 'The Suspended Spectacle of History: The Tableau Vivant in Derek Jarman's *Caravaggio*', *Screen*, 44.4 (2003), 379–403

Vaughan, Keith, *Journals 1939–1977*, ed. Alan Ross (London: John Murray, 1989)

Viart, Dominique, 'Programmes and Projects in the Contemporary Literary Field', in *The Art of the Project: Projects and Experiments in Modern French Culture*, eds. Michael Sheringham and Johnnie Gratton (New York: Berghahn Books, 2005), pp. 172–87

Vickery, Roy, *A Dictionary of Plant Lore* (Oxford University Press, Oxford: 1995)

Vidal, Gore, *Gore Vidal Sexually Speaking: Collected Sex Wrtings*, new edn (San Francisco: Cleis Press, 2001)

—, *Palimpsest: A Memoir*, New Edition (London: Abacus, 1996)

Vogler, Candace, 'Fourteen Sonnets for an Epidemic: Derek Jarman's *The Angelic Conversation*', *Public Culture*, 18.1 (2006), 23–52
Waggoner, Eric, '"This Killing Machine Called America": Narrative of the Body in David Wojnarowicz's *Close to the Knives*', *a/b: Auto/Biography Studies*, 15.2 (2000), 171–92
Walters, Guy, 'Jarman's Desolate Paradise', *The Times*, 8 July 1995
Warhol, Andy, *The Andy Warhol Diaries*, ed. Pat Hackett (London: Pan, 1992)
—, *The Philosophy of Andy Warhol: From A to B and Back Again* (London: Pan Books, 1979)
Wark, Penny, 'A Labour of Love', *The Times*, 19 June 2000
Warner, Michael, ed., *Fear of a Queer Planet: Queer Politics and Social Theory* (Minneapolis: University of Minnesota Press, 1993)
—, *The Trouble with Normal: Sex, Politics and the Ethics of Queer Life* (New York: Free Press, 1999)
Warner, Sylvia Townsend, *T. H. White: A Biography* (London: Jonathan Cape with Chatto & Windus, 1967)
Warwick, Genevieve, 'Introduction: Caravaggio in History', in *Caravaggio: Realism, Rebellion, Reception*, ed. Genevieve Warwick (Newark: University of Delaware Press, 2006), pp. 13–22
Watney, Simon, 'Derek Jarman 1942–94: A Political Death', *Artforum*, 32 (1994), 84–6
—, *Imagine Hope: AIDS and Gay Identity* (London: Routledge, 2000)
—, 'Introduction', in Eric Michaels, *Unbecoming* (Durham, NC: Duke University Press, 1997), pp. xxi–xxv
—, *Policing Desire: Pornography, AIDS and the Media* (London: Comedia, 1987)
—, *Practices of Freedom* (London: Rivers Oram Press, 1994)
—, 'The Spectacle of AIDS', in *AIDS: Cultural Analysis/Cultural Activism*, ed. Douglas Crimp (Cambridge, MA: MIT Press, 1987), pp. 71–86
Watney, Simon, and Erica Carter, eds., *Taking Liberties: AIDS and Cultural Politics* (London: Serpent's Tail, 1989)
Watts, Jonathan P., 'Derek Jarman: Black Paintings at Wilkinson', Galleries Now, n.d., www.galleriesnow.net/shows/derek-jarman-black-paintings (accessed 12 October 2017)
Weeks, Jeffrey, *Coming out: Homosexual Politics in Britain from the Nineteenth Century to the Present* (London: Quartet, 1977)
—, *Sex, Politics and Society: The Regulation of Sexuality Since 1800*, 2nd edn (Harlow: Longman, 1989)
—, *Sexuality and Its Discontents: Meanings, Myths and Modern Sexualities* (London: Routledge & Kegan Paul, 1985)
Weintraub, Karl J., *The Value of the Individual: Self and Circumstance in Autobiography* (Chicago: University of Chicago Press, 1978)
West, Shearer, *Portraiture* (Oxford: Oxford University Press, 2004)
White, Edmund, *A Boy's Own Story* [1982], new edn (London: Picador, 2016)
—, *City Boy: My Life in New York during the 1960s and 1970s* (London: Bloomsbury, 2010)
—, *Genet; with a Chronology by Albert Dichy* (London: Chatto & Windus, 1993)
—, ed., *Loss within Loss: Artists in the Age of AIDS* (Madison: University of Wisconsin Press, 2001)
—, *My Lives* (London: Bloomsbury, 2005)

Wight, Colin, 'Writer in the Garden: Themes – Where Is Paradise?' www.bl.uk/onlinegallery/features/gardens/themeswherepara.html (accessed 30 November 2012)

Wilde, Oscar, *The Picture of Dorian Gray* (1891; repr. London: Penguin Popular Classics, 1994)

Williams, Kenneth, *The Kenneth Williams Diaries*, ed. Russell Davies (London: HarperCollins, 1993)

Wilson, Angus, *Hemlock and After* (London: Secker & Warburg, 1952)

Wiltshire, Susan, *Seasons of Grief and Grace: A Sister's Story of AIDS* (Nashville: Vanderbilt University Press, 1994)

Wittgenstein, Ludwig, *Philosophical Investigations*, trans. G. E. M. Anscombe, new edn (Oxford: Wiley-Blackwell, 1973)

—, *Remarks on Colour*, ed. G. E. M. Anscombe, trans. Linda McAlister and Margeret Schattle (Berkeley: University of California Press, 2007)

—, *Remarks on Colour: Parallel Text*, ed. G. E. M. Anscombe, trans. Linda L. McAlister, new edn (Oxford: John Wiley & Sons, 1979)

—, *Tractatus Logico-Philosophicus*, trans. D. F. Pears and B. F. McGuinness (London: Routledge, 1974)

Wojnarowicz, David, *Close to the Knives* (New York: Vintage, 1991)

—, *Memories That Smell Like Gasoline*, 1st edn (London: Serpent's Tail, 1992)

Wollen, Peter, 'Blue', in *Color, The Film Reader*, eds. Angela Dalle Vacche and Brian Price, new edn (New York: Routledge, 2006), pp. 192–201

—, *Signs and Meanings in the Cinema*, 5th edn (London: Palgrave Macmillan on behalf of the British Film Institute, 2013), pp. 58–96

Wollen, Roger, ed., *Derek Jarman: A Portrait* (London: Thames and Hudson, 1996)

Woods, Chris, *State of the Queer Nation: A Critique of Gay and Lesbian Politics in 1990s Britain* (London: Cassell, 1995)

Woods, Gregory, *A History of Gay Literature: The Male Tradition* (New Haven, CT: Yale University Press, 1998)

—, *Articulate Flesh: Male Homo-Eroticism and Modern Poetry* (New Haven, CT: Yale University Press, 1987)

Woolf, Virginia, 'A Sketch of the Past', in *Moments Of Being: Autobiographical Writings*, ed. Jeanne Schulkind, New Edition (San Diego, CA: Harcourt Brace, 1985), pp. 61–159

Wordsworth, William, 'I Wandered Lonely As a Cloud', in *The Norton Anthology of Poetry*, 4th edn, eds. Margaret Ferguson, Mary Jo Salter, and Jon Stallworthy (New York: W. W. Norton, 1996), pp. 732–3

Wyatt, Justin, 'Autobiography, Home Movies, and Derek Jarman's History Lesson', in *Between the Sheets, in the Streets: Queer, Lesbian, and Gay Documentary*, eds. Chris Holmlund and Cynthia Fuchs (Minneapolis: University of Minnesota Press, 1997), pp. 158–72

Wymer, Rowland, *Derek Jarman* (Manchester: Manchester University Press, 2005)

—, 'Derek Jarman's Renaissance and The Devils (1971)', *Shakespeare Bulletin*, 32.3 (2014), 337–57

Yagoda, Ben, *Memoir: A History*, repr. (New York: Riverhead Books, 2010)

Yourcenar, Marguerite, *Memoirs of Hadrian*, trans. Grace Frick (London: Penguin, 1986)

Zeiger, Melissa, *Beyond Consolation: Death, Sexuality, and the Changing Shapes of Elegy* (Ithaca, NY; London: Cornell University Press, 1997)

—, '"Modern Nature": Derek Jarman's Garden', *Humanities*, 6.22 (2017), 1–12

Filmography

Anderson, Lindsay, dir., *If...* (Paramount Pictures, 1968)
Anger, Kenneth, dir., *Fireworks* (1947)
Benstock, Jes, dir., *The British Guide to Showing Off* (Living Cinema, 2011)
Bistikas, Alexis, dir., *The Clearing* (Royal College of Art, 1993)
Caouette, Jonathan, dir., *Tarnation* (Wellspring Media, 2003)
Cocteau, Jean, *The Blood of a Poet* (Vicomte de Noailles, 1932)
Cole, Julian, dir., *Ostia* (Royal College of Art, 1987)
Davies, Terence, dir., *Death and Transfiguration* (British Film Institute, 1983)
—, *Distant Voices, Still Lives* (British Film Institute, 1989)
'Face to Face: Derek Jarman, with Jeremy Isaacs', *Face to Face*, BBC, 15 March 1993
Ferrara, Abel, dir., *Pasolini* (Capricci Films, 2014)
France, David, dir., *How to Survive a Plague* (Sundance Selects, 2012)
Frears, Stephen, dir., *Prick Up Your Ears* (Samuel Goldwyn, 1987)
Friedkin, William, dir., *Cruising* (Lorimar Film Entertainment, 1980)
Gold, Jack, dir., *The Naked Civil Servant* (Thames Television, 1975)
Jarman, Derek, dir., *The Angelic Conversation* (Channel Four Films, 1985)
—, *Blue* (Basilisk Communications, 1993)
—, *Caravaggio* (British Film Institute, 1986)
—, *Edward II* (Working Title Films, 1991)
—, *The Garden* (Basilisk Communications, 1990)
—, *Imagining October* (1984)
—, *Jubilee* (Megalovision, 1978)
—, *The Last of England* (Anglo International Films, 1987)
—, *The Tempest* (Kendon Films, 1979)
—, *War Requiem* (Anglo International Films, 1989)
—, *Wittgenstein* (Channel Four Films, 1993)
—, and Paul Humphress, dirs., *Sebastiane* (Disctac, 1976)
—, Richard Heslop and John Maybury, dirs., *The Queen Is Dead* (Basilisk Communications, 1986)
Jordan, Mark, dir., 'The Last Paintings of Derek Jarman' (Granada TV, 1995)
Julien, Isaac, dir., *Derek* (Normal Films, 2008)
Kidel, Mark, dir., 'Derek Jarman A Portrait', *Arena* (BBC, 2001)
Kimpton-Nye, Andy, dir., *Derek Jarman: Life as Art* (400Blows Productions, 2004)
Kubrick, Stanley, dir., *Spartacus* (Bryna Productions, 1960)
Peck, Ron, dir., *Nighthawks* (Nashburgh, 1978)
Powell, Michael, and Emeric Pressburger, *A Matter of Life and Death* (The Archers/J. Arthur Rank, 1946)

Russell, Ken, dir., *Savage Messiah* (Russ-Arts, 1972)
—, *The Devils* (Russo Productions, 1971)
Schlesinger, John, dir., *Sunday Bloody Sunday* (United Artists, 1971)
Vertov, Dziga, dir., *Man with a Movie Camera* (Vseukrainske Foto Kino Upravlinnia, 1929)
Wyler, William, dir., *Ben-Hur* (Metro-Goldwyn-Mayer, 1959)

Index

Ackerley, J. R. 12
ACT UP 7, 149, 191, 197, 226
affect 5, 105, 122, 131, 210
A finger in the fishes mouth 9, 20,
    30–9, 87, 104
  'Assisi' 31
  'Fargo 64' 31
  'From Gypsy Mar 1 66' 33
  'Manhattan Lower East Side' 33
  'Patmos – Delos' 33
  'Poem I' 33–5
  'Poem I 1965' 31
  'Poem II' 32–3
'After the Final Academy' (paintings,
    Jarman) 42
AIDS *see* HIV/AIDS
Albert Memorial 127
Alternative Miss World 54,
    57n35
anachronism 61
Anderson, Lindsay 177
androgyny 63
Angelic Conversation, The (Jarman) 4,
    30
angels 45, 56n9
ArtFund 22–3, 221
At Your Own Risk (Jarman) 21,
    89–90, 144, 156, 158, 163,
    166–82, 183, 185, 188, 224
autobiography *see* life-writing

Baroque 66
Bartlett, Neil 9, 151–2, 164n9, 185,
    226
  'A Vision of Love Revealed in Sleep'
    172

Skin Lane 71
*Who Was That Man? A Present for
    Mr Oscar Wilde* 13, 172, 174,
    224
Barthes, Roland 94, 111–12, 114, 146,
    196
Barts Hospital, London 184, 227
Bazin, André 122
Bechdel, Alison 112
Ben-Hur (Wyler) 140
Benjamin, Walter 17
Bildungsroman 40, 47–8
biopic 26, 151, 200, 224
Blake, William 217, 221n7
blood 64, 121, 170
Blue (Jarman) 22, 190–1, 196–7, 201,
    206–7, 224
Borghese Gardens 144
Boyd, Don 153
bricolage 51, 150
British Film Institute (BFI) 47, 103n22,
    151
Britten, Benjamin 4, 25n27
Brown, Ford Maddox 108
Bruckner, Howard 189
Burroughs, William S. 30, 36, 52
Butler, Judith 11, 18–19, 205
Butler, Ken 150, 152–4, 164n11

camp 71, 91, 117, 150, 161
Caravaggio, Michele Angelo Merigi da
    58, 79–80
  Amor Vincit Omnia 108
  Bacchino Malato 62–4, 74
  David with the Head of Goliath
    64–7, 77n28

The Incredulity of Saint Thomas 59, 69–71
The Martyrdom of Saint Matthew 67, 68–70, 74
self-representations 61–6
Caravaggio (Jarman) 58, 59, 74–5, 113, 151
  choice of subject 60–1
  Jarman in 71–3, 83
Cartland, Barbara 169, 179
Certeau, Michel de 11, 26n38
Chatto, Beth 215
Chroma: A Book of Colour (Jarman) 22, 183, 196–212, 224
Clarke, Ossie 52, 83
Clearing, The (Bistikas) 26n31
Cocteau, Jean 13, 122
  The Blood of a Poet 109
Coil 86n9, 211n16
collaboration 6, 88–9, 126, 150, 153, 213
collage 6, 16–20, 22, 30–1, 58–60, 74–5, 90, 162, 166–7, 179, 188, 201–2, 223
  see also montage
Collins, Keith (HB) 36–7, 88–9, 98, 100, 102n1, 119, 123, 126, 132, 135, 143, 161, 168, 183, 186, 191–3, 213, 221, 226
colour 4, 22, 61, 196–9, 202–10
community 8, 21–3, 40, 48–9, 82, 85, 90, 129, 131, 138, 145, 167, 175, 210, 217
  gay 40, 48
  lesbian and gay 170
  LGBTQ+ 149
  queer 6, 49, 129, 138, 170, 197
Continental Baths 54, 57n36
Cook, Roger 71
Crimp, Douglas 191
Crisp, Quentin 12
cross-dressing 156
cruising 54, 79–80, 84, 167, 187, 225

Dancing Ledge, Dorset 40, 44–5
Dancing Ledge (Jarman) 20–1, 34, 40–57, 87–8, 92–4, 104, 114, 143, 175, 188, 225
Davies, Terence 13
Dee, John 38n11, 44–5, 116

Denge Sound Mirrors 125
Derek Jarman's Caravaggio (Jarman) 21, 58–78, 87, 224
Derek Jarman's Garden (Jarman) 22, 100–1, 213–22, 224
Derrida, Jacques 26n35, 32
diary 132–6
Dream of the Rood, The 106, 120–1
Dreuilhe, Emmanuel 15, 19
Driberg, Tom 12–13, 169, 181n5
Dungeness 104, 119, 124–5, 129, 133, 192, 214–15, 217

Eagleton, Terry 26n27, 58
Edward II (Jarman) 4, 29n80, 30, 36, 150, 154, 159, 171
elegy 5, 92, 134, 188–91, 217
Evil Queen (paintings, Jarman) 20, 183–4, 194n4, 224

Fassbinder, Rainer Werner 117, 122
Ficino, Marsilio 4, 201, 203
filmic autobiography 108–9
Fire Island 54, 169, 187
Fireworks (Anger) 109, 117
First World War *see* World War I
Foucault, Michel 69, 164n11
  see also heterotopia
Freeman, Elizabeth 60
Freud, Sigmund 141

Galás, Diamanda 108, 129n9
Garden, The (Jarman) 21, 71, 104–6, 117–27, 129, 134, 174, 217, 226
  dream poet in 117–21
gay history 172, 174
  identity 43, 172
  liberation 187
  see also homosexuality
Gay Liberation Front (GLF) 195n17
gaze 50, 68–9, 79, 139
gender 5, 63, 155–6, 159–60, 205
Genet, Jean 13, 61, 84, 104, 117, 126n2, 187
ghosts 129, 134, 181, 217
Gilbert & George 132
Ginsberg, Allen 30, 52
Goethe, Johann Wolfgang von 47–8, 204–5

Graber, Jody 36, 123, 152, 154, 156–8
grief 15, 27n46, 92, 134, 217–18
Guibert, Hervé 15
Gunn, Thom 32, 125

Hampstead Heath 84, 167, 169, 179, 188, 226
Harwood, Anthony 52–3
HB *see* Collins, Keith
heaven 207
Heaven (London nightclub) 217
Heslop, Richard 127n6
heterosexuality 66, 156, 161, 167, 179, 220
　compulsory 155
heterosoc 167, 178–81
heterotopia 187
history of homosexuality 24n5
HIV/AIDS
　artistic responses to 4, 7, 12, 127n9, 191
　AZT 191, 219
　diaries 133, 137, 184–5
　history of 55
　media portraits of 75, 152, 174
　public perceptions of 3, 91, 133
　representation 6, 101
　self-representation 9, 23, 124–5, 131
　testimony 132–5, 185, 190, 206
　writing 13–16, 19, 92
Hobbs, Christopher 63
Hockney, David 19–20, 52
Holleran, Andrew 55
home movies
　in *The Last of England* 105, 110–15, 120
　see also personal cinema; Super 8
homophobia 3, 47, 83, 138, 149, 151–2, 161, 164n9, 167, 168–70, 173, 223
homosexuality 3, 12, 14, 24n5, 69, 74, 79, 109, 149, 152–3, 158
Houédard, Dom Sylvester 33
Hudson, Rock 14
Hughes, Ted 32

If... (Anderson) 177
Imagining October (Jarman) 34, 194n3
Incandela, Gerald 53, 59, 62, 70

Institute for Contemporary Arts (ICA) 41
Isherwood, Christopher 12

Jarman, Derek
　canonisation 166, 170
　coming out 48–51
　early sexuality 47, 175–8
　HIV diagnosis 24, 90–1, 170
　legacy 8–9, 23, 221
　paintings 20, 42, 170, 181n6
　poetry 9, 17, 22, 26n28, 30–8, 51, 87, 92, 202, 218
　response to HIV/AIDS 4, 7, 12, 88, 133, 137, 149, 170, 178, 191, 206–7
Jordan 45, 52
journals (Jarman's) 103n22, 189
　see also sketchbooks
Jubilee (Jarman) 44–5, 58, 115–16, 120
Julien, Isaac 9
Jung, Carl 42
juxtaposition 6, 16–21, 35, 37, 43–4, 47, 80, 90, 96, 99, 106, 130, 137, 151, 169, 174, 200, 205, 215, 223–4

Kicking the Pricks (Jarman) 21, 79, 80, 82, 87–103, 104, 111–13, 115–16, 175, 219–20
Kincaid, Jamaica 14
Klein, Yves 198–9, 201, 207
Kramer, Larry 55
Kristeva, Julia 26n35, 199

Last of England, The (Jarman, book)
　see Kicking the Pricks
Last of England, The (Jarman, film) 21, 72, 79, 80, 87, 90, 97–8, 104–17, 122–3
　dream poet in 115–17, 120
Lewis, Matthew 141–2
Lévi-Strauss, Claude 51
life-writing 1–2, 5, 8, 10–11, 13, 15, 17–19, 40, 43, 46–7, 87–9, 92, 94–5, 101, 105, 129, 145, 185, 223–6
　queer 11–13
Logan, Andrew 54, 57n35

MacCabe, Colin 36, 150–1, 166
Mackay, James 40, 44–5
magic 215, 219
Man with a Movie Camera (Vertov) 106–8
Mapplethorpe, Robert 189
Marlowe, Christopher, *Edward II* 149–50, 155, 158, 171
martyrdom 66–7, 125
Matisse, Henri 34–5
Maybury, John 127n6
medieval 21, 56n9, 97, 99, 105, 117, 120, 129, 137, 150, 158–9, 171, 214, 223
melancholy 13, 129, 138, 215
memento mori 213, 217
memorial 22, 89, 138, 217–18
Michelangelo 60–1, 65–6, 158, 171, 203
   Judith and Holofernes 66
   Last Judgement 66
Michaels, Eric 15, 136
Mills, Johnny 119, 123
Modern Nature (Jarman) 21, 46, 52, 100–1, 125, 129–48, 176–7, 187, 191–2, 208, 214, 217, 224
Monette, Paul 15–16, 131, 223
montage 5, 18–19, 32, 104, 108, 117
   literary 17
   see also collage

Narcissus 141–2
Nelson, Maggie 198, 204–5
Nighthawks (Peck) 72–3, 83
Nomi, Klaus 55
Nureyev, Rudolf 52, 189

occult 116
O'Pray, Michael 87, 132, 150
Orton, Joe 13, 72–3
Ostia (Julian Cole) 21, 79–86, 224
OutRage! 29n80, 149, 159–61, 163n3, 168
Owen, Wilfred 4, 202

palimpsest 32, 82, 199
Parajanov, Sergei 5, 120, 122
Pasolini, Pier Paolo 7, 52, 79–82, 85, 86n9, 122–3, 187
Pasolini (Ferrara) 86n9

Peake, Tony 30, 37, 42, 47, 73, 82, 126, 131, 186, 220
Pearl 115–17, 120, 220
periperformative 18–19, 201
personal cinema 111, 127n17
phoenix 44
Phoenix House, London 97, 106–7
Piers Plowman (William Langland) 115–16, 120
Pinney, Michael 30
Plato 140, 171, 203–4
Pliny the Elder 141–2
poetry 20–1, 32, 83, 121, 160, 202
postmodern 20, 132, 135, 145
P. P. P. in the Garden of Earthly Delights (Jarman) 79–80, 85n3
Prick Up Your Ears (Frears) 26n31, 72–3, 83
Procktor, Patrick 52, 72–3
Prospect Cottage 22, 34, 118, 125, 129–30, 183, 213
   garden 119, 129, 144, 174, 183, 213–18, 220–1
Proust, Marcel 111
punk 45, 108

Queen is Dead, The (Jarman) 126–7n6
queer cinema 109
   futurity 2–3, 6, 8
   history 3–4, 60, 82, 129, 137, 156, 196, 208, 224
   politics 2, 167, 197, 223
   theory 6, 153, 167
   utopia 7, 187, 226
Queer (paintings, Jarman) 20, 170, 181n6, 183, 194n4, 224
Queer Edward II (Jarman) 21, 58, 149–65, 223–4
Queer Nation 23

Raft of the Medusa, The (Jarman) 183
Rauschenberg, Robert 5
refugees 108
Renaissance 4, 58, 60, 73, 129, 137, 153, 158, 201, 223
Renault, Mary 140
Royal Victoria Docks 99
Russell, Ken 44, 52

Sappho 171
Sebastiane (Jarman) 79, 85, 140, 151, 174, 189
Second World War *see* World War II
Section 28 (Local Government Act 1988) 24–5n13, 57n23, 109, 149, 178
Sedgwick, Eve Kosofsky 3, 19, 136
Sexual Offences Act of 1967 24n5
Shakespeare, William 4, 30, 61, 171
Sissinghurst 144, 219
Sisters of Perpetual Indulgence 149, 166, 170, 174
sketchbooks (Jarman's) 97–101, 107, 130
  see also journals
Slade School of Fine Art 31, 33, 37, 49, 52, 72, 161
Smiling in Slow Motion (Jarman) 21, 52, 100–1, 139, 150, 168, 183–95, 200, 213, 219, 224, 226
Soho, London 151, 207
Sooley, Howard 22, 174, 183–4, 213–15, 218–19, 221
Spartacus (Kubrick) 140
Spender, Stephen 12
St Bartholomew 66
Steede, Patrik 189
Stonewall (organisation) 150
Super 8 26n31, 40, 42, 56n2, 80, 114, 122, 124, 189, 220
  see also home movies
Swinton, Tilda 97, 101, 108, 115–16, 123, 152–5, 201, 210n7, 221

tableau vivant 59, 67
Tarkovsky, Andrei 120, 122
Tarnation (Caouette) 18, 201
Tatchell, Peter 160, 168
Tempest, The (Jarman) 58, 113

Terence Higgins Trust 55
terrorists 123
Terry, Nigel 65–7, 69, 155, 157, 201
Test Dept 82–3, 86n8
Thames river 99
Thatcher, Margaret 88, 108, 142, 149–51, 163n5, 167, 178
time-travelling 137
travel 30–3, 42, 52, 87, 183
traveller 169, 187
Turner, Simon Fisher 201
Twombly, Cy 5, 20, 196

utopia 5, 44, 84, 170

vampires 174

War Requiem (book, Jarman) 58, 151
War Requiem (film, Jarman) 4, 25n27, 30, 34
Watney, Simon 3, 29n80, 91, 112, 151–2, 164n9, 173–4, 178, 186, 224
White, Edmund 3, 12, 14–15, 48, 186
Whitehouse, Mary 169, 179, 182n26
Wilde, Oscar 50, 163n3, 171
Wilson, Angus 13
Wittgenstein, Ludwig 4, 196, 198, 200, 202–5
Wittgenstein (Jarman) 26n27, 117, 200, 224
Wittgenstein: The Terry Eagleton Script, the Derek Jarman Film (Jarman) 4, 58, 203
Wojnarowicz, David 15–16
World War I 24n5, 190
World War II 93, 115, 122

Yourcenar, Marguerite 140

EU authorised representative for GPSR:
Easy Access System Europe, Mustamäe tee 50,
10621 Tallinn, Estonia
gpsr.requests@easproject.com

www.ingramcontent.com/pod-product-compliance
Lightning Source LLC
Chambersburg PA
CBHW050925240426
43668CB00021B/2437